Towards Democratic Renewal

Towards Democratic Renewal: Ideas for constitutional change in New Zealand

Geoffrey Palmer and Andrew Butler

with assistance from Scarlet Roberts

Victoria University Press

TE WHARE WĀNANGA O TE ŪPOKO O TE IKA A MĀUI

VICTORIA
UNIVERSITY OF WELLINGTON

VICTORIA UNIVERSITY PRESS
Victoria University of Wellington
PO Box 600 Wellington
vup.victoria.ac.nz

Copyright © Geoffrey Palmer & Andrew Butler 2018
First published 2018

This book is copyright. Apart from
any fair dealing for the purpose of private study,
research, criticism or review, as permitted under the
Copyright Act, no part may be reproduced by any
process without the permission of
the publishers

ISBN 9781776561834

A catalogue record for this book is available from the
National Library of New Zealand.

Published with the assistance of the New Zealand Law Foundation

Printed by Printlink, Wellington

Contents

1	Why a constitution is important	7
2	Our constitutional vision	12
3	What the public told us	27
4	A Constitution based on principle	50
5	The State and a New Zealand republic	55
6	The Government	69
7	Local government	83
8	The Parliament	91
9	Why New Zealand does not need an upper house	107
10	The Judiciary	124
11	Integrity and transparency	139
12	Bill of Rights	153
13	The Treaty of Waitangi and the constitution	174
14	More people need to know how government works	209
15	Elections are not enough	217
16	Deepening citizen engagement	236
17	The media, information and communication	249
18	How to build a new constitution	256
19	Constitution of Aotearoa New Zealand	284
	Te Pouhere o Aotearoa Niu Tireni	285
	A note on the translation	385
	Afterword	386
	Meetings around New Zealand	387
	Acknowledgements	390
	Index	393

1   Why a constitution is important

In 2016, we published *A Constitution for Aotearoa New Zealand*, a book which proposed a written, codified constitution for New Zealand. We published it in the hope of starting a discussion about the future of New Zealand: who we are and where we're headed. In that purpose, we succeeded. This second book, with its revised proposal for a codified constitution, is in response to what we have learned from participating in this public conversation.

'Constitution' is a word few New Zealanders are accustomed to using. It means the rules under which a democracy like ours governs itself. It is all about who has public powers, what they can do with them, what limits are established upon their use and how human rights are protected. A constitution sets out the basic institutions of government and the core values that guide the work of those institutions.

New Zealand has a most unusual constitution compared with other countries. It has no single document that can be called a constitution. Only three countries in the world find themselves in that condition: New Zealand, the United Kingdom (which is currently experiencing serious constitutional problems) and Israel.

This peculiar New Zealand situation would be fine if there was persuasive evidence that the constitutional settings in New Zealand were ideal. No doubt a considerable number of people believe that there is nothing wrong, so there is no need for change. Indeed, we have heard from a number of people that New Zealand's nebulous, informal arrangements are the envy of many countries around the world.

We beg to differ. We believe there are serious dangers inherent in our current constitutional structures and they need to be overhauled. There remains within them a distinctly colonial tinge that is out of whack with contemporary New Zealand understandings of how political power should be exercised in a democracy.

In truth, the monarchy and its powers are a mystery to most and this is an obstacle to understanding how the system of government works in New Zealand.

The current New Zealand constitution is constantly evolving. It is free to wander where it will according to political developments. The danger is that rights and freedoms of people will be gradually whittled away, that emergencies and shocks may beset us that would require government to trespass not only upon freedoms but also upon democracy itself—and, without greater controls and oversight, it can.

The New Zealand style of government is already authoritarian. In our experience, most New Zealanders are somewhat naïve and complacent in their attitudes to public power. When New Zealand was a small and uncomplicated society it had little need for checks and balances on public power. We were not particularly diverse, and we agreed upon so much. Elections were enough; but they are not now. That is a world we have lost. We need accountability and participation from the people during whole parliamentary terms.

We need a written constitution—one that is not too long, and is easy to understand, which sets out how the major institutions of government are structured, what their powers are, to whom they are accountable and how people's rights are protected. A constitution needs to be used by everyone within and outside government as a guide to how things work. It should be taught in schools to increase understanding of what institutions of government can and cannot do, and the rights of individuals in all of this. Such a document would transform the teaching of civics in New Zealand.

The issues with which government must deal are infinitely more complicated than they were 50 years ago. Climate change is the leading example; we have hardly scratched the surface of what it means for New Zealand in the future. One great weakness of the system of government we have lies encapsulated in that issue. We do not pay sufficient attention to the future or guard against risks that can be readily foreseen. Driven by the three-year election cycle, Governments focus on the present so that the present crowds out the future.

The challenges that New Zealand democracy will face in future are likely to be demanding. Climate change will cause big and disruptive policy changes. Geopolitical developments are also likely to be testing. Terrorism is a threat. Emergencies of one sort or another will occur. Wars and nuclear explosions may occur, as could financial collapse.

Why a constitution is important

The development in the United Kingdom of the Brexit movement and the changes in the United States resulting from the presidency of Donald Trump are changing the ways in which western democracies function.[1] We live in a world in which alternative facts, lies, manipulation of public opinion and 'post-truth' politics distort public discourse. These are dangers indeed and New Zealand does not need them. We even had alleged alternative facts in the 2017 election campaign with claims by the National Party that there was an $11.7 billion hole in the Labour Party's fiscal plans.[2]

Economic nationalism, the manipulation of public opinion through digital means and the influence of immense and powerful multinational corporations on domestic policies all threaten to change the way representative democracy has traditionally functioned. The dangers for democracy inherent in these developments are considerable. It is easy for the voice of the people to become muted and for our liberties and protections to gradually but inexorably disappear. A robust constitutional and democratic framework is a necessary protection. For example, the United States constitution— though we do not advocate a constitutional model that gives judges the final word—has been successful in halting some of President Donald Trump's more extreme tendencies.

New Zealand is one of the world's oldest and most stable democracies, and Kiwis are justifiably proud to live in the first country in the world to adopt universal suffrage and other significant measures. But we cannot rest on past glories.

New Zealand needs to refurbish its own democracy and be vigilant to protect its values. New Zealand is not independent from international trends and cannot afford to be complacent about its democracy. Catastrophes can befall any nation and they must be dealt with. The Christchurch and Kaikoura earthquakes are recent examples. The risks were foreseeable, and could have been better

---

1   The recent book by Colin James *Unquiet Time: Aotearoa/New Zealand in a fast-changing world* (Fraser Books, Masterton, 2017) provides a detailed account of the challenges on New Zealand's horizon.
2   Hamish Rutherford 'National Accuses Labour of $11.7 billion spending Plan Error' *stuff.co.nz* (online ed, 4 September 2017), available at <www.stuff.co.nz/business/96470311/national-accuses-labour-of-117-billion-error-in-its-spending-plan>. Despite the fact that no economist could be found who would support the view, the claim was repeated and was never withdrawn.

guarded against, had the issues been given sufficient priority earlier. An earthquake-prone country should have been better prepared to protect its citizens and infrastructure.

In such a world, the framework that governs decision-making needs to be in good order and condition. It needs to be clear. It needs to be transparent so people know what is going on, rights are protected and corruption is kept at bay. Law and policy need to be designed so they are effective, enforced and competently administered.

Too often in New Zealand our legislation has unexpected and unfortunate consequences. We do not examine the practical effects of much of our law and whether it has achieved the purposes to which it was directed. Too much of it is cooked up in secret with inadequate public participation in its making. Often the public is kept at a distance.

We produce policy blunders that engender poor results. Much time and effort is spent repairing them or dealing with their consequences. Think of the 29 lives lost in the Pike River Mine, a tragedy traced back to bad law, poorly administered. Think about the polluted condition of New Zealand rivers and lakes which have deteriorated rapidly as result of failures of government policy. And think of the mess New Zealand is in with housing, where young people have been priced out of the market and cannot afford homes.

The difficulty with any constitutional discussion in New Zealand is that people struggle to see how it affects them. They vote in elections and think this is about all they can do to influence the way the country is run. They do not see that how power is structured, how it is used and how the remedies against its abuse, can improve their lives. Looked at in this light there is no issue of public policy more important than the constitution; if we get that right, the prospect of better decision-making increases.

We want the powers and functions of the main elements of government set out clearly and authoritatively in a constitution that has been carefully considered and enjoys wide community support. People need to own their constitution and identify with it. At a minimum, it needs to tell us:

Why a constitution is important

- how the **powers of the state** are defined and organised;
- how **Parliament** is elected and by whom, what are its functions and how it works;
- how **Government** is defined, what is the Cabinet and how ministers are appointed;
- what kind of **judicial authority** is vested in the courts;
- how the duties of the **Head of State** are organised as a unifying influence;
- what institutions exist that will promote **integrity and transparency** in public administration, the public service and public finances;
- how human rights and the rights of minorities are protected through an enforceable **Bill of Rights**;
- how Māori constitutional issues and **te Tiriti o Waitangi/the Treaty of Waitangi** are to be respected within what is now a multicultural society;
- what principles should guide **local government**;
- how the mechanisms of **political accountability** work;
- how the constitution should be able to be **amended** to get the right balance between entrenching core values and letting future generations adapt to their conditions.

In this book we set out what we have learned about what New Zealanders think on these issues and explain the changes we have made to our original proposals, reflecting that feedback.

The final chapter of this book contains the text of Constitution Aotearoa, which has been rendered in te reo Māori as well as in English. The two versions appear side by side at the end of this book. The translation was carried out by Kiwa Hammond of AATEA Solutions, assisted by Maakere Edwards, and peer reviewed by Māmari Stephens, senior lecturer at the Victoria University of Wellington Law School. Part of the cost of this process was supported by a supplementary grant from the Law Foundation.

2   Our constitutional vision

Our 2016 book *A Constitution for Aotearoa New Zealand* set out a proposed Constitution for New Zealand. That Constitution aimed to describe in a single, easy-to-read document the bedrock principles by which public power should be exercised, the basic institutions of government, and the rights of individuals.[1]

We did this in order to stimulate debate and to continue the constitutional conversation initiated by the 2013 Constitutional Advisory Panel.[2] We did not expect our proposals to be adopted wholesale, if at all. But we wanted to get people talking about public power in New Zealand: how it is used, and whether we can do better. Previous and better resourced efforts at stimulating this discussion have led nowhere, because there have been no concrete proposals for people to engage with.

Since the publication of the book, we have been on a long and fruitful journey around New Zealand to speak to many people and groups about our ideas and theirs. We have spoken to more than 3500 people. We have received hundreds of submissions through our website (*constitutionaotearoa.org.nz*) and we have had useful engagement with experts on various points of details. Our proposals received publicity through op-ed pieces in many newspapers. All of this has enriched our understanding but not dimmed our vision.

As a result of what we have learned, we have made major changes to our proposals. This was exactly the purpose of asking for submissions. We know that serious public submissions on a concrete proposal can sharpen and increase understanding of where difficulties lie and suggest alternative approaches that may be better. But equally, they

---

1 Geoffrey Palmer and Andrew Butler *A Constitution for Aotearoa New Zealand* (Victoria University Press, Wellington, 2016). We also ran a website: <constitutionaotearoa.org.nz>. Much of the book, and further content including blogs and speeches, is available there.
2 The Panel was established by the National Government in fulfillment of a promise made during confidence and supply negotiations with the Māori Party during the 2008 elections. It was charged with undertaking a review of New Zealand's current constitutional arrangements and seeking the views of the public on various aspects of it. See Constitutional Advisory Panel *New Zealand's Constitution: A Report on a Conversation, He Kōtuinga Kōrero mō Te Kaupapa Ture o Aotearoa* (November 2013).

can help identify areas of substantial agreement. It surprised us how many engaged with us, and many of the submissions were exceedingly detailed and thoughtful. We are indebted to the people with whom we have spoken, to all those who made submissions or contributed blogs, and to those who reached out to us via social media, as well as the experts who have helped us.

Our aim with this project was to kick-start a conversation and provide a resource that can be used as an educative tool about constitutional reform in New Zealand. If New Zealand is to reform its constitutional arrangements, the authors are convinced that it will have to be as part of a government-initiated undertaking to carry out a thorough and properly resourced programme of public education and engagement. Later in the book we outline the way we believe this process should be approached.

In starting a conversation, we have succeeded to a greater degree than we expected. In the end we were unable to speak to all the groups who wanted to hear from us. We are only two people and we have other demands upon our time. Our project attracted much news and other media attention over the 12 months that followed its publication.

Towards the end of our consultation process, the 2017 general election occurred. We did not want the issue of a codified constitution to become part of the election campaign because the nation's constitution is too important to become politicised. For that reason we deliberately curtailed our publicity efforts during the campaign and during the negotiations that followed. Besides, an election campaign cannot effectively deal with an issue of this complexity, although we thought there may be some learning from it to take on board in our final version. Constitutional change requires a properly supported process of its own.

Constitutional issues were little discussed in the election campaign, although there were some policies and statements. One instance did occur that illustrated the importance of human rights.

In the lead-up to the campaign, some commentators questioned the state of New Zealand's democracy, highlighting falling voter turnout at previous general elections (particularly among young people) and suggesting that voters were feeling increasingly powerless and disenchanted. A Massey University survey published in June

2017 showed widespread discontent with New Zealand's system of government.[3]

Human rights issues briefly came to the fore during the campaign when the Deputy Leader of the National Party, Paula Bennett, promised a crackdown on gangs if re-elected. The policy was clearly in breach of the New Zealand Bill of Rights Act 1990, which was admitted by Bennett: 'It probably does breach the rights of some of those criminals.'[4] Bennett was reported as saying some gang members had 'fewer human rights than others', and Prime Minister Bill English said it was good that New Zealand lacked a written constitution, as it gave governments flexibility.[5] The policy was widely criticised.[6] English moved to clarify Bennett's comments, emphasising that the National Party did not believe that some New Zealanders had fewer human rights than others. But the important point is that, without a superior law Bill of Rights, the adoption of such an extreme policy devised in the heat of an election campaign could not be stopped.

Some parties' policies also reflected a mood for change. Gareth Morgan's Opportunities Party (TOP) put forward a 'democracy reset' policy under which it called for a written constitution 'to protect the Kiwi way of life' as well as the re-establishment of an Upper House.[7]

The Green Party called for the entrenchment of the Māori electorate seats,[8] and Green Party Co-leader James Shaw was reported as saying, 'To make the Government fulfil its responsibilities on climate

---

3   Massey University 'Election Survey shows widespread discontent' (June 2017), available at <www.massey.ac.nz/massey/about-massey/news/article.cfm?mnarticle_uuid=9AA7647B-0864-1798-6495-CC7CA330FCAF>.
4   Henry Cooke 'National Party announces $82 million crackdown on methamphetamine use, supply' *stuff.co.nz* (online ed, 3 September 2017), available at <www.stuff.co.nz/national/politics/96442150/national-party-announces-82-million-crackdown-on-methamphetamine-use-supply>.
5   Cooke, above n 4.
6   For example, see editorial comments in 'Editorial: Human rights are for all, including gang members' *The Press* (5 September 2017); and Duncan Greive 'Mask Off: National decides gang members have "fewer human rights"' *The Spinoff* (3 September 2017).
7   The Opportunities Party 'Democracy Reset' (2017), available at <www.top.org.nz/top4>.
8   Green Party 'Green Party will honour Te Tiriti in Government' (press release, 6 August 2017), available at <www.greens.org.nz/news/press-release/green-party-will-honour-te-tiriti-government>.

change, human rights and a host of other things, New Zealand needs a written constitution.'[9]

There was also some mention by Jacinda Ardern, leader of the Labour Party, about New Zealand becoming a republic. She was reported as saying:[10]

> I do think that we should start having the conversation. There are a lot of issues that need to be resolved on that path, and I would have liked the government to have had that conversation when the flag debate came up . . .
> That was the time to say, 'actually, where are we heading? What's the Crown's ongoing relationship with Maori if we transition into a republic? Where will we be in 20 years' time in this regard.'

These are good questions and they are dealt with in this book. There is a great deal of work in carrying out constitutional change and it is a task that tends often to be thought subordinate to more immediate priorities.

Our revised proposals: what we want to change

On a broad level, the new draft of Constitution Aotearoa which we set out in this book is much more streamlined and simpler than our 2016 proposal. We have also reordered the draft. We now start the constitution with a statement of purpose, followed by the Bill of Rights and te Tiriti o Waitangi/the Treaty of Waitangi. This reflects strong feedback that core values should be given top billing. After receiving feedback from various individuals and groups that the first draft was too long, too detailed and too complex, we undertook to pare it back, focusing on principles rather than processes which may not stand the test of time. There are, of course, limits to how far such an approach can go. A constitution is a legal document that needs to speak with as much precision as possible. Otherwise uncertainty will be generated and the basic purpose of writing down the framework of power may be lost.

---

9   Green Party 'Constitutional Lawyer Stands for Greens in Hutt South' (press release, 31 January 2017), available at <www.scoop.co.nz/stories/PO1701/S00201/constitutional-lawyer-stands-for-greens-in-hutt-south.htm>.
10 'Jacinda Ardern in The PM Job Interview: "It's time to talk about a republic".' *The New Zealand Herald* (online ed, 22 August 2017), available at <www.nzherald.co.nz/nz/news/article.cfm?c_id=1&objectid=11908796>.

Many readers of the first draft were clearly not familiar with statutes, passed by the New Zealand Parliament. And there is no reason they should be. Some people, not used to reading legal English, became impatient with our 2016 draft. We sympathise with this, because a basic law such as a constitution needs to be readily understood by everybody. It should be simple enough that schools can teach it without too much difficulty. That is one of the fundamental aims of the project. A constitution is not the exclusive province of lawyers and they are not the most important readers of it: this document and its ethos must live in the hearts and minds of the people.

We have therefore made major changes in this regard. We have completely altered the Preamble, making it contemporary and accessible rather than historical and legal. We have cut down the bulk of what was previously included. And we have made the drafting clearer and more accessible. Much prescription is gone. This has enabled us to shorten the draft considerably.[11] A constitution does have to set out the functions and powers of Parliament, Government, the Head of State and the Judiciary, and our new proposal does this. But much less detail is included now, and we think we have achieved the right balance.

We have also changed a number of other things:

- People are now at the front, reflecting that the State exists to protect the people and their rights.
- We have given the Head of State (to be known as the Guardian or Kaitiaki of the Nation) more powers to make that person an effective protector of the constitution and a better check on legislative power.
- We have reconstituted the institutions of the State and its core —the Government, the Parliament, the Judiciary, the Head of State and local government—and clarified the functions and powers of each.
- We have introduced some new proposals aimed at increasing

---

11 Our draft constitution is not long by international standards. Using English translations of constitutions around the world, available through <www.constituteproject.org>, it is clear that our draft is a great deal shorter than the constitution of India, which covers over 260 pages. It is also considerably shorter than most of the constitutions of South America, many of which have been designed in the last decade (see for example the constitutions of Bolivia and Ecuador).

electoral participation—compulsory voting and lowering the voting age to 16.
- We have changed our approach to other things like te Tiriti o Waitangi/the Treaty of Waitangi and local government.

There are a number of issues we have decided not to change. We are not attempting to move away from our current MMP electoral system, nor to re-establish an Upper House of Parliament. On other matters, we remain of the same view as in our first attempt, such as the need for a superior law constitution and the need for entrenchment of the constitution.

We feel what we have presented in this second draft strikes an appropriate balance between principles and prescription, between things that should require increased scrutiny before they are amended or deleted and things that can be changed through ordinary legislation—though others may disagree. The selection of what to include and what to leave out is a subject on which reasonable minds may differ.

What follows is a summary of the core proposals in our Constitution that would change the status quo. These changes are further examined and explained in the chapters that follow.

Superior law constitution

We propose the constitution should be superior law. That means the constitution sits above all other law, and other laws must comply with it. This feature is commonly found in other countries. It used to be a feature of the New Zealand constitutional system in its early colonial days, but this faded over time. A superior law constitution provides a stable framework of principles and powers for the primary public institutions that make decisions affecting people—the Parliament, the Cabinet and public service, the courts and the Head of State.

The proposed Constitution sets out a clear division of powers between these institutions. It also stops Parliament from changing the basic rules contained in the Constitution by a majority of one.

Entrenched law

We also propose that the Constitution should be entrenched. That is, changes can only be made to the Constitution if a 75 per cent majority of MPs in Parliament agree, or if a change gets more than 50 per cent support in a referendum of the voters.[12] It is very important to appreciate that this entrenchment model will make our constitution harder to amend than is currently the case (at the moment a bare majority of Parliament can change any laws, including constitutional laws) but it will be much easier to amend than the US or Australian constitutions (many submissions that supported our ideas wanted reassurance that Constitution Aotearoa would not lock out future generations' ability to change to their conditions, like in the US and Australia).

Bill of Rights

Under our proposed Constitution, New Zealanders' rights will be better protected. Currently, a bare majority of MPs in Parliament can remove rights or pass laws inconsistent with those rights. As we explained in our 2016 book—and to the surprise of many people at our various public meetings—this power is used regularly in New Zealand. Under our proposal, if 75 per cent of MPs agree, only then will Parliament be able to postpone a court decision to suspend a provision that breaches fundamental rights. This will ensure much closer and more rigorous consideration of human rights issues than previously.

We also propose the recognition of important human rights that are not currently protected by the New Zealand Bill of Rights Act 1990. These include the right to a healthy environment, the right to privacy, the right to property, the right to a free state education, rights for children, some constitutional protection for workers, and the right not to be discriminated against on the grounds of gender identity or expression, or subjected to slavery, servitude or being required to perform forced labour.

Most of the provisions in the Bill of Rights in Constitution Aotearoa are to be found in the New Zealand Bill of Rights Act 1990, but they have been brought up to date to reflect modern developments in international human rights law.

---

12 That is the entrenchment model used in New Zealand since 1956 to protect some core features of our electoral system. See Electoral Act 1993, s 268.

Our constitutional vision

Te Tiriti o Waitangi/the Treaty of Waitangi

Māori rights are extensively recognised in New Zealand law, but the constitutional position of te Tiriti o Waitangi/the Treaty of Waitangi remains unclear. It needs to be clarified. It is not only a subject of controversy, but also of uncertainty as to the precise range of its ambit, 178 years after it was adopted.

A profound national conversation needs to be held to reach better understandings of what is covered by the Treaty and to state those understandings in the constitution so that there is greater clarity around what, in practical terms, the Treaty means in contemporary New Zealand. The proposed constitution provides a process for this to occur.

The Head of State

We should have a Head of State who is a New Zealander living in New Zealand. We should become a republic within the Commonwealth as a majority of nations in the Commonwealth are. We believe the Head of State should be called the 'Kaitiaki' or 'Guardian' of the nation, and in that capacity the Head of State should be given some powers to protect the constitution. The Head of State would be appointed through a free vote of Parliament, requiring the support of two-thirds of MPs. A new function for the Kaitiaki would be to refer to the Supreme Court laws passed by Parliament where the Kaitiaki is concerned they may not be consistent with the Constitution. The Supreme Court would rule on the issue raised after hearing legal argument. Having our own Head of State as a symbol of unity will enhance our identity as an independent nation and help us forge further our own distinct identity.

The State

Our proposed Constitution would legally constitute the state of Aotearoa New Zealand in a new form and provide clarity concerning the powers that it has. Those powers have to be assigned to the Parliament, the Cabinet and public service, the Judiciary and the Head of State. The State would have vested in it all the powers as successor to the Crown in right of New Zealand. The realm of New Zealand would be abolished, as would the royal prerogative.

Parliament

The central democratic institution of the country is Parliament. In it are vested the legislative power and the financial power to tax. It settles the content of legislation, taxation and government expenditure. It is presided over by the Speaker. The Speaker should be elected from among MPs by secret ballot. We are also proposing the introduction of compulsory voting and lowering the voting age to 16. Parliament will have a fixed four-year term, not a three-year term as at present. Within government, business and political circles, there is a widespread consensus that three years is too little time to devise and enact good quality legislation; four years is much more realistic. However, people have—understandably, in the absence of checks and balances—been reluctant to give up the ability to throw out a Government at a general election on a three-year cycle. We believe that if the checks and balances proposed in our Constitution were adopted there would be strong support for a four-year term. Public feedback reinforced this view.

Further, fast law-making has produced mistakes and blunders. The taking of urgency will be restricted so that steps in the legislative process cannot be shortened at the whim of Government. The proposed Constitution improves law-making by requiring advance information about Government legislation and the publication of the Government's legislative programme.

The Government

The executive authority of the State is vested in the Cabinet. The principles governing the functions and powers of the Cabinet and public service are set out in, and limited by, the proposed Constitution. It provides for the role of the Prime Minister and other ministers and their accountability to Parliament.

The way in which the powers are now distributed has enabled the abolition of the Executive Council, which previously we retained. It is simply unnecessary under the proposed arrangements.

Local government

The proposals include a set of principles to provide local government with some constitutional protection. The principles that local government frameworks must comply with are stated. These changes are important because local government is the arm of government nearest the people. It has important functions and is often restricted by central government legislation. Local government often finds itself with inadequate financial resources to carry out its responsibilities.

The Judiciary

The judicial power of the State is vested in the courts. Their constitutional protections and independence remain the same as they are now, in essential respects, as contained in the Constitution Act 1986. The major change is in the creation of a Judicial Appointments Commission, which is provided for in Constitution Aotearoa. The Commission will produce a shortlist of suitable appointees, from among which the Attorney-General will recommend someone for appointment. Since judges have increased powers under the proposed Constitution it is important that their appointment is removed from the political influence of Cabinet.

International relations and defence

Before an international treaty can bind New Zealand, our Constitution provides it must have been approved by resolution of the House of Representatives. Currently this is not the case. Similarly, before New Zealand armed forces are deployed overseas in situations likely to involve the use of lethal force, a resolution must be carried by the House of Representatives.

Integrity and transparency

Constitution Aotearoa provides for reinforcement of key democratic values. The Attorney-General and the Solicitor-General are made responsible for the integrity of the legal system, protecting the rule of law and safeguarding the independence of the Judiciary. Parliamentary control of public finance is laid out in the Constitution. The Auditor-General is the watchdog over the proper expenditure of public money and the power and independence of that office are guaranteed by the Constitution. We have renamed the State Services Commission as the Government Services Commission and made it a commission of three persons. The Government Services Commission, as the supervisor of the public service, is given powers to be exercised independently of Cabinet and to ensure the public service, while serving loyally the Government of the day, is not politicised. The requirement for the public service to give ministers free and frank advice will be constitutionally protected. Officers of Parliament such as the Ombudsman and the Parliamentary Commissioner for the Environment are contained in this part of the Constitution. Official information legislation is required by the Constitution to be strengthened. The police are subject to an important set of constitutional principles by which to hold them to account. The intelligence agencies are required to be regularly reviewed and kept by the constitution within reasonable bounds in order to protect the liberty of the people. The Human Rights Commission is given constitutional status.

Periodic revisions of the Constitution

We propose every 10 years the Constitution must be reviewed. A Citizens Assembly consisting of randomly chosen members of the public must be appointed to ensure ordinary people have a strong voice in recommending changes. In addition, a Constitutional Commission would be convened, containing a mixture of public officials and key office holders who would make recommendations to Parliament for constitutional amendments.

Emergencies

Where emergencies occur, such as actual or imminent threats to national security or public order, or civil emergencies that may flow from natural disasters, there is provision for the Constitution to be suspended subject to important restrictions such as time and approval by the Parliament. These provisions are a significant improvement on the current constitutional position under which anything is possible.

Adoption

The detailed steps we believe need to be taken before any new constitution can be adopted are set out later in the book. They will require an inclusive process of public involvement and conversations before any proposals are finalised or even considered by the Parliament, let alone put to a referendum of the people. The final provision in our proposed Constitution provides that the Constitution must be approved by more than 50 per cent of valid votes cast by electors at a poll conducted under an Act of Parliament for this purpose, and will come into force on a date specified in that Act.

The spirit of democracy

It is important to understand that the legal frameworks any constitution erects must be infused with life and vigour by the human beings who make the decisions within the institutions. Frameworks are important and so equally are the distribution of powers. But these are not everything. The vision and spirit with which public officials approach their tasks are fundamental to increasing the quality of our democracy. Our chapter on deliberative democracy and citizen engagement is fundamental. It is imperative that a new and inclusive approach to the making of public policy and law is developed. New attitudes are necessary to make the structures established by the constitution work well. The government machine must face outwards to citizens, not look inwards, serving its own convenience and comfort. The sense of being disconnected, even alienated, from these processes generates distrust in some segments of the population. That atmosphere must be dispelled. A healthy democracy must serve the common good and not favour particular interests in society, especially those of the most wealthy and powerful.

Democratic renewal

As a result of the submissions, our public meetings and interactions with young people, we became concerned that there was a significant lack of faith in how governmental arrangements worked for people. Things are not looking good in many western democracies and democracy is on the wane in a number of areas of the world. There seems to be a declining faith in the legitimacy of the decisions that are being made. Many feel their voices are neither heard nor heeded. Too many New Zealanders seem to think themselves powerless to influence government actions. It is not just the institutions of government; it is how they are run, how they communicate with people and how they make decisions. We feel these issues have to be addressed by changing the way government works, not merely by altering the constitutional structures, but also by changing the methods of decision-making.

Democratic renewal requires some adjustments to the way business is carried out within government and a new, open and inclusive approach to the making of policy and legislation. To achieve this goal, a written, codified constitution has an important role to play. It will do this by first strengthening institutions; second, by promoting a new sense of citizen engagement with how policy is developed; and third, by imposing boundaries on what government can do and how it must proceed.

The argument for democratic renewal is partly historical and partly institutional. Many people have lost faith in institutions. Our legal and political systems are finding their legitimacy is slipping away. Democracy needs to be thickened and deepened. Institutions will decay unless the public actively own them and trust them. We should move toward a much more deliberative democracy than we have. Several strands of the argument need to be woven together:

- the state of civic understanding and engagement in New Zealand;
- elections and the long march to universal suffrage;
- the rise and fall of mass membership of political parties in New Zealand;
- the changes caused by MMP and the development of multiple political parties;
- the funding of elections, political parties and the role of money;
- the media and the provision of information about government to the public.

Elections are not enough; a proper functioning democracy must work hard to connect citizens better with the government that is carried out in their name. The lines of public discourse and accountability require improvement. There needs to be greater openness and transparency. There need to be more avenues for public participation in decision-making. A new constitutional design can help to achieve these goals.

We think elections and the policy choices that flow from them are important expressions of the collective or aggregated will of the people. We also believe that better techniques of deliberation could refresh democracy and produce better decisions than are often made. One of the prime aims of our proposed Constitution is to contain power and restrict domination of one group or view.

Our constitutional vision

The question of how to encourage civic literacy and to engage and empower the citizenry in democracies is not a simple issue. Functioning as effective citizens requires a skill set. Politics and government are not central to the lives of many people.[13] Increasing trends of not voting must be a concern, however. Voting is a public act, easy to understand and measurable. Measuring and quantifying other forms of civic engagement is more difficult.

Then there is the issue of trust in political institutions, which is a product of many different factors. Once lost, trust is not easily regained. Max Harris, in his recent book *The New Zealand Project*, argues that 'the twin interlocking forces of desensitisation and demoralisation are key to the curtailment of people power' in New Zealand.[14] His diagnosis may lack empirical proof but it does resonate. Measures do need to be adopted that connect citizens more to government, policy and politics, ensuring that they trust government more and take a bigger part in what it does. What is needed are policy choices that increase civic literacy and engagement.

With this in mind, this book and its proposal for a codified constitution have a central focus on democratic renewal, on deliberative democracy and engagement. A constitution is a road-map to how the country operates. The people and the constitution must be in harmony with one another. It is vital, if this project is to succeed, that New Zealanders have trust in their institutions, that government engages with the people and that democratic legitimacy is renewed and refreshed. These ideas are at the core of this, our second draft of Constitution Aotearoa.

Conclusion

Why have we engaged in this project and what do we hope to achieve?

In short, we want better government, increased democratic accountability, stronger rule of law, more public participation in decisions that affect people and greater rights for citizens. Our 2016 book set out an actual draft of the proposed written Constitution and a commentary on the reasons for the proposals. By making a specific

---

13 Henry Milner *Civic Literacy: How informed citizens make democracy work* (University Press of New England, Hanover, 2002).
14 Max Harris *The New Zealand Project* (Bridget Williams Books, Wellington, 2017) at 243.

proposal we thought this would provide a focus for the debate.

We were not suggesting that our views and proposals should prevail. We have remained open-minded as to the precise shape constitutional reform in New Zealand should take. Both of us have had the privilege of direct and hands-on experience with the practical workings of the existing unwritten constitution. For Geoffrey Palmer that has been as law professor, MP, Minister of Justice, Attorney-General, Leader of the House, Deputy Prime Minister and Prime Minister, President of the Law Commission, and as a practising lawyer and QC. For Andrew Butler, it has been as a Government lawyer at the Crown Law Office, arguing some of the most controversial cases of the day, and then acting for private clients with an emphasis on human rights, as well as being an academic teaching public and comparative constitutional law.

It is fair to say we are both insiders in the Wellington legal and policy scene. That does not mean, however, that our views are endorsed in official circles or that we know best. Our ideas are merely proposals. They must be tested in the crucible of public debate and analysis. They must be acceptable to the general public.

We have found in our public discussions away from Wellington that relatively little is known about how we are governed, and frankly there is limited interest as well. In many places we found a lack of knowledge about how Government works, even though Government actions affect everybody's lives. Our 'insider' backgrounds have afforded us the opportunity to see both the strengths and the defects of our current system firsthand. Others do not necessarily see the same weaknesses in the existing state of affairs that we have seen up close, though they have probably seen the poor Government decision-making that results from those weaknesses.

As a country we seem to have lost our mojo when it comes to bold and progressive changes. Our profound belief is that New Zealand could do better with its constitution and its governance. It is not as difficult as many think to change things, even constitutions, for the better. We have every hope of this happening.

3   What the public told us

Our interactions with the public have been substantial and have occurred in many different ways. We met more than 3500 people face-to-face at public meetings across New Zealand. At all of these meetings we engaged in a question and answer session so we could explain our ideas and get feedback on them. We found these engagements invaluable. We were active on social media, including Facebook and Twitter, and were discussed on several Reddit threads. We wrote many op-ed pieces for national and provincial newspapers and on a variety of online media, such as the *Spinoff* and *Newsroom*, which prompted numerous replies and comments. We requested submissions on our proposal via our website *constitutionaotearoa.org.nz*. Other submissions were received through the mail. We also engaged in detailed consultative meetings with groups we thought could provide us with particular expertise. We invited a variety of experts, academics and observers to write blogs discussing their views on aspects of our proposals (including the role of the Head of State, environmental rights, the Treaty of Waitangi, gender discrimination and the voting age, among others), which were then published on our website and Facebook. In addition, we identified and utilised a number of the submissions made to the 2013 Constitutional Advisory Panel set up by the Government.

In these ways we gathered a range of views from many different groups and individuals in the community. The exercise of reaching out has greatly enriched our understanding of the issues. In particular, it has helped us to identify where the points of greatest controversy reside in what we first proposed in *A Constitution for Aotearoa New Zealand*. Members of the public have thought about important issues and expressed their views cogently. We found much significance was to be gleaned from their insights and points of view. We are greatly indebted to everyone who made a submission. We thank you for your time and commitment.

As a result of what we have learned, we have changed our minds on a number of major and minor issues. The reasons for these changes were briefly touched on in the previous chapter and are further developed in later chapters as well.

One feature that became evident from the submissions was a widespread misunderstanding of how our existing systems of government actually work. The level of misinformation was high over matters of detail. For example, some insisted that the Treaty of Waitangi is an instrument for 'apartheid' in New Zealand. How such a position can be advocated in light of New Zealand's colonial history is remarkable and shows that it is not only civics that is not well understood in New Zealand, but also New Zealand history. A submission from Paul Eady told us 'most of us don't even know the basic history of our own country.' Quite a number of submitters clearly had not read the book in which our original proposals were elaborated on.

While we cannot present all the submissions here, what follows is a snapshot of the views we received.[1]

On the idea of a written codified constitution

By December 2017 we had received approximately 440 submissions, including those by people who made several submissions. A key issue raised by the proposals set out in our 2016 book concerned the utility of a written constitution at all. There was strong support from our submitters, with a clear majority of the submitters favouring the aims of the project. A representative sample of those comments follows.

David Scott submitted:

> I think it is a fantastic initiative and document and long overdue. [. . .] I passionately support all the objectives and motivations for having this written constitution; a supreme constitution, inclusive of the Bill of Rights and Treaty, the need for NZ to have its own Head of State, and the abolition of royal powers.

A refrain repeated in several of the submissions came from Heather:

> I didn't realise we didn't have one [a written constitution] till I read the article in the NZ Herald a couple of weeks ago.

Professor Klaus Bosselmann from the University of Auckland told us:

> the proposed constitution strikes the right balance between being pragmatic and easy to understand and being innovative and ambitious.

---

[1] Please note extracts have been edited for clarity. Some names have been shortened or withheld at the request of submitters.

What the public told us

It would sit well amongst constitutions of comparable jurisdictions, but also appears flexible enough to allow enrichment from eco-constitutionalism, arguably the most important area of legal research for achieving sustainability of societies and humanity at large.

Patrick submitted:

codifying the constitution is an excellent idea and there is no reasonable argument against doing so. I think the real issues where reasonable people can disagree is whether it should be superior law [. . .]

Keith Quinn, an author and experienced television and sports commentator, said:

Yes, I would support the recommendation for New Zealand to have a written constitution in one single document. I support that recommendation on the proviso that the constitution encompass the Treaty of Waitangi and the responsibilities that it entails. It is important that New Zealanders know what their rights and responsibilities are as citizens and, just as important undoubtedly, they know where to find them in legislation.

A senior public servant told us:

I am a senior public servant who has worked for 30 years in policy and government work. As such, I strongly support the idea of codifying the constitutional arrangements, both to ensure consistent interpretation and to make them easier to find. Of particular interest to me is lawmaking. I support the proposal to increase the parliamentary term, require a legislative programme, reduce the use of urgency, and improve the oversight of the legislative work.

Richard said:

As an immigrant to NZ I see many things in our society and political world that worry me about a NZ proclivity toward, or susceptibility to, fascism, should the wrong person or faction ever gain control.

Chris Smuts-Kennedy stated:

I think this initiative to produce a Constitution is a great opportunity to help steer our country towards being socially, environmentally and economically sustainable for the long term—for all its people.

Cliff said:

> We really need a check and balance in the system, otherwise 'anything goes' [. . .]

Tony submitted:

> I have become increasingly concerned for our fragile and diminishing rights in recent decades.

James Booth told us that he 'found it astounding that we have not got a formal written constitution.'

Jack Austin submitted, 'Without a Constitution we are all at risk of bad practice, bad policies, and bad government.'

Neville Farquhar said, 'I am very much in favour of a new constitutional structure along the outlines proposed in this forum.'

Lecturer Elizabeth Macpherson, Senior Lecturer Natalie Baird and five of their students, from the Faculty of Law at the University of Canterbury, made a detailed and helpful submission on the draft Constitution, supporting constitutional protection for environmental rights and the justiciability of economic and social rights, and adding to the prohibited grounds of discrimination. On the general features of the proposal they supported 'the entrenched status of the Constitution, the power of the judiciary to strike down inconsistent legislation, the protections of fundamental human rights, the removal of the monarchy as Head of State and (flexible) accommodation of Māori rights, biculturalism and the Treaty of Waitangi.'

Wayne Wedderspoon said:

> For a country that is in so many other respects at the head of the pack, our constitutional arrangements are really embarrassing. Frankly, the whole issue is a no-brainer.

Fiona Jarden argued for a written constitution that is 'a working framework for the exercise of public power in New Zealand on a clear and principled basis.'

Dominic Paul Baron and Steve Baron said:

> We strongly support the proposal to create the first democratic constitution for New Zealand because that is exactly what it will be. Not only will it be ratified democratically by referendum, it will be democratically elaborated.

Hugh argued:

> Given our commitment to democracy and fairness, coupled with the educated nature of our population, it's only right that we should have access to an understandable written constitution.

Dr Dean Knight, Senior Lecturer in Law at Victoria University of Wellington, raised an important point about how far the codification effort should go:

> I have some sympathy for the codification project because at the moment we have the Constitution Act [1986] which is an incomplete outline of some of our important rules, along with other documents which contribute to our constitutional framework. [...] In many respects the devil is in the detail about how far we go with the codification project. I am a minimalist: I am happy to engage in the codification project as it relates to the existing power structures to reflect what is important. In the round, I have some sympathy with attempts to fill out our written constitution in a way that gives it a bit more gravitas and standing.

Of course we received submissions which did not support the idea of a codified constitution.

The Hon Chris Finlayson QC MP made a speech in December 2016 against our proposals,[2] and his suggestion that the document be less prescriptive has seen us simplify the text significantly. In his recent submission to us, he recorded his support for retention of the monarchy and the royal prerogative, and his preference for updating key statutes to make the constitution more accessible—as opposed to undertaking an exercise to codify the constitution.

Alan Willoughby told us:

> Codifying NZ's constitution is both unnecessary and a retrograde step for a country whose lack of a single document written constitution is the envy of many countries in the world. Leave it like it is.

Andrew Beer thought there were other issues more worthy of consideration:

> What we have at present is fine. It's not broken don't fix it. People

---

2 Hon Chris Finlayson, Attorney-General (Keynote address at the New Zealand Law Foundation's 2016 Annual Awards Dinner, Wellington, 29 November 2016).

understand how our country's laws operate. I haven't seen anything in the papers or with the casual discussions that come up at work or that come up socially where anyone has a problem with how NZ law operates. The biggest single problem holding our country back is things like the Resource Management Act 1991. It needs major streamlining, or scrapping altogether. [. . .] It's the low level stuff like that which needs working on.

Dr Edward Willis had the following to say:

Aotearoa-New Zealand does not need a written constitution. Our nation already has an established framework that effectively constrains public power, promotes constitutional stability and provides for credible political commitment to a core set of fundamental principles and values. However, if the people of Aotearoa-New Zealand should choose to adopt a written constitution, fundamental aspects of our constitutional settlement will change. Whether that change is for better or worse is a matter of debate, but any serious reform proposal involving a written constitution needs to take these changes into account. Ideally, the aspects of our current unwritten constitutional arrangements that are valuable should be retained to the extent possible.

Margot argued:

Surely the test of whether or not we need a written constitution is to ask the question—have we done the right thing in the past? My answer is categorically 'Yes', and we don't need one now. [. . .] Over my life I have learned that it is better to have pragmatic solutions to pressing problems, than preordained processes and theoretical answers, which a constitution would endeavour to impose on us.

The point worrying Jane was different but valid:

This may sound like a crazy suggestion but is there any way of getting the writers of Shortland St to pick up and run with your excellent Constitution suggestions? Seems to me the challenge is getting wider take-up—my daughter, a fairly typical bright young mum, would in no way bother herself with the constitution and its importance per se—but under the guise of a Shortland Street viewer she undoubtedly would, if one of their characters expressed an interest in it.

Indeed, we have found popularising the idea of constitutional change is not easy because in order to understand the issues it is necessary to have a grasp of the existing system, and many have only hazy notions about how New Zealand is governed.

Supremacy and entrenchment

Almost all the people who favour a written codified constitution favour the constitution being supreme law; that is to say it would sit above the level of ordinary statues passed by Parliament and would be enforceable so that legislation that contradicted it could be struck down by the courts.

One submitter said:

> I support a New Zealand constitution as superior law. I think it would simplify New Zealand law, and help prevent ambiguities, gaps and contradictions that arise from our current piecemeal approach. It would also serve as the framework for any future legislation.

In the view of Hugo Lawrence:

> I think it is a strong proposal. Currently the constitution has no teeth, and the judiciary has limited effect on the exercise of government power.

Clara told us:

> As long as no party policy is enshrined in the constitution it makes sense for it to be superior law. If there is a superior law in the country we can all know where we stand.

Former Green MP Keith Locke had the following to say on the question of supremacy of the Constitution and the importance of protecting rights:

> A unicameral parliament has too much power and it has the power to rush things through quickly and ignore democratic rights. One of the key questions around superior law would be the provisions around the New Zealand Bill of Rights. At the present time the Bill of Rights can be pretty much overridden.

Bob Newcomb submitted:

> The constitution should be superior to parliament to stop politicians abusing the rights of its citizens. Politicians do not want a written constitution because it means an end to their ability to abuse our rights.

Interestingly, the National Council of Women of New Zealand found that even among their members who were not in favour of a single codified constitution, there was support for making some statutes supreme law:

> A significant number of NCWNZ members supported the proposal that the Judiciary (in the form of the Supreme Court) should be able to override Acts of Parliament that are inconsistent with the New Zealand constitution, regardless of whether it is a single written document or the current set of constitutional documents. They considered that it was acceptable for a 75% majority in Parliament to override a Supreme Court decision as it was important to sustain a balance between judicial and parliamentary power, and specific contextual factors were important in considering these matters.

Many submitters who favoured a codified constitution were also of the opinion that it should be entrenched; that is it would require a special procedure to change or amend the constitution. Gregory Dawes thought that not only should the constitution be entrenched but it should be more difficult to amend than we had proposed in our first draft:

> I strongly support this proposal and congratulate you on the draft Constitution. [. . .] This is a very good idea, not only so that people can know the laws by which they are governed, but also to provide a restraint on the misuse of government power. [. . .] I do not agree that a simple referendum should suffice to change the Constitution. The UK's experience with Brexit shows how dangerous this is. Perhaps a 2/3 majority in a referendum should be required, with perhaps an extra provision that it be a 2/3 majority of votes on both the general and Māori rolls.

Quite a number of people who made submissions on entrenchment felt a simple majority of people at a referendum of the voters (that is, more than 50 per cent of those who participate in the vote) was not a sufficient safeguard. They thought there should be a higher majority required and perhaps a minimum requirement for voter turnout. Philip was one of these:

> I believe in the book you mention a referendum result of >50%. I believe that it should require more than a simple majority in the referendum to make a constitutional change. Internationally Brexit is

a great example (especially with the legal challenges now occurring) of problems arising from a small majority referendum.

Several submitters were advocates of direct voter referenda on many issues, as is required under the Swiss Constitution—not just issues pertaining specifically to amendment of the constitution. Switzerland, however, is a federation and that Swiss model would be difficult if not impossible to operate in the New Zealand political culture. They have not protected some human rights well under the Swiss system. Women did not get the vote until 1971. And recently a referendum banning the building of mosques carried. As Archie told us in a submission:

> [The] Swiss Federal Constitution contains a similar provision, in which a simple majority can ratify amendments via a referendum. In 2009, this resulted in the Swiss Constitution prohibiting the construction of minarets, or towers, on mosques with a popular referendum, despite the strongest recommendations against during the campaign on the grounds it went against the basic principles of the Constitution. This decision, as it can be imagined, drew strong outcry from the Swiss government, other European states and the United Nations but the Swiss government had no choice but to enforce the new article. That is my worry with the proposed constitution's amendment procedures, it does not do enough to protect our rights from whatever fervours may grip the nation. [. . .] only 54% of eligible voters actually did vote, and the 57–42 margin meant that well under half of the of-age population consented with the amendment, yet it had to be enacted.

Emeritus Professor Peter Hogg QC, a New Zealander who became one of Canada's leading constitutional lawyers, had this observation to make:

> I wholeheartedly support the recommendation of a constitutional bill of rights. [. . .]When Canada adopted the Canadian Charter of Rights and Freedoms in 1982, I was much more enthused about the 'patriation' part of the constitutional package (adopting a domestic amending process to free Canada from the residual colonial links with the UK). But, over time, I have learned to love the Charter as well. It has pushed Canada, ahead of public opinion, to do the right thing on a number of important issues, for example, abortion (now unregulated), same-sex rights culminating in marriage, physician-assisted dying, and rights of persons accused of crime, including full

disclosure of the Crown case against them. These developments would probably have occurred anyway, but the Charter advanced the process by giving them a legal nudge as well as making them irrevocable. The effects of a constitutional bill of rights are not radical, but they are generally good.

The four-year parliamentary term and urgency

One of the prime reasons why submitters wanted a written codified constitution was to keep Parliament in order. Many submitters who opposed the idea of a codified constitution still expressed a belief that better law-making processes are necessary. Thus, many submitters favoured both a four-year term and restrictions upon the use of urgency, both of which are designed to avoid hurried and sloppy legislation and to increase transparency and accountability. While both proposals were generally supported, the proposal that the use of urgency when passing legislation in Parliament be restricted to those occasions on which it was supported by a 75 per cent majority of members received surprisingly wide endorsement.

Social media is too various and dispersed to report, but we were struck by one comment on Reddit that said:

> A constitution that prevented urgency unless you have 75% majority of the House would at least ensure that all Bills before the house got a proper debate. Fix most issues by regulating urgency.

There were some submitters who disagreed with these proposals, particularly the suggestion to extend the parliamentary term to four years. Cimino Cole generally agreed with the proposals in Constitution Aotearoa, but did not support an extended term:

> I will live without a written constitution, and believe me I share your passion for a written constitution, rather than vote to relinquish 25% of my enfranchisement.

David Hall said:

> I agree with lengthening the parliamentary term to reduce the impact of law-making with one eye too much on the next general election. But I am not persuaded that extending parliament to four years rather than three years would achieve the outcome that you anticipate—reducing the time pressure for law-making. In my experience, Parkinson's Law (work expands to fill the time available) is very true.

What the public told us

David Herbert Mourant thought that maybe there was a better way of fixing the deficiencies in our law-making processes:

> I do think that a lot of legislation is rushed through. I am not sure whether a four-year parliamentary is desirable. Parliament should meet more often during the year.

Another submitter thought similarly:

> We have more MPs per capita than other countries, plus their staff. When the House is sitting it's often nearly empty. They all turn up to sling arrows across the floor though in the most childish manner and are proud of it. They can rush legislation through the house in an instant when it suits, not a problem. Do they need four years or better time management? To actually turn up for the job and apply themselves to the task at hand and employ more researchers? There are different ways to skin a cat.

Interestingly, a large number of the same submitters who were generally against our proposals for a codified constitution (because 'we already have clarity of the basic rules—one person, one vote; freedom of religion; freedom of assembly etc' or because they were 'suspicious that this [proposal] is a Trojan horse to rewrite the law to confer special rights and privileges to Māori, and to transfer power from the Parliament to the Courts') say they agree with a four-year term and the proposal to clamp down on urgency: 'Yes. The only grounds for "urgency" should be for war, natural disasters or states of emergency.'

One submitter who supported the four-year term said:

> I have to deal regularly with badly drafted, or so over-amended, legislation that it is very hard to understand what Parliament wants me to do. The 3 year term is simply too short. I think 4 years should be about right, it works well in other places.

On limiting the use of urgency by requiring 75 per cent of MPs to agree, he had a more practical concern:

> I wonder though if 75% is too high in an MMP environment. It could effectively prevent urgency under any circumstances. If it were to be 2/3rds (66%) then it would still be hard, but the PM could try to get a few more than her coalition and support parties to vote for it.

Rebecca McMenamin agreed that a four-year term would be 'much better', and supported a restriction on the use of urgency, saying, 'Far too much urgency is being used, it undermines our democratic system (no chance for deliberation or direct participation).'

Another submitter had similar ideas about freeing up opportunities for public input and participation:

> A four-year term makes sense because it allows the government more time to pass quality legislation. It also ensures that the public has more time to evaluate the success of legislation and public policy introduced by the government and pass a more informed verdict when it is up for re-election.

Catherine Cotter took a pragmatic approach to the issue:

> In a three-year term, much time is lost as politicians and the public service, anticipate and recover from elections. It makes the window for transacting the legislative programmes between elections narrow. My worry with a four-year term is the risk of having to 'put up' with poor governments, and especially poor individual ministers, for longer. But it's time to recognise the true opportunity cost of three-year terms.

Andrew Larsen warned against conflating the two issues, saying:

> It seems to me that the proposed four-year term will have no impact on the issue of urgency. In NZ urgency is often used quite cynically to avoid public scrutiny and allow the executive to drive its agenda through parliament. The two issues are separate.

Gregory Dawes supported a four-year term, but on a condition: 'A four-year term is a good idea, provided that we also have the new protections the proposed Constitution would provide.'

On the Republic

The monarchy, to our surprise, did not attract many passionate submissions. It was as if the monarchy as a source of power is fading from the modern New Zealand mind. There is great respect for the Queen and there is an affection for that part of our heritage that is British, but the sentiment is becoming more remote with every passing year.

Of the submitters who took a view on New Zealand moving towards becoming a republic, most were in favour. A small but not

What the public told us

insignificant number were strongly against the idea. The views for moving to a republic were expressed in a number of ways.

Miraz Jordan submitted:

> I think the Monarchy belongs to the past and we should be looking to our future. We need our own head of state, drawn from our own population. I think this person should not only be a 'citizen of Aotearoa New Zealand', but should have been mainly resident here for perhaps 15 or 20 years before their appointment.

David Wright submitted:

> As well as a new constitution there is a proposal for New Zealand to become a Republic. I believe New Zealanders need to get involved in this discussion. I fully support both proposals.

Neville Farquhar submitted:

> The current constitutional arrangements represent the past and not the future. In the continuing evolution of our society, full separation from the crown is inevitable and the appropriate time for this change is when the current monarch dies.

Despite the important constitutional functions retained by the Crown, the royal family are today seen by the majority more as celebrities than political functionaries, and few of our citizens understand what the Crown's responsibilities are, nor care.

David Herbert Mourant told us, 'I do think the monarchy is a bit archaic and that New Zealand needs a Kiwi Head of State.'

Todd Nicholls, a Christchurch lawyer, had a more long-term view:

> I want my children to grow up proud to be New Zealanders and know that they have been blessed to live in one of the most beautiful countries on earth. I want them to know that with a bit of luck they could become New Zealand's Head of State.

Lewis Holden made this point in response to our proposals:

> I think what [Palmer and Butler] have shown us is two things: first, that becoming a Republic is not as complicated as it is made out to be. There are a number of people with vested interests in this debate who want to make it appear all too hard and complicated to change and a lot of effort for very little gain. In reality, it is not very hard. [. . .] Second, what they have shown is that the mindset that goes with the change is the hard part.

Those opposed tended to agree with one submitter who said that:

> Our British Monarchy under God is the best protection we still have to maintain our best and highest cultural heritage.

Stanley Richard Lusby in his submission said, 'New Zealand, like all the constitutional monarchies, has an unwritten constitution in Grace.'[3]

Jane Muir said, 'After reading about the idea to change NZ into a republic [it] is not a good idea at the moment.'

David Brown, on the other hand, argued there is no alternative to the monarchy:

> There isn't a living person in New Zealand who is worthy of being Head of State.

Garth suggested,

> the matter of a republic should initially be separated from whether there is a constitution. [. . .] Like it or not, the majority of 'ordinary' New Zealanders have fallen in love with William and Catherine and will strongly object to your wanting to deprive them of any future role in New Zealand.

Jeff said, 'I have always supported the royal family and Queen Elizabeth as our head of state.'

What did surprise us was the absence of any principled and policy-based arguments for the constitutional monarchy.

Nor was there any analysis of how the royal powers should be exercised or by whom. The constitutional conventions on that matter seemed to be a mystery to most.

Te Tiriti o Waitangi/the Treaty of Waitangi

The range of views on the Treaty could hardly have been wider. Some submitters were clearly in favour of the inclusion of the Treaty in the Constitution; others were unclear on their position or recommended substantial changes, and many of these wanted greater protection for the Treaty than we had provided for; and a number of submitters were clearly opposed to its inclusion at all. Overall, the majority of

---

3 Whatever one's view about religion, clearly in New Zealand there is not and never has been an established church, a position entirely different from that of the United Kingdom's.

What the public told us

submitters who touched on these issues were in favour of some form of recognition or incorporation of the Treaty in the constitution.

Some said the Treaty was producing a system of 'apartheid' in New Zealand. At the other end of the spectrum came the view that the Treaty should be the whole basis for the Constitution and until that discussion has been held no other progress is possible. In between were views that some recognition was necessary for the Treaty but since the document was both old and vague it should not be given direct constitutional effect.

Ken Maynard stated a pungent view echoed by a substantial number:

> The only way to honor Waitangi is to dump this fatally flawed piece of 19th century conveyancing in the trash can. [. . .] be aware Waitangi is so implacably destructive of the national good, if we have to throw out the entire English legal system to get rid of it WE WILL!

David Herbert Mourant submitted:

> There is only one race and that is the human race. I do not think the Treaty of Waitangi is relevant today as New Zealand is becoming more multicultural by the month.

In response to the question of codifying the constitution, Terry said:

> It's fine as it is but we do need to stamp out the racist half truths being put out by maori radicals and half cast 'trash' looking for personal advantage.

Harvey Rosieur, who told us he was of mixed Māori/European descent, wrote:

> I believe that all New Zealanders (those who were born here and those who are legal immigrants) should have equal rights, without exception.

Alan Willoughby told us:

> The Treaty of Waitangi has been misinterpreted in many ways, unintended meanings being derived from words which are eloquent in their simplicity. The only winners have been lawyers, who clip the ticket with each new piece of legislation, every new claim they can persuade part-Maori to lodge. The decrease in the harmony within New Zealand is closely paralleled by the increase in the distance

between the haves (including the part-Maori hierarchy who benefit from the payouts from claims) and the have-nots (largely made up of those part-Maori whom the hierarchy claims to represent), and the increase in the number of lawyers feeding at the public trough.

Another, more extreme view from a submitter who did not want his name disclosed said:

> We as a nation fought for the end of discrimination in South Africa and here are you bastards will and wanting to take our country down that same avenue. No Fuckin' Way. I also am sick and tired of these elite Maori who have turned the treaty bullshit into a business and it is time for all politicians to grow some fuckin' testicles and bring the gravy train to a rapid stop and bury it for ever. If you are such a caring person for the well being of our nation here called New Zealand you will stop all this shit before we have racial wars on hand to deal with as I for one would take up arms to protect what is mine and the standard of living we all enjoy here in New Zealand before all this silly treaty shit happened.

Neil Mercer submitted:

> If it ain't broke there is no need to fix it. But it is necessary to fix it, there needs to be removal of the Waitangi Tribunal in whole as soon as possible to remove the problem created by an appointed panel making pronouncements that are set up to remove the rights of non-maori versus the maori population based on the phrase 'if you think you are a maori then you are a maori' but ignoring the fact that there are few 'maori' with the current premise based on any percentage of maori blood gained from the birth parents no matter how small.

It was evident from quite a number of those who opposed the inclusion of the Treaty in the constitution that they would be happy enough with a codified constitution or some degree of reform aimed at ensuring better governance were the Treaty omitted. For example appreciable numbers of them favoured a four-year term for Parliament.

Of the more moderate views on the Treaty here follows a selection. David submitted:

> I recognise that the most controversial argument for keeping the treaty as an integral part of a new constitution is to keep the guarantee to the 'natives/aborigines' the 'full exclusive and undisturbed possession of their Lands and Estates Forests Fisheries and other properties

which they may collectively or individually possess'. A 21st century constitution should include a revised version of that guarantee taking into account changes over the past 177 years and should include a guarantee of undisturbed possession of their properties for all 21st century New Zealanders who have purchased or inherited their possession legally. A new constitution should abandon that notion of two separate nations.

Racheal McGonigal took the following view:

The Treaty of Waitangi was a document between the 'Crown' and the Maori. If you abolish the 'Crown' then you abolish the Treaty. The Treaty is a founding document and always must be retained as such. But it should never specifically be included in any Constitution. It is too vague and leaves too much open to be argued in Courts and ruled upon by one person, a Judge. The Treaty these days is causing a divide amongst NZers. There are many, both Maori and Pakeha who believe that while it had its place, times change. We need to be encouraging unity of one people, recognising heritage but the Treaty is these days being used to place one above others.

Margot submitted:

Over the last few decades we have made significant progress in addressing the grievances of the past in relation to Maori and the Treaty, without embedding it all in a constitution, which has the potential to trigger more grievances and further expensive litigation—more money for lawyers at the tax payers' expense.

Karl Mattys expressed this view:

The Treaty may be part of the Constitution as an explanatory historical document. I agree fully that past injustices suffered by the original native people of New Zealand, in spite of and contrary to the letter and spirit of the Treaty, should be rectified. However, this process of compensating for past wrongs cannot go on indefinitely. Some form of limit needs to be agreed on and when this limit is reached the Treaty becomes of historic interest only. New Zealand as a Nation needs to eventually treat all its citizens, of all ethnic backgrounds equally, without preference or privilege.

James Booth observed, however:

Regardless of ones views on the Treaty, the realpolitik is that without its inclusion no constitutional reform will get across the line.

Among those who argued for the Treaty to be front and centre of a new constitution was Andrew Barton:

> New Zealand already has a written constitution. It is called te Tiriti o Waitangi. Our written charter is forged between two distinct constitutional practices, Kawanatanga/Legislative Governance and Tino Rangatiratanga/sub-tribal Chieftainship. [. . .] Constitution Aotearoa's commendable and most necessary mission to provoke and ultimately entrench a written charter for our nation appears to not fully recognise the significance of this internationally recognised agreement and considers it constitutionally legal for the practice of Kawanatanga, alone, to oversee and administer such entrenchment. This view is supremely illegal and will further undermine the very foundation of our nation state and sense of nationhood. I implore you, therefore, to please consider the reaffirmation of te Tiriti o Waitangi as Aotearoa/New Zealand's official written charter. A charter that establishes the equal relationship between the constitutional house of Kawanatanga and the constitutional house of Tino Rangatiratanga and gives all peoples equal rights of legal justice and chiefly belonging to this land.

In their submission, the Social Justice Working Group of the Tikanga Pākehā Anglican Diocese of Auckland said:

> We believe that as Kāwanatanga and Pākehā/Tauiwi, we need to develop an informed commitment to the 1835 Declaration of Independence and Te Tiriti o Waitangi as we prepare for a respectful dialogue with Māori about Constitutional Change for our nation.

Miraz Jordan said the following on the Treaty:

> As the key founding document of this country the Treaty should be a fundamental part of the Constitution. How could we consider our Constitution legitimate without it? Whatever the debate about what the Treaty said, the fact that it exists set up a partnership between Maori and the Crown.

Responding to the question of whether the Treaty should be a part of the Constitution, Rebecca McMenamin said:

> Of course it should. The Treaty is our fundamental foundation of the exercise of power. We (pakeha) are tangata tiriti—only here because of the agreement of the Treaty. We should spend more time having korero about Maori-led constitutionalism!

What the public told us

Emeritus Professor Alan Mark of the University of Otago said this:

> Having read the case for and against the inclusion of the Treaty of Waitangi in the proposed Constitution for Aotearoa New Zealand, I further endorse the inclusion of the Treaty in the Constitution. The case made in this statement prepared by the authors/proponents is most comprehensive and fully satisfies me that the inclusion and treatment of the Treaty of Waitangi in the proposed Constitution is fully justified and acceptable.

Ian Langman made this point:

> As you are both well aware, the Waitangi Tribunal has made the most thorough and robust consideration of all available evidence of the circumstances and meaning of the Treaty of Waitangi. Their findings are irrefutable, that Maori have never ceded sovereignty and the Treaty was the establishment of a Sovereign relationship between the two sovereign entities, Maori represented by the 512 [sic] Chiefs and the Queen, the Sovereign of the British. If the Treaty is to be 'honoured', as claimed by all parties, then this must mean that there are two sovereign entities in New Zealand, each having sovereignty over their own subjects, i.e. the Maori Chiefs effecting sovereignty over all who recognise them as Sovereign (to keep it simple I will presume all Maori) whilst the Queen effects sovereignty over all other New Zealanders [(again to keep it simple, non-Maori).

David James made the following point in his submission:

> your proposed constitution is desirable and thorough. It would certainly be preferable to have a constitution set out in one place where it is able to be studied and considered. I have two major reservations, however. One is that you have sought 'to incorporate the Treaty within Constitution Aotearoa', whereas the present call is to harmonise the constitution with Te Tiriti. The result is that your constitution as it stands would improve solely the kāwanatanga side of the equation but without structurally acknowledging the rangatiratanga partnership.

Wally Hicks made this following argument:

> The greatest challenge in creating a Constitution for Aotearoa NZ will be finding a way to fulfil the partnership and true power sharing of Te Tiriti now that (those who identify as) Maori have become only 15% of the total population. What form does such a 'government' take? If

we turn away from this challenge, we will have failed our children, our tamariki, our grandchildren, our mokopuna. [. . .]There's a 'debating technique' used by certain factions concerning Maori representation which I call 'The Stone Age Culture Argument'. It goes hand-in-hand with tag-lines and 'spin' such as 'Maori privilege', 'race-based politics', 'separatism' and 'Tribal elites', and posits the absurd idea that any moves to improve Maori representation in government will result in a return to pre-1840 (supposed) 'Maori' behaviour, often characterised as 'genocide, slavery, cannibalism and infanticide'. 'Stone Age Culture' is a very poor contemporary justification of White Supremacy in my humble opinion.

One anonymous submitter said:

My primary question/feedback is about integrating the Treaty of Waitangi rather than referencing it; as it is one of the 'pieces' that currently demands huge energy and resources to constantly establish and negotiate agreements on so many important decisions and ways of operating in Aotearoa. I believe there is a large number of people who on learning Maori values and principles are deeply drawn to them. How might we integrate the spirit of the Maori text Treaty that was signed; and ultimately navigate a true partnership and collaboration in the principles, values and structures that govern Aotearoa? This is one of the true tests of our maturity as a nation.

John Cody made this observation:

This is to support the direction you have outlined. I think your initiative allows us to clarify the contemporary implications of Article 1[of the Treaty] and introduce a more deliberative approach to governance—often implied in important statutes now but poorly implemented in practice. The international context of sovereignty is also evolving e.g. a call for alternatives to closed 'courts' for adjudicating commercial issues. (As an aside, the 'public excluded' provisions in our own legislation are abused at present, refer for example to the conduct of DHBs.) In due course the conversation you are facilitating will get to core aspects of Article 3 insofar as it refers to social and economic rights. I believe that will place Article 2 in a context that respects rights that go beyond property rights and are probably based on rights of association and principles of subsidiary. In the specific case of the Treaty it is essential that we continue to reduce, as far as is now possible, the impact of rights obtained by conquest and deception. Consequently this is a very important negotiation to continue. Perhaps

What the public told us

this project can be explicitly aligned with the process sketched in the Mutu-Jackson report and any other comparable processes.

Bill Mansfield reached the following pithy conclusion:

> I don't think the inclusion of the Treaty in the Constitution will itself clarify the status, relevance and effect of the Treaty in particular situations. But at this stage of our history it is unthinkable to leave it out. And we need to leave it to the courts to analyse its relevance in individual cases.

The range of views on the Treaty and the intensity with which some of them were expressed have caused us to revise our approach and to require a process to clarify the application of the Treaty. This is discussed in detail in chapter 13.

Other matters of interest

Along with thoughts and opinions on the various proposals included in the first draft of Constitution Aotearoa, the submissions contain a multitude of comments on all sorts of issues which we had not included in our first version. Many of these were raised in our face-to-face meetings with the public as well. Some of these concerns caused us to reconsider our thinking in some areas, or explore new areas of reform. Others, while matters which warrant concern, are not suitable for inclusion in a constitution. A written, codified constitution cannot deal with all the policy issues New Zealand faces. Its prime purpose is to define where the power lies and provide a framework for the limits upon its exercise. Much of the detail for particular policies must be left to the political process that goes into making Acts of Parliament. These law-making methods should certainly be improved as we set out in chapter 8. It is important to avoid clogging up a written constitution with too much specificity on policy issues, just as it is important to provide more checks on public power than we have currently. It is a question of balance in each case.

Included in the list of issues people raised were:

- concerns around the changes to the complaints process for 1080 poison regulation;
- questions around the possibility of including rights *of* nature (rather than just rights *to* nature);
- assisted dying;

- greater provision for quality civics education;
- compulsory voting;
- including a 'not proven' verdict in criminal cases, alongside the current options of 'guilty' or 'not guilty';
- the inclusion of rights to freedom *from* religion, and greater separation of church and state in the Constitution;
- constitutional protection for the Government Statistician;
- greater clarity around language rights for official state languages and greater provision for their use;
- lowering the voting age to 16;
- improving the quality of pre-election debate on party policies;
- concerns around the health of the media;
- issues of digital transformation and digital rights;
- mental health issues;
- the status of women;
- including cultural rights in the Constitution;
- the possibility of reestablishing an Upper House in Parliament;
- greater incorporation of direct democracy in the Constitution;
- concerns around the use and regulation of private prisons;
- including a right to medical treatment in the Constitution;
- including a right to sanctuary in the Constitution;
- intergenerational ethics.

Some of these suggestions we have incorporated (such as the suggestion to lower the voting age to 16, or tweaking our current right to freedom of religion slightly to emphasise the separation of church and state), and more detail on how and why this was done can be found later in the book.

Conclusion

In this chapter we have given a flavour and taste of the submissions on the principal issues that were submitted on by members of the public. There were many other points of detail made in the submissions and where these are relevant they will be discussed at the point in this book where their particular issue arises. In subsequent chapters we have also drawn from a number of the blogposts addressing specific issues published on our website. On the question of a second House in Parliament, on which there were a number of submissions, we have devoted a whole chapter.

The submissions provide useful insight into points of controversy. Resolving the most serious of the controversies through a public and deliberative process with citizen participation will be necessary if an effective constitution is to be adopted. To these approaches we next turn.

4 A Constitution based on principle

The difficulty with any constitutional discussion in New Zealand is that people struggle to see how it affects them. They vote in elections and think that is about all they can do. They do not see that changes to how power is structured, how it is used and the remedies against its abuse can improve their lives. Looked at in this light, there is no issue of public policy more important than the constitution; if we get this right, the prospect of better decision-making increases.

There are a number of things we hope to achieve with Constitution Aotearoa, underpinned by values we think ought to be the basis of any modern country. We set them out in our first book:[1]

Summary of what we hope to achieve with Constitution Aotearoa

1 Accessibility and certainty:

Set out the rules, principles and processes about government in one document so they are accessible, available and clear. Eliminate the need for significant unwritten constitutional conventions and customs that are unclear in important respects. Our Constitution will remove the mystery and provide an accurate map about how we govern ourselves.

2 Education:

Provide a Constitution that will educate people and public decision-makers on their rights and responsibilities. A new Constitution should help people participate in democratic decision-making and provide a better framework for learning about civics. This will help people not born here to understand New Zealand's system of government, and that is a significant need given the increasing ethnic and cultural diversity of New Zealand society. Such a Constitution may help to dispel the disenchantment with politics that seems to afflict us. The Constitution must be trusted by the people.

3 Rule of law:

Anchor public power in a Constitution that will contribute to the rule of law, a concept that is fundamental to a well-functioning representative democracy. Government that is beyond the law

---

1 Geoffrey Palmer and Andrew Butler *A Constitution for Aotearoa New Zealand* (Victoria University Press, Wellington, 2016) at 25–27.

A Constitution based on principle

resembles tyranny. The courts in New Zealand can be relied upon to be fair and follow legal propriety. All must be equal in the eyes of the law. The Constitution embodies principles of legality and fair procedure. An important element of the rule of law is judicial independence and impartiality on the part of judges in supervising the legality of government and promoting the freedom of its citizens.

4 Democratic accountability:

Provide clear means of holding public decision-makers accountable to the public whom they serve on a continuing basis, whether they be ministers, politicians, public servants, the police, the defence forces or the Judiciary. Elections are but one form of accountability. The features of accountability can vary from one government institution to another, depending on the subject matter and particular issues. One form of accountability does not fit all situations.

5 Transparency:

Make decision-making and law-making more transparent so that the public is better able to make judgments about the policies being carried out, and for the same reason, improve the availability of official information.

6 Protection for the rights of citizens:

Ensure that the New Zealand Bill of Rights and te Tiriti o Waitangi/ the Treaty of Waitangi are better observed.

7 A New Zealander as Head of State:

Establish the functions and powers of a New Zealand Head of State.

8 National identity and the preservation of the elements of the system that have served New Zealand well:

Record important elements of New Zealand's national identity and protect basic institutions that are required to serve the public. Provide for development in the future.

9 Protections against the abuse of power:

Restrict and control the arbitrary use of government power by the provision of ample safeguards against wrongful use of that power.

10 The Constitution belongs to the people:

A Constitution must stand above the interests of any particular political party. It must belong to all the people because it is under their will that government must be conducted in a democracy. The aphorism penned by the greatest of American presidents, Abraham Lincoln, in the Gettysburg Address expresses our aim here: 'that government of the people, by the people, for the people, shall not perish from the earth'.

The thing that makes a constitution work is the people who make decisions under it. They need to understand constitutional values, and even a written constitution does not allow all of these principles to be written down in some law or other. Ethics and honesty in those carrying out public functions are vital. However, we think it is important that the constitution begins with a statement of some fundamental values and principles that hopefully all New Zealanders can agree to. The purpose is to state both the objectives of the use of public power and the limits on it, so that those exercising power can be guided by these. Here is what we now propose in Article 1:

1 The objectives of, and limits on, public power

This Constitution confers public power on institutions and public officials of the State to promote the peace, order, and good government of Aotearoa New Zealand for the following purposes:

(1) to ensure that public power is exercised democratically, that is to say, with the participation of people, transparently, accountably, and subject to checks and balances that ensure minorities are protected:

    (a) to secure an environment adequate to equitably meet the needs of present generations in an ecologically sustainable manner and not to impair the rights of future generations to meet their needs reasonably:

    (b) to protect the human rights of all New Zealanders:

    (c) to respect and to enhance the relationship between Māori and the State, and the capacity of Māori collectively to control and influence the use of their resources:

    (d) to advance the public welfare so that all New Zealanders can aspire to, and achieve, fulfilling lives free from poverty, fear, ignorance and violence:

    (e) to foster a community that accommodates difference, respects individuality, yet achieves collective goals for the common good, allowing a fair go to all:

A Constitution based on principle

(f) to recognise that there will be a diversity of views on many questions touching on the public welfare, which need to be resolved through discussion, respectful debate, and decision-making in a range of forums, including central and local government.

Capturing the aspirations that a constitution has for people and their values is no simple task, but we have become convinced it is important. So we have replaced our previous legal and historical account of our constitutional development with a much more aspirational, value-laden and visionary statement:

We the people of Aotearoa New Zealand declare—

We live in a beautiful set of islands in the South Pacific Ocean settled first by Māori migrants from Polynesia, later by settlers from Europe, then joined by people from many other countries and cultures from the Pacific Islands, Asia and elsewhere. We aim to live in an inclusive and just society:

We are committed to governance in the interests of the people of Aotearoa New Zealand from whom all power is derived:

We state our determination to promote human dignity, tolerance and respect for people from diverse cultures and make a commitment to uphold and secure civil, political and human rights, and cultural, economic, and social rights:

We respect te Tiriti o Waitangi/the Treaty of Waitangi as the founding document of the nation:

We value freedom and opportunity for all, fairness, equity, equality, environmental sustainability, kaitiakitanga and tikanga Māori, a sound economy, a strong sense of community and respect for the family, especially the care of children:

We support a clear distribution of power between the Head of State, the Parliament, the Government, and an independent Judiciary with affordable access to justice through courts:

We affirm Aotearoa New Zealand is founded on the principle that the people govern themselves through a democratic system of representative and responsible government based on free and fair elections:

We encourage increased public participation in official decision-making to ensure greater deliberation in the making of major policy decisions:

We wish to live in an open society with a robust, accountable and transparent system of democratic government under the rule of law:

We are a proud and independent nation with our own voice within the community of nations:

We express our desire to build upon our rich constitutional heritage by strengthening our system of democratic, accountable government and adopting this written Constitution.

It is hoped that the combination of a short, aspirational Preamble and the setting out of core values and principles in Article 1 of the draft Constitution will help New Zealanders relate to and take ownership of the Constitution. It also demonstrates key guiding principles for those carrying out functions under the Constitution and exercising public power, and is an indication to newcomers to our country of who we are as a nation and what we hold to be important.

These two things are key, and they guide the rest of the Constitution which follows.

5 The State and a New Zealand Republic

The Realm of New Zealand

In 2016, we proposed that New Zealand should have a New Zealander as Head of State. Currently, New Zealand is a constitutional monarchy. We have a monarch, Queen Elizabeth II, who is Queen in Right of New Zealand. Her mantle is hereditary and will pass down her family line upon her death or abdication of office. We will have no say in who succeeds her, who becomes the next Head of State, representing our country as monarch in right of New Zealand.[1]

The Queen retains and exercises some residual royal powers and appoints a Governor-General as her direct representative to exercise her powers in her role as New Zealand's Head of State.

The Government has become almost synonymous with the Crown, a nebulous concept which in reality exercises most of the powers traditionally held by the old kings and queens of Great Britain.

We think it is time we moved away from the monarchy and became a Republic.

The move to a Republic would, for the most part, make little difference in the day-to-day workings of the country, at least in the way we have proposed. However, two elements of the change would be significant symbolically. The first is that the Crown would be abolished and replaced with the structure of the State, which would draw its power and legitimacy from the people through the Constitution. The second change is that the Queen would be replaced as the Head of State by a New Zealander, who would be appointed for a fixed term to carry out the responsibilities of representing the country of Aotearoa New Zealand, and of guarding the Constitution on behalf of its people.

There is nothing particularly radical in our proposals on this issue. For some years now senior politicians, including at least four recent prime ministers, have said that the abolition of the monarchy is

---

1 Succession is determined by the Act of Settlement 1700, passed in the United Kingdom and referred to in the Constitution Act 1986 (NZ), s 5.

inevitable.[2] Peter Dunne, a long serving MP who retired at the 2017 election, said in a recent speech:[3]

> I strongly believe the time [is] well past for us to have severed the umbilical cord to Grandmother England.
>
> We should be an independent republic within the Commonwealth—like India, or South Africa and the majority of other Commonwealth nations.
>
> It is not just my Irish heritage, but more my sense of pride and confidence in our country and what it can be and that is why I am so staunchly of the belief we can do so much better than continue to bend our knee to a hereditary monarch on the other side of the world.
>
> We have consistently shown over the last thirty years or so, that we can produce many quality New Zealanders to serve as our Governor-General.
>
> There is no reason why we could not do likewise with a non-executive President in that role, and frankly the time for change is long overdue.

Well, if that is true, it is time we faced up to the nature of the alternative. As we pointed out in chapter 3, opposition to our proposal to abolish the monarchy was muted. The submissions we did receive that opposed the move were largely based on sentiment and were a reflection of celebrity culture which has surrounded the young royals, William and Kate in particular. To some degree this opposition also had religious overtones.

We will not repeat the detailed case that we made for change in 2016; it is readily available on our website and in *A Constitution for Aotearoa New Zealand*. Rather, we will concentrate on how our

---

2   David Lange was the first. Former prime minister Jim Bolger thought in 1994 that the momentum for changing the Head of State 'will gather as we identify more with our Asia-Pacific region of the world and as our direct links to Britain decline' (Jim Bolger (8 March 1994) 539 NZPD 121). Helen Clark thought it was absurd to have the Head of State so far away (Stephen Bates 'Republican Pledge Greets Queen' *The Guardian* (online ed, London, 22 February 2002)). John Key has said he thinks a republic is inevitable ('NZ republic inevitable, says Key' *Radio New Zealand* (online ed, New Zealand, 26 November 2008)). In an interview soon before leaving office in 2016 Governor-General Sir Jerry Mataparae said that a republic was 'inevitable', and it was just a matter of when (Rosanna Price 'A Role with a Purpose' *Dominion Post* (New Zealand, 23 April 2016)).

3   Hon Peter Dunne 'Valedictory Address' (Valedictory Address 2017, Victoria University of Wellington Post-Election Seminar, Wellington, 6 December 2017).

proposals have been altered in light of the submissions received.

We have greatly benefitted in this regard from a recent book setting out detailed and meticulous research, by Dame Alison Quentin-Baxter and Professor Janet McLean of the University of Auckland, *This Realm of New Zealand: The Sovereign, The Governor-General, The Crown*.[4]

The importance of this book lies in its account of the entire history of the British Crown in New Zealand. It points out at the beginning that the parliamentary democracy New Zealand takes for granted 'conceal[s] New Zealand's ultimate constitutional underpinnings in the monarchy'.[5] Many of the legal powers in New Zealand are the powers of the Queen, although most of them are not substantively exercised by her or the Governor-General. The whole system is underscored by a series of unwritten constitutional conventions about how power will be exercised so that it can be democratic, recognising that in their origins the powers were anything but democratic. Once the monarchy is removed, a constitutional power vacuum exists. There is no longer any foundation on which the powers of government rest. The monarch must be replaced, and the powers held by the monarch have to be distributed between various institutions of the state.

This Realm of New Zealand concludes with an afterword on how New Zealand might go about becoming a republic if the country was minded to do so. The authors concentrate on the option that transfers the Governor-General's role to a non-partisan Head of State appointed by the Prime Minister or the House of Representatives. They remark that the type of change we have been promoting has a big constitutional result because it 'would also remove its present conceptual core'—the Crown. The authors of the *Realm* say that in theory 'a short operative provision in an Act of the New Zealand Parliament is all that would be required to bring monarchy to an end'.[6] Yet they also say that in reality many other steps would be needed, not least the process leading up to the change and the public involvement in it. And, as they also say, the effects on the law more

---

4 Alison Quentin-Baxter and Janet McLean *This Realm of New Zealand: The Sovereign, The Governor-General, The Crown* (Auckland University Press, Auckland, 2017).
5 At i.
6 At 316.

generally would be substantial and would involve the significant undertaking of re-vesting of powers.

For the present authors, one of the greatest insights we have gained during this whole project is how deconstruction of the Crown in New Zealand requires big shifts of formal power for all the main institutions of government. Looked at in terms of a rational distribution of governmental powers, the monarchy is a source of confusion and doubt. It is an opaque obstacle to understanding the ways the powers of government are exercised and by whom. Essentially, the Crown is a mask the Government puts on to disguise itself when it wants. It functions as a barrier to explaining to people how our democracy works and what the limits on power are.

Clearly for New Zealand to become a republic there must be a significant constitutional exercise carried out and that will require many elements of a written, codified constitution. If we become a republic without a deep programme of public engagement there are likely to be substantial difficulties. There needs to be a Head of State in place of the Queen; that Head of State will need to have functions and powers that are legally defined and limited. It seems unwise to entrust such a transformation to an ordinary statute which can be altered in our single House of Parliament by a majority of one. The obscurity of the present complicated legal position—who has what power and why?—is hard to explain to anyone, let alone to the large number of people who live here but who were not born here and come from other cultures.[7]

A forward-looking constitution would reflect the need to make things clear to people of many cultures and ethnicities, in a society as diverse as New Zealand now is. Once it was largely the British and Māori who lived here; that is no longer the case.

Joseph Romanos, a journalist, made the following point in his submission about New Zealand's changing ethnic make-up:

> It's very important generally; not only because New Zealand's ethnic make-up is changing. It is important that we have a Head of State who unifies our population and symbolises our independence regardless of our changing population make-up. From a sporting perspective,

---

7 Mai Chen *The Superdiversity Stocktake: Implications for Business, Government and New Zealand* (Superdiversity Centre, 3 November 2015), available at <www.chenpalmer.com/wp-content/uploads/Superdiversity_Stocktake.pdf>.

The State and a New Zealand Republic

I don't think that any New Zealand sportsperson is trying to win a Gold Medal for the Queen. I love the Queen; she's been a superb monarch, but New Zealand sportspeople are doing it (trying to win) for their country and New Zealanders are proud of these sportspeople.

If demography is destiny, our present constitutional arrangements miss the bus. They provide a misleading narrative about the real distribution of public power. This is an obstacle to public understanding about how government actually works and leads to a false sense of security, as many believe in checks and balances, which don't actually exist in practice. For example, a number of submitters believed that if the Government tried to pass through Parliament a law that seriously breached human rights, the Queen would step in and refuse to grant Royal Assent to the Bill, meaning it does not become law. This is not the case. While the Governor-General, as representative of the Queen, has this power in theory, it is never exercised; there is a constitutional convention that prevents it.

Further, the vague and mystical concept of the Crown handicaps our search for a distinct national identity in a country that now exhibits superdiversity in its population mix. Mai Chen has conducted an extensive study into the effects of superdiversity on New Zealand's law and institutions. The study points to the need for profound changes in law, government and business to accommodate the current pluralism into a new and distinct cultural blend. This rapid development speaks strongly for a more accessible and inclusive constitution where human rights, cultural rights and the rights of minorities are more strongly protected.

In abolishing the Crown, the proposed Constitution abolishes the Realm of New Zealand. A realm is part of a kingdom, and New Zealand should not think of itself as part of a kingdom. The practical points that arise from the Realm of New Zealand, extending to include the Cook Islands, Niue, Tokelau and the Ross Sea Dependency, are in theory relatively simple to deal with. People will keep their New Zealand citizenship and the degree of association these countries have with New Zealand is up to their own democratic decisions.

Many people in New Zealand seem to believe that becoming a republic would be a difficult, complicated and uncertain step. This is not so. Becoming a republic is relatively simple so long as the political will is present to accomplish it. Ireland accomplished it long ago and in 1937 substituted the monarchy with a written, codified constitution that has worked well. A majority of Commonwealth countries have become republics while remaining within the Commonwealth, and many of them have constitutions, similar to the one we are promoting, which were bestowed on them when the British left. Of the 52 countries that belong to the Commonwealth, 31 are republics, five have monarchs of their own and 16 retain the Queen as Head of State, as in New Zealand.[8]

Not only are the majority of Commonwealth countries republics, most of them have entrenched, written, codified constitutions with entrenched Bills of Rights. Surveying these tendencies in 1964 and weighing them against the traditional British tendency to oppose Bills of Rights, Professor Stanley de Smith found they had been adopted in many of the new constitutions of the Commonwealth. He concluded, '[c]learly, then, there is a close correlation between allegiance to the general principles of constitutionalism and readiness to accept and abide by a justiciable constitutional bill of rights'.[9] Even traditional British opposition to Bills of Rights has weakened; in 1998 the United Kingdom Parliament itself passed the Human Rights Act 1998, a measure that owed much to the New Zealand Bill of Rights Act 1990 and, like that measure, is not superior law.

We are conscious that it has been common in other parts of the world, when making a transition from monarchical government to republican government, to highlight explicitly in the new constitution a bold declaration of the republic. We do not consider this is necessary or appropriate in the New Zealand context. Unlike many other places, the transition in New Zealand is not borne out of any particular sense of resentment about the Crown or rebellious celebration of the shift in form of government. It is simply a reflection of the passage of time and distance and the growing individuality of New Zealand. In these circumstances we think it is much more appropriate that the constitution simply state the new approach to government in a matter-of-fact way that is respectful of the past. We have no doubt the transition can be effected perfectly well.

---

8   See 'Commonwealth of Nations' (23 November 2017) Wikipedia, available at <https://en.wikipedia.org/wiki/Commonwealth_of_Nations>.
9   Stanley de Smith *The New Commonwealth and its Constitutions* (Stevens, London, 1964) at 214.

The deconstruction of the Crown, the creation of the State and the re-distribution of public power

In our first draft of Constitution Aotearoa, we made the following proposals in relation to the State:[10]

- transferring the role of the Crown to the State;
- making the State a new legal entity in New Zealand;
- transferring all Crown assets to the State;
- the State must be bound by the Constitution and the law, its powers should not be unlimited and it must be held responsible for its actions;
- the government of the day exercises the powers of the State (much in the way that it exercises the powers of the Crown at present) and must do so within the legal framework established by the Constitution and the existing law.

Our final proposals regarding the State, as set out in this book, largely achieve the same, though we think that we have managed to do it in a much cleaner and neater way this time around. We have devised a scheme that first establishes the legal personality and capacities of the State of Aotearoa New Zealand. The limits on the powers of the State are set by the Constitution and what it contains. The source of the State's power will derive—as it should in a democracy—from the people. They have the ultimate legal authority, not the monarch. Power is exercised by the institutions of government on their behalf. We have divided the powers of the State between five core institutions, five pillars which support the State and the people within it. Dividing the powers of the State between five different institutions provides protection against excessive concentrations of power. These institutions are:

- the Head of State, to be known as the Guardian or Kaitiaki of the Nation;
- the Parliament;
- the Government;
- the Judiciary;
- Local government.

10 Geoffrey Palmer and Andrew Butler *A Constitution for Aotearoa New Zealand* (Victoria University Press, Wellington, 2016) at 214.

The Head of State

The role of representing the unifying commitment to the Constitution and all the institutions and instruments of the State is vested in the Head of State. The Head of State is to be a non-partisan symbol of unity for the nation, a reflection of who we are and what we value. That person is known as the Guardian or Kaitiaki of the nation. The Head of State is entitled to be informed on the general conduct of the Government and is entitled to information relating to the Government. The Head of State may give advice and comment on affairs of State in private to the Prime Minister or other ministers. The Head of State must also sign all subordinate legislation made by the Cabinet. The Head of State must perform the functions of the office 'as a non-partisan symbol of unity'. The Head of State is responsible for protecting the Constitution. In most things, the Head of State will act on the advice of the Prime Minister, ministers and Cabinet. However, we propose the Kaitiaki also have a new 'referral' power under which they can, having been presented with a Bill to sign into law, and only after consultation with the Prime Minister, refer a Bill of doubtful constitutionality to the Supreme Court to consider the issue. If the Court determines the Bill breaches the Constitution it can direct the Head of State not to sign it into law and the Bill is referred back to Parliament. While this may not occur frequently, it is a useful safeguard and underscores the guardianship or kaitiakitanga dimension of the Head of State's role. In all other cases, the Head of State will act on the advice of the Prime Minister, ministers and Cabinet.

The Parliament

The legislative power of the State is vested in Parliament, whose members are regularly elected by and responsible to the people. Parliament scrutinises, debates and passes legislation, approves Government expenditure and taxation, and provides for the redress of grievances. It votes on motions of confidence or no confidence in a minister or the Government. Parliament's legislative power entails the making and amending of Acts of Parliament which set out the basic laws of the land, for example specifying what behaviour amounts to a criminal offence and what the punishments for offences are. Legislative power includes the making of subordinate laws such as regulations, of which there are hundreds. Parliament carries out much of its work through select committees. Acts of Parliament also currently provide that law can be made by outside agencies such as the various transport authorities, for example the Civil Aviation Authority or the Maritime Safety Authority. These rules are signed off by a minister. The power of Parliament extends to the imposition of taxation to raise money for public purposes and the control and the expenditure of that money through parliamentary approval. Under our proposal, Parliament also votes on Government proposals to commit troops overseas and must approve international agreements such as treaties before Government can themselves commit to them. Parliament is the central democratic institution of the country.

The Government

The Government has the responsibility of running the country, making thousands of decisions every day. The Government is made up of the Cabinet, the Prime Minister and other ministers. We propose that the executive authority of the State be vested in Cabinet and the ministers. It is in these institutions that the executive rests, but its powers and functions must derive from the Constitution itself or an Act of Parliament. The Cabinet members are responsible to Parliament and are questioned and held to account there. The Government may act through the Cabinet, a minister, or any other officer or entity empowered by or under the Constitution. The Executive Council is abolished since it is no longer needed in the absence of a monarch.

The Judiciary

The judicial authority of the State is vested in the courts, whose judges are sworn to uphold the law. Court decisions are subject to appeal and errors are corrected through the appellate structure, with the final appeal being to the Supreme Court. There exists also a statutory mechanism for complaint against the conduct of judges. The Constitution will establish a Judicial Appointments Commission which will ensure that judicial appointments are not political and are 'on merit, having regard to the candidate's personal qualities, legal ability, and experience and the desirability that the judiciary reflect gender, cultural and ethnic diversity.' The Constitution also gives the Judiciary the power to strike down laws inconsistent with or breaching the Constitution. This enhanced constitutional role is discussed in chapter 10.

Local government

Under this Constitution local government will be given a constitutional status that it currently lacks. Where under our present arrangements, a bare majority of Parliament can do with local government what it likes, under our proposed Constitution, local government will be given some constitutional status. Some core principles that govern its relationship with central government will be protected; this will give it some increased autonomy.

Guardian/Kaitiaki of the Nation—A New Zealander as Head of State

The most important function of the Head of State we are proposing will be to act as a symbol of Aotearoa New Zealand; to signify its unity, its legitimacy and its values. Symbols are important, as proven by the 2016 flag debate and subsequent referenda. The national anthem is another such symbol, as is the New Zealand Coat of Arms. Symbols perform a vital function in the life of any nation. They can help to provide a sense of national unity and purpose. They can nourish a belief in the ideals of the nation and give people a sense of aspiration, even destiny.

It is worth pausing to ask: What makes us 'us'? Behind the idea of New Zealand as a nation is the question of our national character, our collective historical experience and some notion of the relationship between the state and the people. Collectively, these add up to the 'civic culture'.[11] It is this civic culture that contributes to the stability of New Zealand and its enduring sense of identity and nationhood. The elements of the culture are often communicated by symbols. The symbols of New Zealand, for example, are different from those of Australia. New Zealand symbols of nationhood must illuminate the experiences of what it is to be a New Zealander.

The monarchy, headquartered as it is in Britain, complicates the

---

11 Gabriel A Almond and Sidney Verba *The Civic Culture: Political Attitudes and Democracy in Five Nations* (Princeton University Press, Princeton, 1963).

development of an identity distinctive to Aotearoa New Zealand. While the monarchy has served us well and we should be grateful for it, in our view the time has come to move on by not only broadening and strengthening our constitutional arrangements but also by allowing our own symbols, such as a home-grown Head of State, space to develop independently.

In 2016, we made the following statement regarding the choices to be made when considering the replacement of the monarchy in New Zealand:[12]

> A Head of State can take various forms, and many different arrangements exist around the world. Here in New Zealand it would be better to have a model that fits into our constitutional tradition as a Westminster-style democracy than to strike out in radical new directions. When deciding on a model, some important issues need to be considered:
> - What powers should the Head of State have?
> - What functions and duties should the Head of State perform?
> - How long should a Head of State occupy the office?
> - How should the Head of State be chosen?
> - What should we call the Head of State?

In our first draft, we answered these questions by saying:[13]

> We are proposing a new Head of State, a New Zealander who lives here, in the place of the Queen reigning over New Zealand. The new Head of State would be called 'the Head of State'. The person would be selected on a free vote in the House of Representatives. The Head of State would enjoy very similar, although not identical, powers and functions to those exercised by the Governor-General now. The term of office would be five years. New Zealand would remain in the Commonwealth. New Zealand has secured many advantages from its British connections over the years and these can be maintained, but we need now a more defined sense of our own national identity as an independent nation in the area of the world in which we live.

Our final proposals set out in our second draft are not too different. We still advocate a five-year term and selection through a free vote in Parliament, though the Head of State will now need a

---

12 Palmer and Butler, above n 10, at 85.
13 At 103.

two-thirds majority of those voting in order to be appointed.[14] For the most part, the Head of State will have very similar powers and functions to those proposed in the first draft, which largely mirrored those currently exercised by the Governor-General on behalf of the Queen. These include acting as a non-partisan symbol of unity for the nation, signing Bills into law, appointing the Prime Minister, conferring honours and awards and representing the country overseas on occasion. These powers and functions are exercised on the advice of the Prime Minister, ministers and Cabinet. We also propose that the Head of State shall be known as the Guardian or Kaitiaki of the Nation. This name was supported by Lewis Holden, a former Chair of New Zealand Republic, in a submission to us.

However, we are proposing one significant change from our first draft. This has come partly as a response to a number of submissions that urged us to give greater powers to the Head of State to act as a further check on the other branches of government that make up the State. It is also partly an attempt to provide a potential means of stopping laws that may breach the Constitution, in an effort to reduce the burden on individuals bringing a claim before the Court once their rights have already been breached.

What we are proposing is a referral power. This is loosely modelled on Article 26 of the Irish Constitution, which allows the Irish President to refer a Bill to the Irish Supreme Court to determine its constitutionality.

This power is set out in draft Article 49:

49 Head of State may refer constitutionality of Bill to Supreme Court
(1) If the Head of State, after consultation with the Prime Minister, is of the view that any Bill passed by Parliament and submitted for the signature of the Head of State may be contrary to this Constitution, the Head of State may refer to the Supreme Court

---

14 Our reasons for having the Head of State appointed rather than elected are set out more fully in chapter 3 of our first book, but in short we wanted to avoid politicising the role, as a Head of State with a popular mandate would be a competing source of authority to the Prime Minister. We have deliberately not set out in the Constitution the process for sifting through names of possible candidates who will be voted on in Parliament for the post. We believe the detail is best left to Members of Parliament to devise a process as this is too much detail for a Constitution that is entrenched and therefore more arduous to amend.

the question whether one or more provisions of the Bill appear to be contrary to this Constitution.
(2) A reference to the Supreme Court under paragraph (1) may not be made later than the tenth working day after the date on which the Bill concerned is presented to the Head of State for signature.
(3) After giving the Head of State, the Government and any other party that the Supreme Court considers should be heard an opportunity to be heard, the Supreme Court must determine the question as soon as practicable and, in any case, not later than the 60th day after the date on which the reference was made.
(4) The Head of State must not sign the Bill concerned if the Supreme Court determines that any provision of the Bill referred to the Court appears to be contrary to the Constitution.

This means that, if within ten working days of being presented with a Bill for signature, the Head of State has concerns that the Bill may breach some aspect of the Constitution, the Head of State may, after consultation with the Prime Minister, refer the Bill to the Supreme Court to determine the issue. The Supreme Court will give the Head of State and the Government an opportunity to present their arguments, and will have sixty days to make a ruling on whether, on its face at the time of consideration, the Bill does or does not breach the Constitution. If the Court determines the Bill does breach the Constitution, the Head of State is barred from signing the Bill into law, and it will be returned to Parliament. If there is no apparent breach, the Head of State must sign the Bill.

It should be noted that, while the signature of the Head of State is required for both primary and secondary legislation to take legal effect, this referral power applies only to primary legislation.[15] That is, while Bills can be referred to the Supreme Court, the Head of State must sign any executive orders or regulations they are advised to sign by ministers. The process will allow the Head of State to raise any issue with ministers concerning the legality of the regulations that

---

15 While we are retaining the requirement that the Head of State must sign off on both primary and secondary legislation for them to have effect, we are not formally recognising the Executive Council, which is currently where the Governor-General is presented with regulations to sign and is briefed by ministers. We believe that, despite this, the requirement for the Head of State to sign executive orders and other forms of secondary legislation has instrumental purpose in maintaining contact between Cabinet and the Head of State and ensures another set of eyes takes a look at them.

require signature, and, of course, this does not mean such regulations cannot be challenged for breaching the Constitution through the ordinary process of challenging such laws. The quantity of secondary legislation is so great it would be overly burdensome to both the Head of State and the Supreme Court if the referral power was extended. The existing checks and balances around secondary legislation, such as Parliament's ability to disallow regulations that are outside the limitations of the relevant primary legislation, and the existing law on challenges in the courts, are sufficient to prevent most instances where secondary legislation may breach the Constitution. Furthermore, challenges to such regulations mounted on constitutional grounds will also be available.

We have not followed the Irish practice whereby if the Court determines there is no breach at the time of consideration, the subsequent Act of Parliament is no longer justiciable on the grounds that it breaches the constitution. Under Article 34 of the Irish Constitution, if a Bill (or any part of it) has been referred by the President to the Supreme Court, and the Court decides that the Bill is compatible with the constitution, no one can take a case challenging the constitutionality of the legislation. We think it is not inconceivable that a situation could arise—once the law is operating in practice—which would show that the legislation in fact does breach a person's constitutional rights, and which was not foreseen when the Court had considered the legislation in the abstract. And if a person's constitutional rights have been breached, they should be able to take the government to court to rectify that.

In Ireland, the referral power has been used 15 times between 1940 and today.[16] While this may not occur frequently it is a useful safeguard, as well as giving the Head of State a more active role as Kaitiaki of the Nation.

---

16 Judgments for each decision by the Supreme Court of Ireland made under Article 26 can be found on the Court's website: <www.supremecourt.ie/SupremeCourt/sclibrary3.nsf/pagecurrent/5A270AE31790620C802575EB003DAC2C?opendocument&l=en>."

6 The Government

The purpose of Government is to govern. The pervasive and comprehensive nature of the powers that a New Zealand Government enjoys are too many to list. The Government has strong executive powers. In New Zealand it is often called the executive government or executive branch of government because it 'executes' the laws, but not all people know what that means. We call it 'the Government' in the proposed Constitution for the sake of simplicity and clarity. The Government makes many public decisions. It sets policy directions and determines priorities. It is the branch of government which makes decisions. Within the Government, the Cabinet and the Prime Minister are the prime sources of authority. The Cabinet is responsible to and accountable to the Parliament. The people elect the Parliament. It is therefore a representative system of government.

The Government is not Parliament. It is not the Judiciary. It is charged with the responsibility of making and executing the thousands of decisions that must be made every day through government departments and agencies. It must administer the law as it stands. It must make policy proposals to Parliament for changing the law where it is unsatisfactory or needs reform. It must manage and control the money. At the top sits the Prime Minister, who presides over a Cabinet of ministers. The Cabinet is the key institution of the Government. The ministers who make up Cabinet meet each week to make all the important decisions about how to run the country. Beyond the ministers and the departments they control, Government also includes the public service and the wider public sector.

Our constitution seeks to define the Government in this way:[1]

68 Constitution and powers of Government
(1) The Government is made up of the following institutions:
    (a) the Cabinet:
    (b) the Prime Minister:
    (c) the office of each Minister designated by Act of Parliament or by the Prime Minister:
(2) All powers exercised by, or on behalf of, an institution of the Government must be authorised by this Constitution or by or under an Act of Parliament.

1 Constitution Aotearoa 2018, art 68.

(3) A person who is authorised to perform any function, conferred by this Constitution or by or under an Act of Parliament on—
   (a) an institution of the Government; or
   (b) a department of the public service, including any statutory officer located within a department; or
   (c) any other institution of the State that is established, otherwise than as a legal entity, by or under an Act of Parliament to implement legislation or policies.

may, for the purpose of taking any action that is required for, or that is incidental to, or consequential on the performance of that function, act in the name of the State and exercise the powers that the State has as a legal entity.

In 2016, our proposals for recognising and improving the key institutions of Government institutions and the framework in which they operate were set out in this way:[2]

> Constitution Aotearoa more clearly sets out the structures and powers of Government and the limits on that, including the roles and function of the Prime Minister:
>
> - the Cabinet is limited to 20 members with up to five for ministers outside Cabinet. The post of Under-Secretary has been abolished:
> - the publication of a Cabinet Manual is required every five years:
> - the House of Representatives will elect the Prime Minister:
> - the Prime Minister's ancient powers of advising on proroguing or dissolving the House will be abolished:
> - the Prime Minister will not be able to be Finance Minister, and the Attorney-General must be a lawyer:
> - the State will be given all powers of government—legislative, executive and judicial. The executive power is exercised by the Government. The Government comprises Cabinet, ministers and the public service.

We also wanted to include 'certain principles in the Constitution to reinvigorate the public service and protect its values'.[3]

To a large extent, our revised proposals follow this same aim of clarifying and setting out the structures and powers of Government and its limits.

We have set out the institutions that constitute Government and

---

2 Geoffrey Palmer and Andrew Butler *A Constitution for Aotearoa New Zealand* (Victoria University Press, Wellington, 2016) at 118.
3 At 175.

established the specific powers of the State that are to be exercised by the Government. We have set out at some length the dynamics and principles relating to Cabinet government because they will continue under what we propose. The essential tasks of the Government and the Cabinet will remain much as they are now. But Cabinet becomes a body established and defined by the constitution itself, not the result of sometimes murky conventions surrounding the exercise of royal powers. The legal power of the Government is vested in the Cabinet. This realistically reflects who actually exercises the power and does away with the need for the major constitutional conventions that govern the system now. A result of this change is that the Executive Council which now exists can be abolished, and it has been dropped from the new draft, though the new Head of State will still have to sign regulations before they become law. We have more clearly delineated the structures and powers of the Government and placed more limits upon it. The superior law Bill of Rights, contained in the proposed Constitution, will serve as a significant check upon Cabinet.

The role and functions of the Prime Minister are clarified and plain to see. Our introduction of a fixed four-year parliamentary term means that the Prime Minister cannot unilaterally cause Parliament to be dissolved and hold an early election. For that to occur Parliament would have to vote by a 75 per cent majority for an early election. This is a reduction in prime ministerial power.

A number of the proposals relating to the Government, which we made in our 2016 book, have been dropped. We have dropped the limit on the number of ministers in Cabinet. We have dropped the requirement that the Attorney-General must be a lawyer, since a Cabinet may not contain a lawyer and there is some history of previous Attorneys-General performing the role admirably despite the lack of a formal legal education. We have also removed the restrictions preventing the Prime Minister from holding the Finance portfolio. The removal of much of this detail is not to say that we do not support those changes to the current system, more that we do not think the Constitution is the right place to effect them.

We have also provided for a Government Services Commission to oversee the public service. It would replace the current State Services Commissioner. We secure the core function of the public service to give free and frank advice to the Government of the day.

Cabinet

As noted earlier, Cabinet is the true seat of Government power in New Zealand. Currently, there is no formal provision for Cabinet; it survives as a constitutional convention and technically doesn't legally exist. Cabinet government in New Zealand is a highly flexible instrument with no two administrations being run in the same manner. This flexibility we wish to maintain, as Cabinets evolve and mutate over time. The biggest influence in its recent evolution has been the introduction of the MMP electoral system. Cabinet government in New Zealand at present is founded for the most part on constitutional convention, not upon law. Constitutional conventions are recognised norms, practices or customs generally followed. Determining with precision whether a constitutional convention exists and what its precise content may be is seldom simple and often the subject of disagreement. The vagueness and mystery surrounding constitutional conventions do not help public understanding of the system and this is a powerful driver of the need for a written constitution. Thus we have walked a fine line in attempting to clarify the situation and set out the most crucial conventions (such as Cabinet itself) clearly and simply, while retaining the flexible nature of the current system.

Cabinet carries out the following tasks:

- administers the laws that have been passed;
- acts as the final decision-maker on all important matters of policy;
- approves the content of many regulations that become laws as part of our system of secondary legislation;
- decides upon the content of all Government bills to be introduced to Parliament—if passed these end up as Acts of Parliament;
- makes decisions on government spending and the use of the country's resources;
- coordinates the administration and gives order to the public service on how to carry out administration;
- behaves in a manner designed to retain the confidence of the Parliament.

These functions will continue under the proposed Constitution as they have in the past. Cabinet comprises a subtle mix of policy determination and political management, always conducted against the background of what may occur in the Parliament. It is the engine room of the Government. It is for this reason that the proposed Constitution provides, 'The executive authority of the State is vested in the Cabinet.'

A core aspect of this form of governance was described by Walter Bagehot long ago. Bagehot described the essence of Cabinet government in his classic exposition of the English Constitution first published in 1867:[4]

> The efficient secret of the English Constitution may be described as the close union, the nearly complete fusion, of the executive and legislative powers. No doubt by the traditional theory, as it exists in all the books, the goodness of our constitution consists in the entire separation of the legislative and executive authorities, but in truth its merit consists in their singular approximation. The connecting link is the Cabinet. By that new word we mean a committee of the legislative body selected to be the executive body. The legislature has many committees, but this is its greatest. [. . .] The Cabinet, in a word, is a board of control chosen by the legislature, out of persons whom it trusts and knows, to rule the nation. [. . .] A Cabinet is a combining committee—a hyphen which joins, a buckle which fastens, the legislative part of the State to the executive part of the State. In its origin it belongs to the one, in its functions it belongs to the other.

The key point is that Cabinet is not only the executive authority, it is an important part of the legislature as well and it proposes and introduces Government Bills, which are usually the most important and far-reaching pieces of legislation to pass through Parliament.

Bagehot's description is at the heart of what distinguishes the Westminster system (like ours) from the United States system and is an indication in itself that Cabinet government produces strong executive government. The doctrine of separation of powers is muted here. Indeed, under the old electoral system of First-Past-the-Post New Zealand was described as 'an executive paradise' because of the nearly complete fusion flowing from a Cabinet formed (usually) by a single party in a unicameral legislature operating in a unitary state. The advent of MMP has slightly lessened that quality in New Zealand, although the power of the Government remains formidable.

We believe that, despite the overlap between the executive and

---

4 Walter Bagehot *The English Constitution* (Fontana, London, 1977) at 65–68.

legislative functions in a Cabinet government, MMP has largely served New Zealand well. We do not wish to change it. We hope, however, that our proposal for a written Constitution can clarify and strengthen the checks and balances which ensures that this system of ours works.

Our proposed constitution sets out the following in relation to Cabinet:[5]

69 Cabinet

(1) This Article establishes the Cabinet.
(2) The Cabinet consists of the persons who hold current warrants as Ministers, but does not include Ministers designated under paragraph (6) or (7).
(3) The Cabinet—
   (a) determines the general direction of the Government:
   (b) develops and implements government policy:
   (c) co-ordinates and directs, subject to any Act of Parliament, the functions of institutions of the government, the public service, and other institutions of the State established to implement legislation or policies:
   (d) initiates and develops Government Bills:
   (e) makes subordinate legislation under authority conferred on it by this Constitution or by Act of Parliament.
(4) The Cabinet is collectively responsible to Parliament for the performance by the Government of its responsibilities.
(5) The Cabinet may appoint any committees that it considers necessary or required to assist the Cabinet in the discharge of its responsibilities; the Prime Minister must report the purpose, membership, and terms of reference of the committees to Parliament.
(6) The Prime Minister may designate Ministers as associate Ministers to the principal Minister in a portfolio with responsibilities delegated by the principal Minister.
(7) The Prime Minister may designate Ministers outside Cabinet with responsibilities designated by the Prime Minister.
(8) The Cabinet must from time to time approve and issue a Cabinet Manual that provides a guide to the processes and procedures of Cabinet.

---

5   Constitution Aotearoa 2018, art 69.

Prime Minister

The position of the Prime Minister can be best understood by regarding that person as the Minister for Co-ordination and Political Leadership. Coordinating the activities of the huge Government machine is a challenging task. The prime instrument of co-ordination is the Cabinet, and the Prime Minister and the Prime Minister's department (known as the Department of the Prime Minister and Cabinet). This has become much more complicated with multi-party Governments that are usually minority Governments under MMP. The Prime Minister is not only manager of the Government but also the chief political manager of the coalition and of the arrangements with other parties for confidence and supply. The Prime Minister is also a party leader, who not only speaks for the Government but for her party caucus as well. This involves a whole range of time-consuming tasks such as attending party functions and conferences, dealing with preparations for elections, helping decide upon issues relating to the election, candidates and their position on the party list at the election, plus a host of other issues big and small.

Currently, to become the Prime Minister, the Prime Minister must enjoy the confidence of the House of Representatives. After an election, parties negotiate to see who can form agreements to command a majority of seats in the House of Representatives. The Governor-General formally appoints the Prime Minister. To remain in office, the Prime Minister must continue to enjoy the confidence of the House. In practical terms that means the Prime Minister must be able to ensure that the Cabinet can command sufficient votes in the House of Representatives to secure money with which to run the Government and carry out its programmes. It does not mean that the Government has to win every vote on every issue or piece of legislation.

It is the Prime Minister who chairs Cabinet and decides the Cabinet agenda and its procedures. It is the Prime Minister who determines the number of ministers and parliamentary under-secretaries, the portfolios those ministers and under-secretaries occupy and whether they sit within or outside of Cabinet. It is the Prime Minister who determines whether a minister should resign. The Prime Minister, using the power to advise the Governor-General, effectively has the power to hire and fire ministers.

The Prime Minister can dominate the Cabinet to a greater or lesser degree depending upon the incumbent's style of operation. Leadership styles vary. However, despite the public appearance that the Prime Minister dominates Cabinet in New Zealand, it is still a highly collective body, more so than the public appreciates. Though each Government functions a little differently, Cabinet usually makes decisions collectively and there is a sense of collegiality around a shared purpose.

We are not changing much in regards to the Prime Minister in our proposed Constitution. We have sought to clarify and formally set out the functions of the Prime Minister, and simplify the appointments process. Under our proposals the Prime Minister is the Head of Government and formally appointed to the office by the Head of State. Parliament will elect the Prime Minister from amongst its members, although in circumstances where Parliament has not yet met after an election, the Head of State may, after the declaration of official election results, appoint as Prime Minster the person who is likely to be supported by a majority of the members of Parliament; as occurred in 2017.

At present, the Prime Minister has no formally assigned duties under New Zealand's constitutional arrangements. The proposed Constitution provides some:[6]

71 Roles, functions, and responsibilities of the Prime Minister

The roles, functions, and responsibilities of the Prime Minister include the following:
  (a) to oversee the execution of the policies of the Government with and through the appropriate Ministers and the public service:
  (b) to act as chair of Cabinet proceedings:
  (c) to make recommendations on Cabinet and other ministerial appointments and determine departmental responsibilities of Ministers:
  (d) to formulate and manage with Ministers the Government's legislative programme in Parliament:
  (e) to be held to account by Parliament for the performance of public duties:

---

6 Constitution Aotearoa 2018, art 71.

(f) to be responsible for the standards of ministerial conduct:
(g) to represent the people and Government of the State of Aotearoa New Zealand overseas:
(h) to perform any other roles, functions, and duties that may be required.

Ministers

Ministers are currently chosen by the Prime Minister and appointed by the Head of State to oversee certain portfolios, often based on their expertise and interests. Government departments are meant to manage a specific sector of public administration (for example, there are education portfolios, primary industries portfolios, portfolios that deal with health, foreign affairs, defence and any number of things that governments must concern themselves with). Ministers generally direct the operations of the government departments they are assigned to by managing their budget and, along with the myriad public servants within the departments, research and draft policy, set the funding and strategic policies for any agencies operating under the department, prepare Bills to go before Cabinet for approval before progressing to the House of Representatives, disseminating information on their activities (whether through freedom of information requests, ministerial responses or answers to written questions) and reporting to Parliament on their activities.

To be a Cabinet minister or a minister outside Cabinet, you are obliged to follow Cabinet decisions, even if you disagree with them. Otherwise you must resign. This doctrine of collective responsibility is based on an important reality. It is well summed up by the aphorism coined by Benjamin Franklin in 1776 in America: 'we must indeed all hang together, or, most assuredly, we shall all hang separately'.[7]

This principle of collective responsibility is an important ingredient of Cabinet's power, and one that our proposed Constitution preserves. Once a Cabinet decision has been taken, all ministers are obliged to support it regardless of their personal views. At base, it is a practical

---

7 Remark to John Hancock at the signing of the Declaration of Independence 4 July 1776 in Elizabeth Knowles (ed) *Oxford Dictionary of Quotations* (7th ed, online ed, Oxford University Press, 2009).

principle. Following the principle of collective responsibility avoids confusion as to what the Government's policy on an issue is. It brings finality to debate. It helps the public to know that it is the collective Cabinet who is responsible and it is they who should be held to account. It helps to provide coherence in Government overall. Furthermore, Cabinet stresses that the House of Representatives must have confidence in the Government as whole.

Ministers are also individually responsible for the decisions they take and are answerable to the House for them. Where they blunder or engage in unacceptable conduct, the Prime Minister can dismiss them. These two doctrines of ministerial responsibility, collective and individual, are an important ingredient of the existing mechanisms of Cabinet's accountability and responsibility to the House of Representatives. Both collective responsibility and individual ministerial responsibility are constitutional conventions or customs. They have no formal legal status under the current system.

The advent of MMP placed two new glosses on ministerial responsibility. Ministers outside Cabinet from support parties may be bound by collective responsibility only in relation to their particular portfolios. They retain the right to vote against the Government on many policies outside those portfolios. As the Cabinet Manual puts it:[8]

> Ministers outside Cabinet from parliamentary parties supporting the government may be bound by collective responsibility only in relation to their particular portfolios, including any specific delegated responsibilities. Under these arrangements, when such Ministers speak about issues within their portfolios, they speak for the government and as part of the government. When they speak about matters outside their portfolios, however, they may speak as political party leaders or members of Parliament rather than as Ministers, and do not necessarily represent the government position.

This applies to the ministers outside Cabinet from the Green Party in the present Government. New Zealand First ministers, however, sit inside Cabinet and are in a different position. Particular 'agree to disagree' agreements may be made which allow ministers within the coalition to maintain, in public, different party positions

---

8   Cabinet Office *Cabinet Manual 2017* at [5.29], and for coalition ministers [5.27].

on particular issues or policies, but in general they are bound by collective responsibility. Even where a coalition Government has an established 'agree to disagree' process, once the final outcome of any 'agree to disagree' issue or policy has been determined (either at the Cabinet level or through some other agreed process), ministers must implement the resulting decision or legislation, regardless of their position throughout the decision-making process. Our proposal reflects much of the current understanding around ministerial positions. Once again we have sought to simplify the existing rules and set out some of the more established conventions so they can be properly enforced. In particular we have formally recognised the principles of ministerial responsibility. Under our proposal, the Cabinet is collectively responsible to Parliament for the performance by the Government of its responsibilities. The Cabinet may appoint any committees that it considers necessary or required to assist the Cabinet in the discharge of its responsibilities; and the Prime Minister must report the purpose, membership and terms of reference of the committees to Parliament.

The Prime Minister may designate ministers and associate ministers in a portfolio with responsibilities delegated by the principal minister. The Prime Minister may designate ministers outside Cabinet with responsibilities designated by the Prime Minister. Ministers are formally appointed by the Head of State on the advice of the Prime Minister. Ministers are individually responsible to Parliament for the proper and efficient execution of that minister's responsibilities.

The public service

The public service is also a critically important part of the Government. The public service is a professional, apolitical body which provides free and frank advice to the Government of the day and delivers core state functions to the people such as health, education and transport services. It has a long and proud history in New Zealand. But it is neither as strong or resilient as once it was. The culture, leadership and spirit of those involved are critical factors in producing a high quality public service.

There has been a decline in the quantity of free and frank advice offered to ministers in recent years. If ministers do not receive free and frank advice there is a real risk that this will promote a tendency to politicise the public service and endanger its independence and adversely affect the quality of advice given and decisions taken. The public service should not be seen as a tool of the Government of the day used to justify policy decisions; rather, it should be an independent service working for the good of the country as a whole. The public service should serve up various options for dealing with issues and the ministers should choose between them: this is how the system is supposed to work.

Under our proposals, the public service is overseen by the Government Services Commission. Here is how the proposed Constitution sets up the public service and the Commission. It is governed by a strong set of principles stated in the constitution itself:

73 Nature and obligations of the public service
  (1) The public service is a career-based service driven by a culture of excellence and efficiency, where appointment and promotion is on merit.
  (2) The first duty of the public service is to act in accordance with this Constitution and the law.
  (3) The public service must act in a spirit of service to the community and with commitment to open democratic government.
  (4) The public service is politically neutral and impartial and serves loyally the Government of the day.
  (5) The public service must provide ministers with free and frank advice.
  (6) The public service upholds the concept of stewardship, that is active planning and management of medium- and long-term interests, along with associated advice.
  (7) The public service and all other institutions of the State must maintain high standards of integrity and conduct.

74 Government Services Commission
  (1) This Article establishes a commission to be known as the Government Services Commission.
  (2) The Government Services Commission consists of three persons who are each appointed for a single fixed term of five years by the Head of State on the recommendation of the Prime Minister, after consultation with the leaders of the political parties represented in Parliament.
  (3) The Government Services Commission—
    (a) is the employer of chief executives of departments of the

public service:
  (b) provides leadership to the public service and all other institutions of the State established to implement legislation or policies:
  (c) supervises standards of integrity and conduct in the public service and any other institution of the State that it is empowered to supervise by an Act of Parliament.
(4) The Government Services Commission makes decisions independently of ministers.
(5) An Act of Parliament must provide for the organisation and governance of the Government Services Commission.

It should be noted the Government owns, controls or has influence over a vast array of other organisations. Many of them are contained in the Crown Entities Act 2004. Some are Crown Agents, some are independent Crown Entities, some are autonomous Crown Entities; then there are Crown-owned companies, school committees and many others. The Government Services Commission is given, in the provision above, some power to intervene in these agencies and exercise leadership over their integrity, conduct and salaries. Such power is lacking at present. The sprawling mass of the state sector that lies beyond the public service deserves attention. Political appointments to boards do not, in our view, provide adequate protection for the public interest. More order and discipline needs to be brought to these more remote agencies, and so the Government Services Commission will have capacity under the proposals to substantially influence some issues. We have long held the view that the best and most accountable form of constitutional organisation for carrying out public purposes is a Department of State, as it enhances the accountability through ministers to Parliament.

Conclusion

The Government is clearly defined by these proposals; its powers and functions are set out and transparent. The accountabilities are established and the limits on its power provided. We hope that in clearing away the cobwebs obscuring the depths of executive function and formally recognising the core rules that underlie Government in New Zealand we can be rid of fictions and state the rules the way they are. In this way, everyone will be able to access and understand the rules under which the Government operates, and hold it to account when things go wrong.

7 Local government

Under our proposed Constitution, local government is the fifth pillar supporting the State. When people think about government, they tend to think about the Prime Minister, ministers, Parliament and party politics. When it comes to local government, many hardly think about it at all, because they don't think it affects them very much. In that belief, they are wrong. In reality, government happens on many levels and touches every aspect of our lives. The level of government closest to the day-to-day lives of most people is local government. People take for granted the important infrastructure provided by local government, such as roads, sewerage, water supply, libraries, community centres and community programmes. Local government functions consume significant resources, raise difficult questions of governance and are of vital importance to communities. Regional councils, for example, have wide-ranging responsibilities for environmental issues, including such matters as water quality, air pollution, public transport and land use.

The main governing statute in this area, the Local Government Act 2002, states that the purpose of local government is:[1]

(a) to enable democratic local decision-making and action by, and on behalf of, communities; and

(b) to meet the current and future needs of communities for good-quality local infrastructure, local public services and performance of regulatory functions in a way that is most cost-effective for households and businesses.

Local government carries out a variety of functions including implementing central government policies on a local scale, managing infrastructure and otherwise dealing with governing on a day-to-day basis. While local government in New Zealand is seen as subordinate to central government, and ultimately is controlled by legislation passed by Parliament, it is nonetheless invested with substantial law-making and regulatory powers. A number of different types of institutions make up local government, including regional councils and territorial authorities. They are often responsible for different

---

1 Local Government Act 2002, s 10.

aspects of local government:[2]

> Regional councils are primarily concerned with environmental resource management, flood control, air and water quality, pest control, and, in specific cases, public transport, regional parks and bulk water supply.
>
> Territorial authorities are responsible for a wide range of local services including roads, water reticulation, sewerage and refuse collection, libraries, parks, recreation services, local regulations, community and economic development, and town planning.
>
> Councils, however, can differ widely in relation to activities they undertake, as long as they have consulted their communities in making the decisions. As a result, there is considerable diversity in the range of activities that councils provide, reflecting the different circumstances that cities, towns and communities find themselves in.

Local governments carry out a variety of health and environmental functions, such as registration and inspection of restaurants and cafés. They often hold substantial amounts of land and carry out public works. They are sometimes engaged in housing activities and encouraging industrial development. They must provide cemeteries. They have functions concerning noxious plants, litter, clean air, animals, offensive trades, wildlife and civil defence. They have important responsibilities concerning the sale of liquor. Local government also has an important function in holding central government to account and acting as a check on its activities. As Local Government New Zealand (LGNZ) said to us in its submission, 'In a governmental system like New Zealand's, without the checks of an upper house or constitutional court, local government plays a critical democratic, as well as functional, role which we cannot take for granted.' It 'provides the democratic machinery for the expression of local opinion on all matters of public policy.'[3]

Local government makes up a vital and continuing feature of governance in New Zealand. It can achieve a great deal for people. In the ever-widening diversity that characterises modern New Zealand there is a great deal of difference between various regions and their

---

2 'Local government basics' Local Government New Zealand (23 June 2017), available at <www.lgnz.co.nz/nzs-local-government/local-government-basics>.
3 John Roberts and Roy Sidebotham *Local Government in the Wellington Region; the challenge of chaos* (Victoria University of Wellington, Wellington, 1968).

attitude to local government. Local government arrangements recognise the differences and allow for different approaches depending on the diverse range of needs of New Zealanders.

The less connection people have to government the less invested they are, and this is detrimental to the system as a whole. A theme we will return to over and over again in this book is the importance of engagement. It is crucial to a properly working government, to an enforceable constitution, to an effective democracy. Thus, while it is important to foster within each unit of local government the idea of community, we also need the converse: empowerment of the people to participate. This becomes difficult when considering that, currently, local government is governed by a vast amount of prescriptive legislation. This, coupled with the troubling pattern of constant amendment of local government legislation by central government aimed at allowing central government to get its own way, makes it difficult for ordinary people to know how to engage with, and participate in, local government.

We tend to vacillate between strong local governments with a wider range of activities and restricting the scope of responsibility of local government to try to ensure they do not get involved in activities that are wide-ranging or novel, even if that is the preference of the local population.

Central government also has a propensity to load up local government with new tasks and new legislation, while providing no funding to carry out those tasks. On this point Dr Jean Drage has observed:[4]

> New Zealand's local government is commonly said to be a creature of statute, which means that its constitutional (or legal) status comes from current legislation rather than being entrenched or guaranteed in a written constitution. As a result, local government's functions and purpose can be changed by a majority vote in Parliament and are not protected by a constitution as is the case in most other developed countries.

In theory, one of the strengths of local government is the opportunity it allows for citizens to be directly engaged in the process

---

4 Jean Drage 'New Zealand's Local Government: Today's Challenges' in Jean Drage and Christine Cheyne (eds) *Local Government in New Zealand: Challenges and Choices* (Dunmore Publishing Ltd, Auckland, 2016) at 3.

of governing their own towns, cities and regions. This practice of self-government should enhance our understanding of citizenship while ensuring public services are responsive to the needs of the communities they are designed to serve. But, if the responsibilities of your local authority are constantly shifting and changing, or there's a lack of credibility and accountability because of continual interference from central government, it is quite understandable that most people would just choose not to bother reaching out. Ultimately, if power comes from the people, local government needs to be secure and protected, as it is the first port of call on many issues of importance to people.

It was on this basis, with the idea of protecting its important constitutional functions, that in drafting our first proposal for a codified constitution in 2016 we included a provision intended to expressly recognise and protect local government:[5]

110 Local Government
   (1) The State must have a strong, democratic, transparent and accountable system of local government based on the following principles:
      (a) the principle of subsidiarity: the provision of services and the solution of problems should take place as close to the citizens as practicable as the nature of the relevant process allows subject to allocative efficiency:
      (b) the power of units of local government to manage their own affairs independently within subject-matters established in Acts of Parliament:
      (c) fostering within each unit of local government the concept of community:
      (d) local government representatives must be democratically elected by secret ballot:
      (e) local government must be open and transparent in its decision-making and accountable to its citizens:
      (f) the financing of local government by the imposition of rates on land and property provided for by Act of Parliament must be accompanied by a revenue-sharing programme with central Government negotiated between central and local Government:
      (g) Parliament may provide special procedures for central

---

5   Constitution Aotearoa 2016, art 110.

government to ensure compliance with the law and the execution of delegated responsibilities, including the appointment of independent Commissioners in accordance with law.

(2) When any new responsibility is placed on local government by or under Act of Parliament, that must be preceded by adequate consultation and estimates of the financial and administrative costs of that new responsibility.

Providing a place in the constitution for local government, as our initial proposal did, was welcomed by Local Government New Zealand (LGNZ). It is the national organisation for local government—representing 11 regional councils, 61 territorial local authorities and six unitary councils—who has the combined powers of territorial authorities and regional councils. LGNZ conducted a workshop for our project in Wellington attended by 16 members of local government from across New Zealand. We discussed some of the difficulties faced by local government today, and got feedback on what we had included in our first proposal. The workshop was followed by a helpful submission from LGNZ.

In its submission to us, LGNZ emphasised what has been the organisation's long-standing position on the constitutional position of local government in New Zealand. It had made a submission on the issue to the 2013 Constitutional Advisory Panel, arguing for constitutional recognition. The submission to us, following the workshop, put the issue in this way:

> LGNZ, on behalf of its members, has consistently argued the need for greater constitutional certainty for local government. The current situation, in which councils operate within a legislative framework that has no constitutional guarantee, has proved itself not only unworkable for good local government but also damaged New Zealand's economic and social performance. Enabling citizens to make meaningful decisions about local matters not only builds social capital it also enhances economic growth, municipal innovation and competition.

The submission goes on to observe that the lack of a secure constitutional position has led to increasing centralisation, which has weakened the ability of cities and districts to make decisions for their own advancement. The result, as explained by LGNZ, has:

... in the view of the World Bank, diminished economic growth. It has also led to frequent, and sometimes idiosyncratic, legislative change to local government's role and powers that has undermined public confidence in the framework and constrained councils' ability to plan for the long term. ... Most concerning is the diminishing autonomy of elected members with recent legislation increasing opportunities for ministers to intervene in local affairs and even over-rule decisions made by elected members.

These weaknesses disclose a serious state of affairs. No system of local government can be robust and effective if its decisions are subject to being overridden, reversed or constantly subject to approval by a higher authority. Issues highlighted at the workshop for inclusion in the constitution were:

- simplicity and passion;
- local solutions to local problems;
- empowerment;
- revenue sharing;
- relationship with central government;
- resourcing nationally imposed costs;
- citizen participation.

Not all of these themes are suitable for inclusion in a constitution—for example, passion cannot be legislated for! But many of the themes are properly the subject of constitutional protection. We have attempted to focus on creating a framework for conversation, between ordinary people and local government, and between local government and central government, which protects enough of the fundamental principles underpinning these relationships to allow this conversation to occur as constructively as possible, but isn't so prescriptive that it dictates the content of those conversations.

A degree of decentralisation can improve governance and deliver services to people that are more responsive and efficient for local needs. We have attempted to forge a set of binding principles to be contained in the Constitution, reflecting the submissions we have received and what we believe to be constitutionally appropriate. We have made some changes to our initial proposal in order to provide for flexibility while incorporating integral principles which a number of submitters, including LGNZ, wanted recognised such as subsidiarity and autonomy.

Subsidiarity requires that public responsibilities should lie with the sphere of government that is closest to the people, unless it is more efficient or effective for them to be the responsibility of governments of larger scale. There was also recognition that some protection for the raising of revenue, whether by rates, other local taxes, or a share of nationally collected revenue (e.g., income tax or GST), needs to be recognised. We have broadened our financial provision after some fears that our initial wording could be interpreted as entrenching property-based taxes as the only possible form of revenue-raising. We have also tried to draft the new provision broadly enough that it could incorporate a range of governance arrangements—including co-governance arrangements with local iwi—and mechanisms of direct democracy. The new provision has been brought forward and placed in a stand-alone Part to reflect its important status in the structure of government.

Here is what we have drafted as a set of binding principles contained in a written constitution with which Local Government legislation and practice must comply. It requires a new relationship between local and central government:[6]

75 Local Government
(1) Aotearoa New Zealand must be divided into defined geographical localities that are governed by local governments under a democratic system of local government based on the following principles:
    (a) the principle of subsidiarity, which means that the provision of services and the solution of issues should take place as close to the citizens as is practicable:
    (b) the principle of autonomy, which means that Parliament should confer on local governments the power and autonomy to manage a substantial share of public affairs:
    (c) the principle of financial sufficiency, which means that the funding of each local government, through financial support, rates, and taxes that it is empowered to raise, should be sufficient for it to function effectively:
    (d) the principle of community, which means that each

---

6 Constitution Aotearoa 2018, art 75.

local government should foster a sense of community and provide for the participation of its citizens in decision-making (including through assemblies of citizens, co-governance arrangements, or other participatory means) to ensure that decisions serve the well-being of the community:

(e) the principle of transparency, which means that local governments should govern in an open and transparent manner and be accountable to their electors.

(2) This Constitution recognises the importance of a sound relationship between the Government and local governments and to that end—

(a) before any new responsibility is placed on local governments by an Act of Parliament or a decision of Ministers, the Government must adequately consult representatives of local governments about the proposed responsibility and provide estimates of the financial and administrative costs of the proposed responsibility:

(b) before introducing to Parliament a Government Bill or a Member's Bill that would change legislation relating to local government legislation or otherwise significantly affect local governments, the Government or the Member of Parliament promoting the Bill must adequately consult representatives of local governments about the contents of the proposed Bill.

There is a long road ahead for New Zealand on local government reform. But it is a road that should be travelled. Local government in New Zealand could be more vibrant, effective and responsive to its communities on local issues if it were provided with a robust constitutional place upon which to stand and more coherent and principled set of legal requirements under which to function. Divided powers between central and local government add to the constitutional protections available to citizens. We hope that in providing for a strong, transparent and accountable system of local government, which has a right to manage its own affairs and is adequately funded, we can improve the system of governance we have here in New Zealand and improve people's ability to participate in their community, and in government more generally.

8   Parliament

The role of elections in any democracy is important: how they organised, how they are run, how they are financed, who can vote and how a Government is formed determine much about the performance of the system of government.

Parliament is New Zealand's central democratic institution. Members of Parliament are elected. A person cannot become a minister without being an MP: this is the democratic connection between the power exerted by the Government and the people. The connection sews the golden thread of democratic legitimacy in the exercise of public power in New Zealand. Our proposals are designed to embed that constitutional fact and enhance it.

The 2016 proposals

We pointed out in our previous book that Parliament has seven key functions:

- to provide a Government;
- to hold Ministers to account;
- to raise the money by which the business of government may be conducted and to approve the expenditure of money;
- to consider and pass Bills into law;
- to provide a place for the airing of grievances;
- to act as a check on the manner in which Government is actually carried out, by virtue of the fact that Cabinet is responsible to the Parliament;
- to serve as a forum for party political contest.

Under the proposals, all of this will continue but in a manner designed to produce more accountability and better law-making.

We set out in 2016 what the main changes to Parliament were under our proposed written constitution:

- a fixed four-year parliamentary term;
- allowing select committees to recommend new legislative proposals to the House of Representatives;
- requiring a 75 per cent majority in Parliament to allow urgency to be taken in passing law;

- more checks and balances, including a stronger Bill of Rights and making more information available before legislating;
- outlining the system of public finance in the Constitution;
- an independent Speaker elected by the House on a personal conscience vote.

Reducing Parliament's power to embark upon any legislative course it wishes without restraint marks the most significant change we have proposed for that institution. It is common to both sets of our proposals. What we said about the doctrine of parliamentary sovereignty in our previous book bears repeating, since our attack on the outdated doctrine remains fundamental to the constitutional purpose of the proposal.

One of the primary constitutional doctrines of the traditional Westminster system of Parliament is parliamentary sovereignty. Although the term is not free from ambiguity, it means that the legal power of Parliament is unlimited. Parliament can legislate without restriction—there is no higher law-making authority. Parliament is supreme. The dangers of such unlimited power are obvious enough and are not tolerated in most democratic countries. Furthermore, the doctrine is unrealistic. Traditionally governments do not do extreme and unreasonable things, because they wish to be re-elected. Nevertheless, the legal power exists here and it would be better, in our view, to accept that the real constitutional principle is not the sovereignty of Parliament but the democratic authority of the people. Democracy is not merely a numbers game. Indeed, in New Zealand there are now generally acknowledged to be some limits on the principle.

For example, as far back as 1956, Parliament passed a law requiring a special parliamentary majority in order to amend the requirement for parliamentary elections to be conducted under a secret ballot. This provision—and there are others critical to the democratic framework, including the current three-year parliamentary term—can only be changed by a 75 per cent majority in Parliament or a referendum of the electors. The same law is now found in the successor Electoral Act 1993.

These requirements for special majorities for very important constitutional safeguards have been universally followed since they were first enacted. It is now generally accepted that such 'manner and form' restrictions, as they are known, are binding and cannot be ignored by a later Parliament. We are building on that tradition in the proposed Constitution to protect more institutions and principles in the same way. Their binding nature means that there are an increased number of matters that cannot be altered by a simple majority. It would seem a sound idea to set out the limits in a formal constitution rather than allow the constitution to be shaped by the remorseless ebb and flow of political developments.

Hiding behind the doctrine of parliamentary sovereignty allows the Government to effectively dominate the House of Representatives, even under our mixed-member system of proportional representation. It also allows Parliament to behave as though it is not bound by the Bill of Rights, which has serious implications for the rule of law.

To say that governments act in the name of democracy is politically naïve and neglects to explore the counterfactual concerning how political decisions are made and enacted.

Governments act to remain in power as long as they can, and they tend to try to get away with whatever they can. The risk is that they will observe no limits so long as there are none. It is a reality in New Zealand that the Government cannot—and should no longer—be relied upon to respect constitutional boundaries. It has the capacity to command resources to influence situations and outcomes to the point where decisions are made not so much in the public interest as in the Government's political interest.[1]

A reduction in the absolute power of Parliament is central to our project, requiring more respect for human rights. It also requires improvement in the way legislation is designed and better scrutiny of the Acts that Parliament is passing.

It is important to note, however, that we have also increased the power of Parliament in relation to the Government. We have made it clear that before an international treaty can be ratified there must be an affirmative resolution in Parliament. If New Zealand's armed forces are to be deployed overseas, where that is likely to involve the use of lethal force, Parliament must by resolution authorise

---

1 For a more developed account of the argument against parliamentary sovereignty, see Geoffrey Palmer 'What the New Zealand Bill of Rights aimed to do, why it did not succeed and how it can be repaired' (2016) 14 NZJPIL 169.

the deployment, and there must be, in front of the Parliament, an Attorney-General's opinion that the proposed deployment would be lawful in terms of both the Constitution and international law. We have therefore sharpened the means by which the Government can be held to account.

Our revised proposals

Our revised proposals for Parliament build on the previous draft, although they are expressed in a simpler form. There are some important changes compared with the present situation. We now define Parliament as the House of Representatives. The Parliament is always in legal existence so that it does not require to be summoned. Its membership changes after elections are held. A Government must have the confidence of a majority of MPs in order to govern.

Parliament meets regularly in accordance with a published timetable on which it has agreed. The proposed Constitution states the purpose of Parliament is to scrutinise, debate and pass legislation; to approve government expenditure, taxation and loans; to provide for the redress of grievances; and to vote on motions of confidence or no confidence in a minister or the Prime Minister. It holds the Government to account.

One big change lies in the proposed four-year fixed term for Parliament. This received substantial support from submitters. The draft is based on the law that was changed to provide for a fixed term in the United Kingdom. But early elections can be held if 75 per cent of MPs pass a motion that there should be an early election. This was done in the British general election held in 2017.

There was widespread support, in our received submissions, for restrictions on the power of Parliament to expedite the passage of legislation under urgency. We had proposed that urgency could only be used if 75 per cent of MPs supported its use. Discussions we had with actors in the system suggested this would never be adopted and was impractical. While we doubt that it is impractical, we believe that much the same advantage can be attained by restricting the use of urgency in another way. Emergencies do occur when urgency for legislation is required. Where an opposition sees advantage in denying urgency in a real situation where it may be it needed, there may be risks in what we had proposed. Requiring a reasoned judgment to be given by the Speaker as to whether a Government motion for urgency is truly justified in the circumstances would restrict its use considerably, but nevertheless ensure that where it was truly required it would be available. So here is what we now propose:

95 Urgency

When a motion for urgency to expedite the consideration of legislation is moved, the Speaker must rule whether it is in the public interest to set aside the ordinary processes of Parliament, including Article 92 [Information concerning Government legislation], because of the particular circumstances stated or referred to in the motion.
The Speaker must give reasons for the ruling.

We adhere to the view that select committees should be able to present legislative proposals to Parliament, as this will reduce the stranglehold the Government in New Zealand enjoys over the legislative process.

We have made one change to the provisions in what is now proposed about the financial veto, contained in Article 54 of the previous draft. We have eliminated it, having reviewed the exercise of the veto against the paid parental leave contained in a member's Bill and vetoed in 2016.[2]

On the method of choosing the Speaker we have made a change. We had proposed that the Speaker would be selected by a free vote, that is to say, where the whips are not operating and each MP makes up their own mind rather than voting along a party line, and we would have deprived the Speaker, so selected, of a vote in Parliament. The purpose of the proposal was to ensure the Speaker was truly a neutral umpire in parliamentary proceedings and was not partial to one party or another. Independence is important in a presiding officer.

We received a very useful submission from Graeme Edgeler, a Wellington lawyer. We set out the detailed research contained in Mr

---

2   In that instance a member's Bill to extend paid parental leave entitlements, which had majority support within Parliament, was killed off by the Government, who used their so-called veto power to stop the measure being enacted. See Jane Patterson 'Paid parental leave: Govt leaves itself open to criticism' *Radio New Zealand* (online ed, 17 June 2016), available at <www.radionz.co.nz/news/on-the-inside/306637/paid-parental-leave-govt-leaves-itself-open-to-criticism>; and (16 June 2016) 715 NZPD 12075.

Edgeler's submission and this has persuaded us to move from a free vote to a secret ballot of MPs as to who should be their Speaker. We have eliminated his footnotes containing the detailed references:

> Election of a Speaker by secret ballot is now common in Westminster Parliaments. The UK House of Commons conducted its first secret ballot for Speaker in 2009 (having adopted rule changes in 2001). Elections for the Speaker of the Scottish Parliament, and for the Presiding Officer of the Welsh Assembly, are also by secret ballot. The Presiding Officer and deputies of the Northern Ireland Assembly are not elected by secret ballot, because of a requirement that election of the Speakers requires cross-community support (a majority of both Nationalist and Unionist members).
>
> The election for the Speaker of the Canadian House of Commons has been by secret ballot for over 25 years.
>
> The election of the Speaker of the Australian House of Representatives and the election of President of the Australian Senate are also by secret ballot, as are such elections in state or territory legislatures in ACT, New South Wales, the Northern Territory, Queensland, South Australia Tasmania, the Legislative Assembly of Victoria (but not the Legislative Council) and Western Australia.
>
> It is time for the New Zealand House of Representatives to follow suit.

We agree and the draft constitution so provides.

Law-making

The provisions relating to law-making are now contained in Part 11 of the proposed Constitution, under the heading 'Fundamental functions of the State'. Those who submitted on law-making had some strong views. One experienced public servant put it this way:

> I am a senior public servant who has worked for 30 years in policy and government work. As such, I strongly support the idea of codifying the constitutional arrangements, both to ensure consistent interpretation and to make them easier to find. Of particular interest to me is law-making. I support the proposal to increase the Parliamentary term, require a legislative programme, reduce the use of urgency, and improve the oversight of the legislative work.

Another public servant, equally experienced and particularly in legislation, had an even bleaker view. He said Parliament was not fit to make law at all and this function should be removed. He gave a list of what he considered to be egregious actions by law-makers and proposed that law should be made by a new Legislation Commission. While we are not prepared to go that far, we do believe there are serious issues to be addressed in this area.

An important feature of the new proposals lies in the revised law-making procedures. The New Zealand Parliament passes a great deal of law and it often passes it too quickly, without sufficient consideration. This leads to mistakes and policy blunders. Given the complexity of modern legislation, more care and greater deliberation is needed, and more public involvement in the fashioning of the proposals.[3]

The revised proposals are briefer and less prescriptive than they were before, but we believe they capture the essential principles required. Our proposal restricting the use of urgency motions, which hurry up the passage of legislation in the Parliament, received widespread support in the submissions we received.[4] But, as explained above, we have amended it—and we are confident it will now achieve the same purpose.

Many improvements required for law-making in New Zealand are beyond the reach of a constitution, but it is worthwhile to set out what those weaknesses are. The responsibilities for legislation in New Zealand are split between the Government and Parliament; it is not easy to determine which branch of government bears the heaviest responsibility for the lack of quality and coherence that some statute law exhibits. This makes sheeting home accountability for the quality and nature of the laws passed by Parliament difficult.

It cannot really be said that there is ministerial responsibility for the statutes passed. In order to sharpen the accountability and make clear who is responsible for what, it is necessary to make transparent what occurs now in the legislative process before a bill comes to the House of Representatives. More openness should also help improve the quality of legislation and the ease of its scrutiny, so long as adequate

3   See also Geoffrey Palmer 'Law-Making in New Zealand: Is there a better way?' (2014) 22 Wai L Rev 1.
4   For a detailed study of the use of urgency in the New Zealand Parliament see Claudia Geiringer, Polly Higbee and Elizabeth McLeay *What's the Hurry? Urgency in the New Zealand Legislative Process, 1987–2010* (Victoria University Press, Wellington, 2011).

time is allowed to get big legislative schemes right. This requires timely publication of the government's legislative proposals. Making the legislative programme publicly available is an important reform. But more than this, a complete reconfiguration of the processes for designing and passing legislation is required to improve quality and make the processes more open and transparent. As a recent analysis of legislation in Europe notes: 'In view of the rule of law and legislation, there are two main challenges for the legislative process in addition to the obvious deficiencies of representative government: transparency and participation.'[5]

We think this conclusion applies to New Zealand. We have addressed it by the following means:

- providing for more information about the design of the legislation before it is introduced into the Parliament;
- ensuring the drafting is accessible and comprehensible;
- restricting the use urgency;
- requiring the publication of the Government legislative programme for each year so people can be warned of what is coming;
- strengthening of the Official Information Act;
- adopting the principles of deliberative democracy that are outlined in chapter 15.

The yin and the yang of the demand for new law in New Zealand is on the one hand legislating too quickly and getting it wrong, or on the other hand going so slowly that important issues lacking political priority remain neglected and the House becomes a bottleneck or choke point for such measures. These two pressures work in opposite directions, but both need to be addressed and integrated into a system that is more flexible. We pass too much legislation in New Zealand quickly, because we have no second chamber and because we can. Further, the pressure of the three-year electoral cycle adds to the legislative speed-wobbles. It is likely that better law would be fashioned in the first place if such things were not possible.

One prime issue relates to our failure to evaluate in any systematic or regular way what the statutes we've passed have (or have not) achieved. Have they worked as intended, or have they produced

---

5 Ulrich Karpen and Helen Xanthaki (eds) *Legislation in Europe: A Comprehensive Guide For Scholars and Practitioners* (Hart Publishing, Oxford, 2017) at 10.

unexpected results? Only if such analyses are carried out can we expect to control some elements in the future. Acts of Parliament are designed to produce a set of policy results into the future. Whether these will be achieved is not capable of being known fully at the time the law is made. Thus, efforts to compare the results that were actually achieved with those expected and desired would seem essential in any rational policy-making community.

The New Zealand approach, however, seems to be to continue legislating in quantity with little attempt to see what actually happens, until something goes sufficiently wrong to require hurried legislative attention. Too often, known and reliable research is not followed or not examined, and seat-of-the-pants reactions and popular sentiments are used to change the law more than careful analysis and evidence. In this age, when there are a variety of social science research methodologies available for examining how legislation has performed in practice, this seems unfortunate.

It is only by carrying out such work that it will be possible to make definitive judgments about the quality of both the policy and the law. Some elements of the process are ineffective, and sometimes legislation misses the mark; the desire for speed is often the cause. The existing tools for designing and processing legislation require improvement. We cannot confidently face the future with the creaking and cumbersome legislative machinery we have. What is to be done?

The most difficult questions are both intellectual and institutional. Even the most gifted public sector analyst cannot foresee the future. Stuff happens. Crises occur. They must then be addressed. Let us summarise steps that could be taken that would improve the way with which legislation is dealt.

We have a vast amount of law and it is increasing exponentially. Steps need to be taken to reduce the bulk and to legislate only when changing the law is legally necessary. There needs to be a comprehensive high-level inquiry into all aspects of the legislative process, with a view to improving it. It should cover policy formation, consultation, drafting, parliamentary scrutiny and evaluation of whether the purposes of the enacted legislation have been met.

Technical scrutiny in the House of Representatives is in urgent need of improvement. Sheeting home responsibility between the Government and Parliament is difficult as matters stand, and the processes of designing legislation within the executive lack transparency. A main committee based on the model of the Australian Commonwealth Parliament's should be adopted to improve the technical scrutiny of legislation in the House. Surprise by supplementary order paper should be stopped—improvements to this were made by the 2017 revisions to the standing orders of the House.

If Parliament is going to process as much legislation as it has been doing, it should sit for more days in the year and more hours in order to properly scrutinise the bills before it. In order to slow the system down and ensure the legislation has been properly designed and considered, a fixed four-year parliamentary term should be adopted. Passing bills through all their stages under urgency without scrutiny will be prevented by the restrictions upon urgency we have proposed.

The revised provisions on law-making in our proposed Constitution follow:

Law-making

91 Legislative procedures
- (1) Subject to this Constitution, a Bill becomes law when it is passed by an affirmative vote of a voting majority of members of Parliament and is signed by the Head of State.
- (2) Subject to this Constitution and any Act of Parliament, any subordinate legislation made by Cabinet becomes law when it is signed by the Head of State.

92 Information concerning Government legislation
At least five working days before introducing to Parliament a Bill that contains a new legislative scheme or a Bill that contains significant or extensive amendments to an existing Act, the Government must make publicly available information concerning the proposed legislation, including but not limited to—
- (a) the detailed nature of the proposals:
- (b) the policy papers relating to the changes:
- (c) the administrative arrangements proposed:
- (d) the fiscal costs of the new measures:
- (e) an analysis whether the proposals comply with this Constitution.

93 Attorney-General to report to Parliament where Bill appears to be inconsistent with Bill of Rights or te Tiriti o Waitangi/the Treaty of Waitangi
(1) Where any Bill is introduced into Parliament, the Attorney-General must bring to the attention of Parliament any provision in the Bill that appears—
   (a) to subject any of the rights and freedoms contained in Part 2 of this Constitution to a limit that cannot be demonstrably justified in a free and democratic society; or
   (b) to be inconsistent with any rights arising from te Tiriti o Waitangi/the Treaty of Waitangi.
(2) The Attorney-General must comply with paragraph (1)—
   (a) in the case of a Government Bill, on the introduction of that Bill:
   (b) in any other case, as soon as practicable after the introduction of the Bill.
(3) The Standing Orders of Parliament must address the case where a provision in a Bill to which paragraph (1)(a) or (b) applies results from an amendment of the Bill, and provide for the attention of Parliament to be drawn to the provision before the Bill is passed.

94 Legislative programme
For each calendar year, the Government must publish its proposed legislative programme.

95 Urgency
(1) When a motion for urgency to expedite the consideration of legislation is moved, the Speaker must rule whether it is in the public interest to set aside the ordinary processes of Parliament, including Article 92, because of the particular circumstances stated or referred to in the motion.
(2) The Speaker must give reasons for the ruling.

96 Legislation to be accessible and comprehensible
(1) All legislation must be drafted in clear and understandable language.
(2) Systems must be in place that allow the people to have ready access to the text of all legislation.
(3) Paragraph (2) applies to subordinate legislation.

97 Subordinate legislation
(1) Acts of Parliament may authorise the Cabinet, a Minister, or other person or body to govern specified matters by subordinate legislation.
(2) Parliament may disallow or amend any subordinate legislation authorised or purporting to be authorised by an Act of Parliament. The manner in which Parliament exercises these powers may be provided for by Act of Parliament or Standing Orders.
(3) Paragraph (2) does not apply to resolutions passed by Parliament or to by-laws made by a local government.

We now examine a number of instances where legislation has been sub-optimal and has led to problems of many types and frustration from those who are subject to the legislation. Such examples are sometimes complex.

1) **Accident Compensation.** New Zealand's accident compensation scheme is a unique system of social insurance that resulted from a visionary Royal Commission Report chaired by Sir Owen Woodhouse in 1967. The scheme provides rehabilitation and compensation to those incapacitated by personal injury. It covers people, without proof of fault, twenty-four hours a day. Over the years, the legislation relating to it has become longer and more complex. It now covers 338 pages of the statute book. The scheme was first enacted in 1972. There was a new Act in 1982, another in 1992, yet another in 1998 and the present one in 2001. And there were many amendments of those Acts. The lines that are drawn in this legislation are technical, difficult and sometimes unfair, particularly where a case falls between the different Acts. The problems facing claimants are formidable. If they read the statute they would have little chance of understanding it. This was a scheme to do away with the need for lawyers when claiming compensation for personal injury. Now lawyers are often needed. The current legislation betrays the vision of the scheme it was fashioned to serve. Constant legislative fiddling with the scheme has produced injustices. Eligibility depends upon which of the statutes the injured person may be subject to, and sorting out the transitional problems as between the various Acts passed over the years is a legal nightmare. The legislation has made aspects of the ACC scheme highly legalistic, and this creates unfairness for some.

2) **The Resource Management Act 1991** has suffered from serious problems resulting from massive numbers of amendments over the years that have destroyed its coherence and added greatly to the complexity and workability of the legislation.[6] The statute was designed to provide environmental bottom lines to test development proposals against the need to preserve the environment. It was designed on the principle of sustainable management, but most environmental indicators have become worse in the life of the statute, especially the quality of water in New Zealand lakes and rivers. The statute has more than doubled in length since it was first enacted. The 2017 amendments were 170 pages in length. Many of the amendments were based on hunch, ideology and presumption, not evidence. The legislative process relating to the latest amendments lasted more than 18 months and was quite unsatisfactory.

3) **Climate change**. The failure to address both the mitigation and adaptation issues in climate change means that New Zealand's climate change law remains manifestly deficient many years after the nature of the risks has become clear and incontestable. Amendments in 2008 to the Resource Management Act disabled that statute from taking into account, in many decisions, the effects of emissions of greenhouse gases. Large changes in the regulatory frameworks have been made due to changes in government, meaning there is no stable regulatory platform. The interests of future generations have been neglected. The Parliamentary Commissioner for the Environment reported in July 2017:[7]

> Between 1990 and 2015, New Zealand's net emissions have risen by 64%, while the UK's net emissions have fallen by 38%. Not all of this difference is due to differences in legislation and policies. Nevertheless, the UK's greenhouse gas curve has bent downward, whereas ours has not.

New Zealand greenhouse gas emissions have increased by 60 per cent since 1990. This is one of the worst records of any OECD country. The Climate Change Response Act 2002 was weakened

---

6 Geoffrey Palmer 'The Resource Legislation Amendment Bill, the Productivity Commission Report and the Future of Planning for the Environment in New Zealand' (2016) 12(4) Policy Quarterly 71.
7 Parliamentary Commissioner for the Environment *Stepping Stones to Paris and Beyond: Climate change, progress, and predictability* (July 2017) at 4.

by two sets of amendments to ensure it was ineffective at stemming emissions. Adaptation to rising sea levels, increased flooding and storms are left to local authorities, with little assistance from central government. The Climate Change Response Act 2002 was amended in 2008 to initiate the Emissions Trading Scheme (ETS). The Act started life as a serious response to the climate change problem, but it has suffered the fate of many statutes in New Zealand. When the Government changed, the Act was massively amended, several times. It has lost coherence. It was substantially weakened, obligations were deferred and the changes favoured emitters.[8]

4) **Human rights**. There has been a failure to adequately address human rights concerns in legislation. On 37 occasions between 1990 and March 2016 Parliament had passed Acts that it was advised were in breach of the New Zealand Bill of Rights Act.[9] What this shows is the dominant power of the Government in the New Zealand Parliament. We harbour concerns about the New Zealand constitutional system which echo those of Professor Margaret Wilson. In a recent and thoughtful book she explained the issue in this way:[10]

> There are three fundamental points to note about New Zealand's constitutional legal architecture. The first is that, like the United Kingdom, it has no formal written constitutional document. The second point is that all constitutional legislation can be amended or repealed by a simple majority of the Parliament. The third point is that the notion of parliamentary sovereignty constrains the scrutiny of legislation by the courts.

Thus, we are led to the conclusion that the institutions of the state lack the capacity to restrain the abuse of executive power. We are increasingly nervous about the fluid nature of New Zealand's 'unwritten' constitution, and the time has come to adopt a codified written constitution that strengthens the Bill of Rights Act, which is an essential step to producing a democracy that is better balanced.

5) **Pike River**. The reckless deregulation of safety standards that led to the death of 29 miners at the Pike River mine on The West Coast

---

8 Geoffrey Palmer 'New Zealand's Defective Law on Climate Change' (2015) 13 NZJPIL 115.
9 Palmer 'What the New Zealand Bill of Rights Act aimed to do', above n 1.
10 Margaret Wilson *The Struggle for Sovereignty: New Zealand and Twenty-First Century Statehood* (Bridget Williams Books, Wellington, 2015) at 18.

is a classic example of defective legislation as well as administrative failure. The Royal Commission into the tragedy found:[11]

The current legislation

The [Health and Safety in Employment Act 1992] placed general and specific duties on employers to ensure the safety of their workers. The aim was to achieve the highest possible level of self-management by employers and the lowest level of compliance cost. The act was based on the reforms recommended by the Robens Committee in the United Kingdom 20 years earlier.

The idea was to replace 'prescriptive' legislation and regulation, which tended to focus on specific hazards in specific industries, with principles that could be flexibly applied to the health and safety hazards confronted by all employers.

The HSE Act imposed a general duty on employers to 'take all practicable steps' to ensure the health and safety of workers. The act promoted the 'systematic' management of health and safety, specified the order in which serious hazards should be managed and provided the regulator with a flexible range of enforcement methods.

Regulations and approved codes of practice

The move towards more self-management by the employer was appropriate but the necessary support for the legislation, through detailed regulations and codes of practice, did not appear. Instead, the opposite happened: such regulations as existed were repealed when the HSE Act came into force. The special rules and safeguards applicable to mining contained in the old law, based on many years of hard-won experience from past tragedies, were swept away by the new legislation, leaving mining operators and the mining inspectors in limbo.

After some years, new mining regulations were issued including, in 1999, detailed requirements in relation to common hazards such as methane. Approved codes of practice or more informal guidance were never issued. The industry, through its association, the MinEx Health and Safety Council, issued some guidance to its members but without endorsement by the [Department of Labour].

As a result New Zealand's regulatory framework for underground

---

11 Graham Panckhurst, Stewart Bell and David Henry *Report of the Royal Commission on the Pike River Coal Mine Tragedy, Volume 1 + Overview* (October 2012) at 32, available at <pikeriver.royalcommission.govt.nz>.

coal mining is years behind those of other advanced countries, including Australia. It does not provide the support that employers and workers need.

Avoiding policy failures and inadequate legislation, and providing better frameworks for designing and considering legislation, are urgent priorities for New Zealand. The 2012 Royal Commission was the 12th into mining tragedies in New Zealand.

We have stressed in this chapter the important parliamentary function of making laws. More care, better information and improved processes are all needed. No doubt a similar analysis could be carried out to improve the way Parliament deals with finance, the control of taxation and how that money is spent.

Statute law has widespread effects on the whole community. Efforts should be made to improve the design of statutes. Such a step could bring the benefit of greater predictability and a reduction in the need for legal advice.

9 Why New Zealand does not need an upper house

Some submitters favoured the reintroduction of an upper house to the New Zealand Parliament. An upper house, we were told, would be an added check on government, and would cause it to think again about its legislative proposals. Submitters said that an upper house could stop governments from abusing urgency, and could ensure that legislation is consistent with the Constitution. Some favoured an upper house with 50 per cent Māori representation as a way of bringing tino rangatiratanga into New Zealand's system of government.

Many of the democracies with which New Zealand tends to compare itself have bicameral[1] Parliaments—including the United Kingdom, Australia, and Canada. New Zealand used to have an upper house, known as the Legislative Council, for almost a century, but it was done away with in 1950. In the years since, numerous attempts have been made to revive the idea.[2] In 1992, an upper house was suggested as an alternative to MMP, and a Bill was introduced to Parliament. During the 2017 election, one political party advocated for an upper house.[3]

We did not recommend an upper house in our 2016 book, and we continue to believe that an upper house would not be in New

---

1 A bicameral Parliament is a Parliament with an upper house (e.g., the House of Lords in the UK) and a lower house (e.g., the House of Commons in the UK).
2 See H Benda 'The Legislative Council' (1949) 1(2) Journal of Political Science 24; DJ Riddiford 'A Suitable Second Chamber for New Zealand' (paper presented to the Eighth Dominion Conference, Dunedin, May 1951), (1951) 27 NZLJ 102; DJ Riddiford 'The Case for a Corporate Upper House: A Reformed Upper Chamber' (1951) 3(2) Political Science 23; GA Wood 'New Zealand's single chamber parliament: An argument for an impotent upper house?' (1983) 36(1) Parliamentary Affairs 334 at 335–336; Andrew Stockley 'Bicameralism in the New Zealand Context' (1986) 16 VUWLR 377; Douglas Graham 'Reflections on the Constitution' [1999] NZ L Rev 561; Whata Winiata 'How Can or Should the Treaty be Reflected in Institutional Design?' in Colin James (ed) *Building the Constitution* (Institute of Policy Studies, Wellington, 2000) at 205; Andrew Geddis 'Parliamentary government in New Zealand: Lines of continuity and moments of change' (2016) 14 I•CON 99; and Gareth Morgan 'Gareth Morgan's Ratana Speech for The Opportunities Party' (Ratana, 24 January 2017), available at <www.top.org.nz/the_opportunites_party_ratana_speech>.
3 The Opportunities Party. See Morgan, above n 2.

Zealand's interests. There are a number of reasons, but the essential point is that there are better, simpler and less expensive ways to improve scrutiny of legislation and to keep a check on government or parliamentary actions that breach the Constitution.

In New Zealand, the Legislative Council was abolished because it was regarded as a failure. It was never a representative or democratic body, and in its 97-year existence it largely failed to hold governments or the lower house of Parliament to account.

The United Kingdom, Australia and Canada have each experienced significant constitutional and political problems with their second chambers that remain unresolved. Efforts at reform have been more or less constant in those countries but without obvious success.[4]

We acknowledge the need for further discussion about the place of tino rangatiratanga in New Zealand's constitution, and we address that issue in chapter 13.

The tortured history of New Zealand's upper house

One of the features of New Zealand's constitutional arrangements is that they have evolved over time in a piecemeal manner. There has never seemed to be an opportunity for the fundamentals of New Zealand's constitutional arrangements to be systematically considered.

The Crown's government in New Zealand began with a Governor assisted by unelected advisors. The 1852 New Zealand Constitution Act established: a House of Representatives; an upper house known as the Legislative Council; and provincial governments. It also provided for 'responsible government', by which the executive was drawn from members of the House of Representatives.

Over the years, as New Zealand moved towards full independence, the provisions of the 1852 Act were gradually removed. The provinces

---

4   See Vernon Bognador *The New British Constitution* (Hart Publishing, US and Canada, 2009), in particular references to the potential for a reformed House of Lords in the United Kingdom in chapter 6; Linda Trimble 'Status Quo Unacceptable; Senate Reform Possible; Abolition by Stealth Anti-Democracy' (2015) 24(2) Constitutional Forum constitutionnel 33 on Senate reform in Canada; and Robin Archer 'From an aristocratic anachronism to a democratic dilemma: an elected House of Lords and the lessons from Australia' (2013) 51(3) Commonwealth & Comparative Politics 267 for a discussion of the lessons to be learned from Australia's history of reforms in this area.

were abolished in 1876. In 1907, New Zealand became a dominion, and in 1947 Parliament adopted the Statute of Westminster Act, granting it full legal autonomy from Britain.[5] The Legislative Council was abolished fairly soon afterwards. The final step in repatriation of our constitutional arrangements was marked by the passage of the Constitution Act 1986, which revoked the application in New Zealand of the 1852 Constitution Act enacted by the United Kingdom Parliament.[6]

Some features of New Zealand's constitutional history—such as the adoption of universal suffrage—are sources of considerable national pride. The history of the Legislative Council, on the other hand, was a tortured one.[7] It was established in 1852 and first met in 1854, reformed many times, often with the aim of neutralising its influence, and was abolished from 1 January 1951.

The essential idea was that it would function in a similar manner to the United Kindom's House of Lords. Bicameral parliaments were part of the Westminster system of government. In constitutional theory, upper houses were supposed to have real influence by revising and improving legislation, providing opportunities for sober second thought by delaying legislation, and acting as something of a check and a balance on the lower house and a brake on the power of the Government. In New Zealand, the theory cannot be seen to have worked out as intended.

We do not need to describe the full history of the Legislative Council, but it is helpful to understand some of the key elements.

The 1852 New Zealand Constitution Act did not define the powers

---

5 JC Beaglehole (ed) *New Zealand and the Statute of Westminster* (Victoria University College, Wellington, 1944). The book comprises five lectures, two by Beaglehole and one by FLW Wood (both historians), and Professor RO McGechan, a lawyer and Professor Leslie Lipson, a political scientist.
6 For an authoritative legal account of how the law developed see Philip A Joseph *Constitutional and Administrative Law in New Zealand* (4th ed, Brookers, Wellington, 2014) at 119–122.
7 The intricate historical steps of the Legislative Council's constitutional dance have been well documented and analysed in the following studies: WK Jackson *The New Zealand Legislative Council: A Study of the Establishment, Failure and Abolition of an Upper House* (University of Otago Press, Dunedin, 1972); and Harshan Kumarasingham *Onward with Executive Power: Lessons from New Zealand 1947–57* (Institute of Policy Studies, Wellington, 2010) at chapter 4. That chapter contains the constitutionally appropriate heading 'Executive Power in Action: the Abolition of the Legislative Council'.

of the Council. Nor did it say how many members the Council should have, except that it should be at least 10.[8] Members were appointed by the Governor, and their appointment was for life.

The appointments system was controversial from the beginning. Some United Kingdom MPs opposed it.[9] So did settlers in New Zealand, who wanted an elected upper house. Thus, the bicameral system began life under something of a cloud and never became a confident and secure body. Indeed, the Council itself debated proposals for its reform more or less continuously over the years.[10]

For much of the 19th century, the Council was reasonably effective in amending and promoting legislation. But, too often, it was less interested in getting the law right than with political manoeuvring and manipulation.

In 1891, the Liberal Government was elected. The Council, dominated by the previous government's appointees, devoted itself to wrecking the Liberals' legislative proposals.[11] The Liberals, in response, appointed new members[12] and pushed through legislation getting rid of lifetime appointments.[13]

The Liberal Premier Richard Seddon, in his long period in office, effectively bent the Council to his will and neutralised its wrecking characteristics.[14] As time went on, it was reduced to a source of patronage for ministers to reward party stalwarts and supporters. It was not perceived as independent. It became irrelevant. It lacked democratic legitimacy or functionality and commanded little public

---

8 For a time, an upper limit on the number of members of the Council was imposed by royal instructions, but that was removed in 1861.
9 See (21 May 1852) 121 GBPD HC 922, where Sir William Molesworth objected to an Upper House composed of Members nominated for life, and to the superintendents being nominated by the Governor.
10 Jackson, above n 7, at 154–165.
11 W Pember Reeves *The Land of the Long White Cloud* (3rd ed, Allen and Unwin, London, 1924); and Leslie Lipson *The Politics of Equality: New Zealand's Adventure in Democracy* (University of Chicago Press, Chicago, 1948) at 357–358.
12 This was a significant moment in New Zealand's constitutional evolution. The Governor at first refused to agree to the Government's request for the appointment of more members. The Government appealed to the Colonial Office in London, which overruled the Governor.
13 Legislative Council Amendment Act 1891.
14 Tom Brooking *Richard Seddon: King of God's Own* (Penguin NZ), Auckland, 2014) at 361.

respect. According to the historian James Belich, it was 'effectively almost castrated' during this time.[15]

When the Liberals lost power in 1912, the Reform Government proposed to reform the Council to make it more democratic and less dependent on party politics.[16] The Legislative Council Act 1914 provided for a 40-member Council elected by proportional representation. The legislation had many merits over the Council's original framework. It could not be swamped by new appointments. It defined the Council's powers, particularly in relation to money Bills and financial matters, and made it subordinate to the House of Representatives.[17]

The Act's main proponent was Sir Francis Dillon Bell, a Wellington lawyer who was appointed Council chair in 1914. His goal, it appears, was to ensure the Council could no longer be swamped by political appointments, and could instead act as a safeguard against hasty legislation and violent swings of the political pendulum.[18]

But the Act was never brought into force. The First World War began soon after the legislation was passed, and a wartime Liberal-Reform coalition government was formed—but the price of Liberal membership was that the legislation not be brought into force unless a further proclamation was issued. That never happened. By the time the war ended, the Reform Government had grown lukewarm about the proposal.

The 1935–1949 Labour Government sometimes said it would abolish the Council, though it never took any steps to do so. On the contrary, like previous governments, it stacked the Council with its appointees. In the late 1940s, opposition politicians began to agitate for the Council's abolition. Many Labour MPs were sympathetic, and the momentum for abolition sparked a series of constitutional changes.

---

15 James Belich *Paradise Reforged* (Allen Lane Penguin Press, Auckland, 2002) at 42–43.
16 See the entry on WJ Gardiner in Claudia Orange and WH Oliver *Dictionary of New Zealand Biography* (Bridget Williams Books Department of Internal Affairs, Wellington, 1993) vol 2 at 35.
17 Jackson, above n 7, at 166–176. Also see William Downie Stewart *Sir Francis H D Bell: His Life and Times* (Butterworth, Wellington, 1937) at 93–104.
18 Downie Stewart, above n 17, at 102, 104. Also see Clifton Webb in discussion in Riddiford, above n 2, at 105.

In 1947, New Zealand adopted the 1931 Statute of Westminster, thereby giving itself full legal independence from Britain and allowing it to amend the UK Parliament's 1852 New Zealand Constitution Act, which had established the Legislative Council in the first place.

A joint committee of the two houses was set up to consider the issue of the second chamber. In 1948 it reported that it was unable to agree on a recommendation.[19] In 1949 the National Party ran in the general election on a platform of abolition of the Council. It won and proceeded to implement its policy. The Legislative Council Act 1914 was finally repealed in 1950, as part of the legislation that abolished the Council on 1 January 1951.[20]

Attempts to revive an upper house

If the main purpose of the Legislative Council was to improve legislation, the verdict of history is that it failed. New Zealand's first professor of political science, Leslie Lipson, argued in 1948 that it must be considered one of the most futile and ineffective second chambers in the world, and had no share in the decisions that really counted.[21]

Lipson's view was that the Council only did useful work through its Statutes Revision Committee, which concentrated on drafting and errors in the text of a Bill. This function, he thought, could be carried out by a Committee of the House of Representatives, as it was after the Council was abolished.

In 1954, Professor KJ Scott delivered an even more devastating judgment on the Council:[22]

> It was not an effective revising body; it did not prevent the passing of hasty and ill-considered legislation; it did not relieve members of the Lower House from the arduous committee work; and it did not represent a distinct interest in the community.

---

19 See *Statements Prepared for the Joint Constitutional Reform Committee* (Legislative Department, Wellington, 1948).
20 Harshan Kumarasingham 'What if the upper house had not been abolished?' in Stephen Levine (ed) *New Zealand as it Might Have Been. Volume II* (Victoria University Press, Wellington, 2010).
21 Lipson, above n 11, at 360.
22 KJ Scott 'Parliament' in JL Robson (ed) *New Zealand: The Development of its Laws and Constitution* (Stevens & Sons, London, 1954) at 38.

But abolition of the Legislative Council did not put to rest debate about bicameralism. Indeed, some of the MPs who voted for abolition hoped another form of upper house would replace it. Another joint committee of the two houses met and, in a 1952 report, recommended a new Senate, with members appointed by leaders of the parties in the House of Representatives.[23] The Labour Party refused to take part in the committee or debate the idea. The proposal went nowhere.

During the rest of the 1950s and the early 1960s, lobby groups continued to agitate for a new second chamber, along with other constitutional reforms.[24] The efforts of constitutional reformers had some effect. They led to the 1956 Electoral Act, which entrenched the right to free and fair elections, and to the creation of the Office of the Ombudsman. One prominent lobby group in the early 1960s called for the adoption of a written constitution,[25] and in 1963 the National Party introduced a proposal for a Bill of Rights, though it did not win support in Parliament.[26]

Throughout this era, only political scientists, lawyers and politicians seemed to take any interest in proposals for a new upper house. At no time was there widespread public demand.

From the mid-1960s, the idea of an upper house faded from political and constitutional debate—but it never quite died. During the late 1980s and early 1990s, as New Zealanders were debating the introduction of the MMP electoral system, the National Party introduced a Bill to the House providing for the establishment of an elected Senate if the public voted to retain the FPP electoral system.[27]

In Parliamentary debates, the Minister of Justice, Hon Douglas Graham, set out a vision for the Senate that steered a middle course between extremes—it was to have power and not be useless, but it would not be co-equal with the lower house and would not able to

---

23 TO Bishop and RM Algie 'Reports of the Constitutional Reform Committee' [1952] IV AJHR I18.
24 Jackson, above n 7, at 202–205; GG Grieve 'Report of the Public Petitions M to Z Committee' [1961] IV AJHR 12–12A; and RE Jack 'Report of the Constitutional Reform Committee' [1964] III AJHR I14. See also L Cleveland and AD Robinson (eds) *Readings in New Zealand Government* (Reed Education, Wellington, 1972) at 14–145 and 183–271.
25 Jackson, above n 7, at 202–205.
26 Jackson, above n 24.
27 Electoral Reform Bill 1992 (209-1); Graham, above n 2, arguing for a 30-member Senate as an alternative to MMP.

produce deadlock, only delay. The House of Representatives would be able to override resistance. This was designed to provide a second opinion and create incentives for Government to make changes to legislation.[28] Many saw the proposal as an attempt to attract support away from MMP. The proposal was referred to a Select Committee, where it was killed.[29]

In the 2017 election campaign, the Opportunities Party proposed a written constitution with an upper house as a central feature. The party's leader, Dr Gareth Morgan, saw the proposed upper house as 'defending our constitution which has at its centre, the Treaty of Waitangi'.[30] He expressed the view that he wanted to take 'sovereignty' away from Cabinet, and saw an upper house as achieving these goals.[31]

> My dream would be that the two treaty signatories are equally represented in the Upper House which—while deferring to the sovereignty of parliament, the Lower House—has the ability to highlight to the public weaknesses in intended legislation, as well as the ability to refer to the Courts issues of constitutional breaches. With the Constitution firmly including the principles of the treaty, this should ensure the interests of both tangata whenua and the other societies that make up the 'New Zealanders', are protected and nurtured.

---

28 (15 December 1992) 532 NZPD 13157, per Hon DAM Graham, Minister of Justice. The National Party put in a substantial amount of work on constitutional issues before and after the 1990 election. A Report of the Electoral Law Reform Committee to the Caucus in September 1990 recommended the party continued its opposition to the introduction of an entrenched Bill of Rights, acknowledged that scope existed for more frequent use of referenda and proposed indicative non-binding referenda of the type that were adopted by statute in 1992, opposed a four-year term while the deficiencies in the electoral system remained and recommended an election Manifesto Commitment to hold a referendum on electoral law matters and to include questions whether a second chamber should be introduced. The Law Reform Division of the Department of Justice produced detailed and extensive issues papers in March 1992 on the establishment of a second chamber. The proposal was well worked through; it was not some casual proposal.

29 (22 July 1993) 536 NZPD 16729, per Hon Murray McCully, Minister of Customs. The lead opposition speaker, the Hon David Caygill, attacked the upper house part of the Bill as a means to trying to prevent MMP being accepted: (15 December 1992) 532 NZPD 13163.

30 Morgan, above n 2, at 3.

31 At 4.

The party's policy set out further details.[32] The proposed upper house would be able to ask the House of Representatives to reconsider legislation it had passed. But its power would be recommendatory only. It would be a power to scrutinise and suggest amendments but not to insist on them. The policy did not say how the membership will be determined, other than to suggest that it may have a mix of appointed and elected members.

The policy has two essential ideas: the creation of a legislative process that is slower and more deliberate; and the protection of Māori interests. These two ideas are both important but they are not necessarily connected.

The arguments, which have been advanced from time to time, to have Māori interests represented in such a chamber on a 50–50 basis face serious difficulties. First, public opinion is unlikely to support such a development. Providing weighted representation for one group in the community is unlikely to be in accordance with democratic theory or politically acceptable, absent a shift in public sentiment. Already there exists a strong view in some portions of the public against the Māori electoral seats. Yet an upper house that specifically involved protecting Indigenous interests would necessarily involve some sort of representational preference.

The case for recognition of Indigenous rights has merit. But how the aim can be advanced through a second chamber is much less sure. The idea has been around at least since 2000, when it was advanced by Professor Winiata, drawing upon reforms within the New Zealand Anglican Church.[33] It has never secured widespread political traction. The proposals for second chambers in New Zealand have been dogged by undemocratic features: first overtones of a landed aristocracy in the early days; and later devising a chamber that could be elected, yet would do useful work, without impeding an elected House of Representatives. No such design has yet appeared that commands the necessary support, and producing such a design looks to be impossible.

---

32 The Opportunities Party 'The Opportunities Party Democracy Reset' <www.top.org.nz>.
33 Winiata, above n 2.

How to improve scrutiny without an upper house

Scrutinising legislation tends to be one of the constitutional tasks of Parliament not well understood by the public. It is not an activity that is obvious to many people. The main constitutional purpose of the Legislative Council was to fulfil this function—to scrutinise, amend and, if necessary, delay legislation in order to make better law. The record in New Zealand is that it failed in this function. Very few people have mourned its passing.

If the goal is to make better law, there are simpler, better and less expensive ways that can be done.

The development of a modern comprehensive select committee system in the 1980s, in which almost all Government Bills are scrutinised and public submissions heard, has given the opportunity to revise legislation in a different way. Select committee scrutiny was in many ways an attempt to mimic what a second chamber would do with legislation. That does not mean, however, that the absence of a second chamber has no consequences. Its absence certainly facilitates the passage of legislation quickly and sometimes without adequate scrutiny.[34]

The issue of checks remains an important one but the goal of achieving an adequate balance can be better facilitated by other mechanisms. While a carefully designed second chamber could scrutinise legislation, it is difficult to see in the New Zealand context how it could avoid either being a political competitor to the House of Representatives or a docile lap dog of the House. It is better to locate the checks and balances elsewhere. A single House of Parliament seems to be here to stay.

A constitutional realist would conclude that developing an effective second chamber in New Zealand at this juncture is impossible. As Professor Philip Joseph observes, it is unlikely the public would support a second chamber; they want a smaller Parliament, not a larger one, as evidenced by a 1999 citizen-initiated referendum.[35] On this latter issue it can be argued that public sentiment is wrong. For a single House to function properly it should not be so easily

---

34 Geoffrey Palmer 'Law-Making in New Zealand: Is there a better way?' (2014) 22 Wai L Rev 1.
35 Philip A Joseph *Constitutional and Administrative Law in New Zealand* (4th ed, Thomson Brookers, Wellington, 2014) at 357.

dominated by the Government, as is the case in New Zealand. And to carry out the scrutiny functions properly, given the quantity of legislation that is passed, more MPs are needed. Legislatures have to be big enough to fulfil their many functions as well as to represent the voters. But let us put that issue to one side.

Public submissions to select committees in New Zealand are a bright point in the system, and this needs to be preserved and enhanced. A tendency has developed of Governments who have the numbers on a committee to use them rather than to engage in debating and refining Bills. This sucks the vitality out of the select committee system. The New Zealand habit of determining everything in secret in caucus is alive and well. A powerful select committee system is essential to a Parliament that has only one House.

A number of factors have combined to make technical scrutiny of Government legislation, through submissions by the public to select committees, less effective now than when the system was established. An example of how the existing House could be reformed to improve legislative scrutiny is contained in the submission of the New Zealand Law Society to the Standing Orders Committee in February 2017. A portion of the submission is reproduced here with footnotes from the original to demonstrate in detail how to overcome some of the problems concerning adequate parliamentary scrutiny of legislation without a second chamber.

The New Zealand Law Society told the Standing Orders Committee in 2017 that quality legislation required some changes:[36]

> ... the Law Society considers that changes to the Standing Orders are needed to enhance the quality of legislation. New Zealand has a tendency to pass too much legislation and often too hurriedly. Unlike most democratic legislatures, the New Zealand Parliament has only one House, and it seems that this has altered the speed with which legislation is progressed. The Standing Orders cannot deal with the problems of the legislative process that arise within the Executive Branch but they can improve the quality of parliamentary scrutiny of Government Bills.
>
> Things have changed over time, including greater pressure on

---

36 Submission of the New Zealand Law Society to the Standing Orders Committee of the House of Representatives (25 November 2016) at [2.2].

parliamentary time, a much-increased legislative load and an MMP Parliament where smaller parties have difficulty resourcing select committees. This has been accompanied by greater complexity of legislative schemes and remorseless pressure on legislative progress, caused in part by the three-year term of Parliaments. Parliament has become more of a legislative bottleneck in the last few years.

Pressure at the Committee of the Whole House stage has seen truncated consideration caused by taking Bills part-by-part rather than clause-by-clause. This has meant the debates are more political and less concentrated on seeing if the actual provisions in the Bill are fit for purpose. It is here where scrutiny breaks down. More openness should also help improve the quality of legislation and the ease of scrutiny, so long as adequate time is allowed to get big legislative schemes right.

On the issue of improved ways to carry out technical scrutiny, the Law Society submission said:

7 The Committee of the Whole—technical scrutiny of legislation

7.1 The Law Society submits that what happens in the Committee of the Whole presents a significant threat to legislative quality.[37]

7.2 Amendments are moved and agreed to by SOP in circumstances that often do considerable damage to the architecture and coherence of Bills. Both opposition and Government members can move amendments with little notice and with no certainty until the last minute whether or not they will be accepted. SOPs can be tabled up until the moment that voting begins on the provisions they propose to amend. SOPs of more than 100 pages are not unknown.[38] Wholesale amendments at this late stage can cause considerable harm, yet there is a reluctance to recommit Bills that are subject to such amendments. Attempts over the years to rectify this feature of the New Zealand process have not proved effective.

7.3 In short, the Committee of the Whole stage is no longer capable

---

37 See David Bagnall 'Problems with New Zealand's Legislative Process, and How to Fix Them' (2009) 24(2) Australasian Parliamentary Review 114, in which he suggests that the conduct of the committee stages of all or most Bills should be conducted in the second chamber without the need for unanimity. See also Palmer, above n 34; See also Geoffrey Palmer and Andrew Butler *A Constitution for Aotearoa New Zealand* (Victoria University Press, Wellington, 2016) at 202.

38 In 2009 a Government supplementary order paper contained 112 pages of amendments to the Climate Change (Moderated Emissions Trading) Amendment Bill.

of ensuring that each provision of a Bill is subjected to close technical scrutiny.

7.4 It is ironic that not only is scrutiny often inadequate, but also that it takes too long. Even uncontroversial changes often wait a considerable time to be passed into law. It promotes the public interest to keep the law up to date and systematically remedy defects and faults in it.

7.5 Structural reform to reduce the legislative backlog in the House and improve the quality of technical scrutiny of legislation should be considered. The Law Society appreciates that this may be beyond the scope of the current review of the Standing Orders but suggests that consideration should be given to introducing a parallel legislative chamber,[39] modelled on the Australian Commonwealth Parliament's Main Committee.[40] That would enable the House to devote more time to legislation and process it in a more considered manner. A committee modelled on the Australian precedent would provide close, detailed scrutiny of a Bill's provisions to ensure they are fit for purpose. Such detailed scrutiny would substitute for the sweeping SOP amendments currently seen at this late stage of a Bill's passage.

7.6 The Commonwealth Parliament's Main Committee, established in 1994,[41] has been successful in alleviating the pressures on the Australian lower house.[42] About a third of all legislation is referred to it.

7.7 The committee stage of Bills that are largely uncontroversial could be taken in this parallel chamber, comprising no more than 30 members, sitting in the old Legislative Council Chamber. It would enable more time and attention to be given to the detail of Bills, with the aim of achieving optimal legislative outcomes. A Bill subject to examination in the Main Committee would revert to the full Committee of the House in the event of significant disagreement. A parallel legislative chamber would mean that the House could deal with two streams of business concurrently.

7.8 Adoption of a parallel legislative chamber would facilitate

---

39 What is meant by parallel legislative chamber in this context is an alternative, for some Bills, for the Committee of the Whole stage provided for at present in Standing Orders. This would allow more rigorous scrutiny by interested MPs. Proceedings could be conducted in the existing Legislative Council chamber.
40 A serious proposal for such a step was made by the then Acting Second Clerk—Assistant of the Office of the Clerk in New Zealand: Bagnall, above n 37, at 114.
41 The Main Committee is now known as the Federation Chamber.
42 Parliament of Australia 'Infosheet 16—The Federation Chamber' <www.aph.gov.au>.

business for uncontroversial measures and improve the quality of parliamentary scrutiny. Such changes would help to alleviate the serious delays to which some measures are subject because they lack political priority.

Recommendation:
That consideration be given to establishing a parallel legislative chamber for the technical scrutiny of Bills and for ensuring that they properly give effect to the purposes of Bills as agreed to on second reading.

Efforts to persuade the Standing Orders Committee to adopt a version of the approach in the Australian Commonwealth Committee have been made for quite some years through the Law Commission, without any action yet having been taken. Geoffrey Palmer, who was Leader of the House when big changes were made to the Standing Orders in the first term of the Fourth Labour Government, was also involved in one of those efforts when President of the Law Commission. He supports the recommendations of the Law Society, set out above, and which he assisted in formulating along with Professor Philip Joseph.

It is a shame that the 2017 Report of the Standing Orders Committee made only cautious changes to the Standing Orders to improve the quality of legislation.[43] The proposal for a Main Committee was not accepted. There was an admission that the Committee of the Whole could perform its scrutiny function better and a new system would be trialled. Such changes are incremental rather than bold, although some of them will be useful. Select committees will henceforth sit during the parliamentary recesses, thereby helping them to devote more time to scrutinising legislation. There were some reservations expressed on the Committee about the use of urgency, although no changes were made restricting its availability. The Committee advocated more pre-legislative scrutiny, but nothing by way of a mandatory rule emerged. One positive proposal was that the Attorney-General will make reports at any time during the legislative process, and the new Standing Order requiring 24 hours' notice to be given of amendments before they are debated is positive.

43 Review of Standing Orders *Report of the Standing Orders Committee* [2017] AJHR I18, see <www.parliament.nz/resource/en-NZ/SCR_74675/70c7a3972ff528fea2a062cc9aad17b6507200c3>.

It turns out in New Zealand that chipping away at improving the legislative process in order to secure better law from Parliament is difficult. Parliament is a very conservative institution and changes its procedures reluctantly. It does not keep up with the times well at all and has been a late adapter of new technology to help with its work. Reform of Parliament is an activity that needs to be pushed hard almost constantly to ensure that the Parliament remains at the forefront of our democracy and does not lose touch with it. There is something about the House of Representatives that reminds people of an English gentlemen's club. The procedures are designed for the convenience of members rather than as a modern way to produce better legislative outcomes. The Government invariably likes things the way they are and Cabinets will resist any reduction in their ability to control things. In a small Parliament, such an approach is destructive of the democratic purpose of the institution and leads to excessive executive power.

The failure of the Standing Orders Committee to address the problems of legislative scrutiny in any decisive manner in the New Zealand Parliament suggests a sense of drift and complacency that fails to recognise the obligations of the House to produce coherent, well-considered statutes that endure and actually work. The select committees these days seem hardly to engage with the public submissions in any serious way and the power of the executive is thereby enhanced.

What is to be learned from this record?

The fundamental reason the second chamber was abolished in the first place and the reason it could not be revived, despite several efforts, lies in the fact that it was contrary to the New Zealand democratic impulse. Proposals for change must run with the grain of New Zealand's constitutional and political culture.[44] What did the chamber represent? The Legislative Council was never elected and it lacked legitimacy for that reason. Political representation lies at the heart of New Zealand democratic politics. As Professor Elizabeth McLeay has put it, 'the relationship between the represented and those who represent should rest on clear democratic principles

---

44 Matthew SR Palmer 'New Zealand Constitutional Culture' (2007) 22 NZULR 565.

of representativeness, responsiveness and accountability'.[45] The Legislative Council could not draw authority from the people directly. It failed on all three counts. New Zealand has traditionally prized direct control over its political representatives. Yet the Legislative Council represented no set of interests. Further, it operated as something of a spoils system of the appointment of favourites to positions that were almost sinecures for the Government of the day.

The prime reason why the final proposal of the select committee failed in 1952 lies in the fact that its members were to be appointed by the Government. If the members were to be elected, they would expect to have power to make significant policy decisions. Should that occur, the prospect for disagreement and confusion between two chambers looked very uninviting to any Cabinet. So, two themes coalesced to produce the result: a strong democratic and egalitarian tradition that said political decision-makers should be elected, combined with a desire of the political elites for strong executive power.

Two proposals, one of which reached the statute books and the other contained in a Bill introduced to Parliament, involved an elected Senate. Yet these proposals, although democratically based, could not command support either. The legislation containing Bell's elected Senate of 1914 never commenced. In 1992 efforts to revive the idea also failed to secure support. This latter may well be partly attributable to mixing up the issue with the change to the electoral system. Further, that Senate was to have been a relatively toothless body for a house with such a complex electoral structure. In the end there just did not seem to be enough for a second chamber to do to make the exercise worthwhile.

The life of the Legislative Council took place for the most part in an FPP electoral system. Majoritarian sentiment was strong. The New Zealand system over time produced Governments with great and dominant executive power. The MMP system was in part a reaction to this sort of authoritarian behaviour; the MMP era has produced a multiparty legislature and put an end to single-party majority Governments for the most part. Further, MMP has produced a much more representative Parliament than ever before, with greater

---

45 Elizabeth McLeay 'Political Connections: Exploring Representation' (Inaugural lecture, Victoria University of Wellington Council Chamber, 11 September 2007).

diversity both in ethnic and political terms.

From this record there can be salvaged some second chamber functions that can, and should be, included in the single chamber we have. The key issue involves scrutiny of legislation—the prime point that proponents of a second chamber point to and which historically remains the major justification for a second chamber. As to further checks and balances, they are probably best designed by means other than a second chamber, and this we have endeavoured to do in our proposed draft constitution.

10 The Judiciary

In our 2016 book we outlined our initial proposals as to the function, structure, appointment process and powers of the Judiciary under a new, codified, supreme-law constitution.[1] As with many of our proposals we were keen to preserve as many of the sound elements of our constitutional tradition, yet to make some changes to ensure a more robust system of checks and balances.

In this chapter we recap the role of the Judiciary and outline in brief the proposals we made, the feedback we received and the changes we propose to make to our new draft constitution as a result.

The Judiciary and the courts

The Judiciary is the third branch in the traditional Westminster structure of government, sitting alongside the Executive (Government) and the Legislature (Parliament). The Judiciary consists of courts (staffed by judges) and tribunals (staffed by judges and/or tribunal members). The core function of courts and tribunals is to undertake the adjudication of disputes and resolve them by reference to the law. In doing so, the Judiciary carries out a vital role as a check and balance on the other two branches of government by overseeing executive action, and interpreting and applying the law made by the legislature. Decisions of the courts and tribunals build up a body of precedent which ensures that similar cases get similar results, and this mechanism allows the law to keep up with society over time. Decisions by the courts are authoritative; they carry the sanction of the state if not respected.

In theory, constitutions do not need to recognise the position or the role of the Judiciary. After all, the New Zealand Constitution Act 1852—which set out parts of our constitution until it was repealed in 1986—made no reference to the Judiciary at all. However, most modern codified constitutions overseas do make reference to the judicial branch, and we think it is extremely important to do so in order to secure its position within the constitutional divisions of power and to ensure the protection of a robust system of checks and

---

1 Geoffrey Palmer and Andrew Butler *A Constitution for Aotearoa New Zealand* (Victoria University Press, Wellington, 2016) at chapter 6.

balances which serve to protect our democracy.

Our 2016 proposals and the feedback we received

In brief, our 2016 proposals were to:

- Guarantee judicial independence from the other branches of government (as the current law does) by only allowing judges to be removed from office on grounds of misbehaviour or incapacity and by preventing reduction of judicial salaries. This allows judges to make decisions without fear of reprisals from Government. These proposals continue the current law. Feedback did not suggest that these proposals were controversial; indeed, the reverse.
- Raise the age of compulsory judicial retirement from 70 (the current law) to 72 (the law prior to 1980). There was mixed reaction to this proposal. Many submitters thought that with increased life expectancy and life function, retirement at 70 was too early. Others, however, saw no pressing need for change. We propose to continue with our initial proposal to raise the age to 72.
- Continue the current structure of the senior courts (being the Supreme Court, Court of Appeal and High Court) and allow legislation to organise other courts and tribunals, within the basic requirements of judicial independence. We received some feedback suggesting that since the District Court is the court in which most Kiwis experience justice (both criminal and civil), it should be explicitly recognised in any written constitution. We have accepted these suggestions.
- Provide for a wholly new system of judicial appointments to avoid potential politicisation of the Judiciary through selective appointment. In particular, we proposed the establishment of a Judicial Appointments Commission, consisting of a range of persons from the legal profession, the Judiciary and non-lawyers.[2] No person could be appointed by the Government to be a judge unless their name appeared on a shortlist prepared by the independent Commission. In determining suitable candidates, the Commission would be required to select on merit, having regard to a candidate's personal qualities, legal ability and experience, as well as the desirability of the Judiciary reflecting gender, cultural

---

2   Constitution Aotearoa 2016, art 64(1).

and ethnic diversity.[3] These proposals were generally well received and we have decided to stick with them.

- Give constitutional recognition to the Waitangi Tribunal and enable courts and tribunals to request an opinion from the Waitangi Tribunal or other established experts where issues arise which relate to te Tiriti o Waitangi/the Treaty of Waitangi or which involve tikanga Māori. This seemed to us to be a logical extension of the courts' ability to request expertise where necessary. We have seen no reason to change our opinion on this.
- Give the Judiciary the power—enjoyed in most western democracies—to strike down legislation that is inconsistent with the Constitution and, in particular, fundamental human rights, separation of powers and the like. We remarked that this power to strike down 'is probably the most significant change we propose, at least in legal terms'.[4] Our new draft still contains these powers, but we have made some changes to the way in which Parliament can respond to such a strike-down. These are discussed in detail below.

In addition to feedback on these aspects of our proposals, broader feedback asked us to explain in more detail how the courts would exercise constitutional jurisdiction. We also were asked to give the new Head of State a more explicit Constitution protection/guardianship role. We have taken onboard that feedback and, as discussed in chapter 5, now propose to permit the Head of State to refer Bills over which there is constitutional concern to the Supreme Court.

Constitutional review of Acts of Parliament

For a number of reasons, we were concerned to ensure that this new check on the otherwise untrammelled power of Parliament was carefully explained and its effects understood.

First, neither of us supported the idea of allowing the Judiciary to have the last word on constitutional matters. We felt that, even though, technically, New Zealand judges actually had the power to strike down laws that were unconstitutional right up till 1986,[5] most New Zealanders did not know this and would regard it as a backward

---

3   Constitution Aotearoa 2016, art 64(2)(b).
4   Palmer and Butler, above n 1, at 20.
5   The grounds on which legislation could be found to be unconstitutional had become very few indeed by 1986.

The Judiciary

step if the uncontrolled rule of Parliament were simply to be replaced by the uncontrolled rule of judges. Second, we anticipated that some people would be concerned at the prospect of introducing a seemingly US-style Judiciary, where the perception is that lots of social issues are ultimately resolved by judges, not legislators, nor indeed the people. Third, we needed to address the question of judicial selection.

Through the 2016 book, our public engagements around the country, many of the opinion pieces we wrote and the submission feedback forms we prepared, we sought to emphasise a number of points about our proposals on the judicial power to strike down legislation.

This idea is not new, even here.

This power is commonplace overseas. Most Commonwealth countries, including Canada, Australia, India, South Africa, the Caribbean Commonwealth and so on, provide for it. So too do almost all of our Pacific neighbours and most European countries, such as Ireland, Germany, Spain and Italy, and in South America it is standard.

Even in the United Kingdom, the courts have the power to invalidate the legislation of the Scottish, Welsh and Northern Irish parliaments. Nor do the courts have to apply Westminster legislation if it is inconsistent with European Union law, though that will likely change when the United Kingdom leaves the European Union.

This same power is one New Zealand courts had under the New Zealand Constitution Act 1852, and one they exercised from time to time (albeit that the grounds upon which they could do so did not include, for example, human rights).[6]

Parliament gave judges a power to strike down changes to certain core features of our electoral law in 1956, unless those changes had been approved by 75 per cent of MPs, or by a binding public referendum.[7] This limited entrenchment model is the model we want to follow. When coupled with the proposal that the Constitution be

---

6 Examples include *In re Gleich* (1879) OB&F 39 (SC, Full Bench) and *R v Lander* [1919] NZLR 305 (CA), in which the Foreign Offenders Apprehension Act 1863 and the Crimes Act 1908, s 224 were found to exceed the then General Assembly's constitutional powers under the New Zealand Constitution Act 1852.
7 Electoral Act 1956, s 189 restricted the amendment or repeal of certain 'reserved' provisions. This has been carried across to the current Electoral Act 1993, s 268.

supreme law, this strike-down power will extend from the ability to strike down legislation on the basis that proper procedure was not followed to change or to create the law (manner and form decisions), to the power to strike down law because it contradicts existing law, that is, the Constitution (substantive decisions). So our proposals are not wholly radical—we have picked up and extended an existing model.

Under many free trade agreements that New Zealand has made with other countries, overseas investors can sue New Zealand before a three-person international arbitral tribunal (effectively a form of international court) if New Zealand legislation breaches those agreements. (These are the so-called Investor State Dispute Settlement [ISDS] clauses that have attracted so much attention during the Trans-Pacific Partnership Trade Agreement (TPPA) discussions.) If successful, the investor is entitled to be paid damages for the losses caused by that legislation. How can it be, we asked, that a foreigner can successfully challenge New Zealand legislation before a court that only contains one New Zealand member (one of the others is nominated by the investor's state, and the third is appointed by the New Zealand and the investor-state member), but we won't allow our own people to challenge the same legislation in front of New Zealand judges?

Contemporary New Zealand judges have significant experience in exercising the power of judicial invalidation. Many of the courts in the Pacific Islands are staffed by New Zealand judges. In almost all of those jurisdictions, the courts have the power of judicial invalidation. If our judges are sufficiently competent to invalidate statutes in our Pacific Island neighbours, why should we think that they would be incompetent to do the same in New Zealand?

Addressing some misconceptions

The introduction of a written constitution enforceable by the Judiciary is unlikely to politicise the New Zealand Judiciary nor diminish public respect for it. For example, in Canada recent public polling has affirmed the high degree of public trust in the Canadian Supreme Court, especially in respect of its work in enforcing the

The Judiciary

Canadian Charter of Rights and Freedoms.[8] And this is despite some of its rulings being controversial and dealing with key social issues such as assisted dying and abortion. Leading constitutional lawyer Professor Alan Page also noted in a 2017 lecture that the fear that greater power would politicise the Judiciary, following the introduction of the Scotland Act 1998 and its amendment in 2016, has not been realised in Scotland.[9] And, of course, our proposals would give a special majority of MPs (75 per cent) the power to override a court decision with which they disagreed—this pressure valve would ensure that, on particular issues where there is a strong parliamentary consensus, the judges' interpretations can be departed from.

We have provided further mechanisms to avoid politicisation by introducing the Judicial Appointments Commission as a wholly new way of appointing judges. It will apply to all judicial appointments, and aims to make the selection and appointments process more transparent and to remove it as far as possible from political influence. In this way we hope to avoid the problems apparent in the United States system, where judges are often appointed based on their political leanings because it is assumed they will look more or less favourably at certain laws as a result.

In a similar vein, New Zealand will not end up with rule by judges. Parliament's power to postpone a court decision and the power to amend the constitution exercisable by a special majority of MPs (75 per cent) or by a simple majority of us, the people, at a binding referendum, will act as powerful checks. But so too will the existence of the text of a constitution. This was a point made powerfully by the Hon John G Roberts Jr, Chief Justice of the United States, at a

---

8 'Vast majority of Canadians trust Supreme Court, including most Tories' *iPolitics* (16 August 2015), reporting on an Angus Reid opinion poll on public trust in public institutions. The poll showed that more than twice as many Canadians expressed a 'great deal' or a 'lot of confidence' in the Supreme Court (61%) as expressed such confidence in the Federal Parliament (28%). See also, 'Canadians have a more favourable view of their Supreme Court than Americans have of their own' *Angus Reid Institute* (17 August 2015), available at <angusreid.org/supreme-court>.
9 Alan Page, Professor of Public Law at University of Dundee 'How we are Governed' (Public address, Victoria University of Wellington, 7 April 2017).

public lecture in Wellington in 2017.[10] When asked whether a written constitution could allow judges to push personal barrows, the Chief Justice said that, to the contrary, the text of a constitution acts as a limitation on judges' ability to bring their own political or personal preferences to constitutional work—a written constitution is more constraining than freeing.

We need greater oversight

The power of judicial strike-down is needed. We have described a number of cases where Parliament have enacted legislation under urgency, or by little more than a bare majority, knowing full well that it was inconsistent with human rights, yet they did so for short term political gain.[11] We expect too much of politicians if we expect them to act in protection of fundamentals all of the time in the face of short-term political pressures. United Nations human rights bodies consistently criticise New Zealand's constitutional arrangements because our courts do not have power to invalidate Acts of Parliament that are inconsistent with human rights. This criticism was repeated as recently as April 2016 by the United Nations Human Rights Committee.[12]

Elections every few years are a useful accountability measure, but far too crude to protect minority rights. Simply put—and at most of our public meetings this was readily accepted by a show of hands— elections are about an individual's money, taxes and spending priorities. There is little interest or relevance in using one's vote to 'punish' a government that has breached a minority's human rights, especially if you're not in that minority group yourself.

Giving judges the power to strike down legislation sets the right

---

10 Hon John G Roberts Jr, Chief Justice of the United States of America, in conversation with Professor Mark Hickford, Pro-Vice Chancellor and Dean of Law at Victoria University of Wellington (Victoria University School of Law, Wellington, 26 July 2017). The full talk can be watched at <www.youtube.com/watch?v=A1mGUVtdoow>.
11 See for example *R v Poumako* [2000] 2 NZLR 695 (CA) (retrospective penalties); *R v Pora* [2001] 2 NZLR 37 (CA) (retrospective penalties); *Attorney-General v Zaoui* [2004] NZSC 38 (access to justice); *Ministry of Health v Atkinson* [2012] 3 NZLR 456 (freedom from discrimination); and *Attorney-General v Taylor & Others* [2017] NZCA 215, 3 NZLR 24 (electoral rights).
12 United Nations Human Rights Committee *Concluding observations on the sixth periodic report of New Zealand* CCPR/C/NZL/CO/6 (28 April 2016) at [9]–[10].

incentives. At present, people can challenge legislation that unjustifiably discriminates against them or that unjustifiably limits their rights under the New Zealand Bill of Rights Act 1990. The mechanism that allows this to occur is called a 'declaration of inconsistency'. In the case of discriminatory legislation, Parliament explicitly provides for the mechanism by means of the Human Rights Amendment Act 2001.[13] In the case of the New Zealand Bill of Rights Act, the courts recently inferred the mechanism from the text of the Bill of Rights.[14] Though declarations of inconsistency draw attention to Acts of Parliament that unjustifiably limit human rights, their effect is limited. The core problem with declarations of inconsistency is that even if an affected person obtains a declaration, it has no direct impact on the legislation. The legislation remains valid.[15] (In our public engagements many people struggled to understand how that could be possible.) The affected person (and others in the same boat) can only hope that Parliament will take notice of the declaration and decide to change the law. How many people would invest time and effort and energy in pursuing a declaration that offers little immediate tangible benefit? Would you?

The answer lies in the evidence. Since 2002, when the Human Rights Amendment Act mechanism came into effect (i.e., 16 years ago at the time of writing) only five cases have been brought. Three were successful; in one case, Parliament was already changing the legislation;[16] in another the government said it would change the law at the next available opportunity—two years later, nothing has happened;[17] and in the third case—which showed how hopelessly outdated and discriminatory the Adoption Act 1955 is—the government said it has no interest in reform; it had other priorities.[18]

---

13 Human Rights Act 1993, s 92J.
14 *Taylor v Attorney-General* [2015] NZHC 1706, [2015] 3 NZLR 791; *Attorney-General v Taylor & Others* [2017] NZCA 215, [2017] 3 NZLR 24. At the time of writing, the decision of the Court of Appeal is under appeal to the Supreme Court.
15 Human Rights Act 1993, s 92K.
16 *Howard v Attorney-General (No 3)* (2008) 8 HRNZ 378 (HRRT).
17 *Heads v Attorney-General* [2015] NZHRRT 12, (2015) 10 HRNZ 203 (HRRT).
18 *Adoption Action Inc v Attorney-General* [2016] NZHRRT 9, (2016) 10 HRNZ 622 (in which Adoption Action successfully argued the Adoption Act 1955 and the Adult Adoption Information Act 1985 discriminated against certain persons on prohibited grounds of discrimination including marital status, sexual orientation, age, race and disability).

This uneven response is hardly likely to encourage citizens to call Parliament to account.

Far better in our view, therefore, to invert the incentives: New Zealanders shouldn't suffer from unjustified laws unless Parliament has seriously reconsidered the issue and decided, notwithstanding the benefit of a court's neutral opinion that the legislation is unjustified, to override the court's opinion. Those steps give incentives for better conduct and ensure better quality, more effective checks.

Recent events—particularly in Brexit Britain and Trump's America—show that the dangers of populism are real. When they arise checks and balances become very important—a constitution cannot stop the election of a Trump, but it can stop one riding roughshod over people's rights.

We found broad support for giving judges the power to strike down legislation, so long as American style judicial review could be avoided. It would be fair to say, however, that not everyone was convinced. Some took the view that 'If ain't broke, don't fix it'. Therein, however, lies the key decision point. To our mind, and those of many submitters, the system is at least vulnerable, if not yet broken. Again, our preference is to recognise the dangers now within the system and seek to improve the checks on parliamentary power before we lose the opportunity to do so.

Constitutional jurisdiction: how it would work

The detail of how courts and tribunals would exercise constitutional jurisdiction attracted a little, but not much, attention in the submissions we received. Some submitters did, however, seek clarification on a number of points. So, we thought we could usefully outline the process here. First, this is what the provision now looks like:[19]

> **109 Courts determine consistency of laws and conduct with Constitution**
> (1) The High Court has original jurisdiction to determine the question whether any law or conduct is consistent with this Constitution.

---

19 Constitution Aotearoa 2018, art 109.

(2) All courts have jurisdiction to determine the question whether any law or conduct is consistent with this Constitution if it arises in the course of proceedings that otherwise fall within their jurisdiction. An Act of Parliament may confer similar jurisdiction upon a tribunal.

(3) When deciding a constitutional matter within its jurisdiction, a court or tribunal—
- (a) if satisfied that any law or conduct is inconsistent with the Constitution, must declare the law or conduct invalid to the extent of its inconsistency:
- (b) may make any order that is just and equitable in order to remedy the consequences or effects of that inconsistency:
- (c) may make any order that is just and equitable to limit the effects of a declaration of invalidity or of a remedial order, including—
  - (i) an order prospectively limiting the retrospective effect of the declaration of invalidity or of the remedial order:
  - (ii) an order suspending the declaration of invalidity or of the remedial order for any period and on any conditions, to allow the competent authority to correct the inconsistency.

(4) Despite anything in this Article, if, in accordance with a declaration under Article 111 [Act may prevail over Constitution for limited period], a provision in an Act of Parliament prevails for the time being over any Article or paragraph of this Constitution, no court may do anything that would be inconsistent with the declaration under Article 111.

(5) If a declaration or order described in paragraph (3) concerns the consistency of an Act of Parliament with this Constitution and is made by a tribunal or by a court other than the Supreme Court, the declaration or order does not take effect unless it is confirmed by the Supreme Court.

(6) The Supreme Court has power to confirm, vary, modify or set aside any declaration or order it is asked to confirm.

(7) The procedure for confirmation by the Supreme Court may be regulated by Act of Parliament.

The basic idea is that—as is the case in many countries in which courts have constitutional review powers—an affected person can raise a constitutional issue in a proceeding in which the court they are appearing before has jurisdiction. For example, suppose you are charged in the District Court with an offence, and you claim that the prosecution obtained key evidence against you in an unconstitutional manner, then the District Court would determine that issue, just as District Courts do thousands of time a year, under the current New Zealand Bill of Rights Act 1990. Say, however, that your complaint was a little different—your claim is that the actual offence with which you are charged is unconstitutional. In that case, you would be saying that the legislation that creates the offence is unconstitutional, or would be unconstitutional if it applied to your circumstances. In that case, the District Court would have power to determine the issue. If it agreed that there would be a breach of your rights, the District Court would see whether the legislation could be read narrowly so as not to interfere with your constitutional rights (all District Courts can do this currently using section 6 of the New Zealand Bill of Rights Act 1990) or, if not, it could decide to strike down the relevant offence. Alternatively, if the District Court regards the issue as too difficult or important or time-consuming for it to decide, it can refer the matter to the High Court.

In any case in which any court decides that an Act of Parliament, or part of an Act, is unconstitutional, its declaration to that effect will not bite until it is confirmed by the Supreme Court. We believe this is an important quality assurance mechanism. In our constitutional theory an Act of Parliament is one of the highest expressions of democratic will; it is only proper that, if that will is to be thwarted, it has the backing of the country's highest court. This confirmatory role for the Supreme Court is similar to the role exercised by the South African Constitutional Court.[20] It appears to have worked well there.

We have also provided explicit power to the courts to modify the remedies available, even where an affected person has established that the Constitution has been breached. So, even where a law is found to be invalid because it breaches the Constitution in some way, the court will have a discretion that allows them to limit the effect of a

---

20 Constitution of the Republic of South Africa 1996, s 172(2)(a).

declaration of invalidity by restricting or suspending its effect. The reason for this is that sometimes a finding of unconstitutionality could have far-reaching implications that will need time to be worked out. Courts in countries like Canada, Ireland, South Africa and so on have powers to modify remedies where the public interest requires it. Similar powers were given to New Zealand courts when the Human Rights Amendment Act 2001 was passed.[21]

Head of State referral of Bill to Supreme Court

In chapters 3 and 5 we discussed a number of submissions that urged us to give a guardian-type role to the Head of State. As a result of those submissions we have proposed that the Head of State be given a power to decline to sign a Bill presented for signature if they are concerned about its constitutionality. As discussed in more detail in chapter 5, in such a case the Head of State must refer the Bill's constitutionality (in whole or in part) to the Supreme Court for a ruling. If the Supreme Court decides the Bill appears to be unconstitutional, the Head of State must not sign it. Otherwise the Head of State must sign.

This Bill referral power, or a version of it, is present in a number of overseas constitutions such as Germany,[22] South Africa[23] and Ireland,[24] among others.

In terms of the process the Court would follow when considering such referrals, overseas practice suggests that the Attorney-General— as chief law officer of the state—would assign counsel to argue for the Bill's constitutionality.[25] Counsel would be assigned by the Head of State or the Court to argue against. Other interested parties could participate if the Supreme Court permits. Consistent with article 77(3) of our current draft Constitution, the Supreme Court would not be bound by its decision on a referral, so, for example, if new facts or legal arguments emerged at a later date that would affect its view of constitutionality, the Supreme Court could strike down legislation even though it had given it a tick of approval on a referral.

---

21 Human Rights Act 1993, s 92O.
22 German Basic Law 1949, art 93(1).
23 Constitution of the Republic of South Africa 1996, s 84(2)(c).
24 Constitution of Ireland 1937, art 26.
25 See for example art 26.1.2 of the Irish Constitution, which directs the Supreme Court to hear arguments by or on behalf of the Attorney-General.

One of our goals with the Constitution Aotearoa project has been to enhance the system of checks and balances. We believe that the Bill referral procedure will be a useful, additional check.

Parliament has the last word

In addition to the ability for Constitution Aotearoa to be amended from time to time (either by a special 75 per cent majority of MPs or by a binding referendum approved by a simple majority of voters), we proposed in our 2016 book that any Act of Parliament that had been invalidated by the Supreme Court could be validated again by a special 75 per cent majority of MPs—essentially, we provided a Parliamentary override mechanism. The relevant parts of our original proposal looked like this:[26]

> **68 Constitutional jurisdiction of the courts and tribunals**
>
> [. . .]
> (4) Where an Act of Parliament has been held or confirmed to be inconsistent with this Constitution by the Supreme Court, within one year of the decision of the Supreme Court, Parliament may enact an Act of Parliament ('the validating Act') that provides that, notwithstanding the decision of the Supreme Court, the Act of Parliament in question shall continue to have effect, subject to such modifications or limitations as are provided for in the validating Act.
> (5) A validating Act described in paragraph (4) has no legal force or effect unless it receives the support of a 75 per cent majority of all members of the House of Representatives.

Our first proposal would have allowed Parliament to enact validating legislation with that special majority within one year of the Supreme Court's decision. If enacted, a validating Act would permit the impugned statute to continue to operate notwithstanding the Supreme Court's decision, subject to such modifications or limitations as provided for in the validating Act.

We received very few comments on the detail of this proposed mechanism. That said, those who were opposed to Parliament ever being able to override the Constitution were, quite naturally, against the provision; those who saw no need for any change to our current

---

26 Constitution Aotearoa 2016, art 68(4) and 68(5).

constitution were, of course, opposed.

For the reasons discussed at length in our first book, we believe the parliamentary override, or notwithstanding mechanism, is useful. Because it is targeted solely on an Act of Parliament that has been invalidated by the Supreme Court, the mechanism is unlikely to be frequently used—we anticipate that it will be quite rare for the Supreme Court to need to exercise the power to strike down. This is a more specific power for Parliament to deal with a particular court ruling, rather than just amending the text of the Constitution itself. The power would be used by Parliament where Parliament does not wish to amend the terms of Constitution Aotearoa, as such, but rather wishes to shield an Act of Parliament from a specific Supreme Court ruling. This could be where, for example, the Supreme Court finds that an Act of Parliament is an unjustified limit on a right guaranteed by the Bill of Rights, but Parliament considers that the limit is justified. In those circumstances there would be no need to amend the terms of the Constitution; everyone agrees that the right itself is fundamental, and it is simply that a significant majority of Parliament disagrees with the Supreme Court's evaluation in this particular instance. Although we expect its use to be rare, we believe the parliamentary override is a useful innovation that strikes a sensible balance.

Our reconsideration of the exact workings of this mechanism has, however, lead us to address two new issues. First, should the notwithstanding legislation have a limited shelf-life? In our view, the answer is yes. Parliament should be required periodically to review the case for validating legislation that the Supreme Court has held to be unconstitutional. This is consistent with the checks-and-balances approach we advocate. In Canada, a notwithstanding clause expires five years after its enactment.[27] We propose a similar period. Thus, under Article 111 of our current draft, an Act which has been passed to validate legislation struck down as unconstitutional by the courts may only prevail over the Constitution for a limited time. The validating Act will cease to have legal effect five years from the date on which it was enacted. If Parliament wishes to continue to enforce a law that the courts have determined contravenes the Constitution, it

---

27 See section 33 of the Canadian Charter of Rights and Freedoms 1982.

will have to pass another validating Act, or amend the Constitution. So, the 'override' provision we proposed in our first draft is now better described as a 'postponement' provision.

Second, should the notwithstanding mechanism apply to a Supreme Court decision that a Bill referred to it by the Head of State under draft Article 49 appears to be unconstitutional? In our view the answer is again yes. But because the Head of State will be prohibited from signing the original Bill, the validating legislation will need to operate in a slightly different way.

As a result of these considerations, the new provision dealing with Parliament's powers in relation to legislation declared constitutionally invalid by the Supreme Court now looks like this:

111 Act may prevail over Constitution for limited period
(1) Parliament may, following a determination under Article 109 that an Act of Parliament, in whole or in part, is inconsistent with this Constitution or a determination under Article 49(3) following a referral of a Bill by the Head of State that a Bill, in whole or in part, appears to be contrary to this Constitution, in an Act that is passed by a majority of 75 per cent of all Members of Parliament, expressly declare that one or more specified provisions which were the subject of the Supreme Court's determination prevail over one or more provisions of this Constitution.
(2) The power conferred on Parliament may be exercised on one or more occasions in respect of the same provisions.
(3) Every declaration, enacted in accordance with paragraph (1), has effect for a period that ends on the day that is five years after the declaration comes into force or such earlier date provided for in the declaration.
(4) No provision of an Act or declaration within an Act of Parliament may prevail over Article 109 or 110 [Entrenchment and Amendment] or 111.
(5) A Bill that contains a declaration described in paragraph (1) may be referred to the Supreme Court by the Head of State under Article 49.

11 Integrity and transparency

In this chapter we briefly discuss the constitutional methods proposed for promoting integrity and transparency within public institutions. In the draft text of the Constitution, Part 10 relates to a number of provisions that strengthen the integrity, accountability and transparency of public institutions. Part 10 also includes the Officers of Parliament: the Ombudsmen; the Parliamentary Commissioner for the Environment; the Auditor-General; and a new addition, members of the Human Rights Commission, who are made officers of Parliament and given added responsibilities to better protect human rights. Another title for this chapter, as it was in the 2016 book, could be 'Safeguards'. It needs to be remembered that many other structural elements in what we propose also provide other safeguards, such as the supremacy of the Constitution itself, the Bill of Rights, and the separation between the Government, the Parliament and the Judiciary.

What we said in 2016

In our first book,[1] we said that public power can be an incredibly coercive and destructive force if used arbitrarily or for improper purposes. In order to minimise the possibility of that occurring, New Zealand has adopted a system of checks and balances within our democratic system to maximise accountability and transparency so as to ensure that those wielding the power in our country cannot abuse it. The Constitution aims to strengthen that system.

We discussed a number of institutions that play a vital role in maintaining those checks and balances and which we believe worthy of constitutional protection. We noted the Constitution cannot contain everything that is desirable and we outlined key normative values to be protected by some of those institutions.

In order to protect the public and democracy from abuses of power by the State, we proposed to include in Constitution Aotearoa the existing institutions of the Ombudsmen, the Auditor-General, Parliamentary Commissioner for the Environment and the Police.

---

1 Geoffrey Palmer and Andrew Butler *A Constitution for Aotearoa New Zealand* (Victoria University Press, Wellington, 2016) at 175–191.

We also recommended:

- setting up a new independent Information Authority to restructure the administration of official information and improve transparency;
- including certain principles in the Constitution to reinvigorate the public service and protect its values;
- reinforcing the constitutional significance of the offices of the Attorney-General and Solicitor-General;
- a revised approach to, and more transparent oversight of, the intelligence agencies;
- constitutional protection for local government;
- establishing a new Constitutional Commission to review the Constitution every 10 years and report on possible amendments.

What we say now

One of these issues, local government, is now dealt with in a separate part of our proposed draft Constitution and is covered in detail in chapter 7. This has been done to recognise what is an underdeveloped segment of New Zealand's constitutional arrangements that needs to be underpinned with a set of principles.

As outlined in chapter 6, we have given specific constitutional protection to the public service to safeguard its independence. We have restructured the State Services Commission into the Government Services Commission, with three Commissioners. The guarantee of political neutrality of the public service is set out there also, as well as the duty to provide free and frank advice to ministers and to safeguard against the challenges of the future. It also obliges all institutions of the Government to maintain high standards of integrity and conduct. In chapter 18, we deal with the Constitutional Commission.

The law officers

The Attorney-General and the Solicitor-General are the Government's law officers. The Attorney is a minister and MP; the Solicitor a highly qualified lawyer who is a public servant. They are the legal advisers to the Government. They have the duty to oversee the Government's litigation, and the Solicitor-General in particular appears in the

Integrity and transparency

courts to argue cases for the Government. The Attorney is the channel of communication between the Judiciary and the Government. The Solicitor-General has obligations to supervise the conduct of prosecutions and criminal appeals. It seems to us important to charge them with the constitutional duty of upholding the integrity of the legal system, to prevent corruption and to protect the rule of law.

83 Attorney-General and Solicitor-General
  (1) The law officers of the State are the Attorney-General and Solicitor-General.
  (2) The law officers are responsible for—
      (a) ensuring the integrity of the legal system:
      (b) protecting the rule of law:
      (c) safeguarding the independence of the judiciary.
  (3) The Solicitor-General alone is responsible for the supervision and oversight of machinery for the criminal prosecutions.

The Police

The Police have coercive power over people that is denied other citizens. This includes arresting them for criminal offences and prosecuting them. It is, therefore, a matter of the most importance that they operate under the law fairly and reasonably, and are held to account when they do not.

The Bill of Rights has substantial application to the activities of the Police and is a restraint upon them. Constabulary independence is a means of ensuring that when prosecutions are being launched there is no capacity for political interference or favouritism. At common law, constables make such decisions independently. For example, ministers cannot give orders about who should be prosecuted and who should not. It is also important that citizens who believe the Police have acted wrongly should have the ability to complain to an independent agency and have the complaint investigated and reported upon. Our proposals concerning the integrity and transparency of the Police are as follows:

104 Police
  (1) An Act of Parliament must provide for the organisation and governance of the Police based on the following principles:
      (a) principled, effective, and efficient policing services are a cornerstone of a free and democratic society under the rule

of law:
   (b) effective policing relies on a wide measure of public support and confidence:
   (c) policing services are provided under a national framework but also have a local community focus:
   (d) policing services are provided in a manner that respects human rights:
   (e) policing services are provided independently and impartially:
   (f) in providing policing services every Police employee is required to act professionally, ethically, and with integrity:
   (g) constables in carrying out their duties and exercising their discretion act under the principle of constabulary independence.
(2) The Police are held to account among other ways by an independent authority established and provided for by an Act of Parliament.

Intelligence agencies

The New Zealand intelligence agencies have recently been the subject of a full review, and new legislation was passed on the basis of the report.[2] Both of the agencies are concerned to prevent acts of terrorism being carried out in New Zealand. They are designed to protect national security generally, New Zealand's international relations and economic wellbeing. They deal in signals intelligence and human intelligence. They have counter-espionage duties.

The Government Communications Security Bureau (GCSB) and the New Zealand Security Intelligence Service (NZSIS) carry out a range of functions. The GCSB guards the Government against cybersecurity threats. The NZSIS vets public servants for security clearances and liaises with overseas intelligence agencies concerning terrorists and persons arriving in New Zealand who may pose a threat. The objectives and functions of both agencies are the same but they use different capabilities to address these.

These agencies operate secretively for the most part. They conduct surveillance over communications and over people as well. They

---

2   Michael Cullen and Dame Patsy Reddy *Report of the First Independent Review of Intelligence and Security in New Zealand: Intelligence and Security in a Free Society* (February 2016); Intelligence and Security Act 2017.

cannot prosecute people; they are not law enforcement agencies. They are required to act within the law and human rights obligations. The agencies must be free from improper influence and be politically neutral. They must not limit freedom of expression in New Zealand. The Leader of the Opposition is regularly briefed on their activities.

The agencies provide intelligence to those who need to know it. That involves cooperation with the Police, the New Zealand Defence Force, the Ministry of Foreign Affairs and Trade, and Customs to facilitate their functions.

Some of the activities of these agencies are very sensitive and intrusive. They require strong supervision and accountability. While there is ministerial responsibility for the activities of the agencies, it is not sufficient, given their secrecy, for the public to be assured that they are behaving properly. The 2016 review found that more checks and balances were required.

The Intelligence and Security Act 2017 contains an elaborate set of oversight mechanisms and checks and balances. The legislation must be reviewed every seven years. Interception of communications is strictly controlled by the issuing of warrants authorised by judicial commissioners. The Act is much better than anything that went before; the agencies were once subject to no legal restraints at all. Both are now departments of state, a much more accountable form of government body. The agencies are now more open and less opaque. A Committee of MPs also examines their performance, although it sits in secret.

Section 3 of the 2017 Act sets out its purpose:

The purpose of this Act is to protect New Zealand as a free, open, and democratic society by—
  (a) establishing intelligence and security agencies that will effectively contribute to—
       (i) the protection of New Zealand's national security; and
       (ii) the international relations and well-being of New Zealand; and
       (iii) the economic well-being of New Zealand; and
  (b) giving the intelligence and security agencies adequate and appropriate functions, powers, and duties; and
  (c) ensuring that the functions of the intelligence and security agencies are performed—

(i) in accordance with New Zealand law and all human rights obligations recognised by New Zealand law; and
(ii) with integrity and professionalism; and
(iii) in a manner that facilitates effective democratic oversight; and
(d) ensuring that the powers of the intelligence and security agencies are subject to institutional oversight and appropriate safeguards.

In 2017, Rebecca Kitteridge, Director of Security of the NZSIS and a person who had previously conducted a review of the GCSB, made an insightful speech about the intelligence agencies. She explained how their approach had changed and in particular how the 'social contract' with the community had changed:[3]

> By 'social contract' I mean on the one hand the licence given by the public to intelligence agencies to operate, and on the other hand the level of information the public expects to know about intelligence activities in return. There are several reasons why the social contract has been shifting.
>
> First, the changes in the threatscape around the world—particularly in relation to terrorism—have meant that security agencies have needed greater powers to detect the activities of terrorists.
>
> Second, changes in technology have given security and intelligence agencies more opportunities and more challenges, with greater privacy implications for New Zealand citizens.
>
> Third, as transparency in government has increased, the public's expectations have changed. People expect to know what the agencies of the state are doing. The public pays for these agencies and there is an expectation that the public will have a say in our activities and how they are conducted.
>
> The outcome of the public debate that has occurred in New Zealand and in other liberal democracies is that there is a new point of balance between the public's right to know and the agencies' need to keep operational activity and capabilities secret. And that is very healthy.
>
> Being more open about what we do reduces the risk that staff will want to expose operational activity that they feel the public should know about. Ultimately it strengthens public trust.

It is clear to us that organisations of such reach and power as

---

3 Rebecca Kitteridge 'Letting in the Light—Increasing Transparency in the New Zealand Intelligence Community' (Transparency International NZ AGM, 30 October 2017) at 4.

the intelligence agencies must have constitutional oversight in any written constitution. The safeguards that presently exist must not be easily diluted and set aside. Ordinary legislation is not a sufficient protection. Here is what we propose:

90 Oversight over intelligence and security agencies
(1) Any intelligence and security agency of the Government must be established by Act of Parliament.
(2) In order to protect the liberty of the people, an Act of Parliament establishing a security and intelligence agency must—
  (a) keep the functions and powers of the agency within reasonable bounds:
  (b) subject the agency to effective oversight mechanisms:
  (c) provide for regular reviews of the agency's functions and powers.

Open government and information

One of the most critical elements in preventing corruption and engaging the citizens in the affairs of the Government lies in the Official Information Act. This Act is the engine of open government, which is such an important value. Public opinion is one of the checks against arbitrary power, but only if people know what is going on. As a famous American Judge Louis Brandeis once said:[4]

> Publicity is justly commended as a remedy for social and industrial diseases. Sunlight is said to be the best of disinfectants; electric light the most efficient policeman.

That is why we have an Official Information Act. We have had it since 1982.

Remember what the Danks Committee said in 1980 which led to the legislation:[5]

- a better informed public can better participate in the democratic process
- secrecy is an impediment to accountability when Parliament, press, and public cannot properly follow and scrutinise the actions of Government

---

4 Louis D Brandeis *Other People's Money and How the Bankers Use It* (Frederick A Stokes Co, New York, 1914) at 92.
5 Committee on Official Information *Towards Open Government, General Report* (Wellington, December 1980) at 14.

- public servants make many important decisions that affect people and the permanent administration should also be accountable through greater flows of information about what they are doing
- better information flows will produce more effective government and help towards the more flexible development of policy. With more information available, it is easier to prepare for change
- if more information is available, public cooperation with government will be enhanced.

Those principles remain sound, but they are being imperfectly executed now. Very few changes have been made to the 1982 Act. The Act is showing signs of its age and it is in serious need of refreshment. Despite two Law Commission reports that have recommended important improvements to it, nothing has happened. There has been clear political resistance to making changes and freeing up further the release of information. There is disquiet about the administration of the Act within the journalistic community.

The then Chief Ombudsman conducted an investigation, published in 2015. She made 48 recommendations for change as to how improvements could be made, but these were strictly connected to administrative and other practices within the bureaucracy. The report contained nothing about legislative improvements.[6] It was not well received by journalists, who generally maintained that it did not go far enough or address the right issues, and neither was it likely to be effective if implemented.

Our conclusion, reached after more than 35 years of the information law in action, is that the present policy settings are inadequate and do not sufficiently serve the interests of transparency in government.[7] Despite the fact that New Zealand has had the Official Information Act since 1982, it is still often difficult to get information about public affairs in a timely fashion.

With some ministers, the Act tends to lack support and acceptance.

6 Beverly A Wakem *Not a Game of Hide and Seek: Report on an investigation into the practices adopted by central government agencies for the purpose of compliance with the Official Information Act 1982* (December 2015).
7 A recent article by Bryce Edwards summarises the key concerns around the legislation and the attempts that have been made to address these issues: Bryce Edwards 'Political Roundup: Will new Government embrace transparency—or run from it?' *New Zealand Herald* (online ed, 27 November 2017), available at <www.nzherald.co.nz/nz/news/article.cfm?c_id=1&objectid=11948427>.

Some simply evade its requirements. Many public servants do not like the Act either, although the former State Services Commissioner Dr Mark Prebble said the Act 'is the best reform that's happened during my whole time in the public service; it has been good for every agency it's been applied in.'[8]

Successive governments have resisted efforts to improve the Act. Yet a strengthened Act would increase protection against corruption and questionable decision-making in both central and local government.

The Law Commission, in a 2012 report, completed a comprehensive and excellent review of the Official Information Act.[9] The Commission made 137 separate recommendations concerning reform of the Act. The Government published its response to the Law Commission's report soon after.[10] The response was seriously disappointing since the policy leaves the law in an unsatisfactory state.

The then Government did not agree with most of the major recommendations. It rejected any recommendations that would have resulted in significant change. Rejected recommendations included: proposals to extend coverage of the Official Information Act to the officers of Parliament, the Parliamentary Counsel Office, the Office of the Clerk, Parliamentary Services and the Speaker; the statutory creation of a new oversight office; and combining the Official Information Act and the Local Government Official Information and Meetings Act into one Act.

The response indicated that reforming the Act was just not a priority. We believe that redrafting the whole Act is essential if real progress is to be made in improving access to official information. Redrafting the Act is not a job for the Constitution. The work has been done and the Act needs to be reconstructed.

One recent court decision, overruling the interpretation applied to the Act by a minister, a government department and the Ombudsmen, illustrates how poor the approach to the Official Information Act has become.[11] Professor Jane Kelsey was a critic of the Trans-Pacific

---

8 Television interview with Dr Mark Prebble (The Nation, TV3, 3 April 2010).
9 Law Commission *The Public's Right to Know: Review of the Official Information Legislation* (NZLC R125, 2012).
10 Government Response to Law Commission Report *The Public's Right to Know: Review of the Official Information Legislation* presented to the House of Representatives 4 February 2013.
11 *Kelsey v Minister of Trade* [2015] NZHC 2497, [2016] 2 NZLR 218.

Partnership Agreement, which had been years in the negotiation and created considerable political controversy. Her argument was that the agreement would impact on New Zealand's sovereignty and that the economic benefits had been overstated. She made an Official Information request for eight categories of documents.

Her requests were refused on the grounds that making the information available would be likely to prejudice the international relations of the Government and damage the economy of New Zealand, and it was necessary to withhold the information on the grounds that it would likely prejudice the Government's ability to negotiate. Furthermore, it would be a burdensome task to go through all the documents, requiring substantial collation and research. On complaint to the then Chief Ombudsman, all the elements of the Minister's refusal were upheld.

When the matter came before the High Court by way of judicial review it was argued that the most basic tasks called for by the Act had not been carried out—the Minister and the officials had not assessed each piece of information requested against the criteria laid down in the Act. There had been instead a blanket refusal. This, it was argued, was a misapplication of the Act because there may have been information in the request that could not properly have been withheld. And the Minister never identified the particular prejudice that would occur.

Justice Collins held that none of the steps required by the Act were undertaken by the Minister. He was required to assess each piece of information requested against the criteria in the Act before the request could be refused. The fact that effort was involved was not an excuse. Good reason needed to exist to withhold information and if there was no good reason, the information should be released. Conclusive reasons to withhold were only engaged if there was a significant possibility of actual harm in New Zealand international relations. Further, the refusal did not provide sufficient explanation as to why the request was refused. The judge quashed the minister's decision and directed him to reconsider it.

Not only had the Minister of Trade and the Ministry of Foreign Affairs failed to properly apply the Act, so had the Chief Ombudsman, by whom a complaint about the Minister's refusal was rejected. As Justice Collins said in his judgment, 'the Act plays a significant role in New Zealand constitutional and democratic arrangements. It is essential the Act's meaning and purpose is fully honoured by those required to consider the release of official information.'[12]

The minister, the government department and the then Chief Ombudsman appeared not to understand the legislation they were applying, despite the fact it had been the law since 1982. How can such a situation arise? Clearly all is not well with the approach to the Act within the Government, and this calls for remedial action. The values of openness and transparency are at stake. The Act needs teeth. That is why we want to see the creation of an Information Authority with power to release information where the openness provisions of the Act have been satisfied.

The Act should be conscientiously enforced. The Ombudsmen have the function of recommending disclosure after complaints. The performance of the office has been spotty and somewhat soft in this regard, although it has improved recently, as evidenced by an address of the Chief Ombudsman Judge Peter Boshier.[13] There needs to be a greater commitment to openness and the Act needs to have teeth that it presently lacks. We think that a powerful commitment to greater openness of government information in a written, codified and judicially enforceable constitution would be a safeguard worth having. It would be a strong nudge to the Government not to game the Act but to improve it.

Transparency International is a respected international watchdog against corruption, both in government and private sector. Transparency International New Zealand made a submission to us urging constitutional protection for freedom of information. They made a technical point about our draft which we have adopted. They supported the establishment of an information authority, but did not support that body taking over the complaints function. They want two separate bodies.

We prefer an Information Authority that has two functions, each of which reinforces the other. The Authority will make decisions

---

12 At [156].
13 Judge Peter Boshier, Chief Ombudsman 'Inside the Ombudsman's Office' (Address to the Institute for Public Administration New Zealand, 4 May 2017), available at <www.ombudsman.parliament.nz/ckeditor_assets/attachments/480/inside_the_office_of_the_ombudsman.pdf?1494215216>.

on release where information has been withheld and a complaint is made. Ombudsmen making decisions is not compatible with the classic functions of that office, in our opinion. On the other side of its work, the Information Authority will provide education and training for agencies and the public. At present the Act does not reach Parliament or the Parliamentary Counsel Office; we do not believe those exemptions are justified. So we have changed that.

89 Official information
(1) An Act of Parliament must give the public as much access as practicable to information held by the Government, public service, institutions of the State, local governments, and by institutions and organisations that are accountable to Parliament, the Government, or to local governments, in order to—
   (a) enable members of the public to participate more effectively in the making and administration of laws and policies:
   (b) promote the accountability of Ministers and elected and unelected officials:
   (c) enhance respect for the law and to promote good governance.
(2) In accordance with these principles, the Act must—
   (a) provide for the availability of official information, and enable individuals and bodies corporate to access information concerning themselves:
   (b) provide for the establishment of an independent Information Authority:
   (c) empower the Information Authority to review decisions to deny information and to release information if it considers that to be right course of action under the Act, with Ministers having no power of veto:
   (d) require the Authority to provide appropriate education, guidance and advice to agencies and the public on the application of the Act.
(3) The Act must also provide for access to information concerning Parliament, including the office of the Speaker, the office of the Clerk, Parliamentary Services, Parliamentary Counsel Office and all officers of Parliament.

Officers of Parliament

The Officers of Parliament are important to maintaining integrity in a number of discrete fields. Their functions are well known except for one new one, so we will not go through them in detail except to say they deserve constitutional recognition.

Elevating the Human Rights Commissioners to the status of Officers of Parliament is designed to increase the attention Parliament gives human rights and to ensure that the legislation it passes respects human rights. The Commissioners' role as parliamentary officers will also enhance parliamentary consideration of social and economic rights. While, as explained in chapter 12, we do not agree that all social and economic rights should be judicially enforceable, we do believe they deserve more attention and that Parliament should be provided with more material on them.

84 Officers of Parliament
(1) Officers of Parliament are appointed by the Head of State on the recommendation of Parliament and are responsible to Parliament.
(2) An Officer of Parliament may report the Officer's findings and recommendations to Parliament.
(3) The following officers continued or established by this Constitution are Officers of Parliament:
   (a) the Controller and Auditor-General, provided for in Article 85:
   (b) the Ombudsmen, provided for in Article 86:
   (c) the Commissioner for the Environment, provided for in Article 87:
   (d) the Commissioners for Human Rights, who are each members of the Commission provided for in Article 88.
(4) An Act of Parliament may establish further Officers of Parliament.

85 The Controller and Auditor-General
(1) An Officer, who may be known as the Controller and Auditor-General, must audit the public accounts of the State and of local governments and report to Parliament to ensure that—
   (a) public monies are properly spent and accounted for:
   (b) taxpayers receive value for money:
   (c) public money is lawfully expended.

(2) An Act of Parliament must provide for the office in accordance with these principles.

86 The Ombudsmen

(1) In order to protect the public from unfair decisions and enhance the quality of administrative decision-making, an Act of Parliament must continue to empower Ombudsmen to investigate administrative actions that affect persons in their personal capacity and are taken by departments of the public service, local governments, and other organisations named by or under the Act.

(2) Parliament must appoint a Chief Ombudsman.

87 The Commissioner for the Environment

In order to enhance the protection of the environment, an Act of Parliament must continue to empower the Commissioner for the Environment to monitor—

(a) the adequacy of the systems established by the Government for managing the environment:

(b) the performance of public authorities in maintaining and promoting the quality of the environment.

88 Commission for Human Rights

(1) In order to enhance the protection of human rights, an Act of Parliament must provide for a Commission for Human Rights to monitor and report on human rights issues and interact with the Government and Parliament. The Act of Parliament may confer other functions and powers on the Commission.

(2) Parliament must appoint a Chief Commissioner for Human Rights. The Chief Commissioner for Human Rights chairs the Commission for Human Rights.

(3) In order to assist the Government and Parliament bring about the rights set out in Article 29, the Commission for Human Rights may assess—

    (a) the social, economic, and health of sections of society and consider whether policy responses are required to progress the realisation of those rights:

    (b) whether proposed policies or Bills are likely to contribute towards, or detract from, realising those rights:

    (c) the impact of existing policies or legislation on the realisation of those rights.

12 Bill of Rights

Under New Zealand's current constitution, the legal protection of human rights is weaker than in many other countries with which we typically compare ourselves. There are two aspects to the issue. First, in New Zealand our human rights are able to be overridden by a bare majority of Parliament. The New Zealand Bill of Rights Act 1990 and the Human Rights Act 1993 are both mere Acts of Parliament. As with almost all other Acts of Parliament[1] they can be amended, repealed or overridden by another Act of Parliament passed by a bare majority. And the courts can do nothing to stop that occurring.

Second, the Bill of Rights and the Human Rights Act are dated. They protect only a relatively narrow set of human rights. So, for example, even though the Bill of Rights says that one of its purposes is to 'affirm New Zealand's commitment to the *International Covenant on Civil and Political Rights* (1966) (ICCPR)', it leaves out significant rights that are found in the ICCPR. The Bill of Rights makes no effort to protect social and economic rights that are guaranteed by the *International Covenant on Economic, Social and Cultural Rights* (1966).

We have had the Bill of Rights for 28 years and have grown accustomed to it. The time has come to take the next step and sharpen its bite.

Should human rights have greater protection?

The submissions we received from members of the public and the feedback at our public engagements were illuminating. It was clear to us that many people had wrongly assumed that human rights could not be easily overridden by the New Zealand Parliament.[2] Many

1   The exception to this statement is that s 268 of the Electoral Act 1993 protects a limited number of features of the current electoral regime from amendment or repeal by a simple majority of Parliament. We discussed this entrenchment in considerable detail in our 2016 book: Geoffrey Palmer and Andrew Butler *A Constitution for Aotearoa New Zealand* (Victoria University Press, Wellington, 2016), at 232–234 in particular.
2   This mirrored the observations of the Constitutional Advisory Panel's 2013 Report which noted (at 54): 'Parliament's ability to amend the [New Zealand Bill of Rights] Act or to pass legislation contrary to the Act with the support of a simple majority of Parliament was of particular concern.'

were genuinely shocked to be told that they could, and that in fact it happens on a regular basis. At our public meetings, attendees were particularly agitated by the treatment of the families of adult disabled persons following the *Atkinson* decision of the Court of Appeal in 2013—see the end of this chapter for a summary of the saga.

Since 1990, the New Zealand Parliament has passed legislation contrary to the Bill of Rights on at least 37 occasions.[3] Some of those occasions have involved serious incursions into human rights. The most egregious instance was Parliament's response to the *Atkinson* case in 2013, passing legislation under urgency which in effect overrode the rights of some of the most vulnerable New Zealanders.[4] It was made an issue of confidence, forcing support parties to vote for it or face the prospect of an early election. Here is what we said in our previous book:

> ... in 2013 Parliament enacted the New Zealand Public Health and Disability Amendment Act in a single sitting day. Its principal effects were first to prevent anyone ever making a complaint to the Human Rights Commission or bringing a court proceeding against any Government family carer policy no matter how discriminatory, and second, to exclude retrospectively the provision of remedies for past discrimination. It followed a decision of the Court of Appeal that had upheld the human rights of some of the most vulnerable people in our community—the disabled and family members who cared for them. There was no warning that the Bill was to be introduced; there was no public consultation on it; there was no Select Committee consideration of it. By any measure, it was a shocking piece of legislation that ousted well-known constitutional protections and removed New Zealand citizens' rights to be free from discrimination in certain cases. Yet it passed in a single sitting day despite almost immediate public outcry. Only another Act of Parliament can alter or remove it. That is how fragile our constitutional system currently is.

We think the Bill of Rights should not be capable of being overridden so easily. At the same time, however, the submissions and feedback also exhibited concern not to let lawyers (i.e., judges) have the final word on such matters. There was concern that judges are

---

3 Geoffrey Palmer 'What the New Zealand Bill of Rights aimed to do, why it did not succeed and how it can be repaired' (2016) 14 NZJPIL 69 at 201–208.
4 *Atkinson v Attorney-General* [2012] 3 NZLR 260 (CA).

sometimes out of touch, and lack the public accountability delivered by an election. The clear message was that stronger legal protection of human rights is important, but there must be limits.

All of this was consistent with the observations made by the Constitutional Advisory Panel in its 2013 report:

> Granting courts the power to strike down legislation has support but is explicitly rejected by a significant grouping. Support can be seen for exploring increased judicial powers that preserve parliamentary sovereignty, new means of public participation and improving parliamentary scrutiny to ensure legislation is consistent with the Act.[5]

In the submission form that we provided to submitters online and in hardcopy format, we asked whether concerns over the power of judges to invalidate Acts of Parliament would be eased by a mechanism that would allow a substantial majority of MPs—75 per cent is the figure we proposed—to override a particular court ruling.[6] Many said this would go some way to meeting their concerns, although a good number did not believe that there should be any override power. As explained in chapter 10, on the Judiciary, the power now is to postpone the prospective effect of a decision for a limited period in the event that this action can command a 75 per cent majority in the Parliament. This will allow for engagement in a later process to amend the Constitution, if that is thought necessary by the Parliament.

In addition, we asked whether people's fears would be eased by providing that—as well as the ability of 75 per cent of MPs to override a specific Supreme Court decision striking down legislation—the same special majority of MPs or the public by a simple majority at a binding referendum could amend the Constitution. Again, many saw this as a powerful limit on judges taking on too much power for themselves. These checks on the Judiciary would mean that, unlike in the United States and, to some degree, Australia, New Zealand's judges would not have the last word on the big issues. To reinforce this point, it is worth noting that in Ireland, which has had an entrenched constitution for 80 years, and where the constitution can be amended

---

5 Constitutional Advisory Panel *New Zealand's Constitution: A Report on a Conversation, He Kōtuinga Kōrero mō Te Kaupapa Ture o Aotearoa* (November 2013), at 56.
6 Constitution Aotearoa 2016, art 68(4), (5).

only by way of binding public referendum, the constitution has been amended 27 times.

The impression we had from our interactions with people at our public meetings, and through the submissions we received from the public, is that a middle-ground of the type we proposed could command considerable support. Introducing judicial review of legislation—particularly insofar as human rights are concerned—would represent a significant step forward in protecting minority rights. But ensuring that the last word would not stay with the judges means that the checkers could be checked. For example, in its submission to us, the National Council of Women of New Zealand stated:

> A significant number of NCWNZ members supported the proposal that the Judiciary (in the form of the Supreme Court) should be able to override Acts of Parliament that are inconsistent with the New Zealand Constitution, regardless of whether it is a single written document or the current set of constitutional documents. They considered that it was acceptable for a 75% majority in Parliament to override a Supreme Court decision as it was important to sustain a balance between judicial and parliamentary power and specific contextual factors were important in considering these matters.

We would urge any serious future proposals for the adoption of a power to strike down Acts of Parliament to cleave to a middle-course of the type we have proposed.

Human Rights Commission

Some suggestions were made to us that the importance of human rights needed to be underscored in a new constitutional arrangement. While the creation of a new power for judges to invalidate legislation was an important step forward, it was also felt that non-judicial mechanisms should be enhanced.

In our revised text we propose that there should be an enhanced Human Rights Commission, giving the Commission constitutional status. Members would be Officers of Parliament appointed by the Head of State on the recommendation of Parliament. As Officers of Parliament, members would be responsible to Parliament and would be able to report to Parliament on their findings. Parliament would appoint a Chief Human Rights Commissioner to chair

Bill of Rights

the Commission. The role of members of the Commission would be similar to that of the Parliamentary Commissioner for the Environment (PCE), established by the Environment Act 1986 and continued as a constitutional officer by Constitution Aotearoa.

Just as the PCE is Parliament's 'person' on environmental issues—assessing and critiquing the Government's performance from an independent perspective—so too the Human Rights Commission should act as an independent and respected source of information and oversight on the Government's performance in respect of human rights. In effect, the current Human Rights Commission would be repurposed and granted explicit constitutional status, thereby enhancing its status and function. And because the Commissioners would be selected by Parliament, there would be increased 'buy-in' to the Commission's work and outputs.

The draft also makes it clear that the Human Rights Commission has power to take or to intervene in litigation concerning civil and political rights (see Article 32). The intervention power is also one we would give to the Commissioner for the Environment, as we make clear later in this chapter (see Article 26(3)).

Should more rights be protected?

Turning from the high-level proposal to entrench human rights so as to prevent them being too easily overridden by a simple majority of MPs, we asked for people's views on what rights should be protected in the new Constitution's Bill of Rights.

To many contemporary young people traditional human rights seem old school. Their concerns revolve around such issues as climate change refugees, protection against the activities of corporate entities, and group or collective rights. There is a new age dawning in this area and human rights law needs to keep up to date.

As noted in the introduction to this chapter, when the New Zealand Bill of Rights Act was adopted in 1990, its proposers were reasonably conservative in what human rights they chose to safeguard: no protection for privacy, for property, for economic or social rights like the right to education, health, social security, professional or workers' rights. And the environmental rights revolution which took off around the rest of the world in the 1990s and 2000s was here in its infancy and not considered for inclusion in the 1990 New Zealand

Bill of Rights Act.

Twenty-eight years later, we feel that the scope of the Bill of Rights needs to be addressed. How could a modern constitution purport to protect human rights and ignore such core modern day rights as privacy and a healthy, sustainable environment? Our own sense that these rights should be included in a revamped Bill of Rights was strengthened by the report of the 2013 Constitutional Advisory Panel, which noted support for a revisit of the scope of the Bill of Rights; that sense was certainly further enhanced by the number of non-governmental organisation submissions to the Constitutional Review Panel that called for the scope of the Bill of Rights to be expanded to include these rights.

Feedback at our public meetings and through the submissions process indicated a strong support for the inclusion of additional rights within the Bill of Rights. In particular, there was strong support for the inclusion of the right to privacy and right to a healthy environment. There was also good support for recognising the right to property in the Bill of Rights. Again this was little surprise—the 2013 Constitutional Review Panel had noted considerable interest in protecting property rights, so long as the drafting was careful.[7]

Public input, submissions and other representations we received persuaded us to make some other relatively minor changes to the proposed Constitution's civil and political rights. We have removed gendered language from the draft Constitution and added freedom from discrimination on the grounds of gender identity and expression.[8] In the provision on religious belief in Article 10 we have made it plain that New Zealand is a secular society.

---

7 Constitutional Advisory Panel, above n 5, at 51.
8 See also the blog on our website from guest commentator Frankie Wood-Bodley, which sets out in detail the rationale behind this inclusion: Frankie Wood-Bodley 'Marginal improvement: the trans* community and discrimination' (6 June 2017) Constitution Aotearoa NZ, available at <http://constitutionaotearoa.org.nz/the-conversation/gender-identity-and-expression/>. Note that *trans** is an umbrella term encompassing people whose gender identity differs to the gender role expected by society due to the sex they were assigned at birth and which commonly includes those who identify as transgender, transsexual, intersex, androgynous, non-binary, genderqueer, takatāpui, fa'afafine, fakaleiti, whakawhine and tangata ira tane.

Socio-economic rights

The most challenging proposal with respect to the Bill of Rights concerned socio-economic rights. Socio-economic rights are those rights that are conferred on people in order to guarantee them a minimum level of material support to sustain themselves within our society—they concern freedom from want, whether that be want of shelter, want of economic sustenance, want of education, want of a safe working environment and so on. At present socio-economic rights receive no protection in the New Zealand Bill of Rights Act 1990. Some of them are, however, given protection in other Acts of Parliament. For example, the Education Act 1989 explicitly gives everyone the right to a free state education up to 19 years of age.[9] The Social Security Act 1964 gives certain rights to particular social benefits.

In our 2016 book we proposed to take steps to recognise some socio-economic rights. First, we proposed that the right to a free state education should be put on a par with other rights guaranteed by the Bill of Rights. Since it is already a free-standing right in the Education Act 1989 (section 3), which has caused no difficulties of application, we could see no harm in it being given constitutional protection. Nothing in the public meetings or submissions moved us from this view. We note, for completeness, that like all rights in the Bill of Rights, the right to a free state education would be subject to reasonable limitation (see Article 33). So, for example, if school zoning continues to be required for some state schools, that system would with little doubt be found compatible, in principle, with the right to education.

Second, we proposed to recognise a significant number of other socio-economic rights in a dedicated Article on socio-economic rights.[10] Those rights included the core rights from the International Covenant on Economic, Social and Cultural Rights (ICESCR), such as the right to an adequate standard of living, housing, food, social security and health (Article 106(a)). They also included some of the human rights longest recognised by international human rights law, being a range of workers' rights first recognised by the

---

9 Education Act 1989, s 3.
10 Constitution Aotearoa 2016, art 106.

Treaty of Versailles (1919), the International Labour Organisation's conventions, and the ICESCR itself. Among them are: the right of workers to undertake collective action, such as collective bargaining for pay and conditions; the right to satisfactory health and safety at work; and the right to earn one's living in an occupation freely entered into (Article 106(d), (e), (f)).

In our 2016 book we proposed that none of these rights should be enforceable as a constitutional right before the courts. Rather, we proposed that these rights should guide the activities of the Government and Parliament. That would leave Parliament to give such rights the force of law as it saw fit—for example, the Employment Relations Act 2000 currently protects the rights to collective bargaining, and to strike, and for employers to lock-out.[11]

Our proposal to create non-justiciable socio-economic constitutional rights was not entirely novel. A number of constitutions deal with similar rights in that way—examples are the constitutions of India, Ireland and Spain. The reasons that inspired those constitutional drafters had some appeal to us. In particular, many socio-economic rights depend for their efficacy on cash. The raising and spending of cash is typically seen as the core concern of politics: politicians should put forward their proposals for how much tax should be imposed, what types of tax should be raised and what the spending priorities should be. Judges do not have legitimacy that comes from election, nor the policy analysis skills to assess what is the right amount of tax to raise. Nor do they have the public service support to determine what policy steps would produce favourable outcomes in such complex areas as employment policy, housing provision and social security.

We were particularly interested in feedback on our proposals for non-justiciable socio-economic rights. We anticipated that a number of progressive elements would criticise us for being too timid, for failing to properly understand how socio-economic rights work and for shutting out those already disenfranchised from a constitutional settlement. In addition, we were conscious of New Zealand's important historical contribution to the international recognition of socio-economic rights through the drafting of the *Universal*

---

11 Employment Relations Act 2000, pts 5 and 8.

Declaration on Human Rights (1948).[12]

We were not wrong. We received a detailed and powerful submission from Josh Opie and Jeff Sissons to the effect that, while they support the project in general, they are strongly of the view that economic and social rights should be justiciable before the courts. In its submission to us, the Human Rights Foundation argued that there would be a number of advantages to allowing all socio-economic rights to be judicially enforceable, including raising public awareness of such rights and enabling New Zealand to enjoy adequate housing, healthcare and income in a 'real' enforceable way, not dependent on whatever legislation is in place from time to time. In their submission to us, a group of University of Canterbury Law School academics and students argued—as did many other submitters—that the international jurisprudence on socio-economic rights has significantly advanced over the last thirty years; there is nothing to fear from justiciability because 'the task of the courts . . . is not to remake a social policy decision of the political branches, but to ensure that in making its decision the government properly took into account any limits on rights, and considered how to mitigate them'. These submitters, and others, have provided a strong analytical case, but we did not feel able to accept such a view at present. We have, however, provided buttressed institutional support for socio-economic rights through our proposal for an enhanced Human Rights Commission (see Article 88(3) in particular).

We have taken on board the feedback we received. As a result, the revised version of Constitution Aotearoa has some different features as it relates to socio-economic rights.

We have proposed to create a new Article that would protect workers' rights and allow them to seek the protection of the courts where legislation unjustifiably limited them. A number of reasons support this. First, these rights have a substantial legal heritage in New Zealand. Second, these particular rights have a hard-edged, individual focus to them, similar to classic civil and political rights; they are of a kind that courts feel comfortable policing. Third, workers'

---

12 C Aikman 'New Zealand and the origins of the Universal Declaration' (1999) 29 VUWLR 1.

rights are judicially enforceable under many overseas constitutions.[13] They do not cause particular concern there and it is hard to believe they would do so in New Zealand.

Not without doubt, we have continued the judicial unenforceability of the other rights (i.e., adequate housing, food, social security and health), leaving it to Parliament and Government to decide how to give effect to those rights. In essence, we remain concerned about whether our courts should be the forum in which such issues are determined.

However, recognising the weight of the arguments in favour of better protection of socio-economic rights, we have proposed a number of features that we believe will make a difference and keep pressure on the political branches to respect core socio-economic rights.

First, we propose that the revamped Human Rights Commission, staffed by Human Rights Commissioners who are Officers of Parliament and headed by the Chief Commissioner for Human Rights, would act as an independent and respected source of information and oversight on Parliament and the Government's performance in respect of socio-economic rights. The Commissioners would have powers to audit Government performance, report to Parliament and raise public concern. The advantage of the Commission over the courts is that it would have the resources, the expertise, the powers and the broad overview necessary to issue authoritative assessments that would create real accountability.

Second, in our revised draft we make explicit that which was implicit in our 2016 book—the Attorney-General's duty to report on Bills that appear to be inconsistent with the Bill of Rights would apply to the socio-economic rights. In doing so, the Attorney-General would be expected to apply international human rights law in assessing consistency of legislation with socio-economic rights. This, in turn, will act as a handbrake on the introduction of Bills that unjustifiably interfere with recognised socio-economic rights.

Third, we propose that the Constitutional Commission—whose function is to undertake a ten-yearly review of Constitution Aotearoa—is explicitly asked to consider the position of the non-justiciable socio-economic rights within the Bill of Rights (Article

---

13 See, for example, Constitution of the Republic of South Africa 1996, ss 22, 23; Constitution of Spain, s 28.

112(3)). Time and experience with mechanisms such as the enhanced Human Rights Commission, the Attorney-General's Bill reporting function, and the Supreme Court's rulings on other rights controversies, as well as developments at the international level, may overcome any residual concern at the constitutionalisation of certain socio-economic rights in New Zealand.

In that regard, we note that when the Australian Capital Territory enacted its comprehensive Human Rights Act in 2004, it declined to immediately recognise socio-economic rights, preferring to leave it to a five-yearly review process to consider whether they should be included. Ultimately, after an extensive research project and community consultation exercise (2009—2011), the ACT Human Rights Act was amended to include a right to education, but no additional socio-economic rights.[14]

Environmental rights

In our first book we included an environmental right. We did this because over the past 20 years there has been a rapid increase in the number of countries protecting the environment by constitutional means.[15] There is a strong connection between human rights and the problems created for humans and other animals by environmental degradation. The model that most influenced our draft was that contained in the South African constitution.

Perhaps one of the most important features of an environmental right lies in its protection of the interests of future generations. New Zealand's three-year electoral cycle is notoriously neglectful of long-range policy issues that can adversely affect people. Climate change policy is the most obvious of these examples, but other environmental issues are not immune from the tendency either. The decline in water quality of New Zealand's lakes and rivers has been hastened by rapid intensification of agriculture, especially dairying, which has caused nitrogen to pollute many rivers.

Almost all the submitters who commented on the environmental

---

14 For a useful summary of this episode, see ANU School of Regulation and Global Governance (RegNet) 'ACT economic, social and cultural rights project' (10 August 2017).
15 David R Boyd *The Environmental Revolution: A Global Study of Constitutions, Human rights and the Environmental* (UBC Press, Vancouver, 2012).

right were in favour of it. There was very little criticism of it, although a number thought it was too weak. One of our submitters, Jolyon Swinburn, said in his personal capacity that there were five benefits of including environmental provisions in a constitution, which we here paraphrase as:

- they can lead to the enactment of stronger environmental laws;
- provide a safety net for gaps in statutory environmental laws;
- raise the profile and importance of environmental protection as compared to competing interests such as economic development;
- create opportunities for better access to justice and accountability;
- and eventually, hopefully, lead to better environmental performance.

This is an accurate account of our aspirations for the environmental right.

We have engaged in consultations with several environmental groups including ECO, the New Zealand Fish and Game Council and the Environmental Defence Society. We have modified our draft as a result of these interactions to give more emphasis to ecological issues and not confine its application to issues concerned only with people. The draft was too anthropocentric and it needed to lean more in the direction of granting the environment rights, as was done in recent legislation concerning the Whanganui River. There is now more emphasis on conservation and biodiversity values; New Zealand's rate of species extinction is very high by international standards. The revised version includes also Māori values. It veers in the direction of giving the environment greater protection and leaves less space for economic development values to trump environmental values.

Two of the submissions we received were particularly helpful. These were from the Environmental Defence Society (EDS), and policy analyst and environmental advocate Claire Browning.[16] Both broadly supported our proposal to recognise an environmental right. The EDS proposed an additional provision to cover 'Rights of Nature'

---

16 Browning's submission was based on her work funded by the Law Foundation *Finding Ecological Justice in New Zealand* (November 2017), available at <www.lawfoundation.org.nz/?p=8419>. The report looked at justice claims for the non-human world, justice between peoples and justice for future generations, concluding that there is a need for progress on all three.

Bill of Rights

which would 'highlight the reciprocal relationship between nature and humans' and more closely align our proposal with Te Ao Māori (the Māori worldview) by reflecting the concept of kaitiakitanga. Claire Browning, on the other hand, advocated against the idea of a nature right, saying, 'while I support the objective for which it might be proposed, I think that, in Aotearoa, we will in time find a better and more effective way to develop this line of thought.' However, Browning did strongly support the use of kaitiakitanga as a guiding principle in relation to environmental law, noting that it is a core value that underpins the recognition and participation of mana whenua in regard to the environment.

We have taken these submissions onboard and have made a number of changes to our initial proposal. As well as removing the wording allowing ecological sustainability to be balanced against economic and social development, we have included a requirement that any measures undertaken for environmental protection must include the concept of kaitiakitanga.

Further, while we have not opted for a distinct nature right, one new feature of the proposal is to empower the Parliamentary Commissioner for the Environment to conduct litigation to safeguard the environmental rights, although it can be expected that this officer would intervene only in the most serious cases. Here is the right as redrafted:

26 Environmental right
  (1) Everyone has the right—
      (a) to an environment that is not harmful to their health or well-being; and
      (b) to have the environment protected, for the benefit of present and future generations, through reasonable legislative and other measures that—
          (i) prevent pollution and ecological degradation:
          (ii) promote conservation and biodiversity:
          (iii) secure ecologically sustainable development and the use of natural resources in a manner that is managed to maintain the equilibrium of the environment:
          (iv) include kaitiakitanga, which is the exercise of guardianship by the tangata whenua of an area in accordance with tikanga Māori in

relation to natural and physical resources.

(2) The Commissioner for the Environment may, if the Commissioner considers it appropriate to do so,—

    (a) conduct litigation to safeguard the rights contained in this Article:

    (b) intervene in litigation in which issues relating to those rights are raised.

Property rights

For the most part our proposed property right attracted little comment, but we did receive a number of useful submissions. One of these was a lengthy piece of legal research on the undesirability of the proposal:[17]

> The right to property proposed by Sir Geoffrey and Dr Butler contains legal uncertainties and ignores political disagreement about the place of property in constitutional reform. Past lawmakers have been mindful there is no consensus in relation to such a right due to the enigma of property as a legal category and its wide-ranging consequences. Moreover, the intuitive conception adopted by Sir Geoffrey and Dr Butler—protection of individual control over valued resources—obscures the nature of property as the product of coercive social relations underwritten by state power. The evolving values and forms of property law complement New Zealand's constitutional arrangements, which provide presumptive protection while recognising the importance of democratic decision-making in the light of the range of stakeholders affected by the creation and regulation of property. But an entrenched right tends to privilege the intuitive and dominant form of property: the commodity.

Claire Browning's submission, on the other hand, supported the inclusion of some security for rights of property, though she expressed a concern that, if not carefully considered, the protection of property rights may led to the establishment of a regulatory takings jurisprudence that would stifle regulation for the public good. On its face value, however, Browning expressed the opinion that 'the current draft is a good statement of the intended position'.

As we have written before on our website, the experience of

---

17 Oliver Hailes 'The Politics of Property in Constitutional Reform: A Critical Response to Sir Geoffrey and Dr Butler' (2017) 15(2) NZJPL 229 at 260–261.

Canterbury homeowners following the devastating earthquakes that affected the region highlights the need for better protection for property rights.[18] The Human Rights Commission Report *Staying in the red zones—Monitoring human rights in the Canterbury earthquake recovery* noted that: 'The right to property is integral to individual autonomy and a free society, and protects individuals from arbitrary or excessive power by the State.'[19] Property rights are linked to housing and also to the right to health and access to information and participation in decision-making. The narrative provided by the Human Rights Commission in its report demonstrates clearly how the Government, by misusing its power, visited hardship and loss of dignity upon these Red Zoners by abandoning them in their hour of need.

We have chosen to retain the provision setting out our proposed property right as it was first proposed. We think that it is drafted in such a way as to avoid the potential problems identified by Browning, and we have heard from a number of submitters and other interested parties that it has substantial support in the business community.

Privacy rights

When the New Zealand Bill of Rights Act 1990 was passed, the drafters excluded the right to privacy, preferring instead only to recognise a subset of that right—the right not to be subjected to unreasonable search or seizure. The view at the time was that a general right to privacy should not be included—notwithstanding that some constitutions did then recognise one—because the right was in the course of development and its boundaries would be uncertain and contentious.

In our 2016 draft, we stated our view that in the intervening years the landscape had changed: there is now a substantial body of case law available here and overseas on privacy and, with the massive digital transformation of our lives, any Bill of Rights that did not

---

18 Geoffrey Palmer 'The proposed constitution, property, and Christchurch' (8 November 2016) Constitution Aotearoa NZ, available at <http://constitutionaotearoa.org.nz/the-conversation/property-christchurch/>.

19 Human Rights Commission *Staying in the red zones—Monitoring human rights in the Canterbury earthquake recovery* (3 November 2016), available at <www.hrc.co.nz/red-zones-report/>.

recognise the right to privacy would be seriously deficient.

Feedback at our public meetings endorsed this view. This wasn't surprising to us, bearing in mind the consistent concern about privacy expressed in public surveys.[20] Our proposal to include a right to privacy in Constitution Aotearoa received strong endorsement from the Privacy Commissioner, John Edwards. In a fulsome submission to us, the Commissioner argued that:

> Constitutional protection of the right to privacy would create a strong legal foundation to navigate accountability in an increasingly complex environment, as the digital transformation of people's lives, business, government and the economy continues and produces vast swathes of personal data and information.

Constitutional protection would 'add to public trust in a data-rich world where public concern about behaviour of government ... has remained high. Constitutional protection may also drive better policy.' And, in addition, he pointed out that constitutional protection of privacy 'would strengthen New Zealand's privacy laws and could therefore have consequential benefits for New Zealand's international standing and international trade'.

More broadly, and in a passage that resonates with an underlying theme of this book, the Commissioner underscored the strong connection between privacy and democracy:

> Privacy is important for a person to be themselves, to think freely, to nurture intimacy, relationships and social interaction, and hereby flourish. In this sense, privacy contributes to the development of personality and citizenship. Privacy helps to preserve the necessary space for individuals to participate in a functioning and healthy democracy. The right to privacy protects aspects of freedom of speech and association that are essential to the functioning of a democratic society and creates the necessary conditions for a healthy public sphere.

We agree. We have left the terms of the proposed privacy right as they were in our 2016 draft.

Children's rights

---

20 See, for example, the survey results available at <https://privacy.org.nz/news-and-publications/surveys/>.

In our 2016 book, we had given some recognition to the rights of children. For example, our Preamble stated that among the values of New Zealand society was 'a strong sense of community, human compassion and the family, especially the care of children'.[21] Article 101(i) repeated the current requirement of section 25(i) of the New Zealand Bill of Rights Act 1990 that a child who is charged with an offence must be dealt with in a manner that takes into account the child's age. Article 94 guaranteed the right to free state primary and secondary education. Article 96 guaranteed the right not to be discriminated against on account of age.

We received some feedback suggesting that a constitution should do more in terms of respecting children's rights than what we had proposed. Among the suggestions made were:

- lowering the voting age from 18 years of age, so as to encourage earlier participation in the electoral process. This has the advantage of making the political processes more responsive to children's needs and engaging younger people in political processes at an early stage of life;
- incorporating all the provisions of the United Nations Convention on the Rights of the Child (1989) (UNCROC);
- recognising the primary consideration principle protected by UNCROC in all court proceedings in which children's interests are affected (such as access).

Having considered the submissions we received, we believe there is a good case to lower the voting age to 16. We have addressed this issue in some detail in chapter 15, on electoral reform.

In addition, we believe that the Bill of Rights should be amended so as to give more explicit recognition to some of the rights of children. In our new version of Constitution Aotearoa, we propose to include some new children's rights:

18 Children's rights
(1) Every child has the right to be free from neglect, abuse, degradation, and exploitative labour practices.
(2) In all proceedings concerning children,—
    (a) the best interests of the child must be a primary consideration; and

---

21 Palmer and Butler, above n 1, at 34.

(b) the child's views must, if practicable, be obtained and given due weight.

The first new right reflects Articles 19 and 32–37 of UNCROC. New Zealand has been a world leader in eliminating exploitative child labour practices; we have not, however, been as successful or as committed to eliminating abuse, neglect and degradation. We believe it is appropriate that a new constitutional settlement set some non-negotiable rights for all New Zealand children, requiring the State to put appropriate legislation, policy and practices in place. The language we have used is drawn from that of section 28(1) of the South African constitution.

The second new right reflects Articles 3.1 ('the best interests of the child shall be a primary consideration') and 12 (child's views should be heard) of UNCROC, which have, in turn, already been recognised in New Zealand legislation (through, for example, sections 4 and 6 of the Care of Children Act 2004, and sections 5(d) and 6 of the Oranga Tamariki Act 1989). Similar protection is to be found in the Victorian Charter of Rights and Responsibilities (section 17) and the ACT Human Rights Act 2004 (section 11). We believe that the primary consideration principle has widespread support and is sufficiently important to warrant constitutional protection.

And, of course, children—as natural persons—will continue to enjoy all the other rights that they enjoy under the Bill of Rights, subject as always to the ability for Parliament to place reasonable limits upon them.

Corporations and human rights

Some concern was raised in submissions about the ability of corporations to enjoy human rights. In a similar vein, concern was also raised about whether large corporates might not be a greater threat to the enjoyment of human rights than the Government.

In our 2016 book we proposed that legal persons (i.e., companies, incorporated societies, charitable trusts boards) should be able to rely on human rights. That is the position currently under the New Zealand Bill of Rights Act 1990 (section 29). However, we explicitly provided that legal persons should not enjoy all of those rights (e.g., the right to life is not something that should be guaranteed to legal persons). We have decided to stick with our original proposals. Many important human rights principles have been established in legal cases brought by corporations—for example, many of the important freedom of expression cases have been brought to court by media organisations; if they were not able to enjoy such rights, the right to freedom of expression would be much impoverished.

As to the power of corporates, the point is well made, but does not require a change in the proposed text of Constitution Aotearoa. First, the point of the Constitution is to constrain the exercise of public power, not to closely regulate private power. Regulation of private power is best undertaken through the democratic institutions such as Parliament. Indeed, a great many of the statutes that have been enacted over the years have such regulation as their primary purpose. Second, and in any event, it is inevitable that in shaping the content of the law, including the common law made by judges, the values in the Bill of Rights will have impact. That is how similar bills of rights operate overseas, and the result is that human rights have some horizontal (i.e., person-to-person) effect. There has been acceptance of this position under the current New Zealand Bill of Rights Act 1990 and there is no reason to think that it will not continue to operate in that way.

Other drafting issues

In our 2016 version of Constitution Aotearoa, the Bill of Rights was located in Part 12, beginning with Article 75. A number of submitters strongly suggested that human rights are so fundamental to our community that it is important they are given much greater prominence in the constitutional text. We have listened to, and agree with, these submissions. In our revised version, the Bill of Rights now appears as Part 2 of Constitution Aotearoa, straight after the pithy statement of core values declared in Article 1. Further recognising the desire for the Bill of Rights to inspire citizens and the state institutions continued (and established) by Constitution Aotearoa, we have reordered the Articles within it. So, some of the technical material (for example, dealing with who is able to claim its protection, or the Attorney-General's special vetting role), comes at the end, not—as it currently does in the New Zealand Bill of Rights Act—at the beginning of the Bill of Rights.

Endnote: The *Atkinson* saga

In submissions we received, and at our public meetings, one of the most striking and tangible manifestations of what is currently wrong with our system of parliamentary sovereignty and the vulnerability of human rights became apparent in discussion of the *Atkinson* litigation. In our 2016 book we discussed aspects of that litigation. Because there was so much interest in it, we summarise the key points of the *Atkinson* saga here in this endnote.

For years, there had been a policy that parents (and resident siblings) who acted as caregivers for their adult, disabled children were not eligible to be paid for the care they provided. So, while non-relatives who undertook such care could be, and were, paid by the Ministry of Health for what they did, parents were not. After years of seeking to have the policy changed, in 2008 a group of parents challenged the lawfulness of the policy under the Human Rights Act 1993. They argued that the policy discriminated against them on the grounds of family status and the policy could not be justified as a reasonable limit on that right in a free and democratic state like New Zealand (that being the test set out in section 5 of the New Zealand Bill of Rights Act 1990).

The parents won before the Human Rights Review Tribunal (2010), the High Court (2010) and the Court of Appeal (2012). In light of these judicial decisions, the ball was put firmly in the Government's court. Clearly a considered response was necessary. A relatively quick consultation exercise was undertaken by the Ministry. Months passed while the Government's next steps were considered.

Then, out of the blue and with no notice, the Government introduced a Bill into Parliament and got Parliament to enact it through all stages of the legislative process within a single sitting day. The legislation was the New Zealand Public Health and Disability Amendment Act (No 2). Its principal effects were: first, to prevent anyone ever making a complaint to the Human Rights Commission or bringing a court proceeding against any government family carer policy no matter how discriminatory; second, in effect, retrospectively to exclude the provision of remedies for past discrimination; third, to permit the Ministry to adopt a paid family carer policy using whatever criteria it considered appropriate. There was no warning that the Bill was to be introduced; there was no public consultation on it; there was no Select Committee consideration of it. It was stated to be a Budget matter, and as a result the then Government's support parties were duty-bound to vote in favour of it or else see the Government collapse. By any measure, it was a shocking piece of legislation which ousted well-known constitutional protections and which was contrary to well-known and honoured constitutional protections. Dr Anne Salmond referred to it as 'shabby' legislation.[22] Professor Andrew Geddis commented that it appeared 'National just broke our constitution'.[23]

The Act in effect took away rights from some of the most vulnerable people in our community—the disabled and family members who cared for them. Yet it passed in a single sitting day, despite almost immediate public concern about it. This is how fragile our constitutional system is.

In our view, this is simply not acceptable. If well-known and accepted constitutional protections are to be departed from, then this should only occur when the public can be persuaded to agree to it, or when there is overwhelming parliamentary support for it.

---

22 A Salmond 'Government or playground bully?' *Pundit* (21 May 2013).
23 Andrew Geddis 'I think National just broke our Constitution' *Pundit* (17 May 2013).

13 The Treaty of Waitangi and the Constitution

In our 2016 book, we proposed to give constitutional recognition to the Treaty of Waitangi. If adopted, this would require Parliament and the Government to give effect to the Treaty, and it would empower courts to interpret the Treaty and enforce it. Because we were proposing that New Zealand would become a republic, we proposed that the State inherit all Treaty responsibilities that currently belong to the Crown.

We made that proposal for two main reasons. First, we believed that the Treaty, as New Zealand's founding constitutional document, and as a key source of the Crown's right to govern, simply had to be included in any codified constitution.

Second, the Treaty is already part of New Zealand's legal and constitutional arrangements. Parliament has enacted many statutes giving recognition to the Treaty, and courts have relied on the Treaty when interpreting statutes. But the Treaty's status differs from one statute to the next. Its legal effect is uncertain. No one can know when it applies and when it doesn't. Incorporating the Treaty into the Constitution would make its legal status clearer.

We had many submissions about the Treaty, and they ranged widely in tone and content. No other topic generated such polarised views, nor as much heat. Many appeared to be comfortable with the approach we had proposed. But some people opposed the Treaty having any place in New Zealand's constitutional arrangements and saw our proposal as ushering in 'a form of apartheid'. Others thought the Constitution should provide much more recognition for Treaty rights, and tino rangatiratanga in particular. Others still felt our proposals would not solve the current legal uncertainty and, in fact, might add to it.

Having reflected on these submissions, our view remains that any constitution must make a place for the Treaty. But we accept that our proposals might not have brought the clarity we were seeking. We also acknowledge that submitters' widely divergent views mean that more discussion is needed to determine what Treaty rights might look like in a modern New Zealand.

The Treaty of Waitangi and the Constitution

We have therefore amended our proposal to provide for a process that will clarify the content and range of the Treaty, while still recognising it as part of our Constitution. Further discussion about this vital aspect of New Zealand's constitutional arrangements will, upon its conclusion, provide more certainty and clarity. It will take some years to sort out. But there would be incentives to do so if the Treaty has constitutional effect. This chapter sets out our reasoning in more depth, and our revised proposal. In essence, we propose that New Zealand faces up to this issue and seeks to resolve it.

Consistent with our approach to the flexibility of the Constitution, future generations will have the capacity to alter the law by use of the amendment powers. In short, if our approach to the Constitution is accepted the Treaty will continue to be central to New Zealand's ongoing constitutional dialogue; no one generation will lock future generations into a fixed view of the Treaty, and each generation will have the chance to address it.

The Treaty's current legal status

The Treaty in international law

Prior to the Treaty, Britain recognised Māori tribes as sovereign over their territories. Britain acknowledged the 1835 Declaration of Independence, in which northern tribes declared their independence and sovereignty.[1] Four years later, when Britain sent Captain Hobson to negotiate the Treaty of Waitangi, the Colonial Secretary's instructions were clear that Māori tribal sovereignty was 'indisputable' and could be given up only with the 'free and intelligent consent' of Māori leaders.[2] Britain's intention was to obtain sovereignty over New Zealand. Its immediate purpose was to obtain the legal power to control British settlement and, in particular, to head off the New Zealand Company, which intended to establish an independent

---

1 Busby's Dispatch of 16 June 1837. See John O Ross 'Busby and the Declaration of Independence' (1980) 14 New Zealand Journal of History 83. See also Matthew SR Palmer *The Treaty of Waitangi in New Zealand's Law and Constitution* (Victoria University Press, Wellington, 2008) at 38–41.
2 Normanby to Hobson (14, 15 August 1839, CO 209/4, 251–82, 157–63) as quoted in Claudia Orange *The Treaty of Waitangi* (Bridget Williams Books, Wellington, 1987 (reprinted 2003)), at 30–31.

colony at Port Nicholson.[3]

The basic elements of the Treaty are well known. Māori signatories recognised the Crown's right of kāwanatanga or government ('sovereignty' in the English text), and the Crown in turn recognised Māori right of tino rangatiratanga or full chieftainship ('full, exclusive and undisturbed possession' in the English text) over their territories. Māori were also promised the same rights and privileges as British citizens.[4]

Modern experts in international law are in broad agreement that the Treaty of Waitangi was a valid Treaty under international law.[5] As Professor Ian Brownlie wrote in 1991:[6]

> There can be no doubt [. . .] that the Treaty of Waitangi presupposed the legal and political capacity of the chiefs of New Zealand to make an agreement which was valid on the international plane.

As such, the Treaty created real rights and obligations in international law. And, under the international law of succession, the rights and obligations undertaken in 1840 devolve in contemporary times to the Crown in right of New Zealand. At international law, the Crown has to honour its guarantees of tino rangatiratanga and equal rights.

Under New Zealand's current constitutional arrangements, rights and obligations arising from treaties cannot be specifically invoked in the New Zealand courts unless they have been incorporated into New Zealand law by Act of Parliament.[7] This notwithstanding the Treaty's binding status under international law. But our courts can and have used the Treaty of Waitangi both as a source of principle and as an aid to interpretation of both statute and common law.

The Treaty in statute law

In the early years of the New Zealand colony, the Treaty had considerable influence over Crown actions in New Zealand. Although the Crown's interpretation differed from that of Māori,

---

3 Orange, above n 2, at 29.
4 At Appendix 2, 257–260.
5 Matthew SR Palmer, above n 1, at 164–168.
6 Ian Brownlie, FM Brookfield (ed) *Treaties and Indigenous Peoples: The Robb lectures 1991* (Clarendon Press, Oxford, 1992) at 8.
7 *Hoani Te Heuheu v Aotea District Māori Land Board* [1941] AC 308 (PC).

The Treaty of Waitangi and the Constitution

it nonetheless took seriously its obligations to protect Māori lands and customary rights. The New Zealand Constitution Act 1852, which established the House of Representatives, also made provision for autonomous districts in which Māori laws would prevail within limits. In the event, these provisions were never used. Over time, as settler politicians persuaded Britain to hand over responsibility for Crown–Māori relations, Treaty rights faded from view. For a very long time, the Treaty received no recognition in New Zealand statute law and very little recognition in public policy.[8]

The Treaty of Waitangi Act 1975 was the first step towards reversing that trend. It established the Waitangi Tribunal and empowered it to inquire into claims that the Crown had caused harm to Māori people by breaching the Treaty and its principles.[9] This measure was, however, subject to a limitation as to time—it could only address Treaty breaches from 1975 onwards.

The Fourth Labour Government extended the Treaty's statutory reach in 1985. It empowered the Waitangi Tribunal to inquire into historical claims as far back as 1840, and those claims have led to numerous settlements which are discussed below.[10]

That Government also incorporated Treaty principles (see below) into several other statutes. The provisions vary in their strength. An early example was the Conservation Act 1987, which contains in section 4 a strong excerpt from the Treaty of Waitangi and provides: 'This Act shall so be interpreted and administered as to give effect to the principles of the Treaty of Waitangi.' Section 4 applies to all decision-makers under the Act.

Even more significant was section 9 of the State-Owned Enterprises Act 1986, which provided:

> Nothing in this Act shall permit the Crown to act in a manner that is inconsistent with the principles of the Treaty of Waitangi.

Over the years, courts have interpreted these statutes and, in so doing, developed a series of Treaty principles which can be applied to other cases. Those principles include: partnership (the Treaty was

---

8 Orange, above n 2, at 136–142, 150–155, 186–190.
9 Treaty of Waitangi Act 1975, ss 5–8.
10 Treaty of Waitangi Act 1975, s 3; Treaty of Waitangi Amendment Act 1985, s 3(1).

a partnership between the Crown and Māori, in which both must act reasonably, honourably and in good faith); active protection (the Crown's right to govern involved a corresponding obligation to actively protect Māori interests, in the nature of a fiduciary duty); and redress (past wrongs give rise to a right of redress). Courts have also found that the Treaty obliges the Crown to consult and make informed decisions.[11]

The Treaty provision in the State-owned Enterprises Act led to a most significant legal case known as the *Lands* case, in which the Court of Appeal unanimously held that the Crown could not transfer assets to state-owned enterprises without establishing a system to consider whether such a transfer would be inconsistent with the principles of the Treaty of Waitangi and therefore unlawful.[12] The result of this legal declaration was the passage of a statute that permitted transfers so long as the titles to the lands in question made it clear they were subject to Waitangi claims.[13] Thus, the rights of claimants were expressly protected.

There is also legal authority on the effect of the Treaty clause in the Conservation Act. In *Ngai Tahu Maori Trust Board v Director-General of Conservation* the tribe held a whale-watching permit and successfully challenged the Director-General's decision to issue a further permit in the same vicinity.[14] The court held the principle of active protection required the Crown to give Ngāi Tahu a 'reasonable degree of preference' when issuing permits, although it did not go so far as to grant iwi a veto over other applicants.

Subsequent governments have extended the Treaty's statutory reach further, for example, by incorporating Treaty references into resource management[15] and local government[16] legislation. About 30 New Zealand statutes contain Treaty references of varying weight, which

---

11 The Waitangi Tribunal has also identified other principles including reciprocity (the Treaty involves reciprocal obligations), mutual benefit, autonomy (the right of Māori communities to manage themselves and their territories and resources), options (the right of Māori to choose whether to live according to tikanga or to assimilate into European communities), and equity and equal treatment.
12 *New Zealand Māori Council v Attorney-General* [1987] 1 NZLR 641 (CA).
13 Treaty of Waitangi (State Enterprises) Act 1988.
14 *Ngai Tahu Maori Trust Board v Director-General of Conservation* [1995] 3 NZLR 553 (CA).
15 Resource Management Act 1991, s 8.
16 Local Government Act 2002, s 4.

need to be considered carefully when dealing with Māori issues that arise under those statutes. The nature of tino rangatiratanga—which was a guarantee of possession and authority over ancestral land and resources—means that Treaty references are particularly evident in environment, conservation and resource management statutes, or in statutes affecting land. But Treaty clauses are also present in public statutes covering health, education, transport and various other matters.

Although the Treaty is recognised in numerous statutes, the Treaty clauses are inconsistent from one Act to another. Some statutes require government agencies to 'give effect to' the principles of the Treaty (as the Conservation Act does);[17] other statutes require agencies to 'have regard to'[18] or 'take into account'[19] those principles, or to consult Māori and involve them in decision-making.[20] Some require government departments or local authorities to comply with Treaty obligations, while others set out specific processes for compliance.[21]

So, the present situation is that the Treaty and its principles are part of statute law for some purposes in New Zealand and not for others, and the Treaty's application is inconsistent from one statute to the next.

Furthermore, under some circumstances courts can consider the Treaty when interpreting a statute even when it is not specifically mentioned. In a 1987 decision, Chilwell J concluded that the Treaty was 'part of the fabric of New Zealand society', and that the Treaty obligations had been explicitly and implicitly recognised in statute law. Where legislation impinged on Treaty principles, the Treaty was therefore 'part of the context' in which that legislation could be interpreted, in accordance with existing principles of statutory interpretation.[22]

---

17 For example, Conservation Act 1987, s 4; Climate Change Response Act 2002, s 3A.
18 For example, Resource Management Act 1991, s 8; Local Government Act 2004, s 4.
19 For example, Marine and Coastal Area (Takutai Moana) Act 2011, s 7.
20 For example, see the New Zealand Public Health and Disability Act 2000, s 4.
21 Marine and Coastal Area (Takutai Moana) Act 2011, s 7; Climate Change Response Act 2002, s 3A.
22 *Huakina Development Trust v Waikato Valley Authority* [1987] 2 NZLR 188 (HC). Specifically, Chilwell J said: 'There can be no doubt that the Treaty is part of the context in which legislation which impinges on its principles is to be interpreted when it is proper, in accordance with the principles of statutory interpretation, to have resort to extrinsic material.'

Treaty settlement legislation

Since 1985, when the Waitangi Tribunal's jurisdiction was extended back to 1840, it has built up a series of rich reports about Crown–Māori relations in New Zealand districts.[23] Many of those reports have been followed by significant settlements of historical claims. In other cases, the Crown and Māori have negotiated directly without waiting for a tribunal inquiry.

All of these settlements become part of New Zealand law. Between 1992 and the 2017 general election, Parliament enacted 59 substantial Treaty of Waitangi Settlement Acts,[24] which settled claims, apologised for the Crown's past wrongs and transferred assets of various types to the claimants. At the time of the 2017 election, seven more Bills had been introduced and were awaiting enactment.

Cumulatively, these settlements have provided Māori with substantial economic assets that have the capacity to support and assist the affected claimant communities.

Many have also provided for Māori participation in decision-making over important resources, such as mountains, lakes and rivers, with which the claimants have ancestral connections. The nature of settlements differ from one region to the next.

One of the most recent settlement Acts passed by Parliament is also one of the most innovative. The Te Awa Tupua (Whanganui River Claims Settlement) Act 2017 not only declared the Whanganui River a living person, but also recognised the river and its tributaries as an indivisible whole which provided both physical and spiritual sustenance to its communities and environment. And it furthermore recognised the 'inalienable' connection between the river and its iwi and hapū, for whom it was a source of both identity and responsibility.[25]

This initiative, which grabbed headlines around the world, was an unprecedented recognition of traditional Māori values and laws in New Zealand legislation.

---

23 Treaty of Waitangi Act 1975.
24 This includes the Treaty of Waitangi (Fisheries Claims) Settlement Act 1992, which provided a nationwide settlement of fisheries claims.
25 Te Awa Tupua (Whanganui River Claims Settlement Act) 2017, pt 2.

Customary title

The Treaty is not the only source of rights for tāngata whenua. In fact, there is a long common law tradition of recognising the rights of Indigenous peoples.

When English common law arrived in New Zealand, one of the principles it brought with it was the principle of aboriginal or native title to land. The essence of this principle is that Indigenous people have rights to possess and use land, and those rights cannot be taken away except with consent. It was this principle that led the Crown, in article 2 of the Treaty, to recognise that Māori had rights to land which could not be extinguished except with their free, informed consent.

This principle was also part of the reason Article 2 (in the English text) granted the Crown a right of pre-emption, which meant only it could buy Māori land. Under English law at the time, only the Crown could extinguish native title. This was done, among other reasons, to protect the requirement for free consent.[26]

This doctrine has since been upheld in New Zealand courts,[27] as well as in the courts of other colonies such as Canada, the United States and Australia.

The so-called 'foreshore and seabed case'[28] in the 1990s arose not from Treaty rights, but from this doctrine of native title.[29] Under English common law, it is assumed that the Crown holds rights to the foreshore and seabed, and could therefore assign rights to others (including, in this particular case, marine farmers). A group of Northern South Island iwi challenged this assumption, arguing that they had pre-existing customary title. The Court of Appeal found that aboriginal or customary title (as it is now called) at common law remained in force until lawfully extinguished. The Crown's title

---

26 This was the legal reason. 'Buy low, sell high' fund settlement was the economic imperative. Both reasons were laid out explicitly in Normanby's instructions to Hobson. English officials didn't see a contradiction between protection and speculative land dealing, because in their view Māori would gain so much civilising influence from the mere presence of Europeans that it more than offset any financial loss.
27 *R v Symonds* (1847) (1840–1932) NZPCC 387, at 390.
28 The seabed is the area of land that is permanently under the sea; the foreshore is the land regularly covered by the tide, including spring tides.
29 *Attorney-General v Ngati Apa* [2003] 3 NZLR 643 (CA).

therefore depended on it proving that to be the case.

The case raised questions about public access to the foreshore and seabed, and the Fifth Labour Government responded in 2004 with legislation that declared the Crown to own the foreshore and seabed, while also making provision for customary activities that had continued since 1840 to be protected.

The National-led government subsequently repealed that Act in 2011, substituting it with a new statute that replaced Crown ownership with no ownership, and provided a mechanism for hapū and iwi to negotiate with the Crown for recognition of customary rights. Among other things, the 2011 statute aimed to 'acknowledge' the Treaty and 'recognise' the traditional authority of hapū and iwi as tāngata whenua over the foreshore and seabed (now known as the marine and coastal area) in their territories.[30] This provided for yet another form in which Treaty rights were acknowledged in statute.

The Treaty in Government decision-making

The law is one thing; Government is another. In recent decades, the Treaty has come to form an important consideration in Government decision-making.

The Treaty provides for a relationship between the Government and Māori, characterised by ongoing discussions and negotiation. Treaty settlements have always been negotiated between Crown and Māori representatives before they are passed into law, and discussions and negotiations also occur in many other areas of government activity.

Likewise, Government decision-making processes set out in the Cabinet Manual[31] require attention to be given to the consequences of decisions that affect Māori interests. For example, it is necessary for ministers who seek Cabinet approval of Bills to be introduced to Parliament to draw attention to any features of the Bill that 'have implications for or may be affected by [. . .] the principles of the Treaty of Waitangi'.[32]

---

30 Marine and Coastal Area (Takutai Moana) Act 2011.
31 The Cabinet Manual is produced by the Cabinet Office in the Department of Prime Minister and Cabinet, and provides guidance on government decision-making processes.
32 Cabinet Office *Cabinet Manual 2017* at [7.65]. For a detailed analysis of the Cabinet decisions on such matters see M Palmer, above n 1, at 215–226.

The Treaty of Waitangi and the Constitution

Different governments have approached issues relating to the Treaty in different ways. For the most part there has been a positive trend in government attitudes towards the Treaty since the 1970s, with focus on developing and strengthening relationships between Māori and the Crown. While this has not always translated into good policy, for example the Foreshore and Seabed Act 2004, successive Governments have made efforts to better recognise the Treaty in everyday decision-making. While there has been increasing consensus within the Parliament on these issues in the last 20 years, recognition of the Treaty is still dependent to a large degree on political decisions. The Treaty is an important part of political constitutionalism as distinct from legal constitutionalism. In order to achieve more stability we need to take further steps.

An excerpt from the Speech from the Throne, delivered by Her Excellency the Rt Hon Dame Patsy Reddy on the State Opening of Parliament after the 2017 election, indicates the growing importance of Treaty relationships to Government operations and gives some insight into what this might look like as historical grievance claims are settled:[33]

> When our forebears signed the Treaty of Waitangi more than 170 years ago they did so in a spirit of cooperation.
>
> Whatever else that agreement might have meant, it was supposed to bring opportunity and mutual benefit for tāngata whenua and settlers alike. It was supposed to provide a place for all peoples in this country.
>
> Instead what followed was a long process of colonisation, in which one of the Treaty partners acquired most of the power and the resources, and the other was sidelined.
>
> For almost 40 years, New Zealand has been addressing past injustices. Most of New Zealand's major iwi are now involved in Treaty settlements. This government is committed to bringing others to completion as quickly and fairly as it can.
>
> It is time to start considering what the Treaty relationship might look like after historical grievances are settled. To consider how we, as a nation, can move forward in ways that honour the original Treaty promise.
>
> A promise of a nation in which Māori values—diverse as they are—stand in their rightful place alongside those of European New

---

[33] Rt Hon Dame Patsy Reddy, Governor General of New Zealand 'Speech from the Throne' (State Opening of Parliament, Wellington, 8 November 2017).

Zealanders and other more recent arrivals.

A nation in which manaakitanga and kaitiakitanga and whanaungatanga inform our decision-making.

A nation in which fairness and equality of opportunity are not just aspirations but facts. And a nation in which all communities are empowered.

Our 2016 proposal

In *A Constitution for Aotearoa New Zealand*, we proposed to incorporate the Treaty of Waitangi into Constitution Aotearoa, thereby making it part of the superior law.

Section 72(1) of our proposed Constitution provided that 'The rights, duties and obligations of Māori under te Tiriti o Waitangi/the Treaty of Waitangi are hereby recognised and affirmed.' Because we were proposing that New Zealand become a republic, section 72(2) provided that all of the Crown's current Treaty duties and obligations would be assumed by the State of Aotearoa New Zealand. Section 72(3) provided that the Treaty 'is considered as always speaking and is to be applied to circumstances as they arise so that effect may be given to its spirit, intent and principles'.

Under our proposal, te Tiriti o Waitangi/the Treaty of Waitangi meant the full texts of the Treaty in Māori and English. These were to be set out in an Appendix to the Constitution.[34]

Our proposal also provided for the Waitangi Tribunal to continue to operate,[35] and empowered the House of Representatives, and courts and tribunals, to seek advice from the Waitangi Tribunal on any issue relating to the Treaty or to tikanga Māori.[36]

The effect of the proposals in our 2016 book would be thereby making the Treaty part of the superior law. This was the approach that was adopted by the White Paper on the Bill of Rights, tabled in the Parliament in 1985.[37] When the New Zealand Bill of Rights Act 1990 was enacted it was as an ordinary statute and the Treaty was not

---

34 The two versions of the Treaty in English and Māori were both set out in the 2016 draft Constitution.
35 Constitution Aotearoa 2016, art 73.
36 Constitution Aotearoa 2016, art 74.
37 Geoffrey Palmer 'A Bill of Rights for New Zealand: A White Paper' [1985–1986] I AJHR A6.

The Treaty of Waitangi and the Constitution

included. The move to incorporate the Treaty into the Bill of Rights was resisted by a number of Māori interests in submissions to the Select Committee at the time.[38] We thought nearly thirty years later this may be appropriate now after many advances have been made in addressing the issues.

We believed the proposals would bring clarity and certainty to the Treaty's legal status. Our proposal would have required Parliament and future governments to recognise the Treaty and give effect to it in a consistent manner. It would have allowed the courts to determine whether laws and government decisions and actions were consistent with the Treaty. It would also have limited opportunities for any future Parliament or government from attempting to alter the text of the Treaty itself.

There were two main reasons for the approach we took. First, we thought it was essential to acknowledge the Treaty's status as a founding document in New Zealand's constitutional arrangements. It was through the Treaty that the Crown obtained Māori consent for the establishment of a government in New Zealand. The system of government we have today therefore owes much to the Treaty. It is part of New Zealand's constitutional arrangements and cannot be ignored.

Second, we wanted to bring some certainty and coherence to the Treaty's legal and constitutional status. As we explained above, the Treaty right now is half in and half out of the law. It is an international Treaty that cannot be enforced in New Zealand unless it is part of domestic law. It is recognised in many statutes, but in ways that are inconsistent. Courts can consider the Treaty in some circumstances but not others. As a result, confusion is rife around when, how and in what situations the Treaty can be applied to. Overall, its legal effect is inconsistent, incoherent and uncertain. We thought that incorporating the Treaty into a superior law constitution would resolve that.

We did not think there were hidden dangers in that course, or that it would significantly alter current approaches to Treaty rights. Successive governments have gained a lot of experience with Treaty issues over the last few decades, and have found flexible and innovative

---

38 Justice and Law Reform Committee 'Interim Report of the Inquiry into the White Paper—A Bill of Rights for New Zealand' [1986–1987] X AJHR I8A.

ways in which to honour the Treaty in contemporary New Zealand, of which the Whanganui River settlement mentioned above is an example. Incorporating the Treaty into a superior law constitution, we felt, would not greatly alter current approaches, other than to act as a check on the temptation to reduce Treaty rights for political expediency.

The courts have built up a large body of case law about the Treaty, and have shown themselves capable of dealing with complex disputes in a way that is even-handed and fair, and does not stifle innovation. We did not think that incorporating the Treaty into a constitution would greatly alter the course of Treaty jurisprudence, other than to bring more certainty and clarity.

What people said about our proposal

Of all of the topics that we included in our proposed Constitution, the Treaty excited the greatest range of opinion. The submissions fell into three broad categories. Some people were opposed to the Treaty having any legal recognition. Others wanted greater recognition of Māori rights. In particular, some called for new institutional arrangements that placed tino rangatiratanga alongside kāwanatanga in what one blogger on our website called 'a constitution sourced in two streams'. Others regarded the Treaty as an important part of New Zealand's constitutional and legal framework, but were reasonably content with New Zealand's current institutions. Most of those submitters had little or no objection to our proposed approach. However, some legal scholars argued that our proposals would not achieve their purpose of bringing clarity and certainty.

Those who opposed the Treaty altogether

One weekend we received a blizzard of similar submissions to our website, all of which said much the same thing: that the Treaty was irrelevant, that it should not be given weight, that it was 'separatist nonsense' and, if truly honoured, would produce a system akin to apartheid. Those submissions argued that there should be 'one law for all', and that tāngata whenua should not inherit any property or resource rights distinct from other New Zealanders.

We responded with blogs on our website setting out our views

The Treaty of Waitangi and the Constitution

on why the Treaty should be in New Zealand's constitution[39] and responding directly to the submissions we had received up until that point.[40]

In essence, those who opposed any inclusion of the Treaty raised five main arguments.

- First, they said that all New Zealanders are equal, and therefore there should be one law for all. The obvious inference was that the 'one law' should be English law as it has been applied in New Zealand, albeit without the recognition for Indigenous property rights, which is an integral part of English common law (as described above).
- Second, they said that recognising the Treaty in a constitution would turn non-Māori into second class citizens. Very few submitters explained how this would occur, although sometimes it was linked to an imbalance in democratic representation. One person put it to us that: 'The Māori people have no right nor need of extra representation in central or local government matters. To give them such, is unfair and an affront to other ethnic groups in New Zealand. It is undemocratic.'
- Third, they argued that the Treaty is an historical document, with no current relevance. Some submitters, for example, argued that the Treaty ceased to have any relevance or effect in New Zealand as soon as the Crown declared its sovereignty over these islands in May 1840. One submitter told us that New Zealand's 'true' constitution was Queen Victoria's November 1840 Royal Charter, which separated New Zealand from New South Wales, established legislative and executive councils, and established courts that would apply 'English law only'. There was no recognition that English law has always explicitly recognised customary property rights and practices.
- Fourth, some submitters told us there was no such thing as Māori; therefore, whatever the relevance of the Treaty in 1840, it has no relevance in modern New Zealand. In contemporary New Zealand no one could show that they were of more than 50 per cent Māori

39 'Why the Treaty should be in NZ's constitution' (2 February 2017), available at <constitutionaotearoa.org.nz/the-conversation/Treaty-palmer-butler>.
40 'Submissions on the Treaty—some reflections' (4 February 2017), available at <constitutionaotearoa.org.nz/the-conversation/Treaty-reflections>.

blood, so the possibility of being Māori had died through dilution.
- Fifth, some said the meaning of the Treaty today is so uncertain, due to court and Waitangi Tribunal interpretations, that nobody knows what it means and what impacts it could have in the future. This uncertainty means it's inappropriate for inclusion in the Constitution.

We responded to these points as follows.

First, all New Zealanders are indeed to be treated equally. That was part of the promise of the Treaty itself: it says that Māori will be given all the rights and privileges of British subjects (Article 3). But part of equality is that Māori have the same right to the protection of their rights and interests before the courts as other subjects. And, by virtue of English law, Māori (like many Indigenous peoples) have rights reflected in the English common law doctrine of native title. This doctrine in fact was reflected in Article 2 of the Treaty, which guarantees to Māori 'the full exclusive and undisturbed possession of their Lands and Estates Forests and Fisheries and other properties' / 'te tino rangatiratanga o o ratou wenua o ratou kainga me o ratou taonga katoa'.

Those promises—of equal treatment and of protection of native title—which in turn reflect English common law—were not honoured. Large tracts of land were wrongly confiscated; other land was purchased using methods that did not reflect and respect the way in which Māori land was held; rights flowing from native title, including associated water, tree felling, fisheries rights, etc., were not respected. In Māori society such rights were held collectively, not individually. The deprivations occurred through a combination of court decisions and legislation.

Some say that, to the extent that this occurred pursuant to the law in force at the time, Māori were treated equally because they were governed by the same lawmakers as non-Māori. But that ignores the guarantee of recognition of Māori rights—rights that were part and parcel of the law recognised by English law in almost all of the colonies that the United Kingdom established—and the associated right to have their rights upheld and recognised in the same way as the Parliament and courts would recognise the rights of non-Māori. Much legislation was passed in order to override those rights.

Second, recognition of the Treaty has not and would not establish Māori as a class of person superior to non-Māori. The Treaty was about recognising the uniqueness of Māori and ensuring that their identity, customs, lands and so on were respected. The history of the law in New Zealand has been that the law has sometimes classified Māori as unique—but in ways designed to make them second class citizens. Examples include the Tohunga Suppression Act 1907, the suspension of habeas corpus during the Waikato War under the Suppression of Rebellion Act 1863, the existence of effectively separate (but unequal) voting systems for Māori and non-Māori (from the end of the 19th century up until 1975, the only Māori who could vote in general electorates were 'half-castes', defined as being people who had one Māori parent and one non-Māori parent).

Much of the recent effort to create Māori representation at local and central government levels has been aimed at recognising both the legacy of separate but unequal participation under the older electoral systems that acted to disadvantage Māori in political life, and also to restore Māori in part to the position they might reasonably expect to have been in had they not been unfairly treated.

Third, the Treaty is relevant to today's circumstances. Its promises underscore why settlements need to occur; promises were broken and trust needs to be fully restored. Its promises also set out a vision for how power might be shared and certain minimum rights and privileges maintained; again that vision is still relevant today. In recognising the contemporary relevance of the Treaty, New Zealand is acting no differently to other countries—Canada, for example, had treaties with aboriginal tribes and today they are part of the relationships between the government and Indigenous people. Indeed, the Canadian Charter of Rights and Freedoms gave explicit protection to those treaties and also to the common law rights of aboriginal title and cultural practices. No one seriously suggests that Canada is as a result practising apartheid. Similarly, the Constitution of India recognises customary law and specifically empowers recognition of the Indigenous tribal communities for administration and legislative purposes.

Fourth, we simply do not agree with people who say that there is no such thing as Māori anymore. The premise is all wrong. Being Māori is about whakapapa. In turn, whakapapa is about kinship, not blood percentages. Most New Zealanders understand that pretty easily, since almost all of us—both Māori and non-Māori—have mixed 'blood' and many ethnic strands, each of which we typically value and cherish. And, moreover, from a legal perspective, recognising the importance of that whakapapa and its significance is compatible with English law because English law recognises the Indigenous system that is used to determine who is within and who is not within a particular group for important purposes such as native title.

Fifth, the work of the Government, the courts, Parliament and the Waitangi Tribunal over the last number of decades has clarified the meaning and effect of the Treaty to a great degree. It is not uncertain, as many claim. But equally as important, it permits contemporary solutions through the flexibility of its principles which focus on process, participation and partnership.

More broadly, we were surprised at the lack of awareness of some of the darker aspects of the history of this land. Wrongs were done; promises were broken; fundamental principles of law and fair treatment were violated. The words said to have been uttered by Hobson at Waitangi—'He iwi tahi tatou,' (translated by some as meaning 'Now we are one people' but by others as 'We are peoples together')—were often relied on by those who opposed recognition of the Treaty.

But the 'one people' concept which appeared to inform their perspective is an assimilationist 'one people' principle—i.e., we will be one people when Māori become like non-Māori. In our view, Hobson's reference to one people was a reference to a people (as in a group of citizens) who live in the one place determined to live with each other in mutual respect and with full recognition of each other's rights. That vision of the words in the Treaty is what we understand to be the promise of the Treaty; it was simply not met. But it can still be, albeit adapted to contemporary circumstances where we all live closely with one another.

Recognising the uniqueness of Māori in our constitutional framework is not at all unusual. In fact, New Zealand (in 2010) became a signatory to the 2007 United Nations *Declaration on the Rights of Indigenous Peoples*.[41] That Declaration (which is legally non-

---

41 United Nations *Declaration on the Rights of Indigenous Peoples* GA Res 61/295, A/RES/61/295 (2007).

binding) has substantial global acceptance.

Articles 3 and 4 are particularly relevant to the rights of tāngata whenua. They provide:

Article 3
Indigenous peoples have the right to self-determination. By virtue of that right they freely determine their political status and freely pursue their economic, social and cultural development.

Article 4
Indigenous peoples, in exercising their right to self-determination, have the right to autonomy or self-government in matters relating to their internal and local affairs, as well as ways and means for financing their autonomous functions.

The Declaration also provides for the right of Indigenous peoples to participate in decision-making in matters that would affect their rights, through representatives chosen by themselves in accordance with their own procedures; and to maintain and develop their own Indigenous decision-making institutions (Article 18).

Where any proposed law or government decision affects the rights of Indigenous peoples, the Declaration imposes an obligation on states to consult and cooperate in good faith with the affected peoples through their representative institutions, in order to obtain their free, prior and informed consent (Article 19).

These are precisely the sorts of measures that the Government, the courts and Parliament have been recognising as rights that flow from the Treaty; in short, Treaty practice increasingly reflects international expectations in this field.

Nor is recognition of the uniqueness of Indigenous peoples an oddity of the United Nations system. As mentioned earlier, native custom and land tenure has long been recognised in English law. In Canada, the Canadian Charter of Rights and Freedoms 1982 (which is part of the Canadian constitution) expressly recognises 'the existing aboriginal and Treaty rights of Aboriginal people of Canada'[42] and also shields aboriginal group rights from being attacked as contrary to the individual rights protected elsewhere in the Canadian Charter.[43]

Canada is not unique; very many constitutions recognise aboriginal

---

42 Canadian Charter of Rights and Freedoms, s 35(1).
43 Canadian Charter of Rights and Freedoms, s 25.

peoples and the importance of protecting their unique rights within the domestic legal system.

Some people who objected to the Treaty's inclusion in a constitution were really opposing historical settlements. They said that whatever happened in the past, they didn't do it, and they didn't think they should have to pay for it. For us, there are several points here. First, we may not have done it, but all of us live with either the fruit and the benefits of the wrongs that were committed in our past, or with the detriments brought about by those wrongs. Second, Māori are unique. Their presence on these islands which we all share is unique to this place. It is the only place where Māori can be Māori. If previous generations of non-Māori could not recognise this, or chose not to, that is no reason for us to follow suit.

Finally, we believe that the Treaty needs to be part of any future supreme law constitution because history has shown that, as a minority, Māori rights will not always be respected. Nor is that a phenomenon of the 19th century; it has happened this century as well. Protection of Treaty and aboriginal rights in the supreme law Canadian constitution has not brought about 'aboriginal privilege' in Canada; recognition of the rights of Māori under the Treaty of Waitangi in a written constitution will not do so in New Zealand either.

Those who thought our proposals would create uncertainty

Another objection to our 2016 approach came from lawyers both experienced in government and also from the private sector. It is based on the judgment that our proposal for a rather minimalist legal incorporation of the Treaty has too many immediate risks of long-term legal uncertainty and indeterminacy.

The argument runs like this: The Treaty is of fundamental importance to every conceivable constitution of Aotearoa New Zealand. But it is important because of its spirit, not because of the actual words that were used in 1840, which are uncertain and partly obsolete. For example, the Article 2 provision granting the Crown a pre-emptive right to buy Māori land is spent.

Therefore, they argued that according constitutional recognition to Treaty rights, duties and obligations would give rise to uncertainty.

Government House, Wellington, where the Governor-General and family live. Many official functions are held here. There is also a smaller Government House in Auckland.

Government House.

The Beehive. Its formal name is the Executive Wing of the parliamentary complex. The Prime Minister's office is on the ninth floor and other ministers are housed in the lower floors. Some ministers are also accommodated in Bowen House.

The Beehive. iStock photo ID 530469027.

Parliament buildings, Wellington. Parliament moved from Auckland to Wellington in 1865. There are four buildings in Wellington that house New Zealand's Parliament. They are: Parliament House, the Parliamentary Library (to the right of the picture), the Beehive (also known as the Executive Wing), and Bowen House, at the corner of Bowen Street and Lambton Quay. In 1918, MPs moved into the building pictured above.

Michal Klajban, CC BY-SA 4.0.

The Legislative Council was abolished by statute in 1950. Since then, New Zealand has not had a second chamber. The room itself remains, however, and is used for a number of ceremonial and official occasions, for example the Governor-General's speech at the opening of Parliament is read there. It has superb acoustics.

Robson, Edward Thomas, 1875–1953. ATL Ref: PAColl-8491.

The Supreme Court, Wellington. The court itself occupies the ground floor, and the five Supreme Court judges have offices and library facilities above. The inside of the court room is striking and well worth a visit. In 2004 the Supreme Court replaced the Privy Council in London as New Zealand's top court.

Ngā Kōti o Aotearoa Courts of New Zealand <www.courtsofnz.govt.nz>

Next Page: News clippings from the publicity surrounding the project.

Should we ditch the royals?

Tony Holman: We need a constitution to protect democracy

Of mice, men and constitutions

Talking about a REVOLUTION

A new book outlines the case for ditching the Queen as our head of state and giving our politicians power for longer. *Michael Donaldson* reports.

NBR In Depth

Order Paper — Rob Hosking

The peri... constitu...

New Zealand's 'intimate democracy' doesn't need the fearful extremism seen in...

Irredeemably policy-c...

When a former prime minister and renowned legal brain says there is too much politics in policy, it pays to listen, writes **David Slack**

Anyone who considers Sir Geoffrey Palmer a dull, policy wonk, should think again, writes David Slack.

LAWN

ISSUE 31 9 SEPTEMBER 2016

+ Law reform, public law

THE QUEST FOR A NEW ZEALAND CONSTITUTION

By Rod Vaughan

Former Prime Minister Sir Geoffrey Palmer QC is on a mission to create a written constitution for New Zealand.

Support essential

I applaud the Palmer and Butler constitutional reform initiative (September 17). It's past time for us as a country to grow up. Let us put 100 years of cringing subservience behind us.

The quality of law-making is rightly criticised and it is to be...

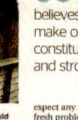

Don't hand law to judges

Written constitution leaves more decisions in the hands of elected legislators than unelected ex-lawyers

Thorough, clear and logical case for NZ constitution

Monday, 10 October 2016

Sir Geoffrey Palmer believes New Zealanders are ready for a shakeup that starts

Proposal to rewrite the rulebook for rulers

Sir Geoffrey Palmer is in it for the long game.

"Surely, we need a head of state who is one of us and who lives here?"
— Sir Geoffrey Palmer

SIR GEOFFREY PALMER: Thinks a written constitution would "boost public confidence in government"

NZ CONSTITUTION

The most important part of the article about a constitution ("Fragile freedoms", September 24) was perhaps the last paragraph. It's easy to believe our essentially liberal social consensus will always be there, but the changing social mix brought about by continued large-scale immigration seems likely to put it under threat. Those of us who have had extensive dealings with immigrants from A... know there is much to l... and admire, but we sho... also remember that man... come here for reasons o... than a love of our West... democratic ways. Many... intolerant of or fail to u... stand the importance o... place of women, the ro... Maori as the tangata wh... the freedom of sexual o... tion, worker's and child rights and our liberal at...

Geoffrey Palmer unfurls his blueprint for a written constitution

LONDON, ENGLAND, UK – JUNE 13 2015: QUEEN ELIZABETH II AND PRINCE PHILLIP DUKE OF EDINBURGH APPEAR IN OPEN HORSE DRAWN CARRIAGE DURING TROOPING THE COLOUR CEREMONY, ON JUNE 13, 2015 IN LONDON, ENGLAND.

The National Business Review / September 16, 2016

Improving quality of government

RIGHT OF REPLY
Andrew Butler

Friday, December 9, 2016

Time for a modern written constitutio...

Former Prime Minister Sir Geoffrey Palmer has recently co-written a book about constitutional law. We print an extract from the book below.

Sir Geoffrey Palmer with wife Margaret photographed in Stratford recently.

Judges should have the power to strike down inconsistent laws

Previous page: Andrew and Geoffrey speaking with students at the UN Youth High Schools Politics Conference at the University of Auckland, 5 August 2017.

Geoffrey with students at South Wellington Intermediate School, 13 September 2017.

Māori Women's Welfare Hui-ā-Tau in New Plymouth, 29 September 2017.

Next page: Andrew and Geoffrey at a public meeting at the University of Auckland, 29 March 2017. Andrew is showing the redacted portions of the Regulatory Impact Statements as they were given to MPs when considering the Bill proposing to reverse the Court of Appeal decision in Atkinson.

Ko WIKITORIA, te Kuini o Ingarani, i tana mahara atawai ki nga Rangatira me nga Hapu o Nu Tirani, i tana hiahia hoki kia tohungia ki a ratou o ratou rangatiratanga, me to ratou wenua, a kia mau tonu hoki te Rongo ki a ratou me te ata noho hoki, kua wakaaro ia he mea tika kia tukua mai tetahi Rangatira hei kai wakarite ki nga tangata maori o Nu Tirani. Kia wakaaetia e nga Rangatira maori te Kawanatanga o te Kuini, ki nga wahi katoa o te wenua nei me nga motu. Na te mea hoki he tokomaha ke nga tangata o tona iwi kua noho ki tenei wenua, a e haere mai nei.

Na, ko te Kuini e hiahia ana kia wakaritea te Kawanatanga, kia kaua ai nga kino e puta mai ki te tangata maori ki te pakeha e noho ture kore ana.

Na, kua pai te Kuini kia tukua a hau, a WIREMU HOPIHONA, he Kapitana i te Roiara Nawi, hei Kawana mo nga wahi katoa o Nu Tirani, e tukua aianei amua atu ki te Kuini; e mea atu ana ia ki nga Rangatira o te Wakaminenga o nga Hapu o Nu Tirani, me era Rangatira atu, enei ture ka korerotia nei.

Ko te tuatahi,
Ko nga Rangatira o te Wakaminenga, me nga Rangatira katoa hoki, kihai i uru ki taua Wakaminenga, ka tuku rawa atu ki te Kuini o Ingarani ake tonu atu te Kawanatanga katoa o o ratou wenua.

Ko te tuarua,
Ko te Kuini o Ingarani ka wakarite ka wakaae ki nga Rangatira, ki nga Hapu, ki nga tangata katoa o Nu Tirani, te tino Rangatiratanga o o ratou wenua o ratou kainga me o ratou taonga katoa. Otiia ko nga Rangatira o te Wakaminenga, me nga Rangatira katoa atu, ka tuku ki te Kuini te hokonga o era wahi wenua e pai ai te tangata nona te wenua, ki te ritenga o te utu e wakaritea ai e ratou ko te kai hoko e meatia nei e te Kuini hei kai hoko mona.

Ko te tuatoru,
Hei wakaritenga mai hoki tenei mo te wakaaetanga ki te Kawanatanga o te Kuini. Ka tiakina e te Kuini o Ingarani nga tangata maori katoa o Nu Tirani. Ka tukua ki a ratou nga tikanga katoa rite tahi ki ana mea ki nga tangata o Ingarani.

(SIGNED.)
WILLIAM HOBSON, Consul & Lieutenant-Governor.

Na, ko matou, ko nga Rangatira o te Wakaminenga o nga Hapu o Nu Tirani, ka huihui nei ki Waitangi. Ko matou hoki ko nga Rangatira o Nu Tirani, ka kite nei i te ritenga o enei kupu, ka tangohia, ka wakaaetia katoatia e matou. Koia ka tohungia ai o matou ingoa o matou tohu.

Ka meatia tenei ki Waitangi, i te ono o nga ra o Pepuere, i te tau kotahi mano, ewaru rau, ewa tekau, o to tatou Ariki.

PAIHIA: Printed at the Press of the Church Missionary Society.

Letters Patent Constituting the Office of Governor-General of New Zealand, 1983.

Archives NZ Reference: R1757751 AAFD 7867 W5145 1

Reprint
as at 3 June 2017

Official Information Act 1982

Public Act	1982 No 156
Date of assent	17 December 1982
Commencement	see section 1

Contents

		Page
	Title	4
1	Short Title and commencement	4
2	Interpretation	4
3	Act to bind the Crown	11
	Part 1	
	Purposes and criteria	
4	Purposes	11
5	Principle of availability	12
6	Conclusive reasons for withholding official information	12
7	Special reasons for withholding official information related to the Cook Islands, Tokelau, or Niue, or the Ross Dependency	13
8	Special reasons for withholding official information related to competitive commercial activities *[Repealed]*	13
9	Other reasons for withholding official information	13
10	Information concerning existence of certain information	15
11	Exclusion of public interest immunity	15

The first page of the Official Information Act 1982 as it appears in the New Zealand statute book.

Reprint
as at 17 May 2005

Constitution Act 1986

Public Act 1986 No 114
Date of assent 13 December 1986
Commencement see section 1(2)

Contents

		Page
	Title	3
1	Short Title and commencement	3

Part 1
The Sovereign

2	Head of State	3
3	Exercise of royal powers by the Sovereign or the Governor-General	3
3A	Advice and consent of Executive Council	4
3B	Exercise of powers and duties by Administrator	4
4	Regency	5
5	Demise of the Crown	5

Part 2
The Executive

6	Ministers of Crown to be members of Parliament	5
7	Power of member of Executive Council to exercise Minister's powers	6

The first page of the Constitution Act 1986 as it appears in the New Zealand statute book.

Reprint
as at 1 July 2013

New Zealand Bill of Rights Act 1990

Public Act 1990 No 109
Date of assent 28 August 1990
Commencement see section 1(2)

Contents

		Page
	Title	2
1	Short Title and commencement	3

Part 1
General provisions

2	Rights affirmed	3
3	Application	3
4	Other enactments not affected	3
5	Justified limitations	3
6	Interpretation consistent with Bill of Rights to be preferred	4
7	Attorney-General to report to Parliament where Bill appears to be inconsistent with Bill of Rights	4

The first page of the Bill of Rights Act 1990 as it appears in the New Zealand statute book.

They also argued that giving constitutional recognition to Treaty rights would put the focus on the text of the Treaty as opposed to its spirit, in a way that is likely to be counterproductive. In their view, what matters is the spirit of the Treaty as reflected in the principles, on which there is now a well-established body of case law.

They felt that giving constitutional recognition to the text of the Treaty could detract from its status as a living document that is always relevant to the way Aotearoa New Zealand is governed. They suggested that the Constitution could recognise the spirit and principles of the Treaty, instead of the actual text.

Other scholars have questioned this approach. In a 2017 *New Zealand Law Journal* article on constitutional reform, Dr Nicholas Smith of Massey University argued that any tidying up of New Zealand's constitutional arrangements ought to make the role and status of the Treaty clearer than it is now, and that recognising existing Treaty principles or jurisprudence in a superior law constitution would not do that.[44] We accept there is some force in Dr Smith's point.

Dr Edward Willis, an advocate of New Zealand's unwritten constitution, made a powerful submission to us concerning the Treaty in which he concluded after analysis:

> The words used to incorporate the Treaty of Waitangi into any written constitution will directly impact on its legal effect and political salience.
>
> New Zealand's unwritten constitution has performed well at accommodating the Treaty in a constitutionally meaningful way despite (and perhaps even because of) its controversial nature.
>
> Traditional approaches to constructing a written constitution are highly unlikely to replicate the unwritten constitution's success in this regard.

So Dr Willis argues as follows:

> As a result any written constitution for Aotearoa-New Zealand that takes the Treaty seriously will be required to adopt a novel approach. More work needs to be done to understand exactly what the detail of this novel approach may look like in practice . . .
>
> He concludes therefore that we should acknowledge how the place

---

44 Nicholas Smith 'Constitutional reform in New Zealand' [2017] NZLJ 270 at 273.

of the Treaty cannot finally be resolved by adopting a constitutional text. We certainly agree with the last point; indeed, precisely because we proposed that Constitution Aotearoa be amendable by special parliamentary majority or binding public referendum, we had contemplated that the constitutional treatment of the Treaty would evolve over time.

We remain convinced that Treaty rights must be recognised in any New Zealand constitution, for all of the reasons explained earlier. What is needed, in our view, is a statement of the existing Treaty and Indigenous rights law in a manner that is clear and transparent, and which brings as much certainty as possible. We cannot put our hands on our hearts and say that our 2016 proposal achieved that.

Second, it would be possible to leave the Treaty out of the Constitution, if that is what Māori wish, and such was their view in the 1980s. But the best evidence available to us now suggests that Māori do want an explicit constitutional recognition of the Treaty; and some would like to see a constitutional transformation inspired by the Treaty, which is addressed in the next section of this chapter. As we have explained above, there are already quite far-reaching ideas being envisaged by some Māori, including abandoning the precepts of the present system of Westminster representative democracy and starting with a clean constitutional slate so as to devise a new constitutional order based on the Treaty of Waitangi and tikanga Māori.

Those who wanted more explicit recognition for tino rangatiratanga

Some people who made submissions argued that any new constitution should make much more explicit provision for tino rangatiratanga and for tikanga Māori (Māori law and values). The essence of this argument was that current institutions and laws did not fully provide for tino rangatiratanga, and that new approaches were therefore needed.

In a blog on our website, Dr Carwyn Jones explained that the Treaty is not only about historical claims, but about current relationships. The original Treaty promises, he wrote, could not be resolved by bringing certainty to the status quo. Rather, what was needed was to give effect to the 'sharing of public power' implied by the guarantees of kāwanatanga (government rights) and tino rangatiratanga (unqualified chieftainship). What was needed were constitutional approaches that were 'truly bicultural, sourced in two streams'.[45]

This, in his view, did not necessarily require the establishment of Māori institutions in parallel to the existing institutions of law and government. But it did require recognition of the validity of Māori law, and acceptance that Māori law and the values that underpin it—such as whanaungatanga, mana, tapu and noa—provided important guidance on who should have power and how it should be exercised, and should inform the development of New Zealand's constitutional arrangements.

Several submitters expressed similar views. Some identified themselves as Māori, but others explicitly told us they were Pākehā who supported a constitutional place for tino rangatiratanga.

Another of the scholars we consulted told us that Māori are seeking 'a place in the constitutional sun'. They did not want to be relegated to the sidelines, as they have been by the way in which the Treaty has operated so far in the system of government. Giving life to the Treaty guarantee of tino rangatiratanga also meant making space for tikanga Māori (the customary system of values and law embedded in Māori society) to develop.[46]

There is a desire also for more opportunities to use distinctive Māori methods of discussion and debate to resolve issues. There exists a long and honourable tradition of Māori organising through rūnanga (ad hoc assemblies called to discuss issues of concern). These use deliberative forms of decision-making, a method we are advocating for the whole process of adopting a written constitution (see chapters 16 and 18).

From what we have heard and read, Māori do not want to be regarded as a sub-group to be marginalised. There should be greater

---

45 Carwyn Jones 'A Constitution "Sourced in Two Streams"' (2 February 2017) Constitution Aotearoa NZ, available at <http://constitutionaotearoa.org.nz/the-conversation/Treaty-jones/>. See more generally Carwyn Jones *New Treaty, New Tradition: Reconciling New Zealand and Māori Law* (Victoria University Press, Wellington, 2016).

46 Richard Benton, Alex Frame and Paul Meredith *Te Mātāpunenga: A compendium of references to the concepts and institutions of Māori customary law* (Victoria University Press, Wellington, 2013).

scope for te ao Māori (the Māori world) to play an important role in the working of government and in the lives of Māori themselves. The energy and aspirations of the Māori culture need to be unlocked and looked at in a different way.

In seeking to reform New Zealand's constitutional arrangements, it is important to appreciate Māori have their own constitutional culture. Developing this culture within the wider confines of a national constitution is no simple undertaking. But it is possible and should be undertaken. The legal scholar Māmari Stephens has identified two key elements of Māori attitudes about civic decision-making and the exercise of power, and therefore of Māori constitutional culture, that could inform future constitutional developments:[47]

> First civic decision-making power ought to be exercised as a means of meeting collective obligation for civic ends. In other words this power ought to be carried out in the exercise of civic collectivism for the good of Māori beyond close kin groups, potentially for the benefit of many or even all Māori. Secondly, civic decision-making ought to be carried out in such a way that provides for substantive group participation and public input. If Māori participation cannot be provided for by way of gatherings or other methods of face-to-face participation, other mechanisms for substantive and direct Māori public input should be found, as occurred by way of Māori adoption of petitions to the Native Affairs Committee.

Some submissions we received asked us to stay away from Treaty issues, at least for the time being, so that Māori can have the conversation among themselves—and in a manner consistent with the approaches outlined by Dr Stephens above—about the Treaty's place in New Zealand's constitution.

Matike Mai Aotearoa: independent Māori constitutional working group

Within Māoridom detailed work on the constitution has been undertaken, in an elaborate project that has been going on a number of years and will continue into the future.

Matike Mai Aotearoa—The Independent Working Group on

---

[47] Māmari Stephens 'A Loving Excavation: Uncovering the Constitutional Culture of the Māori Demos' (2013) 25 NZULR 820 at 842.

Constitutional Transformation[48] was convened in 2010 by Professor Margaret Mutu and Moana Jackson. Between 2012 and 2015, the group held 252 hui, attracting 10,000 people. In 2016, the working group published *He Whakaaaro Here Whakaumau Mō Aotearoa*, a substantial report that has attracted significant support not only among Māori, but also in the wider community.

The working group did not try to fit Treaty rights or Māori constitutional approaches into the current Westminster system of government. Rather, it sought views 'on a different type of constitutionalism that is based on He Whakaputanga [also known as the 1835 Declaration of Independence] and Te Tiriti'. Their vision was not merely for constitutional change, but for transformation.[49]

One of the major outcomes of their hui was that participants wanted a constitution based on fundamental values. In the view of the report's authors, the emphasis on values reflected a desire for a 'more open' constitution based on 'a conciliatory and consensual democracy rather than an adversarial and majoritarian one'.[50]

The report emphasised that further discussion is needed to determine constitutional values, and only then can serious work begin on identifying any institutional changes that might follow. But it identified a number of possible values, as follows:[51]

(1) The value of tikanga—that is the need for a constitution to relate to or incorporate the core ideals and the 'ought to be' of living in Aotearoa.

(2) The value of community—that is the need for a constitution to facilitate the fair representation and good relationships between all peoples.

(3) The value of belonging—that is the need for a constitution to foster a sense of belonging for everyone in the community.

(4) The value of place—that is the need for a constitution to promote relationships with, and ensure the protection of

---

48 The Matike Mai Aotearoa website is: <www.converge.org.nz/pma/iwi.htm#med>.
49 Matike Mai Aotearoa—The Independent Working Group on Constitutional Transformation *He Whakaaaro Here Whakaumau Mō Aotearoa* (2016), available at <www.converge.org.nz/pma/iwi.htm#med>.
50 At 9.
51 At 69.

Papatūānuku.

(5) The value of balance—that is the need for a constitution to ensure respect for the authority of rangatiratanga and kāwanatanga within the different and relational spheres of influence.

(6) The value of conciliation—that is the need for a constitution to have an underlying jurisdictional base and a means of resolution to guarantee a conciliatory and consensual democracy.

(7) The value of structure—that is the need for a constitution to have structural conventions that promote basic democratic ideals of fair representation, openness and transparency.

The report also set out six 'indicative' models for constitutional change, based on the idea that the Treaty provided for distinct Māori and Crown spheres of influence. By 'indicative', the authors meant these were not recommendations—they were approaches that had emerged from their consultation, and 'simply indicate the range of possibilities that are available for those who really want a good faith honouring of Te Tiriti'. In setting out these models, the authors hoped to provide some options for future discussion, and recognised that much more work would be needed before any single model was considered for adoption.

The models are:[52]

(1) A tricameral or three-sphere model consisting of an iwi/hapū assembly (the rangatiratanga sphere), the Crown in Parliament (the kāwanatanga sphere) and a joint deliberative body (the relational sphere).

(2) A different three sphere model consisting of an assembly made up of iwi, hapū and other representation including Urban Māori Authorities (the rangatiratanga sphere), the Crown in Parliament (the kāwanatanga sphere) and a joint deliberative body (the relational sphere).

(3) A further three-sphere model consisting of an iwi/hapū assembly (the rangatiratanga sphere), the Crown in Parliament (the kāwanatanga sphere) and regional assemblies made up of iwi, hapū and Crown representatives (the relational sphere).

---

52 At 104–105.

(4) A multi-sphere model consisting of an assembly of iwi/hapū and other Māori representation (the rangatiratanga sphere) and the Crown in Parliament (the kāwanatanga sphere). It also includes a relational sphere which would have two parts—a constitutionally mandated set of direct iwi/hapū/Crown relationships to enable direct iwi/hapū–Crown decision-making plus a unitary perhaps annual assembly of broader Māori and Crown representation.

(5) A unicameral or one-sphere model consisting of iwi/hapū and the Crown making decisions together in a constitutionally mandated assembly. This model does not have rangatiratanga or kāwanatanga spheres. It only has the relational sphere.

(6) A bicameral model made up of an iwi/hapū assembly and the Crown in Parliament. This model has distinct rangatiratanga and kāwanatanga spheres but has no provision for a relational sphere.

Matike Mai Aotearoa does not yet have a final set of proposals. It seems that a Māori Constitutional Convention will be called in 2021 to further the discussion. Dialogue with the Crown is also planned. The 2016 report identified 2040, 200 years after the signing of the Treaty, as 'a good year to set as a goal for some form of constitutional transformation'.

We received quite a number of submissions saying that we should adopt the process outlined by Matike Mai Aotearoa. For example, the Te Tiriti Bi-cultural Committee of the New Zealand Association of Psychotherapists voiced its support for a constitutional transformation process along the lines set out in the working group's report.

Some of the people working on Matike Mai Aotearoa are opposed to our proposal to incorporate the Treaty into a superior law constitution. As we understand their concern, they see our approach as premature, and as prejudging the outcome of debates yet to be held. What we propose involves some big changes to New Zealand's constitutional arrangements, including a new Head of State, a superior law constitution, entrenched human rights, more power to the courts and much more. But it also retains much of what we have now; it remains a representative democracy with Cabinet government and a unicameral parliament. Our proposals do not amount to a transformation in the sense that Matike Mai Aotearoa seems likely to advocate.

At this stage it is difficult to see how the Matike Mai Aotearoa ideas might work in practice, simply because there is much more discussion to be completed before they are fully developed. It is also difficult at this stage to see how much political support the project might get among Māori leaders, politicians and non-Māori.

But we acknowledge the intention behind the project—to recognise that the Treaty provided the foundation for government in these islands and is therefore central to the design of any new constitutional arrangements.

Matike Mai Aotearoa is also an important piece of evidence that the status quo is unsustainable. There is a point at which the ideas it expresses, or even more challenging ones, will come onto the political agenda. We believe that it is preferable to begin the discussion before a crisis point is reached. Many of the ideas within the Matike Mai Aotearoa report are rich in conception. They deserve to be discussed to see what concrete proposals can emerge from them.

A modified proposal for dealing with the Treaty

For the many reasons discussed above, we believe that the approach we took in 2016 needs to be modified.

We continue to believe that the Treaty needs formal recognition in any new constitution, firstly because of its importance to New Zealand's constitutional arrangements and secondly in order to provide clarity and certainty. But we also acknowledge that our 2016 proposals did not necessarily achieve those objectives, and furthermore—if adopted without much more discussion to bridge the large gaps that currently exist—could have become a source of considerable tension. A constitution should express what unites us, not what sets us apart.

Our modified proposal seeks to achieve both goals—clarity and certainty, and proper recognition of the Treaty's legal and constitutional status—by new means.

To provide certainty and clarity about current law, Article 37 of our new Constitution for Aotearoa New Zealand specifically recognises and affirms the Treaty rights already in existence and for persons of Māori descent.

But recognising existing rights is not enough. Any new constitutional arrangements must reflect the Treaty's role as a founding document and source of legitimacy for government power. And they must also recognise the ongoing existence of rights and obligations (albeit unclear in ambit) derived from the Treaty under international law. Under current arrangements, these rights exist in the law but cannot be enforced except where they are explicitly provided for.

As we explained above, both our 2016 proposal and our new one inevitably transfer to the Courts responsibility for fleshing out the specific details of what the words of the Treaty mean in a modern context. The Courts have a long history of dealing with Treaty principles and rights in ways that are positive, have been absorbed smoothly into the broader legal and political context, and have not been costly. We believe the Courts could be trusted with further responsibilities in this regard in the future. But we are strongly of the view that, when it comes to fleshing out modern meaning for the Treaty in a constitutional context, a political process involving negotiation is also required. Only if the politicians cannot succeed will it be necessary to rely on our new provision—as a backstop. Securing greater clarity and certainty about the Treaty is an important aim.

The essence of our proposal, therefore, is that New Zealanders have a proper conversation on what the Treaty means now. That can be accomplished by having extensive and official dialogues with both Māori and other communities using the techniques of deliberative democracy detailed in chapter 16 and 18. The intricate issues could then be considered separately from the other constitutional issues contained in the draft. A thorough process that produces better community understanding could lead to greater clarity. Such a process is necessary if we are to put conflict behind us and provide a clear and certain path forward. So, our new approach is to commit to the Treaty and work out detailed provisions through a rigorous public deliberation process.

This option is put forward on the basis that a commitment to the Treaty is constitutionally necessary, but it will take significant effort to achieve clarity and certainty, and to find some kind of reasonable common ground among the many various views that currently exist. The process will be time-consuming and complicated, but it is worth undertaking in order to put an untidy situation behind us and start with an agreed position. Here is our revised text:

37 Te Tiriti o Waitangi/the Treaty of Waitangi

(1) The rights that persons of Māori descent enjoy at the commencement of this Constitution as Indigenous people under te Tiriti o Waitangi/the Treaty of Waitangi are hereby recognised and affirmed.

(2) On the commencement of this Constitution, all rights, duties and obligations of the Crown in right of New Zealand under the Treaty and under Treaty settlement agreements and related statutes vest in and are assumed by the State.

(3) Time and space need to be devoted to developing more precise content on what tino rangatiratanga and the other undertakings in the Treaty mean in the modern context and what express provision should be made in this Constitution to protect those interests with sufficient clarity and certainty.

(4) As soon as practicable after the commencement of this Constitution, Parliament must select a Panel of Distinguished Persons and Kaumātua to recommend to Parliament—
  (a) changes to this Constitution relating to te Tiriti o Waitangi/the Treaty of Waitangi; and
  (b) if the Panel thinks it appropriate, any other legislative or policy measures.

(5) The Government must provide support to conduct hui for Māori and the community as a whole, using rūnanga and other methods of deliberative democracy, to produce reports for consideration by the Panel.

(6) No later than seven years after the commencement of this Constitution, the Panel must present to Parliament a report that sets out the Panel's recommendations for adopting—
  (a) more express provision for te Tiriti o Waitangi/the Treaty of Waitangi in this Constitution; and
  (b) any other policy or legislative measures that the Panel considers appropriate.

(7) Parliament must, within 18 months of receiving the report of the Panel, consider it and determine—
  (a) the form and content of the required constitutional amendments (if any) that it considers are required; and
  (b) if the Panel has made other recommendations, whether those recommendations should be proceeded with.

(8) Any amendments to this Constitution to give effect to Article 37(7)(a) must follow the process for amendments set out in Article 110 [Entrenchment and Amendment].

38 The Waitangi Tribunal
(1) There continues to be a body known as the Waitangi Tribunal, which is provided for by an Act of Parliament.
(2) Where issues arise that relate to te Tiriti o Waitangi/the Treaty of Waitangi or that involve tikanga Māori, the Parliament, the courts, and tribunals have the power to request an opinion from the Waitangi Tribunal on those aspects of the matter.

It is important to note the language that Treaty rights are 'recognised and affirmed'. The same language is used in the Canadian Charter of Rights and Freedoms (section 35) which is superior law. The Canadian courts have drawn on that provision to uphold aboriginal interests and rights. Their jurisprudence is not radical. We believe that, in light of the provision that we have made for the panel of Distinguished Persons and Kaumātua, our courts will yield the ground to political processes—at least in the early days of Constitution Aotearoa—but will use Article 37(1) whenever Parliament or Government seek to unreasonably pare back current Treaty-based outcomes. That, in our view, is appropriate.

In our view it will take a substantial period and many meetings all around New Zealand to secure the necessary understanding to allow further constitutional progress to be made. But while the discussions need to be thorough and not hurried, they must be finished. Future generations can carry the conversation forward from the base established after the Panel has reported and Parliament has acted on its report.

Our current proposal has similarities to one made by the Royal Commission on the Electoral System in 1986. In discussing the history of Māori participation in the electoral system, and of Māori constitutional issues more broadly, including the Treaty of Waitangi, the Royal Commission concluded:[53]

> We are convinced [. . .] that it is time the questions were addressed in a comprehensive and systematic way. We recognise the effective

---

53 Royal Commission on the Electoral System 'Towards a Better Democracy' [1986–1987] IX AJHR H3 at 112.

protection of Maori rights and the appropriate recognition of the constitutional position of the Maori people will not be easy to resolve. But the issues will not become any easier as time passes, and we think it desirable to face the problems before their resolution becomes even more difficult. They will not be solved once and for all, and there will, in our view, need to be ongoing processes under which the issues can continue to be handled in the light of experience, and new solutions devised as new problems arise. We think it vital that there be a commitment by Parliament and Government to establish and coordinate mechanisms and processes which adequately recognise the constitutional position of the Māori people and which have the support of the Maori people themselves. It is particularly desirable that these mechanisms and processes have the support of all parties in Parliament, and that the Maori participants in any discussions are chosen on a widely-representative basis.

We have described here why we have changed our approach to Treaty and customary rights in the revised version of the proposed Constitution. There is no short way around the issues and they need to be faced. As Dr Carwyn Jones has observed, 'with no direct legal enforceability . . . the Treaty rights are always in a slightly precarious position.'[54]

Incorporating the Treaty in a superior law constitution will ensure that those rights cease to be in precarious position. But in order to accomplish this we need to go through a process that involves framing provisions that can be agreed on and are clearer than the present position. That is not a process that can be hurried, since the community engagement needs to be prolonged and thorough, and the product needs to be adopted into the Constitution.

While there is dispute about what Māori gave up in 1840, the present need is to concentrate on some principles applicable to life on these islands now that can endure into the future. Should the processes we propose reach no result, the Treaty under the provision we have drafted remains legally enforceable.

A multicultural society

Any improvement to the constitutional position of Māori should proceed on the understanding that New Zealand's population profile

---

54 Carwyn Jones, above n 45, at 13.

is changing rapidly. New Zealand is now one the most pluralistic and diverse societies on earth. A constitution has to protect the rights of everyone. Demography is transforming New Zealand and this will change many things about how we live. It will certainly impact New Zealand's sense of its own identity. The composition of the New Zealand population is changing quickly and the high level of shared values that used to be a feature of New Zealand is breaking down. Statistics New Zealand project the following ethnic populations by 2038:[55]

European or other:	3.43–3.82 million
Māori:	1.00–1.18 million
Asian:	1.06–1.26 million
Pacific:	0.54–0.65 million

Professor Paul Spoonley, a distinguished professor from Massey University, underlines the point:[56]

> In coming years, the European/Pakeha population will decline as a percentage of the total population. Maori will continue to grow in size but remain about the same percentage, while Pasifika communities will become a slightly larger part of the New Zealand community.
>
> But it is the Asian population that will grow the most. Already one-quarter of Aucklanders identify with an Asian ethnicity. These communities are growing three or four times faster than any other. By the mid-2020s, the Asian population of New Zealand will overtake the Maori population in size.

The consequences of such diversity mark a considerable departure from the traditional New Zealand, which had a population that

---

[55] Statistics New Zealand 'Ethnic Diversity projections to rise' (media release, 18 May 2017), available at <http://archive.stats.govt.nz/browse_for_stats/population/estimates_and_projections/NationalEthnicPopulationProjections_MR2013-2038.aspx>. For a developed analysis of the implications of these trends see Mai Chen *The Superdiversity Stocktake: Implications for Business, Government and New Zealand* (Superdiversity Centre, 3 November 2015). See also Mai Chen *Superdiversity, Democracy and New Zealand's Electoral and Referenda Laws* (Superdiversity Centre, 3 November 2015). In the wake of this work there has been established in Auckland the Superdiversity Centre for Law, Policy and Business. For Statistics New Zealand's projections, see Liz MacPherson 'National Ethnic Populations Projections: 2013(Base)–2038' (21 May 2015) Statistics New Zealand <www.stats.govt.nz>.

[56] Paul Spoonley 'Welcome to the new New Zealand' (14 November 2014) *Massey University* <www.massey.ac.nz>.

was largely European (mainly British) in origin with a substantial Māori minority. Our heterogeneity needs to be celebrated, but it also requires clear frameworks that do not rely on vague and old promises that are hard to apply in the modern world. Something concrete is required.

As New Zealand becomes more diverse, individual human rights will become more important. Those rights have to be elevated in order to be adequately protected and respected. Greater diversity requires greater tolerance and greater protection.

An entrenched Bill of Rights will assist with this—especially the provision that protects the rights of people from an ethnic, religious or linguistic minority to enjoy their culture, to profess and to practise their religion, or to use the language of that minority.

Conclusion

The state of knowledge on Treaty issues within the general community suggests to us that greater efforts need to be made to teach in our schools the complicated and fascinating history of New Zealand and particularly the clashes between the Crown and Māori during the New Zealand wars and the unjust land confiscations. Many of the injustices done during the colonisation of New Zealand and by the settler governments left a stain on the reputation of the country and a lingering sense, particularly in the minds of Māori, that justice requires a more comprehensive statement of Māori rights than presently exists. While modern New Zealand was not founded on slavery, it was to a considerable degree founded on systematic injustice concerning the acquisition of land and suppression of custom.

Breaches of human rights occurred in colonial times that could never be tolerated today. One egregious example will suffice: that of events at Parihaka, Taranaki, in 1881. This Māori village was a centre of non-violent and passive resistance to the land confiscation policies of the government. On 5 November 1881, the village was destroyed by 1600 government troops, while several thousand Māori sat quietly. Women were raped. The Parihaka leaders were arrested and detained without trial for 16 months. Here were blatant breaches of the rule of law and the right to a fair trial. The detentions could be authorised only by the rapid passage of oppressive statutes in clear violation of

The Treaty of Waitangi and the Constitution

the existing legal norms.[57] The detained people were then imprisoned in South Island jails far away from Taranaki. The Hon Christopher Finlayson, who tendered the government apology on 9 June 2017, described the events then as 'shameful'. Among other things he said:

> A few short years after guaranteeing to Māori the undisturbed possession of any lands they wished to retain, the Crown began systematically to dispossess the tangata whenua of Taranaki of their lands. By purchase deed, force of arms, confiscation and statute, the Crown took the rich lands of Taranaki and left its people impoverished, demoralised, and vilified. The Crown reiterates the apologies it has made to iwi of Taranaki for its many failures to uphold the principles of partnership and good faith that the Treaty of Waitangi embodies, and for the immense harm those actions have caused to generations of Māori in Taranaki.

The settlements of many grievances under the umbrella of the Treaty of Waitangi have gone some distance to remedy wrongs, but the issues also need to be considered from a constitutional point of view. Where issues remain, they must be resolved before progress can be made. We have not been good in the past in conducting the conversation on these matters: people get upset and tend to adopt extreme positions. The answer does not lie in extreme positions. It lies in tolerance, dialogue and understanding.

In her submission to us, Dr Judith Pryor drew our attention to an extract from a Waitangi Tribunal report which we think is worth repeating here:[58]

> unless it is accepted that New Zealand has two founding cultures,

---

57 The Maori Prisoner Trials Act 1879, The Confiscated Land Inquiry and Maori Prisoners Trials Act 1879, the Maori Prisoners Detention Act 1880 and the West Coast Preservation Act 1882. For the Crown's 2017 apology for these events and the campaigns that preceded them, see the remarks of the Hon Christopher Finlayson on 9 June 2017, available at <parihaka.maori.nz/reconciliation-ceremony-9th-june-2017>.
   Of even greater significance were the injustices that flowed on from the decision to send military forces to the Waikato even though no act had taken place that justified war. This action caused the Waikato War of 1863–1864. See Vincent O'Malley *The Great War for New Zealand: Waikato 1800–2000* (Bridget Williams Books, Wellington, 2016).
58 Waitangi Tribunal *Ko Aotearoa Tēnei: A report into claims concerning New Zealand laws and policies affecting Māori culture and identity* (Wai 262, 2011) at xviii.

not one; unless Māori culture and identity are valued in everything government says and does; and unless they are welcomed into the very centre of the way we do things in this country, nothing will change. Māori will continue to be perceived, and know they are perceived, as an alien and resented minority, a problem to be managed with a seemingly endless stream of taxpayer-funded programmes, but never solved.

We cannot ignore our history, neither can we change it. But we can acknowledge that history in shaping our shared future. We must come to terms with our history through a process of information, reflection and reconciliation. We are not governed by the dead hand of past events. Neither can we ignore the effects of those events in shaping our attitudes and approaches. For these are the things that have made us who and what we are. The relationship between the races in New Zealand will not be determined by the Treaty of Waitangi. It will be determined by the attitudes of individuals and by a collective sense of justice, fairness and tolerance. By facing up to these issues we will be stronger for it.

14 More people need to know how government works

New Zealanders have a low level of civic knowledge—knowledge about public affairs, the constitution, the primary institutions of government and the rights and duties of citizens—and do not necessarily see themselves as participants or engaged in their own governance. Most people concentrate on their jobs and day-to-day lives, which seldom directly intersect with government, politics, governance or public policy. Many people have neither the time nor the inclination to follow political and policy matters closely. They rely on their elected representatives to do it for them. They will take some interest at election time, and most will vote, but increasing numbers neither register nor vote. This is particularly the case for young people.

A number of demographic categories can be discerned:

(1) Political people comprising MPs, high party officials, elected local government officials, political commentators and media people. Party members who are active can be regarded as in this group.

(2) Government officials and employees in the wider state sector, many of whom work with ministers and Parliament in the development and execution of policy and who know intimately how the system of government works. Approximately 45,000 people are employed in the public service. About 13 per cent of the total New Zealand workforce is employed in the wider state sector: in Crown entities, the defence force, the education service, the police, universities, the health agencies and many others in such state-owned enterprises. Many of those further out from the centre will have limited knowledge and exposure to the development of policy and ministers.

(3) Pressure groups and lobby groups who take an interest in policy outcomes and actively work to urge and persuade governments to adopt particular policies. Business New Zealand, Manufacturing New Zealand and Federated Farmers are prime examples, but there are many others in the business arena. Other sectors of the economy, Māori

organisations and civil society spawn a large number of groups who wish to influence government policy. They often have significant and permanent organisations to monitor and interact with Government and parliamentary Select Committees. It is hard to estimate the number of people who belong to these organisations, but much of the influence lies in the hands of those who manage them.

(4) The general public who take a reasonable interest in public affairs and government decisions, but do not devote much time to issues and seldom become active or make representations to government. Many will have contact and connection with government agencies through education, the benefit system, the medical system and the criminal justice system.

(5) Members of the public who are not interested in the system of government except for a few specific issues that directly affect them. They will usually vote in general elections but that is often the extent of this group's civic involvement.

(6) Those members of the public who take little or no interest in the system of government, do not vote and tend to be turned off by anything involving the government and its machinery. They may be people who suffer significant deprivation and poverty. Day-to-day survival is their prime preoccupation and they have no time or resource for anything else.

Categories 1, 2 and 3 work closely with the current system and have experiential knowledge of how it works. The ability of category 3 to effect change is limited.

It is a fair conclusion to say that the vast bulk of the voting population falls into categories 4, 5 and 6 above. They have little contact with the development of public policy or the democratic system of governance in which Cabinet and Parliament sit at the apex.

Two recent government reviews of New Zealand's constitutional arrangements both reported that New Zealanders had scant understanding of how the system of government works.

In 2005, the Constitutional Arrangements Select Committee recommended that:[1]

---

1 Constitutional Arrangements Committee *Inquiry to review New Zealand's existing constitutional arrangements* (10 August 2005) at 5.

To foster greater understanding of our constitutional arrangements in the long term, increased effort should be made to improve civics and citizenship education in schools to provide young people with the knowledge needed to become responsible and engaged citizens.

In its response, the Government agreed that more should be done to continue to improve civics and citizenship education in schools, but nothing significant has occurred.

The 2013 report of the Constitutional Advisory Panel recommended that New Zealand develop a national strategy for civics and citizenship education in schools and in the community, including the unique role of te Tiriti o Waitangi/the Treaty of Waitangi, and assign responsibility for the implementation of the strategy.[2] They reviewed the available material for teaching the necessary elements and concluded that there was no strategic leadership in the field and there was a shortage of resources. They stated: 'It seems that the current fragmented approach means that no one agency or group of agencies has taken responsibility for ensuring that New Zealand citizens can easily access information about how our government operates and how to participate effectively.'[3]

While we have found in the *New Zealand Curriculum*[4] useful elements that relate to citizenship values, we nevertheless believe the document is far too broad and is noteworthy for steering clear of politics, Cabinet and Parliament.

Research by Katy Lang, based on 2008 data and published in 2010 by the Ministry of Education, concludes that New Zealand Year 9 student achievement on civics and citizenship knowledge is 'above the international average, although our performance was below a number of other OECD countries'.[5] We believe this is too optimistic a view. A report published by the McGuinness Institute in 2016, *Proceedings*

---

2 Constitutional Advisory Panel *New Zealand's Constitution: A Report on a Conversation, He Kotuinga Korero mo Te Kaupapa Ture o Aotearoa* (November 2013) at 98.
3 At 15.
4 'Social Sciences' *The New Zealand Curriculum Online*, see <http://nzcurriculum.tki.org.nz>.
5 See Kate Lang and Sharon Cox 'What do New Zealand students understand about civic knowledge and citizenship? Results from the International Civic and Citizenship Education Study' (Minsitry of Education, 2008), available at <www.educationcounts.govt.nz/__data/assets/pdf_file/0011/85871/What-do-NZ-Students-understand-about-civic-knowledge-and-citizenship.pdf>.

of the Civics and Media Project, a Report of three workshops held in 2015[6] provides a broader picture.

The official theory is that civic and citizenship education is a topic embedded in the principles, values and key competencies of the current curriculum. However, civics and citizenship and political literacy are not taught systematically. Citizenship education is a 'highly contested area of curriculum, teaching and learning.'[7] Teachers need more help and support with teaching materials to assist in this challenging area. Without a concerted effort in this regard, there is a risk our democracy will descend into apathy and non-participation through lack of knowledge, unfamiliarity and alienation.

We have both taught public law at university level for many years in New Zealand. We have been struck by how little even the second-year law students know about how they are governed. In 2017, Geoffrey Palmer asked his Advanced Public Law course at Victoria University what they had learned of civics, government and the constitution at school. The single student who had received such instruction received it in Australia. A leading constitutional lawyer in Canada, Emeritus Professor Peter Hogg, who attended Nelson College at the same time as Geoffrey Palmer, wrote: 'You will recall that we learned nothing about these matters at Nelson College or anywhere else until we were taught constitutional law by Colin Aikman and read Ivor Jennings excellent little book (which of course was about the UK).'[8] Such a state of affairs is insufficient to produce a thriving democracy. A constitution is not a document to be kept in a dark back-room, shrouded in obscurity. Neither should it be the sole preserve of lawyers, historians or political scientists. The person in the street should know the fundamentals. Political literacy is a necessary skill for survival in a democracy.

Change for civics education has not occurred in any meaningful

---

6 See 'Proceedings of the Civics and Media Project: A report on the three workshops held in 2015' (McGuiness Institute, May 2016), available at <www.mcguinnessinstitute.org/wp-content/uploads/2017/02/20170227-Civics-and-Media-Booklet-WEB.pdf>.
7 Bronwyn Hayward and Bronwyn E Wood 'Editorial' [2016] 3 Set (New Zealand Council for Educational Research, Special Issue: Civics, Citizenship and Literacy), at 1.
8 Email commenting on *A Constitution for Aotearoa New Zealand* from Peter Hogg to Geoffrey Palmer (17 August 2017).

or real sense. Nor has the issue resolved itself. The authors were worried by the misconceptions about our system of government that many people demonstrated at the public meetings we held around New Zealand. For example, a significant number of people at our meetings expressed the belief that if Parliament attempted to pass a law that might contravene human rights, or be otherwise 'bad law', the Governor-General as the Queen's representative in New Zealand would be honour-bound to refuse to give Royal Assent to the legislation and thus prevent it becoming law. This cannot occur. The Governor-General must act upon ministerial advice. So, when we discussed the *Atkinson* case at our public meetings (see chapter 12), very many people were genuinely shocked that the New Zealand Public Health and Disability Amendment Act 2013 could become law; they had wrongly believed either that it was not possible for Parliament to pass a law so blatantly contrary to human rights, or that the Governor-General could and should have refused to sign it into law. Clearly, such basic misconceptions as to how our democratic system works are not healthy.

And, of course, the concept of civics needs to be broader than merely learning about how the institutions of government work, important as that knowledge undoubtedly is. A group of New Zealand political scientists chaired by Associate Professor Bronwyn Hayward of the University of Canterbury have formed a group called 'Civics, Political Citizenship and Literacy'. Here is what their website defines as the three necessary ingredients:

What is Civics?
In political science, civics is used broadly to refer to the knowledge, skills and shared expectations of citizens who participate in, and sustain, democracies.

What is Citizenship?
It is both a legal status and lived experience. In legal terms citizenship is conferred on those in a community who hold rights to make claims and seek support from a community (the right to vote, to assemble, the right to access to education, health and social needs for example) and in turn have legal responsibilities to sustain and maintain that community, (through for example, paying taxes, obeying laws, voting and becoming informed).

However citizenship is also the outcome of lived experience, of being, belonging and participating in a community, in ways that support, maintain and enable a community to function effectively.

What is Political Literacy?
The ability to understand and interpret information about how and why community decisions are made (or not made), to support citizens to think critically, and make informed choices or take action where necessary, (often in cooperation with others), to advance particular concerns and interests, while also considering the possible consequences and impacts of these choices and actions for themselves and others.

We are convinced that all these elements are required to be taught in the education system in order to produce fully functioning citizens in a democracy. As one political scientist has concluded: 'Expanding the public's voice is essential to have a democratic polity and broadly improves the quality of governance. The dilemma for democracy is to embrace a more active public, while ensuring equality of political voice at the same time.'[9]

If we had a written constitution, public education on these topics would be much easier and would be likely to help dispel the levels of ignorance that exist. The point was powerfully made by a young university student, Peter McKenzie, in a blog on our project's website:[10]

> Another way we can support the development of such a culture is to implement comprehensive civic education in our schools. At the moment, most students are only taught about our political system during Year 9 and 10, after which it becomes voluntary in the form of 'Social Studies'. Students will spend the rest of their lives living within this system, and yet most are taught only the bare surface details of it. It seems only logical that we should expand this subject out to cover Years 11 to 13 as well, so that students can develop a comprehensive understanding of their place within our democracy.
>
> The way we teach civics must change as well. It is no longer good

---

9 Professor Russell J Dalton 'Is citizen participation actually good for democracy?' (25 August 2017) The London School of Economics and Political Science: British Politics and Policy, available at <http://blogs.lse.ac.uk/politicsandpolicy/is-citizen-participation-actually-good-for-democracy/>.
10 Peter McKenzie 'Why a constitution alone is not enough' (21 June 2017) Constitution Aotearoa NZ, available at <http://constitutionaotearoa.org.nz/the-conversation/constitution-alone-not-enough/>.

enough to simply sit our students down and lecture them about dusty figures from history, or old statutory relics. Instead we must embrace the new wave of experiential teaching, which encourages students to actively get involved.

It is not a requirement that people have to have any particular knowledge or skills in order to vote. Equality is a key feature of democracy. Every person's vote is worth the same as every other person, whether the person is part of the political elite or someone who knows nothing about politics or government. But basic knowledge about how the system works will enhance the capacity of voters to make informed decisions and also to understand the other elements of democracy. These include such important ingredients as the rule of law, Parliament, the Bill of Rights and the ability of people to secure attention from government when they need it. Civics, citizenship and political literacy can be powerful instruments over time to strengthen the democratic character of government in New Zealand, if combined with a constitution that allows for greater citizen participation and deliberation over important decisions. It is to be hoped that greater knowledge of the system of checks and balances which makes up our system of government will result in greater levels of public trust and legitimacy.

People can influence outcomes if they are well organised and persistent. Community activism has become more common. Barack Obama learned much of his politics as a community organiser in the city of Chicago. Community engagement can be an important way to promote change. As one British community activist in London puts it in a book he wrote recently on how to procure change:[11]

> Start with what makes you angry. If you want change, you need power. You build up power through relationships with other people based on common self-interests. You break the big problems you share down into specific issues-and then you're ready for action. Action is what turns people power into change.

Constitution Aotearoa has as an important educative function. A constitution will provide instant and accessible guidance on the elements of the system of public power and its institutions. It

---

11 Matthew Bolton *How to Resist: Turn Protest to Power* (Bloomsbury, London, 2017) at 77.

will educate people and public decision-makers on their rights and responsibilities. A new constitution should help people participate in democratic decision-making and provide a better framework for learning about civics, citizenship and political literacy. More importantly, it will help people not born here to understand New Zealand's system of government, and this is a significant need given the increasing ethnic and cultural diversity of New Zealand society. Such a constitution, and the discussion that will necessarily precede its adoption, may also help to dispel disenchantment with politics and government.

15 Elections are not enough

While elections are vitally important in a democracy, they are by themselves not sufficient to ensure that democracy functions effectively. There are values that can be lost easily unless further steps are taken. While the mixed-member proportional electoral system (known as MMP) functions well, in our view, there are some disturbing trends. Voter turnout has been declining and at the last election was slightly less than 80 per cent of those who were enrolled[1]—and, of course, even though enrolment is compulsory in New Zealand, the reality is that many people do not enrol. We are particularly concerned about the numbers of young people who are not involved in voting. For this reason we have decided that the voter age should be lowered and voting made compulsory, as set out in this chapter. We also argue there should be more transparency surrounding political donations to political parties and increased regulation of the rules that political parties function under. We have not engaged with the technical details of the existing MMP system and changes that could be made to it, nor have we discussed the Māori seats.

The 2017 election and MMP

In the submissions we received from the public it was noteworthy that there was little, if any, opposition to MMP, which began to function in 1996. Yet there was a flurry of discontent in the media about the operation of MMP following the 2017 election. This was because although the National Party secured 44.4 per cent of the vote (the highest proportion), the party is not in government. While we have had MMP since 1996, there remains strong elements of first-past-the-post (FPP) thinking in New Zealand. What needs to be appreciated is that numbers matter. Government has to be able to command a majority in Parliament on confidence and supply. The National Party could not do so after the election because New Zealand First would not support National but preferred Labour to lead the Government. The Green Party would not support National either. National's previous

---

1 'Voter Turnout Statistics' *NZ Electoral Commission* see <www.elections.org.nz/events/2017-general-election/2017-general-election-results/voter-turnout-statistics>.

support parties, the Māori Party and United Future, were wiped out in the election. What we know about MMP is that while in theory it can deliver a majority government to one party, it does not do so in practice. To suggest that National has been hard done by flows from a misunderstanding about how proportional representation works. It is not flawed, as critics allege; it is democratic. But to form the Government under MMP, you need more than 50 per cent support for you and your allies. This the National Party did not achieve.[2]

In the proportional representation system of MMP, the seats in Parliament result from the share of the party vote secured. But unless 5 per cent of the vote is secured there is no representation, unless a candidate wins an electorate seat. Each elector has two votes, one for the party and one for an electorate member. The key element in the new Parliament is that National, despite its electoral result, cannot command a majority in the House of Representatives on confidence and supply, and thus cannot lead the Government. The majority rules, and such is what democracy requires. The system is still not well understood in some quarters despite the fact that the first election occurred under it in 1996 and there have since been seven elections. This would support the case we make elsewhere in this book: better public civic education is needed.

There is no constitutional convention, rule or expectation that the party with the largest number of seats must lead the Government; there is no 'moral authority' to govern. To do so, a Government must be able to command a majority in the Parliament on confidence and supply. Some have argued that the negotiations should first have been conducted with the National Party and only after they failed should negotiations with Labour have begun. There is no rule about this either. These negotiations have been going on at every election from, and including that of, 1996. New Zealand has, over the years, developed its own way of doing things when it comes to forming a government after an MMP election which is quite different from the previous FPP system. The majority rules, and that is what democracy

2 Nor is this phenomenon unique to New Zealand. Germany held federal elections in 2017 under the MMP system a week later than New Zealand. Even though her party, the Christian Democratic Union, received the largest percentage of the vote, Chancellor Angela Merkel had by the conclusion of 2017 been unable to get sufficient parliamentary support to get over 50 per cent support in the Bundestag.

requires. Some people thought it was not fair that New Zealand First should have a share of the Government since they polled only 7.2 per cent of the vote. This overlooks the fundamental feature of MMP: the Government must be able to command a majority in the Parliament on confidence and supply. Indeed, this has always been true, but it was usually achieved in general elections automatically under the FPP electoral system. As Brenda Midson wrote in an editorial recently published in the New Zealand Law Journal:[3]

> National received 44.4 per cent of the party votes. In other words, 55.6 per cent of voters did not want National to govern. It does not matter that those voters did not all vote for the same party—in fact, the very purpose of MMP is to allow for smaller interests to be represented ... the representation of smaller interests does not mean that the minority rules (which is not to say that this would always be a bad thing)—it is just that the majority is not a homogenous group (in the sense of being made up of people who all vote the same way).

The 1986 Royal Commission's persuasive report was an important factor in the promotion of change. It concluded the old FPP system was unfair but there were other factors at work too.[4] The adoption of the new system can also be attributed in part to a wish for more responsive government and better representation. Massive government changes to the organisation of the economy, made between 1984 and 1992 and led by both Labour and National, undoubtedly contributed to the mood for change as well. There was a sense of betrayal in the electorate; that the economic changes were too quick, too hurtful and too market-oriented. The referenda indicated a lack of trust in the two main political parties who had pursued economic policies they thought were necessary at the time for the health of the country. The change in the electoral system offered the opportunity for broader representation than had been achieved by the two big parties, with their declining mass memberships. The previously close connection between the two main political parties and the people was beginning to fray.

Another interpretation of the adoption of MMP was the idea that

---

3 Brenda Midson 'Democracy, MMP, and the mandate to govern—a brief refresher' [2017] NZLJ 343.
4 Royal Commission on the Electoral System 'Towards a Better Democracy' [1986–1987] IX AJHR H3.

the electorate was tired of powerful executive government that did not heed their desires sufficiently. Given that New Zealand has only a small single house in its Parliament, there were insufficient checks and balances against unbridled executive power. In New Zealand the executive used to control virtually everything that Parliament did; not what it said, perhaps, but certainly what was decided there. MMP put the brakes on the system, to a degree, because the chance of one party securing a majority alone under the new electoral system was remote.

The new electoral system was one of the most important changes in New Zealand's constitutional history;[5] MMP altered the political incentives. The old two-party duopoly was broken.[6] It is highly unlikely, now, that single party majority governments can be formed. Thus confidence and supply agreements or coalitions, or both, are necessary to secure a government under MMP. Representation in the House of Representatives is proportional to the percentage of the party vote that a political party received at the polls. The MMP system has, to a degree, caused the legislative process to slow down while the Government searches for the numbers to pass measures. Inter-party negotiations are the norm on many occasions. Majority support in the House of Representatives is necessary for legislation, taxation and appropriation. Strangely, however, the capacity of Cabinet to secure its will has not been impaired nearly as much as was predicted.[7]

The surprising feature about the introduction of MMP is not how much Cabinet government has changed, but how little. The co-ordinating and controlling role of Cabinet in New Zealand has not been diminished to any appreciable degree. Cabinet makes the decisions. What has changed is the style of management and the development of techniques to deal with coalition and confidence and supply agreements. The need to hunt for support for the introduction

---

5   For an in-depth look at how the New Zealand electoral system has changed over time, see the comprehensive history: Neil Atkinson *Adventures in Democracy: A History of the Vote in New Zealand* (University of Otago Press in Association with the Electoral Commission, Dunedin, 2003).
6   The adoption of MMP certainly caused a proliferation of political parties to develop. There were seven parties represented in the Parliament from 2014–2017. From 2017, the number has dropped to five.
7   Geoffrey Palmer 'The Cabinet, the Prime Minister and the Constitution' (2006) 4 NZJPIL 1.

and passage of Government Bills to the House is a big change.

The effect of MMP on Cabinet government has been to blunt the hard edge of Cabinet decision-making by adding into the mix increased amounts of political policy pluralism. Power has to be shared more than it used to be. There is more representation of diverse policy views within the Cabinet decision-making system, and politicians of different outlooks and philosophies have had to work together more. The primacy of Cabinet and its processes remain under MMP, but their dominance is reduced and there is room for more flowers to bloom. The Prime Minister and their Cabinet colleagues have to convince more than their own party in order to produce change. Particularly noteworthy, compared with the classical Westminster model, has been the loss of complete control over legislative outcomes. Cabinet no longer controls the fate of Government Bills, although it remains the most significant actor in the legislative process of Parliament.

While MMP has reduced, to some extent, the capacity of the Government to control and dictate to the Parliament, it has also enhanced and added to the powers of the Prime Minister because the Prime Minister must manage the agreements that keep the Government in office. The power of the Prime Minister has been increasing incrementally in all Westminster democracies since the Second World War, as government has become more intricate and multi-faceted. In many ways the system is much more presidential in style than it used to be, and this is partly a result of television and new social media.

The House of Representatives itself, however, is much more diverse in its representation than it was formerly. More women, more Māori, more ethnic minorities and more political ideologies are on offer—generally the House is much more representative of the population. The legitimacy and representational aspects of the House must be judged to have improved greatly. Yet connection to the voters and the level of public engagement with politics is still a problem.

Party discipline in the New Zealand Parliament has traditionally been very strong. Elected members seldom vote against the party position agreed in the Caucus room and enforced by the Whips. This feature, when New Zealand had an FPP system, made New Zealand resemble what Lord Hailsham called 'an elective dictatorship'.[8]

But outside the Caucus room and Parliament there has been a more deeply concerning development relating to our political parties: membership decline. Professor Raymond Miller writes of New Zealand political parties: 'Whereas one in four voters once belonged to a political party, today it is closer to two in a hundred.'[9] It has been estimated by political scientists that, in 1954, 290,000 New Zealanders belonged to political parties, of which there were essentially only two: National and Labour. This amounted to 26.4 per cent of the votes cast at the general election. By 1984 that was down to 170,000, or 8.8 per cent of the votes cast; by 2002 they estimated it to be 50,000, or 2.4 per cent of the votes cast.[10] Now it is probably considerably lower. These days parties are dominated by political elites to a much greater degree. Effective control of the parties is in the hands of a very few people. This is what the German political scientist Michels in 1915 called 'the iron law of oligarchy'.[11] It is for these reasons that political parties cannot be regarded as the faithful carriers of the public interest and require greater regulations.

Despite this decline in membership, National and Labour remain the two main political parties in terms of voting behaviour in recent elections. But, to a large extent, they are now both cadre parties rather than political parties with a mass membership base. That is to say, they are dominated by an elite group of political activists. This has consequences for citizen engagement with the machinery of government and governance. Fewer people have an involvement with the issues that concern political parties and they feel less connection with the system.

There has been another consequence to MMP. In times gone by, election manifestos were pored over by the public at election time. National and Labour put up competing programmes and the

---

8 Lord Hailsham *The Dilemma of Democracy: Diagnosis and Prescription* (Collins, London, 1978) at 9. He was writing of the British Constitution.
9 Raymond Miller *Democracy in New Zealand* (Auckland University Press, Auckland, 2015) at 175.
10 Ian Marsh and Raymond Miller *Democratic Decline and Democratic Renewal: Political change in Britain, Australia and New Zealand* (Cambridge University Press, Cambridge, 2012) at 228.
11 J Blondel *Political Parties: A Genuine Case for Discontent?* (Wildwood House, London, 1978) at 11.

electorate judged between them at election time. These specific policy promises tended to be regarded as a binding 'mandate'—that is to say, parties felt obliged to follow through on those commitments if they were elected Government.[12] Professor KJ Scott wrote in 1962:[13]

> We can now state the current conventions. Save in emergency, legislative powers should be used only in accordance with the government party's election platform. As each party has a broad platform, this allows a good deal of latitude. The principle on which the limitation rests is that the New Zealand system of government is in one of its aspects a system of representative government in the sense that the electors choose not only between rival candidates but also between rival sets of policies.

How the political world has changed with MMP. Such a convention, which was never complete because of the unpredictability of events, has now been destroyed. Even the larger parties' policy pledges cannot necessarily be delivered upon.

The Government does not have an automatic majority in the House. So, the process of policy bargaining that takes place after an election as part of the Government formation process can cancel some policies out at the beginning of an administration and rule others in. This, in turn, means that voters have less ability to predict the policy effects of their voting in advance of the election or indeed after it. And since many policy negotiations take place in secret, there is a certain level of disengagement, and in some ways less accountability, than under the older system. The key point is that the Government now often struggles to claim its actions have democratic legitimacy, as clear policy mandates no longer exist.

The 2017 election campaign was an illustration of policy pluralism arising from elections. Parties inside Parliament and some outside made numerous specific policy promises. One might think the voters would have difficulty gaining any coherent idea of what would happen after the election. Many of these policies appear to have been generated quickly in order to garner electoral support. They were advanced to show what each party thought should be the priority issues.

12 Richard Mulgan *Politics in New Zealand* (2nd ed, Auckland University Press, Auckland, 1997) at 257.
13 KJ Scott *The New Zealand Constitution* (The Clarendon Press, Oxford, 1962) at 51.

What was interesting in 2017 was how the three political parties that now make up the Government—Labour, New Zealand First, and the Greens—developed an extensive set of policy undertakings during their negotiations based on their respective campaign promises. This has provided an ample policy programme that will be sufficient for a full parliamentary term. The publicly announced policy agreements give a good indication of the policy direction of the Government and this was encapsulated in the Speech from the Throne in November 2017.[14]

Evidence-based policy can easily suffer in such a policy environment. Bad decisions can be made and bedded in. When it comes to the hard business of governing after the election it is likely that special interests could have increased influence to advance their causes, given that securing support within the MMP Parliament cannot be guaranteed, as once it was. To some degree, MMP has increased the lottery aspect of policy choice after the election. This makes imperative a strengthened system of working through the detail afterwards in an open and consultative manner, as is required by some features of the proposed Constitution.

The task of political leadership under MMP remains clear. The Government's policies have to be carefully framed and have broad appeal. They must be communicated well to the public. The public needs to be involved in the policy discussion. The Parliament must consider policy and legislative proposals put to it by the Government carefully and rigorously. Every effort must be made to unite the country around the direction that has been chosen.

Turnout, voting and young people

One indication of voter disenchantment lies in low rates of voting in general elections. There has been a steady decline in voter turnout in New Zealand general elections since the mid-1980s. The voices of those who do not vote are not heard. In 2014, the official turnout

---

14 New Zealand Labour Party 'Coalition agreement NZ First and Labour' (press release, 24 October 2017); Green Party 'Greens sign agreement to govern based on shared values' (press release, 24 October 2017); and Rt Hon Dame Patsy Reddy, Governor General of New Zealand 'Speech from the Throne' (State Opening of Parliament, Wellington, 8 November 2017).

Elections are not enough

was 76.2 per cent; up from 74.2 per cent in 2011.[15] In 2017, it was up to almost 80 per cent. The 2011 turnout was the lowest since 1887. The real turnout rate is worse because of the failure of many to enrol as voters. While it is legally required that voters enrol, the law is not enforced as a practical matter. It has been reported that no one has been prosecuted for non-enrolment in respect of the 2008, 2011 and 2014 elections.[16]

Professor of Comparative Politics at Victoria University of Wellington Jack Vowles, and others, have analysed the trends closely and report that about a third of the increase in 2014 over 2011 is illusory, because in 2014 the enrolment rate was down by just over 1 per cent.[17] The increase in 2017 compared with 2014 can similarly be deflated when taking lower enrolment into account, but only by a very small amount. This means the level of voting is overstated. The persistent gap is largely contributed to by the group aged between 18 and 29 and ethnic minorities. Young men are less likely to vote than young women. These trends suggest to us that the case for compulsory voting in New Zealand is a strong one. Turnout will go up, the views of the whole community will be better represented in an MMP Parliament, and political parties will have an incentive to adopt policies that appeal to the entire community. We do not want to get to the point in New Zealand when political parties decide to make it harder to become registered to vote and also actually to vote, as the Republican Party has been doing in the United States for some years. There are connections, in the view of Vowles and his co-authors, about rising inequality and voter turnout. Whether there is progressive disempowerment in the electoral system of those on low incomes remains an issue to be nailed down. In the outpouring of literature in the United Kingdom following Brexit, there have been calls to improve the nature and quality of British democracy. Professor AC Grayling has argued that not only is a written constitution required there but also that:[18]

---

15 Jack Vowles, Hilda Coffé and Jennifer Curtin *A Bark but No Bite* (ANU Press, Canberra, 2017) at 242–280.
16 Catrina Williams 'Commission votes not to prosecute' *The Dominion Post* (6 September 2017).
17 Vowles and others, above, n 15, at 245.
18 AC Grayling *Democracy and Its Crisis* (Oneworld, London, 2017) at 187.

Voting should be compulsory for all citizens, and the voting age should be sixteen. Civic education on the political and governmental system should be obligatory in schools for pupils aged fourteen and above.

Lowering the voting age

In submissions on our original proposals, there were strong arguments for lowering the voting age in New Zealand from 18 to 16. We considered these submissions carefully and have concluded there is real merit in them. Accordingly, we have changed our proposed Constitution.

We had a very helpful submission from Victoria University of Wellington student Hai Xin Huang, who also wrote a blog on the topic, available on our website, and we have relied heavily on this for what we have said below.[19] Hai Xin argued that there is a strong case for lowering the voting age to 16:

> The fundamental importance of voting rights in a democratic country means that they should be widely enjoyed by citizens. Just as the voting age was lowered from 21 to 20 in 1969, and then to 18 in 1974, it might be appropriate in the present time to lower it to 16. This concept of adaptability in the law to respond to changing demographics lends strong support for lowering the voting age, in addition to the ideal of consistency in the law in its treatment of rights.

One argument for lowering the voting age to 16 is simple consistency with the other rights and responsibilities that are conferred at the same age: for example, the age for leaving school, paying tax, consenting to sex and marriage, and obtaining driving and gun licences.[20] The fact that 16-year-olds have these rights and responsibilities indicates that, in the eyes of the law, they are considered able to make responsible and rational choices.[21] Surely voting rights in a democratic country are fundamental.

However, those against lowering the voting age raise concerns about

---

19 Hai Xin Huang 'A lower voting age would be fairer and more consistent' (3 August 2017) Constitution Aotearoa NZ, available at < http://constitutionaotearoa.org.nz/the-conversation/voting-age-hai-xin/>.
20 Community Law Manual Online 'Legal ages: when you can do what' Community Law <www.communitylaw.org.nz/community-law-manual/chapter-9-youth-rights/legal-ages-when-you-can-do-what-chapter-9>.
21 Alex Folkes 'The Case for Votes at 16' (2004) 41(1) Representation 52 at 53.

the lack of political maturity of young voters, referring to a lack of political interest and knowledge, which might lead to an uninformed vote choice.[22] There is little New Zealand research on such topics, but overseas surveys indicate otherwise. For example, a survey carried out during the 2014 Scottish independence referendum found that 16- to 17-year-olds showed similar political interest as adults, used a variety of information sources and engaged in extensive discussions with family and friends.[23] Austrian survey results also showed no significant difference in political interest between 16- to 17-year-olds compared with older first-time voters in general elections.[24]

Naturally, the rate at which political maturity develops varies from individual to individual. Lowering the voting age to 16 would enable politically mature 16- to 17-year-olds to fully participate in the democratic process. For those slower to develop political maturity, the experience of voting should help.

Lowering the voting age to 16 has the potential to reverse the trend of low youth participation and improve overall participation. Helena Catt, former Chief Executive of the Electoral Commission, argues that 'the most likely way to stop the decline in adult political participation is for students to acquire the habit at school'.[25] This raises the importance of better civics education, which is the topic of another chapter.

Compulsory voting

Compulsory voting rests on similar arguments concerning democratic engagement and participation. The Elections Singapore website

---

22 Eva Zeglovits and Julian Aichholzer 'Are People More Inclined to Vote at 16 than at 18? Evidence for the First-Time Voting Boost Among 16- to 25-Year-Olds in Austria' (2014) 24(3) Journal of Elections, Public Opinion and Parties 351 at 353.
23 Jan Eichhorn and others 'Young people's attitudes on Scottish Independence' (Research project funded by the Economic and Social Research Council, University of Edinburgh, 2014).
24 Zeglovits and Aichholzer, above n 22, at 253.
25 Helena Catt and Peter Northcote 'Prompting participation: can a personalised message to the newly enrolled have an impact on turnout?' (paper presented to the Australasian Political Studies Association Conference, University of Newcastle, September 2006) at 10.

contains this strong statement:[26]

> Voting is compulsory in Singapore as it is as much a fundamental right of citizenship as it is a civic responsibility to be exercised by citizens to choose and elect their leaders in a democracy. All Singapore citizens whose names are in the registers of electors have to cast their votes on Polling Day.

It is also compulsory to vote in Australian federal elections and has been since 1924. Section 245 of the Commonwealth Electoral Act 1918 provides: 'It shall be the duty of every elector to vote at each election.' Small fines are imposed for breach of the law. When compulsory voting was introduced at the federal level in 1924 the turnout went up from 50–60 per cent of registered voters to over 90 per cent, where it has remained.[27] The Australian law does not compel a person to vote. It compels the voter to turn up at the booth, but she can spoil her vote and vote informal. Thus, in Australia it amounts to a compulsory attendance law.[28] Belgium has the oldest compulsory voting law, introduced in 1892, even before universal suffrage. Argentina, Brazil and Chile all have what are known as compulsory voting laws. Indeed, the research shows that a total of 25 countries, inhabited by more than 700 million people, have them.[29]

Elections are about candidates and policy choices. In a democracy everyone 'must have equal and effective opportunities for making their views known to the other members as to what the policy should be'.[30] Compulsory voting ensures the results are a better reflection of what the views of the people are.

The arguments against compulsory voting are based on personal freedom. While people are entitled to vote they should not be obliged

---

26 'What Should I Do If I Did Not Vote in a Past Election?' *Singapore Elections Department* (24 May 2017), available at <www.eld.gov.sg/voters_compulsory.html>.
27 Lisa Hill 'Compulsory voting, much like democracy, beats alternatives' *The Conversation* (online ed, 29 January 2015), available at <https://theconversation.com/compulsory-voting-much-like-democracy-beats-the-alternatives-34765>.
28 George Williams, Sean Brennan and Andrew Lynch *Australian Constitutional Law and Theory: Commentary and Materials* (The Federation Press, Sydney, 2014) at 656–664.
29 Bart Engelen 'Why Compulsory Voting Can Enhance Democracy' (2007) 42 Acta Politica 23, at 26.
30 RA Dahl *On Democracy* (Yale University Press, New Haven, 1998) at 37.

to do so. They should have freedom, for whatever reason, not to vote. They may have any variety of reasons for their preference and they ought not to be required by the law to do something they do not want to do. If one has freedom to choose whom to vote for, one should have the freedom not to choose. For example, a voter may not like any of the candidates or parties on offer at the election.

In our view, while the libertarian argument has merit, this issue is one of those where the public benefit outweighs the personal detriment. Habits are important to participation; and socially created and sustained habits sustain a sense of community and ownership. This sense is at the heart of a thriving democracy, and so turnout is important. In the extensive political science literature on the subject, it is uncontested that compulsory voting raises the turnout, which has been decreasing in most western countries for some years, including New Zealand. We already have in New Zealand compulsory registration to be on the electoral roll. How can we logically insist on one and not the other? Indeed, the research shows that even in those countries that have compulsory voting which is not actively enforced, the existence of such laws encourages compliance. Italy and Turkey are such countries.

Voter turnout is fundamental to democratic legitimacy. If no one voted at a New Zealand general election, democracy would become unworkable. The more people who do not vote, the less representative the result of the election becomes, and the less legitimacy that decisions taken by the system will enjoy. Low turnout suggests democracy in trouble. Raising the turnout at elections minimises social and economic inequalities in electoral participation. This means the interests of all citizens, including the less privileged ones, are registering in the electoral system.

The argument that it is wrong to compel people to attend the polling station does not hold water. In a democratic society citizens have obligations too. Surely asking them to vote once every three or four years, thereby giving them a say in the system of government, is not too much to ask. One duty of living in a democratic society is to support democracy by participating in the making of democratic choices. It can be seen as a measure that strengthens the system of government and enhances the legitimacy of the decisions that are taken. People who wish to abstain can cast an informal ballot and that in itself will be a political message. People who stay away from the polls do so for many different reasons, however, and it is hard to infer any general motive for it. It would also be possible to add on the ballot paper a choice for 'none of the above'. This would cater to those voters who cannot find a candidate or party they support.

The danger with low turnouts is that it will lead to voting only by those with strong or even extreme political views. Moderation and a check on extremism and polarisation is likely to result from compulsory voting. The nature of the New Zealand MMP electoral system, in which the character of the government is highly sensitive to voter preferences, makes the argument even stronger.[31]

It is interesting to note that three recent New Zealand Prime Ministers support compulsory voting in New Zealand.[32] This would indicate their desire to promote health in the democratic system. We are convinced by these arguments and we have included in the Constitution a provision stating that it is the duty of every person who is eligible to register and to vote at each parliamentary election. As in Australia, such a provision means the voter would have to turn up the voting place and have their name marked off, but could indicate disapproval at the electoral offering by casting an informal vote.

Elections and money

Funding for political parties tends now to be sourced from corporations, trade unions and wealthy individuals, rather than from mass party membership, which no longer exists. In such a situation there are risks that the voices of ordinary people will be drowned out by corporate and business interests. Serious issues also exist about funding that derives from foreign sources.

The manner in which the funding of political parties by business has developed in the United States has much to do with the present state of political discontent in that country.[33] The decision is

---

31 Anthoula Malkopoulou *The History of Compulsory Voting in Europe: Democracy's Duty?* (Routledge, London, 2015).
32 Craig McCulloch 'Former PMs support compulsory voting in NZ' *RNZ* (online ed, 7 April 2017), available at <www.radionz.co.nz/news/political/328358/former-pms-support-compulsory-voting-in-nz>; see also Guyon Espiner and Tim Watkin *The 9th Floor: Conversations with five New Zealand Prime Ministers* (Bridget Williams Books and Radio New Zealand, Wellington, 2017).
33 *Citizens United v Federal Election Commission* (2010) 558 US 310.

anchored in the idea that freedom of expression must be protected. It has been interpreted to allow corporations and wealthy individuals to spend unlimited amounts of money on election campaigns. It has encouraged a most unhealthy relationship between members of Congress and donor corporations. Whether this is the case in reality, the general perception is that there is a quid-pro-quo arrangement involved. The development results in unrestricted outside spending on political campaigns, by corporations and very rich individuals alike. This is at a time when wealth and income disparities in the United States are at high levels. The undemocratic character of this development is obvious and is to be avoided.

Following the constitutional shambles in the United Kingdom that was Brexit, Professor AC Grayling has argued that '[t]here should be complete transparency about which individuals and organizations are involved in election campaigning, on what basis and by what methods'.[34]

New Zealand law regulates political party funding to some extent, attempts to limit the expenditure of money on elections, and purports to require transparency in political donations. There are ways to avoid many of these requirements.[35] In the 2017 general election, a party's election expenses during the regulated period, which was from 23 June until 22 September, could not exceed $1,115,000 including GST. The limit was adjusted up $26,200 for every electorate seat contested by the party. The main expenses parties incur relate to advertising and other promotional material. The cost of opinion polling is not included. Donations to political parties must be reported to the Electoral Commission and donations of more than $15,000 are required to be declared in the party's annual return of donations and names declared for donations above that amount. Parties cannot retain anonymous donations exceeding $1500. Parties are not permitted to retain donations of more than $1500 made by overseas persons or corporations.

Separate limits are also imposed on expenditure in electorates

34 Grayling, above n 18, at 187.
35 Andrew Geddis *Electoral Law in New Zealand: Practice and Policy* (2nd ed, LexisNexis NZ, Wellington, 2013). This book contains an excellent analysis of the extensive system of law regulating the conduct of elections in New Zealand and criticism of the adequacy of that law. It is a complex and extensive body of law that cannot be dealt with in detail in this book.

in New Zealand. Expenses for a candidate in an electorate seat for 2017 during the regulated period (23 June to 22 September) must not exceed $26,200 including GST. It is an offence to spend more than this. Political parties represented in Parliament also receive an element of state funding for their activities. For example, the state pays the salaries of MPs, their travel costs and their staff support.

Furthermore, broadcasting facilities were made available to the parties free of charge for many years. This was altered for the 2017 election onwards by the Broadcasting (Election Programmes and Elections Advertising) Amendment Act 2017. The effect of the measure was summarised by the Associate Minister of Justice Hon Mark Mitchell:[36]

> The Bill will modernise some election broadcasting rules to give political parties more flexibility. It removes the requirements for parties' opening and closing addresses, and for Television New Zealand and Radio New Zealand to provide free time for these. These were an outdated format, and it is important that resources made available for political parties to engage with the public at election time can be used as effectively and efficiently as possible. The bill allows parties to advertise more flexibly by enabling them to use their funding allocations under the Broadcasting Act for internet advertising. It is particularly important, in light of declining voter participation, that political parties can engage effectively with the public in the most relevant media.

Public money was appropriated by Parliament for the purpose. There are arguments that more state funding would avoid the impression that elections may be influenced by which party has the most money. There are also arguments that once a party secures parliamentary representation it is advantaged in staying there compared with a party that has no such representation due to the funding arrangements available to incumbent MPs in Parliament. There is a strong case for tightening the donation and spending law for elections in New Zealand.

Professor Andrew Geddis's book finds there are serious gaps in the law when it comes to regulating party funding and disclosure of donations. He concludes 'this disclosure regime is so riddled with

---

36 (15 March 2017) 720 NZPD 16700.

loopholes as to operate on a virtually voluntary basis; any donor who wished to keep her or his identity secret could do so easily and completely legally.'[37] The rules are easy to evade. Limits on election expenses imposed by the law have defects in them as well. Yet those who decide on the content of the law are MPs who have more direct interest in the issue than in almost every other matter they legislate on. As Dr Gareth Morgan and his party highlighted in the 2017 election campaign, the disparity in support between political parties represented in Parliament and those who lack such representation is marked. Morgan, who is wealthy, financed much of his party's campaign, as did Colin Craig for the Conservative Party campaign in 2014. In our view the case is reasonably strong for having the rules on these matters set by an independent organisation, such as the Electoral Commission, to avoid partisan political advantage.

We also think the law should require political parties to publicly report their membership numbers periodically so that the public can know to what extent they speak for many, and how extensive their support is. It would also be transparent to require parties to report publicly on their finances and these should be available for public inspection.

There is a strong case for changing the law so limits on expenditure extend throughout the electoral cycle. Non-citizens and businesses not registered in New Zealand should not be permitted to donate money. Individual donations below $5000 could be given tax credits and matched by state funding to encourage small donors. A basic level of state funding should also be available to support party organisations outside Parliament. It may be a good idea to provide all parties in Parliament with funds to commission their own regular polling, focus groups and consultants, or at least bring the costs of polling into campaign expenditure limits.

In many parts of the world political parties are corrupt. Transparency International reports that they are the most corrupt institutions internationally, as found by their surveys.[38] Many of them, even in Europe, are widely regarded in this way. It would be

---

37 Geddis, above n 35, at 156.
38 Deborah Hardoon and Finn Heinrich *Global Corruption Barometer 2013: Report* (Transparency International, July 2013), available at <www.transparency.org/gcb2013/report>.

prudent in New Zealand to ensure that we have sufficient regulation and oversight for political parties to ensure they do not develop in this way, particularly so when the MMP system confers such a central role to political parties. The degree of regulation is too light and the recommendations of the Royal Commission on the Electoral System in 1986 should be revisited. The rules of parties need outside scrutiny. The current provisions about the decisions on party lists and candidates are remarkably loose and unsatisfactory. The room for manipulation is substantial and the courts have not intervened in decisions.[39] Section 71 of the Electoral Act 1993 provides:

> *71 Requirement for registered parties to follow democratic procedures in candidate selection*
> Every political party that is for the time being registered under this Part shall ensure that provision is made for participation in the selection of candidates representing the party for election as members of Parliament by—
> (a) current financial members of the party who are or would be entitled to vote for those candidates at any election; or
> (b) delegates who have (whether directly or indirectly) in turn been elected or otherwise selected by current financial members of the party; or
> (3) a combination of the persons or classes of persons referred to in paragraphs (a) and (b).

A better system of regulation is necessary because the effect of these rules upon the democratic process and the identity of the people who become MPs is profound. Political parties and their activities have an enormous impact on the system of government and they cannot any longer be regarded as private organisations free to do as they like. We have not included these proposals in the revised draft Constitution because this would foreclose the debate on what they should be and who should decide. Nevertheless, we regard the issue as urgent and important.[40] The changing nature of society, political parties and

---

39 *Payne v Adams* [2009] NZAR 417 (HC) is a decision that appears to restrict what is already a narrow provision. See also *Takerei v Winiata* HC Hamilton CIV-210-4190-1071 2 March 2011 in which it was ruled that even breaches of a party's own rules will not invalidate the candidate selection process unless the breach is so severe as to amount to procedural unfairness.

40 Geoffrey Palmer *New Zealand's Constitution in Crisis—Reforming our political system* (John McIndoe, Dunedin, 1992) at 128–149.

MMP requires more regulatory attention.

Conclusion

This chapter has dealt with a number of measures which could be used to improve the quality of elections, since regular elections are a necessary feature of any democracy. Turnout of voters is a critical element to ensure that election results have legitimacy in the eyes of people. A Government that commands a majority in the Parliament needs to be as representative as it can be of the population as whole. For this reason we have argued for lowering the vote age to 16 and for compulsory voting, on the Australian model.

Actual elections themselves are not enough, especially when campaign financing and party discipline are taken into account; associated changes to political parties and their regulation need to be made as well. There are signs that MMP, despite it the fact it began in 1996, is not well understood and too many voters who are registered do not vote and too many people do not register. First-past-the-post thinking is still alive and well. Political parties do not have the mass memberships they once had in New Zealand and party discipline is strict. Membership and party finances need to be regularly disclosed. No campaign contributions from overseas sources should be accepted and there should be much stronger disclosure rules identifying who donates. Political parties require regulatory attention.

Further, the policy pluralism of MMP makes it essential that the public are involved in policy discussions constantly, not just at election time. While elections are a necessary and desirable feature of democracy, alone they are not a sufficient condition for a strong democracy. The act of voting itself is not enough, unless other conditions are present. This is a theme that is further developed in the next chapter, which deals with other methods of public engagement.

16 Deepening citizen engagement

Democracy can be characterised in different ways. There are three main approaches:

- Some see democracy as the mechanism by which a society arrives at decisions where a key element is that voters determine who will exercise the power on their behalf. This is achieved by using the institutions of competitive voting to arrive at a collective and rational view of competing policy choices and the identity of the decision-makers.
- Another view focuses on the need to improve the techniques of deliberation so that the decisions made are better informed, better considered and more acceptable to more people. Under this approach, elections are useful, but not sufficient. Alternative techniques and forums need to be used to gauge public opinion.
- A third view says that, since democracy is about the distribution of power and managing power relations, the real point is to minimise domination. Various restraints must be placed upon the exercise of democratic power to avoid excesses and domination.[1] According to that view, expectations about what democratic government can realistically achieve should be limited. Domination means, in this sense, the illegitimate exercise of power—where a person or a group shape agendas, limit options and influence peoples' preferences and wishes. This is where checks and balances and accountability come in. Governments themselves are a significant source of domination and this needs to be recognised in any adequate democratic constitutional framework.

The three approaches are not necessarily mutually exclusive. Indeed, there is more than a grain of truth to be gleaned from each of them.

Our own approach incorporates elements of all three approaches. We think elections and the policy choices that flow from them are important expressions of the collective or aggregated will of the people. And ultimately, in a complex society we will simply not always agree, so we must find a way to make decisions that people will respect, even

---

1 Ian Shapiro *The State of Democratic Theory* (Princeton University Press, Princeton, 2003) at 3.

if they do not necessarily like them. We also believe that improved techniques of deliberation can refresh democracy and produce better quality decisions than are often made by the institutions established by a constitution where adequate deliberation is absent. One of the primary aims of our proposed constitution is to contain power and restrict domination by one group or view.

The question of how to encourage civic literacy and to engage and empower the citizenry in democracies is not a simple issue. Functioning as effective citizens requires a skill set. Politics and government are simply not perceived by many people to be central to their lives.[2] Although there is a need for other methods of democratic participation aside from voting in elections, increasing trends of not voting must be a concern. Voting is a public act, easy to understand and measurable. Measuring and quantifying other forms of civic engagement is more difficult. Then there is the issue of trust in political institutions which is a product of many different factors. Once lost, trust is not easily regained. Max Harris in his recent book *The New Zealand Project* argues that 'The twin interlocking forces of desensitisation and demoralisation are key to the curtailment of people power' in New Zealand.[3] His diagnosis may lack empirical proof but it does resonate. Measures do need to be adopted that connect citizens more to government, policy and politics, ensuring that they can trust government more and take a bigger part in what it does. What is needed are policy choices that increase civic literacy and engagement.

The theme in this chapter is the level of connection and engagement between the citizen and the elected representatives who make the decisions, and how this relates to the level of legitimacy government institutions are viewed with. While voting is often regarded as the main form of political engagement and the easiest method of having a voice in the governing of the country, election results are neither an accurate nor a sufficient reflection of the views of the voters on specific policy issues. There needs to be what some political scientists have called 'democratic renewal', to reach out by new methods to

---

2 Henry Milner *Civic Literacy: How informed citizens make democracy work* (University Press of New England, Hanover, 2002).
3 Max Harris *The New Zealand Project* (Bridget Williams Books, Wellington, 2017) at 243.

consult and have dialogue that enriches policy and public debates before big decisions are made.[4] The purpose is to reconnect citizens with the political system.

There is a burgeoning overseas literature that explores better ways to connect citizens with their governments. Brexit in the United Kingdom and the election and behaviours of President Donald Trump have quickened public interest in the nature of democracy. The complacency around democracy has certainly been shaken. Democracy is a difficult form of government to manage at the best of times, but it can easily develop into a soft form of fascism under the twin pressures of populism and social instability. By 'fascism' we mean authoritarian nationalism in which opposition is supressed and government control largely unlimited. The old-fashioned view of representative government was expressed by the British political philosopher Edmund Burke who, in a speech to the electors of his Bristol constituency following his election in 1774, said:[5]

> [. . .] it ought to be the happiness and glory of a representative to live in the strictest union, the closest correspondence, and the most unreserved communication with his constituents. Their wishes ought to have great weight with him; their opinion high respect; their business unremitted attention. It is his duty to sacrifice his repose, his pleasures, his satisfactions, to theirs; and above all, ever, and in all cases, to prefer their interest to his own. But his unbiased opinion, his mature judgment, his enlightened conscience, he ought not to sacrifice to you, to any man, or to any set of men living. These he does not derive from your pleasure; no, nor from the law and the constitution. They are a trust from Providence, for the abuse of which he is deeply answerable. Your representative owes you, not his industry only, but his judgment; and he betrays, instead of serving you, if he sacrifices it to your opinion.

This appears to modern eyes a rather patrician and undemocratic approach. It does not sit well with modern sentiments. Yet there is an important piece of wisdom in Burke's point. He believed in deliberation. He wished to listen to the arguments and consider them.

---

4   Ian Marsh and Raymond Miller *Democratic decline and democratic renewal: political change in Britain, Australia and New Zealand* (Cambridge University Press, Cambridge, 2012) at 289–317.
5   AMD Hughes (ed) *Edmund Burke Selections* (Clarendon Press, Oxford, 1921) at 62–65.

After hearing other points of view, he would decide what line to take. When there is time for deliberation in an independent assembly in which many points of view are expressed decisions will be better.[6] While the electors of Bristol voted him in, he was a member of Parliament charged with considering the good of the whole country. The debate preceding the expression of the collective mind was important to him.[7] This is the very reverse of tumult and populism.

There has been extensive research on deliberative democracy in recent years. The idea has reached a stage where it can be usefully deployed in the actual practice of governing and making policy decisions.[8] Two Australian scholars have recently published a valuable book on deliberative democracy, examining whether, and how, the law of politics can match deliberative democratic ideals.[9] They say:[10]

> [. . .] deliberative democracy, properly understood and applied, offers an holistic approach that can in some instances rise above apparent competitions between values. Democratic values are not locked in ineluctable conflict. Deliberative democratic understandings can assist us to accommodate the disparate normative commitments of the law of politics. This accommodation does not magically erode all tension within political values. But it does offer a more enriched understanding of politics and governance as something more than a jungle of individuated rights, a numerical notion of equality, or an elite game (understandings associated with naïve, siloed approaches to liberty, equality and integrity).

The concept of deliberative democracy has several important features:[11]

- deliberation is for all people, it is not elitist; many methods of involvement such as citizen juries or assemblies can find out the views of different groups and contribute in an inclusive way to the

---

6   GH Sabine *A History of Political Theory* (3rd ed, George G Harrap, London, 1951) at 513.
7   Ernest Barker 'Burke on the French Revolution' in Ernest Barker *Essays on Government* (2nd ed, Clarendon Press, Oxford, 1951) 204 at 222.
8   Nicole Curato and others 'Twelve Key Findings in Deliberative Democracy Research' (2017) 146(3) Daedalus 1.
9   Ron Levy and Graeme Orr *The Law of Deliberative Democracy* (Routledge, New York, 2017).
10 At 196.
11 Curato and others, above n 8.

resolution of issues
- it is realistic and actually works across a range of governmental institutions
- proper deliberation is essential for democracy as it can help reach agreement and prevent destabilisation of the decision-making processes
- deliberation is more than discussion and is directed to exchanges of views aimed to reach a practical judgment
- deliberative democracy involves many forms of communication from many groups
- deliberative democracy has a nuanced view of power and can influence how coercive power is exercised and what decisions are made
- deliberation is useful for many purposes and is not necessarily aimed at producing consensus; it should recognise pluralism and the legitimacy of different values, preferences and judgments
- participation and deliberation go together, and deliberations can be scaled up in various ways to enhance political participation
- to transform positions by deliberation takes time and reflection as views change over time and as a result of the deliberation and exposure to information
- deliberation helps to break down polarization, ensuring all sides are involved
- deliberative democracy can be used in deeply divided societies and help to bridge gaps between different groups within those societies
- many different research methods are available to advance deliberative democracy, both quantitative and qualitative.

While perfection can never be reached by using these techniques, progress could be made in thickening, strengthening and enhancing the nature of our democracy by better deliberation, rendering the results more acceptable to more people and better thought through. The deliberations must be authentic and inclusive. Communication and the media have a big role to play in these processes.

Respect for those with opposing views, reciprocity of consideration and reflection are the important elements. In the end, decisions have to be taken and not everyone will agree with them. But more of our political discourse and decision-making could be deliberative in a way that opens government up to more diverse influences and better information. The policies will then be infused with better reflection about which there has been discussion. In these discussions some people will have changed their minds. The knowledge of different people in different spheres is pooled in such processes and all brought to bear upon the issue in question. While not everyone will want to deliberate and participate, it is true that participation and deliberation go together.

Listening is an important element of this. It will enhance the legitimacy of the decisions when they are taken. And they will be better decisions and therefore better outcomes for people. Such processes will break down the appeal of simple solutions to complex problems advanced by populist politicians.

This idea of deeper engagement between those with ultimate decision-making power and everyone else is not a new idea in New Zealand—in fact it is a very old one. While modern conception of deliberative democracy may seem novel, for centuries Māori used techniques involving participation and collaboration as part of their decision-making process. Indeed, many of the methods of deliberative democracy are similar to the methods of communication and discussions that are so much a feature of Māori culture. Within Māori legal traditions power is very decentralised, Rangatira exercise very little executive authority and must develop strong relationships and engagement skills to maintain legitimacy.[12] Collective decision-making is particularly prevalent when it comes to civic participation:[13]

> Māori communities and collectives have developed and expressed a distinct civic whanaungatanga, or civic collectivism, that speaks to a Māori ongoing quest to use public power for purposes that benefit Māori far beyond their own immediate kin group, potentially including all Māori. In this context, decision-making by Māori for such civic ends usually provides for substantive collective participation and public input, by way of large gatherings and other methods of

---

12 Carwyn Jones *New Treaty New Tradition: Reconciling New Zealand and Māori Law* (Victoria University Press, New Zealand, 2016) at 67, 70.
13 Māmari Stephens "To Work out their own Salvation': Māori Constitutionalism and the Quest for Welfare' (2015) 46 VUWLR 905, at 915. See also Māmari Stephens 'A Loving Excavation: Uncovering the Constitutional Culture of the Māori Demos' (2013) 25 NZULR 820; and Māmari Stephens 'Māori constitutionality (and the Treaty of Waitangi)' (2013) Māori LR 8.

face-to-face participation, or for substantive and direct Māori public input.

Rūnanga (collective committees or group processes whereby decisions are reached and disputes settled, with the use of tikanga Māori),[14] and hui in particular have long, honourable traditions of facilitating collaborative and constructive conversations and relationships, and providing a way of making important political and social decisions while allowing the opportunity for people to have their voice be heard.[15] At hui everyone talks and discusses; different views are heard and considered. In determining how we can utilise ideas of deliberative democracy, New Zealand should actively engage with Māori legal traditions, which can greatly strengthen these practices. It is hoped that re-discovering and re-invigorating such methods will go some way towards reducing the degree to which cynicism surrounds democracies these days.

Deliberation emphasises that democracy is much more than the counting of votes. This point has been powerfully made by a Dutchman, David Van Reybrouck, with the provocative title *Against Elections: The Case for Democracy*.[16] People are both in favour of democracy and they mistrust it. If 'democracy' comprises only of elections, then participation and dialogue on particular issues tend to be lost. Most Western democracies are representative democracies—that is, they are governed by a select few who are chosen (through elections) to represent the interests of all the people within that country. Many of these countries are now suffering from what Van Reybrouck terms 'Democratic Fatigue Syndrome'—a crisis of both legitimacy and efficiency characterised by:[17]

> low voter turnout, high voter turnover, declining party membership, governmental impotence, political paralysis, electoral fear of failure, lack of recruitment, compulsive self-promotion, chronic electoral

---

14 Stephens 'Māori Constitutionalism and the Quest for Welfare', above n 13, at 922; see also Vincent O'Malley 'English Law and the Maori Response: a Case Study From the Rūnanga System in Northland, 1861–65' 116 The Journal of The Polynesian Society 7.
15 Stephens 'Māori Constitutionalism and the Quest for Welfare', above n 13, at 922–923.
16 David Van Reybrouck *Against Elections: The Case for Democracy* (Bodley Head, London, 2016).
17 At 16.

fever, exhausting media stress, distrust, indifference and other persistent paroxysms . . .

After identifying the syndrome, Van Reybrouck goes on to posit a diagnosis: Western representative democracies are in crisis because it is 'assume[d] that the representation of the people in a formal consultative organ is inextricably bound up with elections.'[18] In other words:[19]

> we have all become electoral fundamentalists, despising those elected but venerating elections. Electoral fundamentalism is an unshakeable belief in the idea that democracy is inconceivable without elections and elections are a necessary and fundamental precondition when speaking of democracy. Electoral fundamentalists refuse to regard elections as a means of taking part in democracy, seeing them instead as an end in themselves, as a holy doctrine with an intrinsic, inalienable value.

Thus, when Western nations talk about the process of 'democratisation' in war-torn countries like Iraq or Afghanistan, 'what they really mean is this: they must hold elections'.[20] This is despite the fact that elections do not automatically foster democracy and may indeed prevent or destroy it in states that are fragile by exacerbating violence, ethnic tensions and corruption.

That is not to say that elections are not useful or important. They have often made democracy possible and they provide a relatively efficient way of selecting representatives to govern. However, we seem to have forgotten that other forms of participation exist, and that in the interests of legitimacy, some efficiency may need to be sacrificed by seeking greater public input; 'Representative democracy is in essence a vertical model, but the twenty-first century is increasingly horizontal'.[21] Interactive conversation between the governed and the decision-makers seems more difficult to conduct now.

So, what's the solution then? What can be done? Van Reybrouck champions 'deliberative democracy' that we have discussed above. He defines this as follows:[22]

18 At 37.
19 At 39.
20 At 39.
21 At 57.
22 At 109.

Deliberative democracy is a form of democracy in which collective deliberation is central and in which participants formulate concrete, rational solutions to social challenges based on information and reasoning.

It has its origins in Athenian democracy in ancient Greece and combines political equality and deliberation.

The search is for a more equal distribution of political opportunities. The Greeks filled many public offices in all branches of government for a limited period by drawing lots. There are of course serious problems associated with filling public offices on a random basis. Questions of competence for the job would surely arise, and there could be practical problems in building up a sense of civic duty to encourage participation in the system—witness how hard it can be to ensure people turn up for jury duty at the courts. But the decision-makers in our political system should not be seen as some sort of aristocracy just because they are elected, the only ones able to make decisions which affect all our lives. There are important institutions we use where the people are chosen randomly, juries in criminal cases being perhaps the best example in New Zealand. The system obliges people to sit in court and decide, sometimes after lengthy trials and listening to the Judge sum up, whether one of their fellow citizens is guilty of a criminal offence.

There is a need to strike out and find new ways to allow democracy to develop in different ways. As Professor Quentin Quentin-Baxter said, 'Constitutions are as devoid of function as an empty seashell unless there is life within them'.[23] On a very basic level, a constitution is just a piece of paper – the only thing that can protect society is an actual belief in the value and legitimacy of that piece of paper. A constitution is a people's document and the system only works if people believe it works, and for people to believe in it they need to know they can trust it, and to trust it they need to feel they are listened to.

Trust is at the heart of any successful nation. Trust breeds legitimacy, and legitimacy breeds loyalty; it is 'a reservoir of goodwill that allows the institutions of government to go against what people may want

---

23 RQ Quentin-Baxter 'Themes of constitutional development: the need for a favourable climate for discussion' (1985) 15 VUWLR 12 at 27.

at the moment without suffering debilitating consequences,'[24] one that 'allows people to maintain confidence in institutions' long-term decision-making' even if they do not agree with all decisions made by the institutions.[25]

Sarah Kerkin says that institutions can be designed for legitimacy. She suggests that to maximise legitimacy, institutions should be based on a 'triangle of trust' model, the three key features being transparency, accountability and participation. We talked at length in *A Constitution for Aotearoa New Zealand* about how our proposed Constitution aims to strengthen the system of checks and balances in government to increase accountability, and about how its proposals around law-making and official information hope to increase transparency in the system. Now, we need to talk about the third piece of the puzzle: participation.

There exists a spectrum of engagement: from low-end consultation that often appears more one-way than true reciprocal participation. More direct forms of democratic participation play only a very limited role in the New Zealand context.[26] We have a very narrow view of engagement in government for the most part, focusing largely on a bare minimum of consulting key stakeholders and potentially giving reasons for final decisions, but often without showing any of the process in between or allowing for any wider form of public engagement. This may be in part due to a 'reluctance of governments, used to being able to advance their policies through an all-powerful parliament, to trust the people's judgment on some issues.'[27]

Kerkin discusses how *participation* promotes acceptance of the framework of legal rules, social norms and decisions made within that framework—it increases buy-in as a decision involves not only being heard, but also *listened to*.

Democracy is a fragile flower and needs careful nurturing. It faces

---

24 James L Gibson *Overcoming Apartheid: Can Truth Reconcile a Divided Nation?* (Russell Sage Foundation, USA, 2004) at 289.
25 Sarah Kerkin "'Here There Be Dragons': Using Systems Thinking to Explore Constitutional Issues' (Doctoral Thesis, Victoria University of Wellington, 2017); and Sarah Kerkin 'Designing for legitimacy: systems perspective' (2017) 15(1) NZJPIL 67.
26 Andrew Geddis *Electoral Law in New Zealand: Practice and Policy* (2nd ed, LexisNexis, Wellington, 2014) at 306.
27 At 306.

many challenges in an increasingly uncertain world. Some current trends in New Zealand suggest we should not be complacent. We have a rich democratic tradition. It has stood us in good stead. But it cannot be taken for granted. If we do not take action to strengthen it from attack, it will wither. Brexit and Trump are just the best known international examples, but the existence of attacks and their corrosive effects on the body politic are there to be seen on other societies in places that New Zealanders would often assume would be resistant to democratic decline. So now is the time to take stock and renew our strong democratic heritage.

The elements of concern revolve around a number of factors. In the 2014 election, 700,000 electors who were enrolled did not vote and that was only slightly improved in 2017. Opinion polls suggest that there is quite widespread discontent with how government is working for people. During our public meetings following publication of *A Constitution for Aotearoa New Zealand* we were regularly told of discontent by members of the public. Many told us in plain language—some colourful, some more diplomatic—that they had had, in essence, a gutsful of not being listened to by government; a gutsful of being treated as consumers, not citizens. This latter comment was a repeated theme of public comment at our meetings.

There is a dislocation between the politicians and the public. The politicians conduct a dialogue with each other in Parliament, but it is a dialogue that increasingly does not reach the mass public. Younger people in particular seem to be turned off by political parties and many voters have scant understanding of how the system of government works.

Money matters in politics and there is concern that big corporate interests have too much say and that vested interests secure their own advantage at the expense of the common good. There has occurred also a transformation of the media by the emergence of a multi-media digital environment that is having profound effects upon journalism and threatens to reduce the traditional constitutional role of the media.

Economic policy dominates a great deal of decision-making in politics, but modern critiques of economic analyses suggest that the approaches have been defective:[28]

---

28 Joe Earle, Cahal Moran and Zach Ward-Perkins *The Econocracy: On the Perils of Leaving Economics to the Experts* (Penguin Books, Great Britain, 2017) at 150.

... economics underpins a technocratic system that marginalises citizens and restricts their ability to engage with economic issues. Econocracy is a system where some have access to economic knowledge and authority and others do not. While improving the quality of experts would undoubtedly be good for society, the wider system will still be incompatible with democracy and with some of our most deeply cherished political beliefs. Therefore ... we need more than just better experts; we need a new relationship between experts and society. This entails a new culture of open and inclusive economic dialogue that all citizens can take part in.

Our democracy concentrates too much on voting and not enough on deliberation. The development of a deliberative democracy, drawing on modern research as well as Māori legal traditions, would likely invigorate the system of government and public confidence in it and develop a democracy that is uniquely New Zealand. In this process a written codified constitution can play an important role. And the most important feature of the debate about it lies in the principle of democratic renewal. As Matthew Palmer has written '[t]here is a still strong streak of *authoritarianism* in New Zealand constitutional culture.'[29] Yes, there is and it comes from our colonial period. Renewing our democracy can expand and develop our constitutional culture and make it less authoritarian, more open and more inclusive.

Such a development requires a new approach to transparency in government institutions and openness in policy-making.[30] Our executive government system in New Zealand is too much of a closed system. Our system of government is also highly centralised and can be unresponsive to the wishes of the people it serves. It is here where open government is such an important value. Public opinion is one of the checks against arbitrary power, but only if people can find out what is going on. Open government is also a safeguard against corruption.

Democratic renewal requires a more rigorous policy of open government. Taking democracy for granted and being apathetic about

29 Matthew SR Palmer 'New Zealand Constitutional Culture' (1997) 22 NZULR 565 at 576.
30 Max Rashbrooke *Bridges both ways* (Institute for Governance and Policy Studies, Victoria University of Wellington, June 2017). This book makes bold proposals for transforming the openness of New Zealand government.

it imperils its future. The New Zealand political scientist Bronwyn Hayward in answer to an inquiry from a nine-year-old girl named Dora, who asked her what democracy was, said:[31]

> It's listening Dora, listening every day to people who aren't like us and making decisions together in ways that include everyone, when we can't agree, the decision respects others. It's a pretty wonderful thing Dora, but it needs lots of courageous, creative, caring citizens just like you to make it work.

Barack Obama, when discussing democracy and constitutions, said he saw democracy not as a house to be built but as a conversation to be had. A constitution organises the way we argue about our future. The constitution is:[32]

> ... designed to force us into a conversation, a 'deliberative democracy' in which all citizens are required to engage in a process of testing their ideas against the external reality, persuading others to their point of view, and building shifting alliances of consent.

Few truths are eternal and things change. Our type of democracy needs to be changed and adjusted to better cope with the challenges that beset it. Deepening our citizen engagement will help with that.

---

31 At this point we acknowledge our debt for the helpful comments we have received on an earlier draft of this chapter from Associate Professor Bronwyn Hayward from the University of Canterbury.
32 Barack Obama *The Audacity of Hope* (Three Rivers Press, New York, 2006) at 92.

17 The media, information and communication

Effective and constant communication between those who make the decisions and those who are subject to them is highly necessary in a democracy. There is evidence, however, that the channels of communication are breaking down. No doubt there are many reasons for this, but one factor must be the crisis in the traditional news sources resulting from the digital revolution destroying the traditional media business model, particularly for newspapers.

In 1828, long before most people could vote, Lord Macaulay observed of the Parliamentary Press Gallery in the United Kingdom: '[t]he gallery in which the reporters sit has become a fourth estate of the realm.'[1] Accurate reports of what the MPs said and did were communicated to the world at large through the press.

In New Zealand, many newspapers flourished in the 19th century. Newspapers carried lengthy accounts of what was said in Parliament and this continued up to the 1970s. Parliament began to be broadcast over the radio in the 1930s and still is. All proceedings in the Chamber are televised live now and available on Sky Television, a pay service, and have been for some years. When television began, current affairs interviews became frequent.

But the media landscape has changed drastically over time. Television news had a significant impact on political reporting— leading politicians seemed more human than when their views were only available from the written word or on the radio. The medium became the message. Radio and television began to compete with newspapers. Advertising revenue fell due to competition, first from broadcasting and then, catastrophically, from the internet. Newspaper circulation began to decline seriously.

Meanwhile, there has been inevitable cost-cutting in the face of declining revenue. While newsroom numbers were cut heavily, most

---

1 *The Oxford Dictionary of Quotations* (3rd ed, Oxford University Press, Oxford, 1979) at 323. Edmund Burke was even more emphatic on the importance of the media: 'There are three estates in Parliament but in the Reporters' Gallery yonder there sits a Fourth Estate more important far than they all. It is not a figure of speech or witty saying, it is a literal fact, very momentous to us in these times.'

newspapers maintained reasonable staff numbers in the press gallery. But what they reported on changed drastically. The focus of coverage shifted away from what happened in the House of Representatives as the media pursued an entertainment focus instead of hard political news.

There have been big changes in the patterns of news media ownership in New Zealand over the past 30 years. The news industry. and thus the profession of journalism, has shrunk. Most newspapers, with the notable exception of the *Otago Daily Times*, are now owned by foreign-controlled companies. One significant development for political journalism in recent years was the closure of the cooperative news agency the New Zealand Press Association. This reduced the amount of political reporting.

The main free-to-air news channels now are TVNZ and TV3. The former is owned by the state but operated as if it were a private organisation with few elements of the public interest. The latter, known as MediaWorks, with its associated news service Newshub, is owned by an American private equity company. Radio New Zealand (now called RNZ) is a public broadcaster operating under a Charter, and Māori Television is also a significant public broadcaster. Meanwhile, Facebook and Google, the digital giants controlled by massive multinational companies, are eating into the revenues of the New Zealand news media.[2]

How the New Zealand news media will develop in the future is difficult to know, but the changes are likely to be profound. Many New Zealand journalists are concerned about the trends, but no clear consensus has emerged about what the future of journalism is.[3] The media in New Zealand has become highly fragmented with a proliferation of platforms offering news. The decline of traditional news sources, the demise of the New Zealand Press Association, the arrival of blogging and the proliferation of alternative sources of news

---

2 Gavin Ellis 'The Media we want by 2020' in 'The Media' (unpublished 2017 paper supplied to Geoffrey Palmer).
3 Emma Johnson and others (eds) *Don't Dream It's Over: Reimagining Journalism in Aotearoa New Zealand* (Freerange Press, Christchurch, 2016). A Law Commission Report designed to assist with some of these issues met with no approval from the then Government: Law Commission *The News Media meets 'New Media': Rights, Responsibilities and Regulation in the Digital Age* (NZLC 128, 2013).

and views on the internet all seem to have made it more difficult for the public to know what is actually going on. Political reporting, long-form journalism on policy, and detailed reporting of public documents and legislation have declined noticeably as the media has pursued entertainment and celebrity culture to keep up circulation, viewers and audiences.

The internet has meant that a vast amount of information is now available, much more than before. But people do not know what to make of it and cannot devote the time and effort to find out what it all means. These days the media cover Parliament only if it is newsworthy—this tends to mean the sensational or bizarre. Select Committee proceedings are usually ignored unless something out of the ordinary is involved. It is hardly surprising that busy people these days know less about what is going on in the political system than used to be the case. Serious and even profound policy changes frequently attract little attention compared with the trivial, the sensational and clickbait.

The rise of social media has given alternative access to information and many conversations concerned with policies and political developments. These could be used for widespread citizen participation in policy development if properly deployed. However, social media, as it works at present in New Zealand, often appears to limit the range of material seen by the average person because users tend to exchange information with like-minded 'friends'. People choosing to access only information that interests them are not exposed to the wider range of news and opinion that they used to see in daily newspapers or more in-depth television news bulletins. Facebook, Google and Twitter have created echo chambers in which people are happiest with a replica of their own thoughts and voices. Indeed Facebook and Google supply news without paying those who write it. This increases the financial difficulties of news organisations.

Nonetheless, social media and the internet allow voices to express themselves and link up with others. Entirely new systems of communication and publicity are developing that make political messages less dependent upon the traditional media. New news platforms can be established, as they have been in New Zealand with *Newsroom* and the *Spinoff*. New systems of publicity and communication have sprung up through the internet. Different methods of political campaigning are available to reach different parts of the public and engage them. Views are not selected and censored through reticulation in the traditional media, as they used to be. The gatekeepers have gone. How all of this influences the psychology of voters in making their choices is probably largely unknown so far. For example, how much real influence does the Twitter-sphere have, in fact? Do we know? The new methods provide new ways of conducting political campaigns, reticulating information and securing public support for views, and they are democratic in the sense that there are few barriers to communication. What we have lost, however, is likely to be substantial, and what we have gained remains largely unknown.

A recent analysis concluded that the civic and democratic function of the media in New Zealand to provide information on which to base opinions and collective political decisions remains, but somewhat dismally, as follows:[4]

> What has changed is the media ecology, which has been destabilised by disruptive technologies and rapacious financial interests.

What is called 'big data' has a different effect. Political parties in New Zealand have always used the habitation indexes of the electoral rolls to canvass for party support, record their findings and use those to assist in getting people to vote by contacting them during the election period. Over time this has become more sophisticated. Now overseas campaigns, not only political, develop detailed information about citizens to inform the political strategy a party should follow and to guide tactical decisions.[5] Many different sources of data are used, including information gathered from consumers. Mining big data to assist political campaigns has become a controversial subject. It involves computing power, mathematical models and quantitative analysis.

While some of these techniques had been used in Barack Obama's political campaigns, they really became controversial when used in the Brexit campaign in the United Kingdom and the Trump campaign in 2016. A firm based in the city of Cambridge in the United Kingdom,

---

4   Gavin Ellis and Peter A Thompson 'Restoring Civic Values to the News Media Ecology' (2016) 12(2) Policy Quarterly 37 at 40.
5   David W Nickerson and Todd Roger 'Political Campaigns and Big Data' (2014) 28(2) Journal of Economic Perspectives 51.

called Cambridge Analytica, assisted both the 'Leave' campaign in the United Kingdom and President Trump's campaign in the United States. The essence of the marketing method appears to have been sending individualised messages to voters based on data analysis of their preferences. Apparently, some of the techniques used are similar to those used by military forces to persuade civilian populations. It was an exercise in finding 'persuadable' voters and sending them messages.[6] This is based on the view that the voter is a sort of consumer and the successful candidate a product. Whether these techniques should be regulated by electoral regulators has become a live issue. These techniques can be used to discover the state of public opinion on many social, economic and cultural issues. In this respect, there are positive features of the developments.[7] But they may well need to be regulated, as are other aspects of the electoral system, in order to prevent abuse.

In this transformed media and political environment, politicians themselves strive for political oxygen to secure the attention of the media. They are also extensive users of social media. Politicians go to great pains to polish their image and cultivate the art of impression management. Television has made this more common. It is all about the image created and it seems personality has become more important than policy. More and more, the test of how people will vote seems to be determined by whether they would like to have a beer with the party leader they see on television. They will know the names of very few MPs indeed, only the leaders. Politics has become much more presidential than it used to be. It is no surprise that much political debate now takes place on social media, such as Facebook and Twitter. Campaigning now seems to revolve more around the content in the social media aimed at giving selected people messages they may want to hear. Traditional campaign methods such as addresses at public meetings have become somewhat endangered, although they still occur.

6 Carole Cadwalladr 'The great British Brexit robbery: how our democracy was hijacked' *The Guardian* (online ed, 7 May 2017), available at <www.theguardian.com/technology/2017/may/07/the-great-british-brexit-robbery-hijacked-democracy>.
7 It should be noted as well that the media in New Zealand are beginning to use big data for analysis of such things as the performance of schools and crime statistics. Such analysis can aid public understanding of complex policy issues.

Governments in New Zealand know the media matters. Virtually every MP watches the 6pm news on television. The media set significant portions of the political agenda by deciding what issues they will report upon. Virtually every minister has a media adviser. Government departments have many of them. Messages and information are carefully controlled. There are far more spin doctors in the Beehive and government departments than there are members of the Parliamentary press gallery. There are approximately 50 full members of the Parliamentary press gallery at present. In 2014, there were 288 people employed as communications specialists in the public service. Consultants are also extensively used, but the official statistics do not contain information relating to their numbers. People employed in the public relations industry in New Zealand now outnumber journalists by a significant ratio. Dr Gavin Ellis estimates this ratio at four or five public relations people for one journalist.[8] No doubt ministers need skilled journalists to help get their messages across, but in these relationships considerable efforts are made on both sides to manipulate the message. Cause and effect between all elements of the media and public opinion is not easy to assess.

The concentration by governments on trying to secure a favourable image to assist the public reception of their policies and to assist their re-election prospects has become an activity now highly developed in New Zealand. A counterweight to this might lie in better methods to consult the electorate and discuss the details of the policies and decisions in the first place. The media is trying to counteract the tendency towards infotainment in some instances by setting up teams of investigative journalists to plumb serious issues such as defence, corrections and prisons, foreign corporation tax avoidance, suicide and mental health.[9]

The media has been a centre of power in the political system, but that power is now being dispersed and diluted. The media's function traditionally has been of a constitutional dimension. It has been a check and a balance on the exercise of public power. How it will work in the future must remain a matter for speculation. One of the

8 Information and analysis supplied to us by Dr Gavin Ellis. We are grateful to Dr Ellis for considerable assistance with this chapter.
9 For an analysis of the media see generally Gavin Ellis *Complacent Nation* (Bridget Williams Books, Wellington, 2016).

challenges of our age is to find ways to strengthen the New Zealand media and journalists. They dig out information on poor policies, blunders and abuse that the elected officials and public servants would rather not see the light of day.

There is a role for government policy decisions to strengthen the media, its integrity and its viability. Strong public broadcasting would be the place to start. It is likely changes in broadcasting policy will result from the new Labour-led government elected in 2017. The crisis in the media also suggests there is a need to examine new checks and balances located elsewhere. In this regard, better and more timely availability of information to the public through the Official Information Act is required, as we have provided for in the proposed Constitution. An informed public is critical for the health of any democracy.

18 How to build a new constitution

How to structure a conversation

If New Zealand is to have a serious conversation about whether to revise its constitutional arrangements, engagement by both the Government and Parliament will be necessary. But of utmost importance will be the engagement of the public. This book and its predecessor are the work of two private individuals. Neither the first nor the second set of proposals for a codified constitution enjoy any special weight other than what benefit flows from our combined experience. And there are other ideas and proposals out there besides those we have devised. All options have to be explored further, with deep public engagement, before any decisions can be taken. Nevertheless, the proposals in this book have been tempered and revised in light of the numerous public submissions received.

Two official Government-led inquiries into these issues, one in 2005 and one in 2013,[1] resulted in no action and no change, though the 2013 inquiry had recommended the Government continue the constitutional conversation. We reasoned that the public appetite for change should be explored further. What we have concluded from our experience with public meetings and the approximately 440 submissions we have received is that there exists a public appetite to address these issues.

A question we have been asked repeatedly since embarking on this project in 2016 is: 'Even if people like your proposals, even if we do *want* change, how are we actually going to *get* a new constitution?' This chapter will address how to take the next steps in a way that is open, constructive and positive.

Constitutional change is conceived by us as a contributor to democratic renewal and as a tool to guard against the problems that currently afflict other western democracies, the symptoms of which include declining voter turnout at elections, increasing intolerance and disrespect, a feeling of mistrust in government decisions and

---

1 See Constitutional Arrangements Committee *Inquiry to review New Zealand's existing constitutional arrangements* (10 August 2005); and most recently the Government-commissioned report from the Constitutional Advisory Panel *New Zealand's Constitution: A Report on a Conversation, He Kōtuinga Kōrero mō Te Kaupapa Ture o Aotearoa* (November 2013).

their legitimacy, a failure of many young people to vote, a lack of transparency and lack of information. In other words, the decisions made these days in representative democracies are not perceived as pursuing the common good. So even where they do objectively serve the common good, many people are sceptical.

The essential character of any process that considers constitutional revision lies in the need for it to be inclusive. In writing this chapter we have benefitted considerably from a thesis written by law student Rebecca McMenamin.[2] She argues that three elements are required to meet the test for inclusivity:

- ownership of the process by the people;
- representation in the process;
- public oversight, meaning transparency and consultation.

New Zealand has never in its history had a process like this to consider—from first principles—how it is governed. It is time we tried it.

The danger with projects concerning constitutional design is that they can become dominated by political elites who have their own interests to preserve and who may cut out or severely limit the participation and representation of the population in the process. However, if you exclude those currently in power from participating at all, you run another kind of risk—that of not fostering the kind of political buy-in required to actually achieve the change sought. So a pragmatic balance has to be found.

In a striking passage in her thesis, McMenamin offers this insight:[3]

> It can be hard to strike the proper balance between limiting the role for political elites (to strengthen democratic legitimacy) and not alienating them (to increase the likelihood of enactment). Excluding politicians enhances the likelihood of long-term thinking, which is necessary for constitution-making. Moreover, excluding politicians makes it easier to de-politicise difficult or controversial issues. Constituent assemblies may be able to progress this kōrero when ordinary politics cannot. However, total exclusion from citizen-led constitution-making would

---

2 Rebecca McMenamin, 'Inclusive Constitution-Making: Lessons from Iceland and Ireland for Aotearoa New Zealand' (LLB(Hons) Thesis, Victoria University of Wellington, 2017).
3 At 20–21. Footnotes omitted.

be unattractive to politicians and detrimental, if not fatal, if Parliament retains the power of ratification. Including politicians is a 'strategic consideration more so than a principled one, although not entirely'. There is still some instrumental benefit of including politicians in a constitution-drafting body. Just as inclusive constitution-making educates citizens, it also educates those who will be implementing the constitution and therefore are interested in its workability. Including politicians does not limit the constituent assembly's power to reconfigure or recreate the constituted institutions; rather, it brings a reality-check from people with national governance experience.

For New Zealanders, there is a real issue embedded in that passage. We are used to Parliament making all the law. We have had referenda on a limited number of constitutional issues, such as MMP, which resulted from a 1986 Royal Commission report. While the 1986 report involved extensive public consultation and the taking of submissions, there was no direct-people participation that modern constitutional literature suggests is desirable. The Royal Commission was established by political elites, its members were experts, and while it did consult the public, ultimately the decision to implement had to go through Parliament before being referred to a referendum. To make the process truly inclusive, in the sense of a citizen-led process using techniques of deliberative democracy, represents a significant change in our modern law-making culture and particularly our methods of constitutional change. While this is not entirely new to New Zealand (as discussed in chapters 13 and 16, collaborative decision-making has long been a core feature of Māori constitutionalism), it is not widely used.

New Zealand tends to regard constitutional change as requiring no more than what is required for ordinary legislation because under the existing arrangements it is ordinary law.[4] This attitude results from the fact we do not have a constitution in the sense that other countries

---

4   There was no public referendum or major consultative or engagement exercise when we adopted the Statute of Westminster 1947, which allowed the New Zealand Parliament to amend the New Zealand Constitution Act 1852 without the involvement of the UK Parliament; or when we abolished the Legislative Council in 1950, which meant that from then on we only had one house in Parliament; or when the Constitution Act 1986 was enacted; or the Privy Council was abolished as the highest court for New Zealand in 2005 and replaced with the Supreme Court of New Zealand.

do. As a result, constitutional issues are things that elites and experts debate, not all New Zealanders. This feeds apathy and contributes to the general lack of constitutional literacy, which undermines people's ability and desire to engage at the level of inclusive constitution-making.[5]

So it is a big leap to go into an inclusive constitution-making process. It is for this reason that we believe putting the whole drafting process into the hands of a citizen-led constituent assembly is unlikely to work here given its novelty, and indeed the novelty of discussing constitutional issues at all. Further, as noted above, some involvement from political elites is necessary to achieve change. Nevertheless, we believe the process must be as inclusive and have as much real citizen involvement as possible. What follows is an effort to thread our way through the undoubted problems in getting such a process going at all.

Any process to consider new constitutional arrangements can be structured in a variety of ways. Before progress can be made the public has to be systematically engaged in the debate. There exist narrow issues and broad ones; from questions of which values we want to underpin our institutions, to whether we think a constitution should include a specific age for the retirement of judges. The key threshold issue becomes: Do we think that the advantages of a written, codified constitution outweigh the disadvantages? While the authors think 'yes', for many this is not a simple question. Despite the odd character of the New Zealand arrangements in terms of international comparisons, we are used to them and, for most people,[6] they have not produced major disaster or crises—or at least not yet.

There is a range of big and vital issues on which opinions will differ to a greater or lesser extent. These topics include:

- whether to become a republic and, if yes, how the former royal powers should be distributed;
- what a New Zealand Head of State might look like and what powers they should have;
- whether the power of Parliament should be limited and how;

5 McMenamin, above n 2, at 25.
6 The caveat reflects the harsh effects that some New Zealanders have suffered as a result of not having political power from time to time, for example Māori, disabled people, members of the LGBTQ+ community, and so on.

- the place of te Tiriti o Waitangi/the Treaty of Waitangi;
- the incorporation of tikanga and Māori constitutional law;
- whether increased power should be given to the courts;
- whether to give greater weight to our Bill of Rights and whether to include new rights;
- the powers of the Head of State;
- whether to increase the Parliamentary term from its current three years to, for example, four years;
- the constitutional position of local government;
- whether we should have a second chamber of Parliament;
- how to achieve increased transparency and availability of government information;
- whether any future constitution should be supreme law, or entrenched;
- the process for amending the constitution.

Some submitters have told us that because all these issues are significant they should be dealt with one at a time. In their view we should break down our proposals and advocate for incremental changes, such as first, extending the Parliamentary term, then becoming a Republic, and so on. While that view has some attraction, it overlooks the organic nature of a constitution. Each part of government—Parliament, the Government and the Judiciary—has a relationship to every other part. The powers need to be distributed and designed in such a way as to produce societal harmony rather than dissonance.

Since 1852 New Zealand has looked at the issues separately. This approach is the enemy of coherence. While this piecemeal approach may work for some (for example, the Irish system has developed through incremental change since 1937), this takes place in the context of countries with already-written and relatively well-functioning constitutions that undergo merely periodic revision. These countries have in the past undertaken the task of examining themselves and determining what kind of arrangements they want. We have not. Our system still significantly reflects the outcomes negotiated between settlers and the United Kingdom colonial office in the 1850s.

The system needs to be analysed as a whole, within a truly New

How to build a new constitution

Zealand democratic framework. Take republicanism, for example. There is substantial support for New Zealand to become a republic. But if such a change is carried out in isolation from the rest of the elements of the constitution, there will be a lack of integration. The legal powers of the Queen pervade every branch of government. Severing this connection would leave these powers untethered and uncertain. So becoming a republic is a constitutional move that cannot be carried out without dealing with the issues in other branches and locating the royal powers and functions somewhere.

Below those big issues sit many detailed provisions, most of which did not excite much opposition in the public submissions we received. These include such issues as:

- a Judicial Appointments Commission to select judges;
- a Constitutional Commission to revise the constitution every 10 years;
- the exercise of the foreign affairs, defence and international treaty powers;
- an environmental right in the Bill of Rights;
- whether there should be a right to private property;
- what to do about parliamentary privilege;
- whether there should be restrictions on the use of urgency in Parliament;
- better legislative procedures;
- the method of selecting the Speaker of the House;
- principles to govern the security agencies

A third category of issues sits below these first two. They are technical legal issues that are of practical importance, but many of them are obscure and of limited public interest. These issues must be dealt with because the constitution is a legal document that is enforceable. Thus, a degree of precision is necessary and sometimes this is a turn-off for laypeople reading the provisions. We have, as far as possible, used plain language and a logical order and people who are interested should be able to follow the draft easily enough.

One significant issue in all of this relates to the choice to be made between retaining the institutions and processes that have served New Zealand well enough while making significant adjustments, or starting with a constitutional clean slate. It is conceivable we could begin with a blank sheet of paper and develop an entirely new constitution from first principles. That is not an approach we favour, however, because it seems to us impractical due to the amount of work it would require. We also think it is unnecessary; many aspects of our current system work well, and we think it would be difficult to attract sufficient support and acceptance from the public if we did not retain familiar institutions. Though we are not perfect, New Zealand does have a highly developed system of government in what is now one of the world's oldest democracies.

Moreover, the machinery of government cannot be totally replaced on a wholesale basis without significant disruption. All constitutional systems require a legislature, an executive and a judiciary. Our approach has been to retain a great deal of what now exists; the Constitution Act 1986, the New Zealand Bill of Rights Act 1990, and many other features of our existing arrangements are reflected in what we propose. We have added additional safeguards but have also built upon what has gone before. Whether that is a sound approach has to be tested against other approaches that may be on offer.

A plan to advance upon

In 2005 a constitutional review exercise was carried out by a Parliamentary Select Committee chaired by the Hon Peter Dunne. In 2013, as the result of an initiative from the Māori Party, a conversation was conducted by a Government-appointed panel under the chairmanship of Sir Tipene O'Regan and Professor John Burrows QC.[7] Neither report produced any discernible action or change. This was disappointing, since the conclusion of the O'Regan/Burrows panel was that there was public appetite to undertake an ongoing constitutional conversation. Currently, there is also another constitutional reform project running parallel with ours. Matike Mai Aotearoa is a grassroots, Māori-led group initiating and continuing conversations about constitutional transformation with Māori.

The conventional way to approach the building of a new constitution would be to appoint a Commission of Inquiry, a step that would have to be taken by the Government of the day. The best precedent for this would be the 1986 report of the Royal Commission

---

7 Constitutional Arrangements Committee, above n 1; and Constitutional Advisory Panel, above n 1.

on the Electoral System, which produced the MMP electoral system. The composition of such a Commission would need to be carefully weighed. And while it would be possible to commence the process in that way, there would need to be sufficient funding to provide an extensive programme of public engagement.

The option is worth considering seriously. This is a familiar process in New Zealand.[8] It has been used to undertake investigations into important reforms in New Zealand such as not only the introduction of MMP, but also the adoption of the Accident Compensation scheme,[9] the regulation of genetically modified organisms[10] and the investigation into the Pike River mine disaster.[11] Alone, however, such an inquiry would be insufficient. The programme of public engagement surrounding it would be of vital importance. Furthermore, given its vast scope, the programme of engagement should probably be organised separately, using the modern connecting mechanisms that are available with digital media. The methods of engagement employed are critical to developing a sense of public trust in the process and the legitimacy of the outcome.

In this connection, it is timely to remember one particular recommendation of the 1986 Royal Commission on the Electoral System after conducting a detailed analysis of the position of the Māori minority within the electoral system. The Royal Commission made a broad constitutional recommendation that has never been implemented:[12]

> Parliament and Government should enter into consultation and discussion with a wide range of representatives of the Māori people about the definition and protection of the rights of the Māori people and the recognition of their constitutional position under the Treaty of Waitangi.

8 See DG Jamieson *A finding list of New Zealand royal commissions of inquiry, together with some departmental and special commissions and committees of inquiry* (New Zealand Library School, Wellington, 1961).
9 AO Woodhouse *Report of the Royal Commission of Inquiry into Compensation for Personal Injury in New Zealand* (Government Printer, Wellington, 1967).
10 Thomas Eichelbaum *Report on the Royal Commission on Genetic Modification* (July 2001).
11 Graham Panckhurst, Stewart Bell and David Henry *Report of the Royal Commission on the Pike River Coal Mine Tragedy* (October 2012).
12 Royal Commission on the Electoral System *Towards a Better Democracy* [1987] IX AJHR H3 at 112.

This recommendation is as valid today as the day on which it was made. These issues lie deep in New Zealand's history, politics and government, and they need careful, sensitive kōrero and discussion not only with Māori but with other sectors of the population. We have found deep fissures of opinion in some quarters about these issues and it would be disastrous if unbridgeable gaps developed between various segments of the population on the issue of te Tiriti o Waitangi and related Māori rights. Polarisation must be avoided and understanding fostered. This can only be done by a properly funded, well-organised system of public engagement.

Our suggestion is that, in addition to the programme recommended by the Royal Commission in 1986, there should be deeper public engagement by way of citizen assemblies or citizen juries on a number of the issues that arise in building a new constitution.

A thorough and properly funded programme over a period of two years should be planned and structured in order to tease out all the issues in a systematic and carefully documented manner. In order to assist the process throughout the two years, a Constitutional Engagement Group should be established that comprises people expert in the techniques of public engagement, through social media in particular.

We have some suggestions for what this programme might look like. We anticipate a choice between two approaches, with the difference falling on where in the process a consideration of Treaty issues takes place. As we have said, the treatment of the Treaty is the most controversial issue we encountered. Thus we propose two options: start with the broad outline of the constitution first, or start with the Treaty.

As may be clear from our provision relating to the Treaty in our new proposal, with its stepped programme of conversation and the discussion in chapter 13, we favour the first option. There are a significant number of problems within our democracy which we believe require urgent attention, and we anticipate the process of conversation and reconciliation centered around the Treaty will take a few years longer than other issues. In saying that, we understand the desire of a significant proportion of submitters not to continue with a constitutional conversation until Treaty issues have been properly addressed, as there is a belief that it could prejudice these discussions by precluding some options for resolution. It is also arguable that progress on reaching some shared understandings on Treaty issues with a reasonable degree of consensus will help progress on other issues. However, the ultimate decision is not up to us.

Keeping in mind that a national conversation about the Treaty, as proposed by the 1986 Royal Commission on the Electoral System, could occur at two different points in the process, a programme for constitutional change could look something like the below.

Phase One

The first phase should be a structured and thorough engagement with New Zealanders designed to locate and define the values framework favoured by the population and the general principles that should inform a constitution. This can be conducted by meetings, social media and interactive means of engagement. Discussion could be stimulated by short issue statements. Extensive use should be made of social media and other online interactive tools in this regard.[13]

If New Zealanders decide to pursue the second option discussed above and seek to settle the Treaty question at the outset, Phase One should also include a structured and thorough engagement with Māori to find out how they see the expression of te Tiriti o Waitangi in the modern world and what place they believe it should have in New Zealand's constitutional arrangements. One way this could be achieved is through collaboration with Matike Mai. A parallel exercise would need to be conducted simultaneously to find out what non-Māori communities believe about the Treaty. As we have observed, reaching finality on these issues is likely to take years, but we believe that is where the process should begin. In what has become a multicultural society, efforts must be made to ensure all views are heard and heeded.

---

13 For example, Design+Democracy's app 'On the Fence' was used by thousands of people in both the 2014 and 2017 general elections to help sort through the policies of various political parties to see which party your personal values most aligned with. The Law Commission is also experimenting with different ways of encouraging and receiving submissions; as part of their review of the Property (Relationships) Act 1976 they have created an interactive website with educative material and different ways to tell your story or submit on issues <http://prareview.lawcom.govt.nz/>.

If New Zealanders chose to pursue the first option and leave a deeper discussion of the Treaty until after a general constitutional framework has been adopted, this engagement process would then take place over time as we have discussed in chapter 13.

Phase Two

The results of these inquiries should be reported to a Constitution Committee established by Act of Parliament.[14] The Committee could comprise:

- 12 MPs selected by their parties in proportion to their strength in the House of Representatives;
- 12 experts in constitutional issues drawn from relevant academic disciplines, the public service and the Judiciary;
- 24 members of the public randomly selected from the electoral roll who agree to serve and who come from the regions of New Zealand in proportion to the population in those regions, of whom at least three should be from the Māori electoral roll;[15]
- Five mayors drawn from local government, nominated by Local Government New Zealand.

The chair should be a respected public figure who is knowledgeable but apolitical, perhaps one of our retired Governors-General.

While this arrangement could take any number of forms, we

14 Our thoughts on what we term 'the Constitutional Committee' are based around the proposals of Robert Blackburn. He was heavily involved in the United Kingdom's report on the UK Constitution: see House of Commons Political and Constitutional Reform Committee *A New Magna Carta* (Second Report of Session 2014–15, 10 July 2014). See also Robert Blackburn 'Enacting a Written Constitution for the United Kingdom' (2015) 36(1) Stat L R 1 at 20. A version of this model was used recently in Iceland when it attempted to rewrite its constitution: see Thorvaldur Gylfason 'Chain of Legitimacy: Constitution Making in Iceland' (presented at the 'Perspectives on Constituent Assemblies' conference, Columbia University, 1–2 April, published as CESifo Working Paper No. 6018, July 2016); Thorvaldur Gylfason and Anne Meuwese 'Digital Tools and the Derailment of Iceland's New Constitution' (CESifo Working Paper No. 5997, July 2016); and Hélène Landemore 'Inclusive Constitution-Making: The Icelandic Experiment' (2015) 23(2) The Journal of Political Philosophy 166, discussed below.

15 There are arguments for increasing this number. Further, the nomination selection for Māori members may need some thought, as there are potentially issues of mana that arise through randomly selecting Māori representatives that do not arise with regards to randomly selecting from the general roll.

How to build a new constitution

feel this strikes an appropriate balance between public engagement and encouraging buy-in from political elites, as well as not directly involving so many members that it becomes extremely difficult to coordinate and make decisions.

The results of the process undertaken in Phase One—designed to excavate New Zealand's values framework—would form the touchstone or sounding board for the efforts of the Constitutional Committee going forward; those results would inform the choices of the Committee in deciding to investigate some potential reforms rather than others.

The exercise should be supported by a high-quality secretariat that has sufficient financial support from Government to make the exercise effective. This body could be termed the Constitutional Engagement Group. The process needs to be open and transparent, with interactive social media being involved.

Phase Three

At Phase Three the Committee would undertake an engagement process assisted by the Constitutional Engagement Group in the various stages of its work, including:

- citizens' juries and/or assemblies, focus groups and multiple forms of engagement including physical meetings, email, video streaming of meetings and social media such as Facebook and Twitter;
- members of the Committee may travel in smaller subgroups to kōrero around the country (either on general or specific issues) and report back to the Committee on findings;
- a number of drafts of proposed changes to our constitutional arrangements would be discussed and improved after further consultation; all the drafts would be open and published.

Phase Four

The Committee's prime purpose would be to report on what changes should be made to New Zealand's constitution and how these should be structured and legally expressed. The work of the Committee should relate to how all the issues can brought together and whether constitutional change should be made and the degree to which it should be written down.

In the event that a Bill was required, the Chair would give instructions to drafters from the Parliamentary Counsel Office (PCO), who have vast amounts of experience in drafting instruments that will have legal effect. As noted above, these drafts would likely go through several iterations as the public respond to them.

Once a final draft had been agreed on, the Chair would present to the House of Representatives a detailed report setting out the findings of the Constitution Committee and the reasons for its recommendations, together with a draft of the changes it may recommend.

Phase Five

Any draft Bill would then likely be referred to Select Committee for consideration, where it would be available for further public scrutiny. It would then be up to the Government and Parliament to decide whether or not the proposals should go to a referendum for adoption by the people. We anticipate this process requiring a timeframe of two to three years.

We have had some comment on this suggested process from Rebecca McMenamin, who said the following:

> These ideas are complicated by the self-interested political elites idea [discussed above], and also the idea that there are some issues so politically thorny that no Government really wants to touch them (for example, abortion in Ireland,[16] perhaps Treaty constitutionalism in NZ) [so] that constitutional reform may be discussed by the Constitutional Committee, then Select Committee but still withheld by the Government for political reasons.
>
> [There are] tensions between representative democracy (we elect you, you do what you think is best) versus direct democracy (we elect you, but if it's so important then we want a say, automatically, rather than at your discretion). I think that technology and being able to

---

16 Note that recently in Ireland the use of a Citizens' Assembly on constitutional reform has encouraged politicians to address the regulation of abortion in Ireland, something that may well not have occurred without the legitimation and political cover provided by the Assembly's identification of the issue as one that needs to be addressed: see Ronan McGreevy 'Citizens' Assembly backs abortion rights in wide range of circumstances' *The Irish Times* (23 April 2017); and Mary Minihan 'Abortion referendum set for May or June of next year' *The Irish Times* (25 September 2017).

access leaders in a way that the people never could before is changing democracy such that 'legitimacy' requires a level of direct democracy.

I think there is something important to be said for automatic referenda on a programme of constitution-making [...]—similar to the Commission's recommendation that referenda ought to be held on major constitutional issues. Maybe something like Iceland's multi-question referenda. [...]

Chile has done something interesting where the appointed/governing body has devised four possible options of process for the way forward in their current constitution-making experience and is using referenda to get citizen endorsement from the outset.

This issue of interference from political elites is significant, and it is a tendency that needs to be guarded against as much as possible. While we are attracted to the open-textured methods of constitution-making that have been employed in some places overseas, we doubt that it is possible in the New Zealand political culture, as it now exists, for those methods to be adopted in their entirety. They could be adopted, but it will require political will.

We found it fascinating that MP Golriz Ghahraman was worried about domination by political elites. In her submission to us she said:

> I would very much like us to have a superior law constitution, but I would like this to emerge after a very open, participatory, broad-based consultation process. It needs to be very open with the public, including Iwi. So I almost don't want us as politicians to take a very specific position. An example is who should be New Zealand's Head of State and in what way should they be elected? I very much want us as a country to have a conversation about things like 'what the constitution means to us' and 'what does nationhood mean to us' and get the principles right. That should be the starting point because (as a nation) we have never really had a constitution.

Only after a process that will last several years should a set of proposals for change be contained in a Bill passed through Parliament and then put to a referendum of the people. While referenda are not generally a good idea in a representative democracy like ours,[17] for substantial constitutional change such referenda are both necessary and essential to provide legitimacy. Such was how MMP was adopted. The Royal Commission, after analysing the issues in 1986, said:[18]

> In general, initiatives and referenda are blunt and crude devices which need to be used with care and circumspection. Their frequent use would amount to a substantial change in our constitutional and political system. They would blur the lines of accountability and responsibility of Governments and political parties, and blunt their effectiveness.

The Commission recommended, however, that referenda 'ought to be held on major constitutional issues'.[19] And they went, to some pains, to set out the processes that should govern their conduct. In each case, special legislation should be passed specifying the issues to be asked and the procedures to be used in conducting the campaign and the poll. The result should be binding on Parliament and the text of the proposed changes would be included in the Bill passed by Parliament authorising the referenda. At the referendum the proposals would simply be voted up or down.

What is proposed here is an open and novel way to make constitutional policy. There are experiences from overseas that New Zealand can learn from, in terms of methods of public engagement that give proposals a legitimacy and engender a sense of public trust and ownership, which are essential to the continued survival and health of a constitution.

Future revisions of the constitution?

If this process does result in a new constitution, a question will arise as to how the public may continue to be engaged in its development and

---

17 While true that referenda can add legitimacy to constitutional decisions in particular, if not properly executed they can fall prey to issues including those relating to the ill-informed electorate, the deliberative and participatory deficit, elite control, lack of accountability and responsibility, and tyranny of the majority. They are also costly and time-consuming and thus impractical for use in day-to-day decision-making. See Georgia Whelan 'Of Demagogues and Dictators? The Redemption of Constitutional Referenda in New Zealand' (LLB(Hons) Thesis, University of Wellington, 2017).
18 Royal Commission on the Electoral System above n 12, at 175.
19 At 180.

evolution into the future. We have been conscious throughout this project of the importance of keeping a constitution relevant and up to date with developing trends. This is the reason we have made it easier to change than some well-known constitutions.[20] The mechanism that will be adopted for revisions is therefore an important topic and we will briefly describe here what we propose. This is intended to echo the process set out above to adopt a constitution, but in a more permanent form.

112 Periodic revisions of Constitution
(1) The Constitution must be reconsidered every ten years, although changes may be made at other times.
(2) An Act of Parliament must establish a commission to consider amendments to this Constitution ('the Constitutional Commission').
(3) Particular consideration must be given to the question of the appropriate position of social and economic rights in this Constitution, and whether the list of grounds of discrimination prohibited under Article 16(1) is adequate.
(4) Every ten years, following the year in which this Constitution comes into force, Parliament must appoint representatives of the political parties represented in the Parliament to be members of a commission.
(5) The number of representatives of each political party serving as members of the Constitutional Commission must be proportionate to the political party's strength in the Parliament.
(6) The other members of the Constitutional Commission are the Head of State, the Speaker, the Chief Justice, the Chairperson of the Waitangi Tribunal, the Chief Ombudsman, the Controller and Auditor-General, the Solicitor-General, the Chair of the Government Services Commission, the Commissioner for the Environment and the Chief Commissioner for Human Rights.
(7) After the representatives of the political parties are appointed to the Constitutional Commission, an Assembly must be convened of 100 citizens randomly selected from the electoral

---

20 To amend the constitution of Australia, for example, amendments have to be passed by an absolute majority of both houses of the federal Parliament or by one house twice, *and* passed at a referendum by a majority of the people as a whole *and* by a majority of the people in a majority of the states. From the feedback we have received, we believe a more flexible constitution is much more likely to find favour with New Zealanders.

roll from each region in approximately the same proportion as the proportion of the population of that region bears to the total population of Aotearoa New Zealand.
(8) The Assembly must be adequately supported by the Government and must consider and report on how the Constitution is working and what improvements could be made.
(9) Within six months after being convened, the Assembly must report to the Constitutional Commission on the Assembly's findings.
(10) In considering any recommendations for constitutional amendments, the Commission must take into account the report of the Assembly, but is not restricted to the matters raised in that report.
(11) No later than one year after the appointment of representatives of political parties, the Constitutional Commission must report its finding and recommendations to Parliament.

There are many different ways in which a process for constitutional revisions could be configured and we doubt that we have decided on an arrangement that will survive without adjustment. We have not been prescriptive about numbers, but it needs to be understood that, the larger the group, the more difficult the decision-making will be and the harder it is to secure clear, widespread consensus.

What follows is a more detailed discussion of the techniques of citizen engagement that can be used to make more meaningful and effective the processes of both the Constitutional Committee and the Constitutional Commission, which will precede the decision by the electors at a referendum whether to opt for constitutional reform or not.

Overseas models for citizen engagement

The kinds of processes we are proposing may be somewhat novel in the New Zealand context, but around the world countries are every year trialling new methods of citizen engagement in an effort to increase legitimacy and renew their faltering democracies. Among the measures that have been trialled in the search for some way to

How to build a new constitution

increase participation and reinvigorate democracy are:[21]

- Ireland's Constitutional Convention in 2013 comprising 66 lay people chosen by lot and 33 politicians, who were charged with looking at eight articles of the Irish Constitution to consider options for reform or repeal.
- A National Assembly of 1,500 Icelandic citizens, followed by the establishment of a Constitutional Assembly of 25 citizens elected by their peers to draft a new Constitution for Iceland.
- Canada's attempts to reform electoral law in British Columbia through a random sample of 160 citizens. The Province of Ontario did a similar thing in 2006–2007.

These experiments offer some useful suggestions for how we in New Zealand might carry out a successful programme of engagement, now and in the future. We turn first to the Irish example since it is a country similar to our own, with a Westminster tradition and similar population size and culture.

Ireland

Ireland already has a written constitution that requires the consent of the people before major change is undertaken. Before any amendment is made to the constitution it must be approved by a majority of those who vote in a referendum of the people. To ensure voters are well informed, information on the proposals and their effects is made available by a publicly funded, independent Referendum Commission.[22] Despite this, there has been a recent push for more active forms of engagement, as there has been across the globe since the 1990s, particularly as technology has made this easier.[23]

In June 2011, a pilot Citizens' Assembly was held through the *We the Citizens* initiative. *We the Citizens* was established in 2011 following a general election in which political reform featured heavily during

---

21 For more on this see David Van Reybrouck *Against Elections: The Case for Democracy* (Penguin Random House, United Kingdom, 2016), which investigates why democracy is declining and looks at studies and trials from around the world to suggest ways to remedy this.

22 Referendum Act 1998 (Ireland), as amended by the Referendum Act 2001 (Ireland). See generally <www.refcom.ie>.

23 Joe Humphreys 'Why Ireland's citizen's assembly is a model for Europe' *The Irish Times* (27 November 2016).

the campaign. The intention was to feed deliberately and publicly into the political reform agenda and to ignite citizen involvement in Irish democracy.[24] It tested whether a more participatory form of democracy could work in Ireland at a time when people felt adrift and disconnected from power.

It was decided that the agenda for the citizens' assembly should be set by Irish citizens rather than those organising the project. To this end a series of regional evening events were held around Ireland in May and early June 2011 to 'discuss the visions of ordinary citizens of what kind of Ireland they would like for the future'.[25] The themes that emerged from these events formed the basis of the citizens' assembly held in June. The assembly had 100 members, comprising a good representation of Irish society.[26] During the assembly, participants were put into groups of eight, with a trained facilitator and a note-taker at each table, with some assembly-wide discussion as well.

According to *We the Citizens*: 'After the assembly, participants showed a greater interest in politics, expressed more willingness to discuss and become involved in politics, and felt more positive about the ability of ordinary people to influence politics.'[27] The model was later used as a template for the Irish Constitutional Convention, first established in late 2012 and repeated in 2016.

The Irish Constitutional Convention was established in 2012 in fulfilment of the coalition government's 'Programme for Government', published soon after the 2011 election.[28] The Convention consisted of 100 members: 66 ordinary citizens selected at random by a survey company, 29 members of the Irish parliament, four members of the Northern Ireland Assembly and a chairperson. It was tasked with examining eight specific issues, including the reduction of the presidential term of office to five years, lowering the voting age, provisions for same-sex marriage and increasing the role of women

---

24 David M Farrell, Eoin O'Malley and Jane Suiter 'Deliberative Democracy in Action Irish-style: The 2011 We the Citizens Pilot Citizens' Assembly' (2013) 28(1) Irish Political Studies 99 at 100; *We the Citizens* homepage: <www.wethecitizens.ie>.
25 At 102.
26 At 103.
27 *We the Citizens* homepage: <www.wethecitizens.ie>.
28 David M Farrell 'Deliberative Democracy, Irish style: Ireland's Constitutional Convention of 2013' (2014) 34 Inroads 110 at 111.

in public life and politics. With a small budget and a deadline of one year to complete its work, the Convention held its first formal session on the weekend of 26–27 January 2013.

A further Citizens Assembly was established in 2016 as a non-political forum for examining ethical and moral issues, including, notably, whether to repeal Ireland's eighth amendment, which restricts access to abortion. This assembly was made up of 99 members chosen randomly to represent the views of the Irish electorate, chaired by Justice Mary Laffoy, a Supreme Court judge.

The assembly heard testimonies over six months from medical, ethical and legal experts, as well as from women with direct experiences of unplanned pregnancy, before voting in the ballot on 23 April 2017. The vote indicated 64 per cent were in favour of change.

Justice Laffoy presented her report on the assembly process and its recommendations to the Irish parliament in June 2017.[29] It deals with a massively controversial issue. It recommends, among other things, that termination of pregnancy restrictions should be removed. This report has been considered by a Committee of the Irish Parliament and there is likely to be a referendum on proposals to amend the Irish constitution in May or June 2018. If constitutional change emerges from this process, it will be a great tribute to the institution of deliberative democracy, which the assembly's report described in the following way:[30]

> In deliberation, citizens exchange arguments and consider different claims that are designed to secure the public good. Through this conversation, citizens can come to an agreement about what procedure, action, or policy will best produce the public good. Deliberation is a necessary precondition for the legitimacy of democratic political decisions. Rather than thinking of political decisions as the aggregate of citizens' preferences, deliberative democracy claims that citizens should arrive at political decisions through reason and the collection of competing arguments and viewpoints. In other words, citizens' preferences should be shaped by deliberation in advance of decision making, rather than by self-interest.

29 Republic of Ireland *First Report and Recommendations of Citizens Assembly, the Eighth Amendment of the Constitution* (29 June 2017), available at <www.citizensassembly.ie/en/The-Eighth-Amendment-of-the-Constitution/Final-Report-on-the-Eighth-Amendment-of-the-Constitution/Final-Report-incl-Appendix-A-D.pdf>.
30 At [103]. We described the essence of deliberative democracy in chapter 16.

It appears there is a pattern emerging in Ireland of undertaking extensive programmes of deliberative democracy prior to voting on fundamental constitutional law. Ireland has been characterised as 'a country that trusts its citizens rather than fearing them'.[31] One may wonder what would have happened had the United Kingdom undertaken a similar exercise before deciding to conduct a referendum around Brexit.

If the assembly process is open and transparent and participatory, it will have a stronger chance of carrying legitimacy and in bolstering a belief that ordinary citizens have a real say in the laws and governance of their nation. Deliberative democracy has been shown to generate change in people's opinions.[32] It can create a shared sense of accomplishment and ownership of decisions, even if not everyone agrees to the final outcome.

Iceland

While it is important to keep in mind the limitations relating to how much help New Zealand can gain from studying the Icelandic experience given their extremely small (0.33 million) and largely homogenous population, the Icelandic example of deliberative democracy is remarkable for a number of reasons, not least because:[33]

> for the first time in human history, a country's foundational text (or at least a draft proposal for it) was written with the more or less direct participation of its people . . .

Iceland began the process of redesigning its constitutional arrangements by holding a number of one- or two-day national assemblies, which were attended by up to 950 people selected largely at random from the electoral roll. The assemblies were asked to consider whether Iceland in fact needed a new constitution. After a declaration in the affirmative, a Constitutional Council was formed to represent the citizens, made up of 25 'ordinary' (in that they were non-political) people elected by the citizens, through a Single Transferable Vote from a roster of 522 candidates. After only four

---

31 Humphreys, above n 3.
32 Jane Suiter, David M Farrell and Eoin O'Malley 'When do deliberative citizens change their opinions? Evidence from the Irish Citizens' Assembly' (2016) 37(2) International Political Science Review 198.
33 Landemore, above n 14, at 167.

months the Council produced a draft text which was unanimously agreed to by all Council members and subsequently approved by two-thirds of the voters in a public referendum.

What was remarkable about the process as a whole was the level of transparency and engagement fostered and maintained throughout almost the entire process. There was public input upstream in the form of national assemblies tasked with identifying the value framework of the Icelandic people and the general principles that should inform a new constitution. There was public input downstream in the form of the referenda to approve or disapprove the resulting draft text:[34]

> The most open and directly participatory part of the Icelandic constitutional process, however, took place midstream of the process, during what has traditionally been the most secretive moment in the history of past constitutions: the writing of the draft itself. The twenty-five members of the Council, far from isolating themselves from popular input, regularly posted online, for the world to see and for the Icelandic people to read, the version of the draft they were working on. All in all, they posted twelve drafts, all at various stages of completion. Anyone interested in the process could post comments and send feedback using social media like Facebook and Twitter, or using regular email and mail. In fact, foreigners themselves were free to participate if they could find a way (e.g., Google Chrome) to overcome the language barrier.

While it was likely partly a result of the fairly representative Council, achieved through direct voting, rather than through Government appointment, one of the primary reasons behind the overwhelming popular support of the draft constitution was due to the ability of the model to allow for a wide variety of public engagement. The public must be able to witness, observe, and thus make up their minds about, the activities of the actors engaged in the process. This increases the apparent legitimacy of the draft by fostering a sense of public ownership of the document, as it acts like a window 'opened in the walls of the constitutional assembly and more generally onto the whole constitution-writing process.'[35]

While ultimately the process in Iceland did not result in a new constitution, that was largely due to political failings rather than a lack

34 At 174.
35 At 179.

of public engagement or support, or a lack of democratic legitimacy. In garnering that support and legitimacy, the media aspect behind the development of Iceland's draft constitution was crucial. The Council invited outsiders to participate through a specially designed interactive website as well as through social media.

The way in which people engage with each other, and with their communities at large, is changing.[36] As technology develops so too do the means of engaging directly with different communities in different ways. In order to increase engagement, a range of methods will need to be deployed to reach as many people as possible, including the traditional formal submissions and physical meetings, but also using new forms of media such as Facebook and Twitter.

The Icelandic experiment is an excellent example of how this can work. It had a Council Facebook page, as well as individual member pages; a Twitter account; an interactive website designed to underscore the popular nature of the constitution-making exercise as opposed to constitution-making by politicians and their lawyers; the use of online translation software; live video-streaming of some Council sessions; a YouTube account with speeches and interviews with Council members; all culminating with 'a total number of 3600 comments received in addition to some 320 formal suggestions from citizens, which were all discussed and answered by the three committees of the Council'.[37] Compared to the formal submissions, there were significantly larger numbers engaged through new media.

All twelve iterations of the draft produced by the Council were put on the internet for public scrutiny and debate, whether via Facebook, Twitter, email or snail mail. Volunteers translated the document into other languages, giving the Council the added benefit of advice from constitutional experts across the globe.

Ultimately, the process worked because:[38]

> the fact that regular citizens could peek in the constitution-writing process, be kept apprised of the modifications on a regular basis, and receive personal emails from the Council members in response to their suggestions and comments may have increased the perceived

---

36 Manuel Castells *Networks of Outrage and Hope: Social Movements in the Internet Age* (Polity Press, Cambridge, 2012).
37 Gylfason and Meuwese, above n 14, at 14.
38 Landemore, above n 14, at 176.

legitimacy of the draft, by creating a sense of ownership of the document in the larger population, including amongst those who did not even try to participate in the experiment, but, crucially, knew they could have if they had been so inclined or had found the time.

In New Zealand there are already private groups attempting to foster this engagement in constitutional design. Groups like Design+Democracy have been formed in response to a growing recognition that our current system is inadequate when it comes to engagement, particularly with young people. Design+Democracy works in partnership with government and other organisations to develop apps that encourage participation in issues relating to government.[39] Examples include the 'On the Fence' app, referenced earlier at n 13, which provided a user-friendly, interactive method of discovering how the users values and beliefs measured up against those of candidates running for public office, and 'Ask Away', an online platform that allows users to ask questions directly to political parties or individual politicians, with popular questions capable of being 'voted up' by users so they are more likely to be seen by those answering the questions.

Other, more traditional means of engagement and consultation are, of course, still necessary when engaging in the reform process, as there are always some 'unconnected citizens' who are excluded altogether if the process relies too heavily on internet-based digital tools.[40] Social movements are, after all, made of individuals: 'At the individual level, social movements are emotional movements ... the big bang of social movement starts with the transformation of emotion into action.'[41] Creating an environment through numerous engagement efforts, which foster enthusiasm and make people feel they are able to participate and that they will be heard, is the key to successful constitutional reform.[42]

---

39 Design+Democracy is a research unit established within Massey University's College of Creative Arts and is accessible through its website: <designdemocracy.ac.nz>.
40 Gylfason and Meuwese, above n 14, at 12.
41 Castells, above n 36, at 12.
42 See Scarlet Roberts 'Constitution Aotearoa—Hopeless Dream or Possible Reality? An analysis of the hurdles facing major constitutional reform in the New Zealand Context' (LLB (Hons) Thesis, Victoria University of Wellington, 2016); and McMenamin, above n 2.

Incompletely Theorised Agreements

Much of the democratic process is devoted to resolving disagreement. Disagreements can be disabling for both societies and governments. It is important that they be resolved and the processes we have advanced in this chapter should assist in resolving many of them.

Yet in many cases when it comes to change, there will be disagreement and dissent. 'One of the key goals of democracy's constitution is to solve the problem of enduring disagreement.'[43] And in this case, given the nature of constitutional design and its pervading influence over the lives of all New Zealanders, it becomes doubly important to ensure that the issue of disagreement is addressed and faced.

This does not mean that change can only go forward if everyone agrees 100 per cent; 'solving' the problem of enduring disagreement does not require for no disagreement at all. Disagreement is natural; it is part of democracy, and it would be detrimental to attempt to ignore that. Rather, it should be acknowledged and accepted from the beginning. The problem emerges when groups becoming polarised in their beliefs.

How, then, do we ever achieve change if we know that not everyone will always agree? The answer lies in the idea of incompletely theorised agreements:[44]

> Very frequently constitution-making becomes possible through this form of incompletely theorized agreement. Many constitutions contain incompletely specified standards and avoid rules [. . .]

These agreements, which are incompletely theorised in the sense that people who accept the principle in general do not need to agree on what it entails in particular cases to move forward, necessitate a certain level of engagement and participation. To avoid polarisation the agreement must establish institutions that promote deliberation among people with different points of view, so that all sides feel their beliefs are valid, and they have been listened to:[45]

> Group polarization is often the source of deliberative trouble.

---

43 Cass R Sunstein *Designing Democracy: What Constitutions Do* (Oxford University Press, Oxford, 2001) at 9.
44 At 56.
45 At 9 and 51.

> Incompletely theorized agreements are often the solution to deliberative trouble. And it is especially important for a diverse democracy to create institutions to ensure that governmental power is not available only to segments of society, and to promote deliberation among people who would otherwise like to talk only to like-minded people. [. . .] One of the key goals of democracy's constitution is to solve the problem of enduring disagreement—by promoting exposure to multiple perspectives, by proliferating the points of access to government, and by finding productive courses of action when disagreements cannot be solved.
> [. . .]
> [This process] enlists silence, on certain basic questions, as a device for producing convergence despite disagreement, uncertainty, limits of time and capacity, and (most important of all) heterogeneity. Incompletely theorized agreements are thus an important source of successful constitutionalism and social stability; they also provide an important way for people to demonstrate mutual respect.

These sorts of agreements are common across South American constitution-making. We feel it also suits our own common-law tradition of having principles that are interpreted over time, as well as New Zealand's long practice of evolution rather than revolution in constitutionalism. New Zealanders have already recognised the need for deliberative processes when discussing the constitution, given the complex nature of the issues involved and the different priorities and interests different individuals or groups will likely have. The 2013 Constitutional Advisory Panel stated in its report that it found:[46]

> support for deliberative and consensus-building processes, which may be more suitable than a referendum to achieve the complex balancing of priorities and interests required and to ensure that minority views are considered.

What we have done here is take on board this view and ensure that a process is devised to manage disagreement so that all views are weighed and considered before any action is finally taken. Nothing like this has been done before in New Zealand, but we think it would be therapeutic for the body politic and would assist the society in deciding what it stands for and how this should be expressed in constitutional terms. Furthermore, it can be done

---

46 Constitutional Advisory Panel, above n 1, at 13.

relatively inexpensively. The Irish Citizen's Assembly was run on very economical lines.

The way forward

So, where to from here? Having set out our vision of the process that should be followed in reforming New Zealand's constitution, what can people do to get it started?

The first and most important thing people can do is publicly support the move for change. You don't need to agree with all of our proposals, but if you want change, the best way to get it is to convince MPs and political parties in charge of the current system that there is a demand for it. The best way of doing this is writing to your local MP. This is an extremely underrated and underused method of engaging with government. Your MP was voted in by you, to represent you. They are accountable to you if they do not live up to this responsibility. If you want change, you need to tell them.

Besides the direct route, there are other avenues to make your voices heard. Matthew Bolton, a member of the United Kingdom's Citizens United group and a key driver behind the UK's living wage campaign, has recently published a short book which essentially acts as a 'how to' guide for effective campaigning.[47]

Here is a good place to remember an old Māori proverb, which applies as much to constitution-making (and maybe even more so) than anything else:

> *He aha te mea nui o te ao*
> *What is the most important thing in the world?*
> *He tāngata, he tāngata, he tāngata*
> *It is the people, it is the people, it is the people.*

It is people who make constitutions work. You are the people; it is now up to you.

---

[47] Matthew Bolton *How to Resist: Turn Protest to Power* (Bloomsbury Publishing, London, 2017).

19 Constitution of Aotearoa New Zealand

Preamble

Part 1 Principles

Part 2 The Bill of Rights

Part 3 Te Tiriti o Waitangi/the Treaty of Waitangi

Part 4 The State

Part 5 The Head of State / Kaitiaki of the Nation

Part 6 The Parliament

Part 7 The Government

Part 8 Local Government

Part 9 The Judiciary

Part 10 Integrity and Transparency

Part 11 Fundamental functions of the State

Part 12 Status and revision of Constitution

Part 13 Emergencies

Part 14 Miscellaneous Provisions

19 Te Pouhere o Aotearoa Niu Tireni

Kupu Whakataki

Wāhanga 1 Ngā Mātāpono

Wāhanga 2 Te Pire Tika Tangata

Wāhanga 3 Te Tiriti o Waitangi/The Treaty of Waitangi

Wāhanga 4 Te Whenua Rangatira

Wāhanga 5 Te Upoko o Te Whenua Rangatira / Te Kaitiaki o te Motu Whānui

Wāhanga 6 Te Pāremata

Wāhanga 7 Te Kāwanatanga

Wāhanga 8 Kāwanatanga ā-Rohe

Wāhanga 9 Te Hunga Whakawā ā-Ture

Wāhanga 10 Te Ngākau Tapatahi me te Taiahoaho

Wāhanga 11 Ngā āheinga matua o te Whenua Rangatira

Wāhanga 12 Te tūnga me te whakahoutanga o te Pouhere

Wāhanga 13 Ngā Ohotata

Wāhanga 14 He Āheinga Anō

Preamble

We the people of Aotearoa New Zealand declare—

We live in a beautiful set of islands in the South Pacific Ocean first settled by Māori migrants from Polynesia, later by settlers from Europe, then joined by people from many other countries and cultures from the Pacific Islands, Asia and elsewhere. We aim to live together in an inclusive and just society:

We are committed to governance in the interests of all the people of Aotearoa New Zealand from whom all power is derived:

We state our determination to promote human dignity, tolerance, and respect for people from diverse cultures and make a commitment to uphold and secure fundamental freedoms and human rights, including cultural, economic, and social rights:

We respect te Tiriti o Waitangi/the Treaty of Waitangi as the founding document of the nation:

We value freedom and opportunity for all, fairness, equity, equality, environmental sustainability, kaitiakitanga and tikanga Māori, a sound economy, a strong sense of community and respect for the family, especially the care of children:

We support a clear distribution of power between the Head of State, the Parliament, the Government, and an impartial and independent Judiciary:

We affirm Aotearoa New Zealand is founded on the principle that the people govern themselves through a democratic system of representative, accountable and responsible government based on free and fair elections:

We encourage increased public participation in official decision-making to ensure greater deliberation in the making of major policy decisions:

Kupu Whakataki

Ko tātou nei, ko te iwi o Aotearoa Niu Tireni, kei te whakapuaki–

Ka noho tātou ki tētahi huinga moutere ātaahua kei Te Moana Nui a Kiwa, i nōhia tuatahitia e ngā tīpuna o te iwi Māori i heke mai ai i reira, ā, nō muri mai i tau mai ngā kainoho Pākehā nō Ūropi, kātahi ko Tauiwi mā nō ngā whenua maha, nō ngā ahurea maha o ngā moutere o Te Moana Nui a Kiwa, o Āhia hoki, o whenua kē atu hoki. Ko tō tātou whāinga kia noho tahi hei porihanga whaiuru, hei porihanga whai tika:

Ka pūmau tātou ki te tikanga o te mana ārahi hei painga mō ngā tāngata katoa o Aotearoa Niu Tireni nō rātou ngā mana katoa i ahu mai:

Ka whakapuaki tātou i tō tātou māia kia toko ake i te tū rangatira o te tangata, i te ngākau māhaki hoki, i te whakaute hoki ki ngā tāngata nō ngā ahurea maha, kia ngākau titikaha hoki ki te hāpai, ki te whakamau hoki i ngā māhorahoratanga matua me ngā tika tangata, tae atu ki ngā tika ahurea, ki ngā tika kia whai ōhanga hoki, ki ngā tika pāpori hoki:

Ka whakaute tātou i Te Tiriti o Waitangi/The Treaty of Waitangi hei puka whakapūmau mō te motu whānui:

Ka uara tātou i te māhorahora, i te mea angitu hoki mō ngā tāngata katoa, te tōkeke hoki, te taurite hoki, te ōritetanga hoki, te ukaukatanga o te taiao hoki, te kaitiakitanga hoki me te tikanga Māori, he ōhanga kaha, he whakaaro nui mō te hapori me te whakaute mō te whānau, tae rawa atu ki te manaaki tamariki:

Ka tautoko tātou kia mahea te tuaritanga o te mana whakahaere i waenga i Te Upoko o Te Whenua Rangatira, i te Pāremata hoki, i te Kāwanatanga hoki, me tētahi Hunga Whakawā ā-Ture, he matatika, he motuhake hoki:

Ka whakaū tātou ka takea mai a Aotearoa Niu Tireni i te mātāpono mā te iwi anō rātou e ārahi ā-kāwana mā tētahi pūnaha manapori ka whai māngai, ka noho haepapa hoki, ka whai haepapatanga hoki te kāwanatanga mā ngā pōtitanga e māhorahora ana, e tōkeke ana hoki:

Ka akiaki tātou kia whaiuru te iwi whānui ki ngā whakatau ōkawa kia whakaū ai ka nui ake te whakaaroaro i ngā whakatau matua mō te kaupapa here:

Ka tino hiahia tātou ki te noho ki tētahi porihanga māhorahora me tētahi pūnaha

We wish to live in an open society with a robust, accountable and transparent system of democratic government under the rule of law nationally and internationally:

We are a proud and independent nation with our own voice within the community of nations:

We express our desire to build upon our rich constitutional heritage and accordingly adopt this written Constitution.

Part 1 Principles

1 The objectives of, and limits on, public power

(1) This Constitution confers public power on institutions and public officials of the State to promote the peace, order, and good government of Aotearoa New Zealand for the following purposes:
   (a) to ensure that public power is exercised democratically, that is to say, with the participation of people, transparently, accountably, and subject to checks and balances that ensure minorities are protected:
   (b) to secure an environment adequate to equitably meet the needs of present generations in an ecologically sustainable manner and not impair the rights of future generations to reasonably meet their needs:
   (c) to protect the human rights of all New Zealanders:
   (d) to respect and enhance the relationship between Māori and the State, and the capacity of Māori collectively to control and influence the use of their resources:
   (e) to advance the public welfare so that all New Zealanders can aspire to, and achieve, fulfilling lives free from poverty, fear, ignorance, and violence:
   (f) to foster a community that accommodates difference, respects individuality, yet achieves collective goals for the common good,

pūioio, tētahi pūnaha noho haepapa hoki, tētahi pūnaha taiahoaho hoki o tētahi kāwanatanga manapori i raro i te ritenga o te ture ā-motu, ā-ao hoki:

Ko tātou nei, he whakahī, he motuhake hoki tō tātou motu whānui, he reo ake tō tātou i waenga i te hapori o ngā whenua o te ao:

Ka whakapuaki tātou i tō tātou tino hiahia ki te whakakaha ake i tō tātou hītori pouhere, nā whai anō ka whāia tēnei Pouhere ā-tuhi.

Wāhanga 1 Ngā Mātāpono

1 Ko ngā whāinga me ngā herenga kei te mana whakahaere tūmatanui

(1) Ka tuku tēnei Pouhere i te mana whakahaere tūmatanui ki ngā hinonga whakahaere me ngā āpiha tūmatanui o te Whenua Rangatira kia hohou ai te rongo, kia rangimārie ai hoki te noho, kia pai ai hoki te mahi kāwanatanga mō Aotearoa Niu Tireni mō ngā aronga e whai ake nei:

    (a) kia whakaū ka manapori te whakamahinga o te mana whakahaere tūmatanui, me kī, me te whaiuru a te iwi, te taiahoaho hoki, te noho haepapa hoki, e ai ki ngā hihiratanga me ngā whakatautika kia whakaū ai ka whakamarumarutia a ngāi tokoiti:

    (b) kia mau tētahi wāhi whita hei whakatutuki matatika nei i ngā matea o ngā whakatipuranga o nāianei i roto i tētahi āhuatanga ukauka hauropi me te kore taupēhi i ngā tika o ngā whakatipuranga e haere mai nei, kia āta whakatutuki hoki i ō rātou matea:

    (c) kia whakamarumaru i ngā tika tangata o ngā tāngata katoa o Aotearoa Niu Tireni:

    (d) kia whakaute, kia whakarākai hoki i te hononga i waenga i ngāi Māori me te Whenua Rangatira, me te āheitanga o te katoa o ngāi Māori ki te whakahaere, ki te whakaawe hoki i te whakamahinga o ō rātou rawa:

    (e) kia kōkiri whakamua i te toiora tūmatanui kia whai ai, kia whakatutuki ai ngā tāngata katoa o Aotearoa Niu Tireni i ngā oranga whai hua he pōhara kore, he mataku kore hoki, he kūare kore hoki, he patu kore hoki:

    (f) kia whakatītina i tētahi hapori ka whai wāhi ngā rerekētanga, ka whakautehia te tū takitahi, engari ka takitini hoki te whakatutuki whāinga mō te katoa, ka tōkeke hoki kia whai hua

allowing a fair go to all:
(g) to recognise that there will be a diversity of views on many questions touching on the public welfare, which need to be resolved through discussion, respectful debate, and decision making in a range of forums, including central and local government.

Part 2 The Bill of Rights
Life and security of the person

2 Right not to be deprived of life

(1) No one may be deprived of life except on such grounds as are established by law and are consistent with the principles of fundamental justice.
(2) No one may be condemned to death or executed.

3 Right not to be subjected to torture or cruel treatment

Everyone has the right not to be subjected to—
(a) torture; or
(b) cruel, degrading, or disproportionately severe treatment or punishment.

4 Right not to be subjected to medical or scientific experimentation

Every person has the right not to be subjected to medical or scientific experimentation without that person's consent.

5 Right to refuse to undergo medical treatment

Everyone has the right to refuse to undergo any medical treatment.

6 Right not to be held in slavery, servitude nor to be required to perform forced or compulsory labour

Everyone has the right not to be held in slavery or in servitude nor to be required to perform forced or compulsory labour.

ko tēnā, ko tēnā:
(g) kia whakaū he kanorau ngā tirohanga mō ngā take maha e pā ana ki te toiora tūmatanui, me whakatau rawa mā te matapaki, mā te tautohetohe whai whakaute hoki, mā te whakatau hoki i roto i te whānuitanga o ngā wāhi, tae atu ki te kāwanatanga ā-motu me te kāwanatanga ā-rohe.

Wāhanga 2 Te Pire Tika Tangata
Te oranga me te whakamarutanga o te tangata

2 Te tika kia kaua e whakamatea

(1) Kāore te tangata e whakamatea, atu i ngā wā ka whakaturetia, ka hāngai hoki ki ngā mātāpono hōhonu o te mana ture.
(2) Kāore te tangata e whakawāngia kia mate, e patua rānei kia mate.

3 Te tika kia kaua e whakamamaetia, e tūkinotia hoki

Kei te tangata te tika kia kaua e—
(a) whakamamaetia;
(b) tūkinotia rānei, e whakaitingia rānei, e takahia kinotia kia pāhikahika te putanga rānei, e hāmenetia rawatia rānei.

4 Te tika kia kaua e whakamātauria mahi rata nei, pūtaiao nei hoki

Kei te tangata te tika kia kaua e whakamātauria mahi rata nei, pūtaiao nei hoki me te kore whakaae a taua tangata nei.

5 Te tika kia whakakāhore i te maimoatanga mahi rata

Kei te tangata te tika ki te whakakāhore i ngā maimoatanga mahi rata katoa.

6 Te tika kia kaua e mauheretia kia noho hei taurekareka, hei tonotono, hei kaimahi ka pēhia, ka herea rawatia ki te mahi

Kei te tangata te tika kia kaua e mauheretia kia noho hei taurekareka, hei tonotono rānei, hei kaimahi ka pēhia rānei, ka herea rawatia rānei ki te mahi.

Democratic and civil rights

7 Electoral rights

Every citizen who is over the age of 16 years—
  (a) has the right to vote in genuine periodic elections for Parliament and for local government; and
  (b) is qualified for membership of Parliament and local government.

8 Freedom of thought, conscience, and religion

Everyone has the right to freedom of thought, conscience, religion, and belief, including the right to adopt and to hold opinions without interference.

9 Freedom of expression

Everyone has the right to freedom of expression, including the freedom to seek, receive, and impart information and opinions of any kind in any form.

10 Manifestation of religion and belief

Aotearoa New Zealand is a secular state in which every person has the right to manifest that person's religion or belief in worship, observance, practice, or teaching, either individually or in community with others, and either in public or in private.

11 Freedom of peaceful assembly

Everyone has the right to freedom of peaceful assembly.

12 Freedom of association

Everyone has the right to freedom of association.

13 Right to privacy

  (1) Everyone has the right not to be subject to arbitrary or unlawful interference with that person's privacy, family, home, or correspondence.
  (2) Everyone has the right to be secure against unreasonable search or

Ngā tika manapori, ngā tika hiwhiri hoki

7 Ngā tika pōtitanga

Kei ngā kirirarau katoa pakeke ake i ngā tau 16—
  (a) te tika kia pōti i ngā pōtitanga tūturu, kauteatea hoki mō te Pāremata, mō te kāwanatanga ā-rohe hoki;
  (b) he whai tohu hoki hei mema Pāremata, hei mema kāwanatanga ā-rohe.

8 Te māhorahora o te whakaaro, o te ngākau manako hoki, o te wairuatanga hoki

Kei te tangata te tika mō te māhorahora o te whakaaro, mō te ngākau manako hoki, mō te wairuatanga hoki, mō te whakapono hoki, tae atu ki te tika kia whai atu, kia whai whakaaro hoki me te kore raweke.

9 Te māhorahora ki te whakapuaki whakaaro

Kei te tangata te tika mō te māhorahora ki te whakapuaki whakaaro, tae atu ki te māhorahora ki te rapu, ki te whiwhi hoki, ki te tuku hoki i ngā momo pārongo me ngā momo whakaaro katoa.

10 Te whakatinanatanga o te wairuatanga, o te whakapono hoki

He whenua rangatira here kore ki tētahi hāhi kotahi a Aotearoa Niu Tireni kei te tangata te tika ki te whakatinana i te wairuatanga, i te whakapono rānei mā te karakia, mā te whai, mā te tikanga, mā te whakaako, takitahi mai, hei hapori rānei me tangata kē, tūmatanui nei rānei, tūmataiti nei rānei.

11 Te māhorahora o te huihui rangimārie

Kei te tangata te tika mō te māhorahora o te huihui rangimārie.

12 Te māhorahora o te tōpūtanga

Kei te tangata te tika mō te māhorahora o te tōpūtanga.

13 Te tika o te noho tūmataiti

  (1) Kei te tangata te tika kia kaua e pāngia te tūmataiti o te tangata, o te whānau rānei, o te kāinga rānei, o ngā whakawhitinga kōrero a taua tangata nei, ki te raweke tīpokapoka noa, ki te rāwekeweke takahi ture rānei.
  (2) Kei te tangata te tika kia noho haumaru i te rapunga take kore, i te mau

seizure, whether of the person, property, or correspondence or otherwise.

14 Freedom of movement

(1) Everyone lawfully in Aotearoa New Zealand has the right to freedom of movement and residence in Aotearoa New Zealand.
(2) Every citizen of Aotearoa New Zealand has the right to enter and remain in Aotearoa New Zealand.
(3) Everyone has the right to leave Aotearoa New Zealand.
(4) No one who is not a citizen of Aotearoa New Zealand and who is lawfully in Aotearoa New Zealand may be required to leave Aotearoa New Zealand except under a decision taken on grounds prescribed by law.
(5) Every citizen of Aotearoa New Zealand has the right to a passport.

Equality, non-discrimination, and minority rights

15 Equality before the law

Everyone must be treated as equal before the law, including before the courts and tribunals, and must be given the equal protection of the law.

16 Freedom from discrimination

(1) Everyone has the right to freedom from discrimination on the grounds of sex, gender identity and expression, sexual orientation, colour, race, language, ethnic or national origins, marital or family status, religious or ethical belief, disability, age, political or other opinion, or employment status.
(2) Measures taken in good faith for the purpose of assisting or advancing persons or groups of persons disadvantaged because of discrimination on the grounds listed in paragraph (1) do not constitute discrimination.

take kore rānei, ahakoa i te tangata, ahakoa i te wāhi rānei, ahakoa i te whakawhitinga kōrero rānei, ahakoa i mea kē atu rānei.

14 Te māhorahora o te hāereere

(1) Kei te tangata kei roto i Aotearoa Niu Tireni i raro i te ture, te tika mō te māhorahora o te hāereere, o te noho hoki i Aotearoa Niu Tireni.

(2) Kei te kirirarau o Aotearoa Niu Tireni te tika ki te uru mai, ki te noho mai tonu i roto i Aotearoa Niu Tireni.

(3) Kei te tangata te tika ki te wehe atu i Aotearoa Niu Tireni.

(4) Kāore te tangata ehara ia i te kirirarau nō Aotearoa Niu Tireni kei roto hoki ia i Aotearoa Niu Tireni i raro i te ture ka panaia atu i Aotearoa Niu Tireni, atu i ngā wā ka whakatauria e ai ki te ture.

(5) Kei ngā kirirarau katoa o Aotearoa Niu Tireni te tika kia whai puka uruwhenua.

Te ōritetanga, te kore whakatoihara, me ngā tika o ngāi tokoiti

15 Te noho ōrite i raro i te ture

Ka noho ōrite ngā tāngata katoa i raro i te ture, tae atu ki ngā kōti, ki ngā taraipiunara hoki, ā, me pērā rawa te ōrite o te whakamarumaru i raro i te ture.

16 Te noho māhorahora i te toihara

(1) Kei te tangata te tika kia noho māhorahora i te toihara ka whiua i runga i te hōkakatanga, i te tuakiri huanga rānei, i te whakapuaki huanga rānei, i te aronga hōkaka rānei, i te tae o te kiri rānei, i te kāwai iwi rānei, i te reo rānei, i te mātāwaka rānei, i ngā takenga i whenua kē rānei, i te āhua mārena, i te āhua o te whānau rānei, i te wairuatanga rānei, i te whakapono matatika rānei, i te hauā rānei, i te pakeketanga rānei, i te tōrangapū rānei, i whakaaro kē atu rānei, i te āhua o te taimahi rānei.

(2) Ka whāia ngā tikanga ka mahia i runga i te ngākau pai hei āwhina, hei hāpai i ngā tāngata, i ngā rōpū tāngata rānei e noho taumaha ana i te toihara e ai ki ngā kōrero e rārangitia ana i roto i te rerenga (1) ehara ērā i te toihara.

17 Rights of minorities

A person who belongs to an ethnic, religious, or linguistic minority in Aotearoa New Zealand must not be denied the right, in community with other members of that minority, to enjoy the culture, to profess and practise the religion, or to use the language, of that minority.

18 Children's rights

(1) Every child has the right to be free from neglect, abuse, degradation, and exploitative labour practices.
(2) In all proceedings concerning children,—
    (a) the best interests of the child must be a primary consideration; and
    (b) the child's views must, if practicable, be obtained and given due weight.

Liberty, arrest, detention, and criminal process

19 Liberty of the person

Everyone has the right —
    (a) to liberty and security of the person, and must not be deprived thereof except in accordance with the principles of fundamental justice; and
    (b) not to be arbitrarily or unlawfully arrested or detained.

20 Rights of persons arrested or detained

(1) Everyone who is arrested or who is detained under any enactment—
    (a) must be informed at the time of the arrest or detention of the reason for it; and
    (b) must have the right to consult and instruct a lawyer without delay and to be informed of that right; and
    (c) must have the right to have the validity of the arrest or detention determined without delay by way of *habeas corpus* and to be released if the arrest or detention is not lawful.

17 Ngā tika o ngāi tokoiti

Me kaua rawa e kati te tika o te tangata nō tētahi tokoiti mātāwaka, he wairuatanga ake tō rātou rānei, he reo ake tō rātou rānei kei roto i Aotearoa Niu Tireni, e noho hapori ana me tāngata anō nō taua tokoiti, kia noho pai i roto i te ahurea, kia whakapuaki, kia whai hoki i ngā tikanga o taua wairuatanga hoki, kia whakamahi rānei i te reo o taua tokoiti.

18 Ngā tika tamariki

(1) Kei ia tamaiti te tika kia māhorahora i te whakangongo, i te tūkino hoki, i te whakaiti hoki, i ngā mahi whakahāwini i te tamaiti kia whakamahia.

(2) I roto i ngā whakahaerenga katoa e pā ana ki te tamariki,—

    (a) me mātua whakaaro rawa mō te tamaiti me ngā painga mōna;

    (b) me whiwhi rawa hoki, me āta whakaaro rawa hoki mō ngā whakaaro o te tamaiti ki ōna taumata e taea ana.

Te noho here kore, te mauhere, te here tonu, me te hātepe taihara

19 Te noho here kore o te tangata

Kei te tangata te tika—

    (a) kia noho here kore, kia noho haumaru hoki te tangata, ā, nā whai anō me kaua rawa e whakaeo, atu i ngā wā e ai ki ngā mātāpono hōhonu o te mana ture;

    (b) kia kaua rawa hoki e mauheretia, e herea tonutia rānei i runga i te tīpokapoka, i te kore whai rānei i te ture.

20 Ngā tika o te hunga ka mauheretia, ka herea tonutia rānei

(1) Ko te tangata ka mauheretia, ka herea tonutia rānei i raro i tētahi whakaturetanga—

    (a) me whakamōhio rawa i te wā ka mauheretia, ka herea tonutia rānei, mō te aha hoki te take;

    (b) me āhei rawa hoki te whai tika kia kōrero tahi me tētahi rōia, kia tohutohu hoki i tētahi rōia i taua wā tonu, kia whakamōhiotia mai hoki mō taua tika;

    (c) me āhei rawa hoki te whai tika kia whakatauria te pono o te mauheretanga, o te herenga rānei, i taua wā tonu mā te tikanga o te *habeas corpus*, ā, kia tukuna kia haere mehemea kāore te mauheretanga, te herenga tonu rānei i te whai i te ture.

(2) Everyone who is arrested for an offence has the right to be charged promptly or to be released.
(3) Everyone who is arrested for an offence and is not released must be brought as soon as possible before a court or competent tribunal.
(4) Everyone who is arrested or detained under any enactment for any offence or suspected offence must have the right to refrain from making any statement and to be informed of that right.
(5) Everyone deprived of liberty must be treated with humanity and with respect for the inherent dignity of the person.

21 Rights of persons charged

Everyone who is charged with an offence—
   (a) must be informed promptly and in detail of the nature and cause of the charge; and
   (b) must be released on reasonable terms and conditions unless there is just cause for continued detention; and
   (c) must have the right to consult and instruct a lawyer; and
   (d) must have the right to adequate time and facilities to prepare a defence; and
   (e) must have the right, except in the case of an offence under military law tried before a military tribunal, to the benefit of a trial by jury when the penalty for the offence is or includes imprisonment for two years or more; and
   (f) must have the right to receive legal assistance without cost if the interests of justice so require and the person does not have sufficient means to provide for that assistance; and
   (g) must have the right to have the free assistance of an interpreter if the person cannot understand or speak the language used in court.

22 Minimum standards of criminal procedure

Everyone who is charged with an offence has, in relation to the determination of the charge, the following minimum rights:

(2) Kei te tangata ka mauheretia mō tētahi mahi taihara te tika kia wawe te whai heitara, me tuku rānei kia haere.
(3) Me wawe rawa hoki te mau mai te tangata ka mauheretia mō tētahi mahi taihara, kāore hoki i tukuna kia haere, ki mua tonu i te aroaro o tētahi kōti, o tētahi taraipiunara whai mana rānei.
(4) Me whai tika rawa te tangata ka mauheretia, ka herea tonutia rānei i raro i tētahi whakaturetanga mō tētahi mahi taihara kua mahia, ka whakapaetia pea rānei i mahia, kia noho wahangū, kia whakamōhiotia hoki mō taua tika.
(5) Me whakatangata rawa, me whakaute rawa te tangata ka noho here kore i te whakaeo, i runga i te tū rangatira ake o te tangata.

21 Ngā tika o ngā tāngata ka whai heitara

Ko te tangata ka whai heitara mō tētahi hara—
(a) me wawe rawa te whakamōhio, me ngā kōrero whakamārama mō te āhua me te pūtake o te heitara;
(b) me tuku rawa hoki kia haere i runga i ngā ritenga me ngā āhuatanga e taea ana, māna arā kē tētahi take anō kia mau tonu;
(c) me whai rawa hoki te tika kia kōrero tahi me tētahi rōia, kia tohutohu hoki i tētahi rōia;
(d) me whai rawa hoki te tika kia whai wā, kia whai wāhi hoki ki te whakarite i tētahi wawaonga;
(e) me whai rawa hoki te tika kia whakawāngia mā tētahi hunga whakawā ā-ture i ngā wā e rua tau neke atu te roa o te mauheretanga o te whakawhiunga mō te hara, atu i ngā wā ka whakamātauria tētahi hara i raro i te ture ngārahu i mua tonu i te aroaro o tētahi taraipiunara ngārahu;
(f) me whai rawa hoki te tika kia whiwhi āwhina ā-ture me te utu kore mehemea me pērā kia ea ai ngā whāinga o te mana ture, waihoki kāore he rawa o te tangata hei tuku āwhina;
(g) me whai rawa hoki te tika kia āwhinatia e tētahi kaiwhakawhiti reo ā-waha mō te utu kore mehemea kāore te tangata i te mārama, i te āhei hoki te kōrero i te reo o te kōti.

22 Ngā paerewa mōkito o te tukanga taihara

Ko te tangata ka whai heitara mō tētahi hara, kei a rātou ngā tika mōkito e whai ake nei, me kī, e ai ki te whakataunga o te heitara:

(a) the right to a fair and public hearing by an independent and impartial court:
(b) the right to be tried without undue delay:
(c) the right to be presumed innocent until proved guilty according to law:
(d) the right not to be compelled to be a witness or to confess guilt:
(e) the right to be present at the trial and to present a defence:
(f) the right to examine the witnesses for the prosecution and to obtain the attendance and examination of witnesses for the defence under the same conditions as the prosecution:
(g) the right, if convicted of an offence in respect of which the penalty has been varied between the commission of the offence and sentencing, to the benefit of the lesser penalty:
(h) the right, if convicted of the offence, to appeal according to law to a higher court against the conviction or against the sentence or against both:
(i) the right, in the case of a child, to be dealt with in a manner that takes account of the child's age.

23 Retroactive penalties and double jeopardy

(1) No one is liable to conviction of any offence on account of any act or omission which did not constitute an offence by such person under the law of Aotearoa New Zealand at the time it occurred.

(b) No one who has been finally acquitted or convicted of, or pardoned for, an offence may be tried or punished for it again.

Fair process

24 Right to justice

(1) Every person has the right to the observance of the principles of natural justice by any tribunal or other public authority which has the power to make a determination in respect of that person's rights, obligations, or interests protected or recognised by law.

(2) Every person whose rights, obligations, or interests protected or

(a) te tika kia whakawāngia i runga i te tōkeke, i roto hoki i tētahi huinga tūmatanui, i tētahi kōti motuhake, matatika hoki:
(b) te tika kia whakawāngia me te tatari kore:
(c) te tika kia noho ānō nei he harakore tonu tae atu ki te wā ka whakaaturia kua mahi hara e ai ki te ture:
(d) te tika kia kaua e uruhia kia tū hei kaiwhāki, kia whāki atu nōna ake te kino:
(e) te tika kia tae ā-tinana atu ki te kōti, kia whakatakoto hoki i tētahi wawaonga:
(f) te tika kia whakamātau i ngā kaiwhāki nā te taha whakawhiu i whakatū, kia āhei hoki te tono atu, te whakamātau hoki i ngā kaiwhāki nā te taha wawaonga i whakatū pērā i ō te taha whakawhiu āhuatanga:
(g) te tika kia whai painga i te hāmene iti iho te kaha, mehemea ka whiua mō tētahi hara ka panonihia te hāmene mai i te wā i mahia te hara tae atu ki te wā o te whakawhiu:
(h) te tika, mehemea ka whiua mō tētahi hara, kia īnoi atu ki tētahi kōti nui ake te mana e ai ki te ture, hei tono pīra mō te whiunga, mō te whakawhiu rānei, mō aua āhuatanga e rua rānei:
(i) te tika, mehemea he tamaiti, kia whakawāngia me te whai whakaaro mō ngā tau o te tamaiti.

23 Ngā hāmene o mua me te tukurua

(1) Kāore te tangata e whiua anō mō tētahi hara, mō tētahi hapa rānei a te tangata mehemea ehara taua mahi i te hara e ai ki te ture o Aotearoa Niu Tireni i te wā i mahia ai.
(b) Kāore te tangata kua whakatauria rawatia ake he harakore, kua whiua rānei, kua murua rānei tētahi hara, e whakawāngia anō, e hāmenetia anō mō taua hara.

Hātepe tōkeke

24 Te tika kia whai mana ture

(1) Kei te tangata te tika kia hāpainga ngā mātāpono o te mana ture me te pono e tētahi taraipiunara, e mana tūmatanui kē atu rānei, kei reira te mana whakahaere ki te whakatau i runga i ngā tika, ngā herenga rānei, ngā pānga rānei o te tangata, ka whakamarumarutia, ka whakaūngia rānei i raro i te ture.
(2) Kei te tangata kua pāngia ōna tika, ōna herenga rānei, ōna pānga rānei

recognised by law have been affected by a determination of any tribunal or other public authority has the right to apply, in accordance with law, for judicial review of that determination.

(3) Every person has the right to bring civil proceedings against, and to defend civil proceedings brought by, the State, and to have those proceedings heard, according to law, in the same way as civil proceedings between individuals.

Property

25 Right to property

(1) Everyone has the right not to be deprived of their property except in accordance with the following principles:
    (a) deprivation must not occur except under an Act of Parliament:
    (b) deprivation may occur only under a law of general application and in pursuit of a public purpose or public interest:
    (c) deprivation must not be arbitrary:
    (d) deprivation by way of expropriation must be subject to the prompt payment of just and equitable compensation.

(2) Deprivation in pursuit of a public purpose or public interest includes, but is not limited to—
    (a) the carrying out of public works (whether or not the works are undertaken by a person or body referred to in Article 31):
    (b) taxation, and the levying of rates or charges:
    (c) the benefit of public health, resource management, the environment, public transport, the integrity of the financial sector, law enforcement, family relationship purposes, or any other aspect of the common good.

ka whakamarumarutia, ka whakaūngia rānei i raro i te ture, e tētahi whakatau a tētahi taraipiunara, a tētahi mana tūmatanui rānei, te tika ki te tono atu e ai ki te ture mō tētahi arotake whakawā ā-ture i taua whakatau.

(3) Kei te tangata te tika kia kōkiri i tētahi whakahaerenga ā-hiwhiri mō tētahi take, whakahē atu rānei, papare atu rānei i tētahi whakahaerenga ā-hiwhiri ka kōkirihia e te Whenua Rangatira, kia rangona hoki aua whakahaerenga, e ai ki te ture, pērā i ngā whakahaerenga ā-hiwhiri a tētahi tangata ki tētahi tangata.

He Rawa

25 Te tika kia whai rawa

(1) Kei te tangata te tika kia kaua e noho whakaeo i ōna rawa atu i ngā wā, e ai ki ngā mātāpono, e whai ake nei:
  (a) me kaua rawa te whakaeo e tinana ai, atu i ngā pānga e ai ki tētahi Ture Pāremata:
  (b) ka tinana pea te whakaeo i raro i tētahi ture pānga whānui anake, hei whai atu hoki i tētahi aronga tūmatanui, i tētahi pānga tūmatanui rānei:
  (c) me kaua rawa e tīpokapoka te whakaeo:
  (d) me whai rawa te whakaeo ā-raupatu rawa mā te utu wawe i tētahi pānga hakaea e tika ana, e matatika ana hoki.

(2) Ko te whakaeo mā te whai i tētahi aronga tūmatanui, i tētahi pānga tūmatanui rānei, tae atu rā, engari kāore i te herea e te—
  (a) mahi i ngā mahi tūmatanui (ahakoa āe rānei, ahakoa kāore rānei ka mahia e tētahi tangata, e tētahi rangatōpū rānei ka kōrerotia i roto i te Whiti 31):
  (b) tāke, me te whakaeke i ngā reiti, i ngā utu rānei:
  (c) painga o te hauora tūmatanui, o te whakahaeretanga o ngā rawa rānei, o te taiao rānei, o ngā waka tūmatanui rānei, o te ngākau tapatahi rānei o te rāngai tahua, o te hāpai ture rānei, o ngā kaupapa rānei e pā ana ki te hononga whānau, o tētahi atu āhuatanga rānei e whai painga ai te katoa.

The Environment

26 Environmental right

(1) Everyone has the right—
   (a) to an environment that is not harmful to their health or well-being; and
   (b) to have the environment protected, for the benefit of present and future generations, through reasonable legislative and other measures that—
      (i) prevent pollution and ecological degradation:
      (ii) promote conservation and biodiversity:
      (iii) secure ecologically sustainable development and the use of natural resources in a manner that is managed to maintain the equilibrium of the environment:
      (iv) include kaitiakitanga, which is the exercise of guardianship by the tangata whenua of an area in accordance with tikanga Māori in relation to natural and physical resources.
(2) The Commissioner for the Environment may, if the Commissioner considers it appropriate to do so,—
   (a) conduct litigation to safeguard the rights contained in this Article:
   (b) intervene in litigation in which issues relating to those rights are raised.

Social and Economic Rights

27 Right to a State education

Every person who has attained the age of five and is under the age of 20 is entitled to free enrolment and free education at a State primary or a State secondary school.

28 Labour relations

Every worker has the right—
   (a) to resort to collective action in the event of a conflict of interests, including the right to strike:
   (b) to enjoy satisfactory health and safety conditions in their working environment:

Te Taiao

26 Te tika taiao

(1) Kei te tangata te tika—
(a) ki tētahi taiao kāore e pā kino i te hauora, i te toiora rānei o te tangata:
(b) kia whakamarumarutia hoki te taiao, hei painga mō ngā whakatipuranga o nāianei, e haere mai nei rānei, mā ngā whakaturetanga e taea ana me mahi kē atu—
  (i) hei ārai parahanga, hei ārai hoki i te whakaiti hauropi:
  (ii) hei toko ake i te whāomoomo, i te rerenga rauropi hoki:
  (iii) hei whakamau i te whanaketanga toitū ā-hauropi, hei whakamahi hoki i ngā rawa māori i runga i tētahi āhuatanga ka whakahaeretia kia pai ai tonu te mauri o te taiao:
  (iv) ka whai wāhi te kaitiakitanga, he kaupapa tiaki nō te tangata whenua o tētahi wāhi, e ai ki ngā tikanga Māori, e pā ana ki ngā rawa māori, ki ngā rawa ōkiko hoki.
(2) Mā te Kaikōmihana mō te Taiao e mahi ēnei e whai ake nei, mehemea e ai ki ngā whakaaro o te Kaikōmihana he tika kia pēnei, arā,—
(a) kia whai i tētahi take ture hei tiaki i ngā tika kei roto i tēnei Whiti:
(b) kia uru ki roto i te whai i tētahi take ture e pā ana ki ngā take whai pānga e ahu mai ai aua tika.

Ngā Tika Pāpori, Ngā Tika Ōhanga hoki

27 Te tika kia whai mātauranga i te Whenua Rangatira

Ka whai mana te tangata kua eke ki te rima tau te pakeke, ā, kei raro tonu i te 20 tau te pakeke kia whakaurua, kia kuraina me te utu kore ki tētahi kura tuatahi, ki tētahi kura tuarua rānei o te Whenua Rangatira.

28 Ngā hononga mō te mahi

Kei te kaimahi te tika—
(a) kia tū kotahi i ngā wā ka puta mai tētahi taupapatu whāinga, tae atu ki te tika kia porotū:
(b) kia pai ngā āhuatanga hauora, ngā āhuatanga haumaru hoki i roto i tōna wāhi mahi:

(c) to earn their living in an occupation freely entered upon.

29 Rights relating to standard of living and health

In making provision for the social and economic welfare of the people, Parliament and the Government must be guided by the following non-justiciable rights:
    (a) everyone should enjoy an adequate standard of living, which encompasses adequate food, clothing, and housing:
    (b) everyone who requires social support should have access to a system of social security that provides financial and other support and clearly establishes the entitlements that may be claimed:
    (c) everyone should be able to enjoy the highest attainable standard of physical and mental health.

Application of Bill of Rights

30 Rights affirmed

The rights and freedoms contained in this Part are adopted and affirmed.

31 Application

This Bill of Rights applies only to acts done—
    (a) by the legislative, executive, or judicial branches of the State; or
    (b) by any person or body in the performance of any public function, power, or duty conferred or imposed on that person or body.

32 Powers of the Commission for Human Rights to conduct litigation

The Commission for Human Rights may, where it considers it appropriate to do so—
    (a) conduct litigation to safeguard the rights contained in this Part:
    (b) intervene in litigation where issues relating to the rights contained in this Part are raised.

(c) kia whai oranga ia i tētahi umanga mahi ka whāia noatia.

29 Ngā tika e pā ana ki te taumata oranga me te hauora

Hei whakarite āheinga mō te toiora pāpori, mō te toiora ōhanga hoki o te iwi whānui, me ārahi rawa te Pāremata me te Kāwanatanga e ngā tika here kore ki te ture e whai ake nei:

(a) kia pai noa te noho o te tangata ki tētahi taumata oranga, tae atu ki te kai pai, ki te kākahu pai hoki, ki te whare pai hoki:

(b) kia āhei te tangata me whai tautoko oranga ka tika, te whakauru ki roto i tētahi pūnaha whakapūmau oranga e tukuna ai te tautoko ā-pūtea me tautoko kē atu hoki, ā, ka mahea hoki ngā whiwhinga ka āhei te tono atu:

(c) kia āhei te tangata te noho pai i roto i ngā painga o te hauora tinana, o te hauora hinengaro hoki.

Te whakatinana i te Pire Tika Tangata

30 Te whakaū i ngā tika

Ka whāia, ka whakaūngia hoki ngā tika me ngā māhorahoratanga o tēnei Wāhanga.

31 Te whakatinana

Ka hāngai tēnei Pire Tika Tangata ki ngā mahi ka mahia—

(a) e ngā kāwai hanga ture, e Te Rūnanga Kāwanatanga rānei, e ngā kāwai whakawā ā-ture rānei o te Whenua Rangatira;

(b) e tētahi tangata rānei, e tētahi rangatōpū rānei i roto i ngā mahi i tētahi āheinga tūmatanui, i tētahi mana whakahaere rānei, i tētahi kawenga ka tukuna, ka whakatauria rānei ki runga i taua tangata, i taua rangatōpū rānei.

32 Ngā mana whakahaere o Te Kāhui Tika Tangata kia whai take ture

I ngā wā ka whakaarotia e tika ana kia mahi pēnei, ka āhei Te Kāhui Tika Tangata te—

(a) whai take ture hei tiaki i ngā tika kei roto i tēnei Wāhanga:

(b) kia uru ki roto i te whai take ture e pā ana ki ngā take whai pānga e ahu mai ai aua tika i roto i tēnei Wāhanga.

33 Justified limitations

The rights and freedoms contained in this Part may be subject only to such reasonable limits prescribed by law as can be demonstrably justified in a free and democratic society.

34 Rights preferred

Wherever an enactment can be given a meaning that is consistent with the rights and freedoms contained in this Part, that meaning is preferred to any other meaning.

35 Legal persons entitled to benefit of rights and freedoms

(1) Except where the provisions of this Part otherwise provide, the provisions of this Part apply, so far as practicable, for the benefit of all legal persons as well as for the benefit of all natural persons.

(2) Articles 2 (right not to be deprived of life), 3(a) (right not to be subjected to torture), 4 (right not to be subjected to medical or scientific experimentation), 5 (right to refuse to undergo medical treatment), 6 (right not to be held in slavery, servitude nor to be required to perform forced compulsory labour), 7 (electoral rights), 14 (freedom of movement), 19 (liberty of the person), and 20 (rights of persons arrested or detained) do not apply to legal persons who are not natural persons.

36 Other rights and freedoms not affected

An existing right or freedom must not be held to be abrogated or restricted by reason only that the right or freedom is not included in this Part or is included only in part.

Part 3 Te Tiriti o Waitangi/the Treaty of Waitangi

37 Te Tiriti o Waitangi/the Treaty of Waitangi

(1) The rights that persons of Māori descent enjoy at the commencement of this Constitution as Indigenous peoples under te Tiriti o Waitangi/the Treaty of Waitangi are hereby recognised and affirmed.

33 Ngā herenga ka parahautia

Ka pāngia noatia ngā tika me ngā māhorahoratanga kei roto i tēnei Wāhanga e ngā herenga e taea ana ka tohua e te ture e whakapuakina mai ai i roto i tētahi porihanga māhorahora, manapori hoki.

34 Ngā tika ka tino hiahiatia

I ngā wā ka whai kōrero whakamārama tētahi whakaturetanga e hāngai ana ki ngā tika me ngā māhorahoratanga kei roto i tēnei Wāhanga, koirā te kōrero whakamārama ka tino hiahiatia i ō ērā atu kōrero whakamārama.

35 Ngā tāngata ā-ture e whai mana ana kia whai painga i ngā tika me ngā māhorahoratanga

(1) Atu i ngā wā ka tuku āwhina atu ngā āheinga o tēnei Wāhanga, ka hāngai ngā āheinga o tēnei Wāhanga, ki ōna taumata e taea ana, hei painga mō ngā tāngata ā-ture katoa, hei painga hoki mō ngā tāngata tūturu katoa.

(2) Kāore e hāngai ki ngā tāngata ā-ture ehara rātou i te tangata tūturu ngā Whiti 2 (te tika kia kaua e whakamatea), 3(a) (te tika kia kaua e whakamamaetia, e tūkinotia hoki), 4 (te tika kia kaua e whakamātauria mahi rata nei, pūtaiao nei hoki), 5 (te tika kia whakakāhore i te maimoatanga mahi rata), 6 (te tika kia kaua e mauheretia kia noho hei taurekareka, hei tonotono, hei kaimahi ka pēhia, ka herea rawatia ki te mahi), 7 (ngā tika pōtitanga), 14 (te māhorahora o te hāereere), 19 (te noho here kore o te tangata), 20 (ngā tika o te hunga ka mauheretia, ka herea tonutia rānei) hoki.

36 Ngā tika me māhorahoratanga kē atu kāore e pāngia

Me kaua rawa tētahi tika tūturu, tētahi māhorahoratanga tūturu rānei e tārewahia kia whakakorengia rānei, e ārikarikatia rānei nā te mea kāore i whai wāhi i roto i tēnei Wāhanga, kei roto rānei tētahi wāhanga anake.

Wāhanga 3 Te Tiriti o Waitangi/The Treaty of Waitangi

37 Te Tiriti o Waitangi/The Treaty of Waitangi

(1) Ka whakaūngia, ka whakaūngia anōtia hoki ngā tika kei ngā uri Māori i te tīmatanga o tēnei Pouhere hei iwi taketake i raro i Te Tiriti o Waitangi/ The Treaty of Waitangi.

(2) On the commencement of this Constitution, all rights, duties and obligations of the Crown in right of New Zealand under the Treaty and under Treaty settlement agreements and related statutes vest in and are assumed by the State.

(3) Time and space need to be devoted to developing more precise content on what tino rangitiratanga and the other undertakings in the Treaty mean in the modern context and what express provision should be made in this Constitution to protect those interests with sufficient clarity and certainty.

(4) As soon as practicable after the commencement of this Constitution, Parliament must select a Panel of Distinguished Persons and Kaumātua to recommend to Parliament—
   (a) changes to this Constitution relating to te Tiriti o Waitangi/the Treaty of Waitangi; and
   (b) if the Panel thinks it appropriate, any other legislative or policy measures.

(5) The Government must provide support to conduct hui for Māori and the community as a whole, using rūnanga and other methods of deliberative democracy, to produce reports for consideration by the Panel.

(6) No later than seven years after the commencement of this Constitution, the Panel must present to Parliament a report that sets out the Panel's recommendations for adopting—
   (a) more express provision for te Tiriti o Waitangi/the Treaty of Waitangi in this Constitution; and
   (b) any other policy or legislative measures that the Panel considers appropriate.

(7) Parliament must, within 18 months of receiving the report of the Panel, consider it and determine—
   (a) the form and content of the required constitutional amendments (if any) that it considers are required; and
   (b) if the Panel has made other recommendations, whether those recommendations should be proceeded with.

(8) Any amendments to this Constitution to give effect to Article 37(7)(a) must follow the process for amendments set out in Article 110.

(2) I te tīmatanga o tēnei Pouhere, ko ngā tika katoa, ko ngā kawenga katoa, ko ngā herenga katoa o te Karauna i heke iho mō Niu Tireni i raro i te Tiriti, i raro hoki i ngā whakataunga Tiriti, me ngā ture whai pānga, ka noho ērā, ka riro hoki ērā i te Whenua Rangatira.

(3) Me tuku wā, me tuku wāhi hoki ka tika hei hanga kōrero e mārama ake ana mō te tikanga o te tino rangatiratanga me ētahi atu āhuatanga i roto i te Tiriti e ai ki te horopaki o nāianei, ā, he aha ngā āheinga me whakapuaki i roto i tēnei Pouhere hei whakamarumaru i aua pānga kia mārama pai ai, kia mōhio pai ai hoki.

(4) Whai i muri atu i te tīmatanga o tēnei Pouhere, ki ōna taumata e taea ana, me kōwhiri rawa e te Pāremata tētahi Kāhui Amorangi, Kāhui Kaumātua hoki hei tuku tūtohunga ki te Pāremata—

    (a) mō ngā panoni ki tēnei Pouhere e pā ana ki Te Tiriti o Waitangi/ The Treaty of Waitangi;

    (b) mehemea ka whakaaro hoki te Kāhui i ngā wā e tika ana, mō āhuatanga ture kē atu, mō āhuatanga kaupapa here kē atu rānei.

(5) Me tuku tautoko rawa e te Kāwanatanga hei whakahaere hui mā ngāi Māori me te hapori katoa, mā te whakamahi rūnanga, mā te whakamahi i huarahi kē atu hoki mō te manapori whai whakaaroaro, hei whakaputa pūrongo kia whakaarotia e te Kāhui.

(6) Me kaua e hipa atu te whitu tau mai i te tīmatanga o tēnei Pouhere kia tāpaea e te Kāhui tētahi pūrongo e whakatakoto ana i ngā tūtohunga a te Kāhui kia whāia—

    (a) he āheinga kaha ake mō Te Tiriti o Waitangi/The Treaty of Waitangi i roto i tēnei Pouhere;

    (b) he kaupapa here anō hoki, he āhuatanga ture anō rānei e tika ana ka whakaarotia e te Kāhui.

(7) I roto i ngā marama 18 mai i te whiwhinga o te pūrongo a te Kāhui, me whakaaro rawa, me whakatau rawa hoki e te Pāremata—

    (a) te āhua, te kōrero o roto hoki o ngā whakahoutanga pouhere e whāia ana (mehemea arā ētahi) ki ōna whakaaro me whai atu;

    (b) mehemea he tūtohunga anō hoki a te Kāhui, āe rānei, kāore rānei ka whāia aua tūtohunga.

(8) Me whai rawa e ngā whakahoutanga o tēnei Pouhere hei whakatutuki i te Whiti 37(7)(a), te hātepe mō ngā whakahoutanga ka whakatakotoria i roto i te Whiti 110.

38 The Waitangi Tribunal

(1) There continues to be a body known as the Waitangi Tribunal, which is provided for by an Act of Parliament.
(2) Where issues arise that relate to te Tiriti o Waitangi/the Treaty of Waitangi or that involve tikanga Māori, the Parliament, the courts, and tribunals have the power to request an opinion from the Waitangi Tribunal on those aspects of the matter.

Part 4 The State

39 The people of Aotearoa New Zealand

(1) The country known as New Zealand in the English language or Aotearoa in te reo Māori is referred to in this Constitution as 'Aotearoa New Zealand' or 'the country'.
(2) By virtue of this Constitution, the people of Aotearoa New Zealand determine that they are represented by and governed through an independent, democratic State that functions under the rule of law.

40 The territory of Aotearoa New Zealand[1]

(1) The territory of the country comprises—
    (a) all the islands of Aotearoa New Zealand, including the internal waters of those islands:
    (b) the Territorial Sea, as defined by legislation.
(2) The State has the sovereign rights and jurisdiction recognised by international law in and over the marine areas that constitute the country's contiguous zone, exclusive economic zone, and continental shelf.
(3) The State is responsible for governing the Ross Dependency.
(4) An Act of Parliament may specify the boundaries of the Ross Dependency or of any of the marine areas referred to in paragraph (2).

41 The State of Aotearoa New Zealand and the authority of its principal institutions

(1) The State of Aotearoa New Zealand is an entity that has the rights,

---

[1] Issues regarding the Cook Islands, Niue and Tokelau will need to be addressed. Abolition of the monarchy and the Realm of New Zealand, of which they are a part, will have constitutional consequences that will need to be discussed with them and accommodated.

38 Ko Te Rōpū Whakamana i Te Tiriti o Waitangi

(1) Ka tū tonu tētahi rangatōpū e kīia nei ko Te Rōpū Whakamana i Te Tiriti o Waitangi, ka tukuna e tētahi Ture a te Pāremata.

(2) I ngā wā ka puta mai tētahi take e pā ana ki Te Tiriti o Waitangi/The Treaty of Waitangi, e pā ana ki ngā tikanga Māori rānei, kei te Pāremata, kei ngā kōti hoki, kei ngā taraipiunara hoki te mana whakahaere ki te tono kupu whakatau i Te Rōpū Whakamana i Te Tiriti o Waitangi mō aua āhuatanga o te take.

Wāhanga 4 Ko Te Whenua Rangatira

39 Ko ngā iwi o Aotearoa Niu Tireni

(1) Ko te whenua ka mōhiotia ko Niu Tireni ki te reo Ingarihi, ko Aotearoa ki te reo Māori, ka kōrerotia i roto i tēnei Pouhere ko 'Aotearoa Niu Tireni', ko 'te whenua' rānei.

(2) Mā tēnei Pouhere e whakatau ai ngā iwi o Aotearoa Niu Tireni he māngai ō rātou ka ārahi ā-kāwana hoki i a rātou mā tētahi Whenua Rangatira motuhake, manapori hoki e mahi ana i raro i te ritenga o te ture.

40 Te takiwā o Aotearoa Niu Tireni

(1) Ko te takiwā o te whenua, ko—
   (a) ngā moutere katoa o Aotearoa Niu Tireni, tae atu ki ngā wai ō-roto whenua o aua moutere:
   (b) te Takiwā Moana, ka tautuhia i roto i ngā ture.

(2) Kei te Whenua Rangatira ngā tika mana motuhake, ka whai mana hoki kia whakaūngia e te ture ā-Ao i roto, e kape ana hoki, i ngā takiwā ahumoana ka whai wāhi i roto i te rohe tūtata, i te rohe ōhanga motuhake hoki, i te paenga paparahi hoki o te whenua.

(3) Ka noho haepapa te Whenua Rangatira mō te ārahi ā-kāwana i te Ross Dependency.

(4) Mā tētahi Ture a te Pāremata e āta tohu ai ngā taupā ake o te Ross Dependency, o ngā takiwā ahumoana rānei ka kōrerotia i roto i te whiti (2).

41 Ko te Whenua Rangatira o Aotearoa Niu Tireni me te mana o ōna hinonga whakahaere matua

(1) He hinonga te Whenua Rangatira o Aotearoa Niu Tireni he tika ōna,

powers, and capacities of a natural person of full age and capacity and that exclusively operates through institutions and instruments established or recognised by this Constitution or by Act of Parliament.

(2) All powers of the State derive from the people of Aotearoa New Zealand and must accordingly be conferred by this Constitution or by or under an Act of Parliament.

(3) The authority of representing the unifying commitment to this Constitution of all institutions and instruments of the State is vested in the Head of State, whose functions are performed to protect the Constitution.

(4) The legislative power of the State is vested in Parliament, whose members are elected by and responsible to the people.

(5) The executive authority of the State is vested in the Cabinet, which is responsible to Parliament.

(6) The judicial authority of the State is vested in the courts whose judges are sworn to uphold the law.

(7) The authority to undertake and regulate activities within local districts is vested in local governments in terms specified by or under Acts of Parliament.

42 The State is the successor of the Crown in right of New Zealand; Royal Prerogative abolished

(1) The State is the successor of the Crown in right of New Zealand.

(2) On the commencement of this Constitution, all powers and rights of the Crown in right of New Zealand, and all assets of the Crown in right of New Zealand including, without limitation, natural resources, land, minerals, personal property, and money, vest in the State.

(3) On the commencement of this Constitution, all liabilities and obligations of the Crown in right of New Zealand are assumed by the State.

(4) Paragraph (2) affects the land law doctrines of tenures and estates only to the extent that the State takes the place of the Crown for the purpose of the continued application of those doctrines.

(5) All powers formerly exercisesable by Ministers under the authority of the royal prerogative are abolished from the commencement of this Constitution.

he mana whakahaere ōna, he āheinga ōna pērā ki tētahi tangata tūturu pakeke te hanga, pakeke hoki te āheitanga, ā, ka kawe i āna mahi mā ngā hinonga whakahaere, mā ngā puka hoki ka whakatūria, ka whakaūngia rānei e tēnei Pouhere, e tētahi Ture a te Pāremata rānei.

(2) Ka takea mai ngā mana whakahaere katoa o te Whenua Rangatira i ngā iwi o Aotearoa Niu Tireni, ā, nā whai anō me tuku rawa e tēnei Pouhere, e tētahi Ture a te Pāremata rānei, i raro rānei i tētahi Ture a te Pāremata.

(3) Ka riro ki Te Upoko o Te Whenua Rangatira te mana hei kanohi mō te takohanga whakakotahi ki tēnei Pouhere o ngā hinonga whakahaere katoa, o ngā puka katoa o te Whenua Rangatira, e mahia ai ōna āheinga hei whakamarumaru i te Pouhere.

(4) Ka riro ki te Pāremata te mana whakamana i te whakature o te Whenua Rangatira, e pōtihia ai ōna mema e te iwi, ā, ka noho haepapa ki te iwi.

(5) Ka riro ki Te Rūnanga Kāwanatanga te mana matua o te Whenua Rangatira, ka noho haepapa ki te Pāremata.

(6) Ka riro ki ngā kōti, ka tuku oati ngā kaiwhakawā ki te hāpai i te ture, te mana whakatau o te Whenua Rangatira.

(7) Ka riro ki ngā kāwanatanga ā-rohe i āta tohua ki ngā ritenga e ngā Ture a te Pāremata, i raro rānei i ngā Ture a te Pāremata, te mana ki te mahi, ki te whakahaere hoki i ngā mahi i roto i ngā takiwā kāwanatanga ā-rohe.

42 Ka riro ki te Whenua Rangatira te mana Karauna o Niu Tireni; ka whakakorehia te Kawa Upoko Ariki o Ingarangi

(1) Ko te Whenua Rangatira te kairīwhi o te mana Karauna hei mana mō Niu Tireni.

(2) I te tīmatanga o tēnei Pouhere, ko ngā mana whakahaere katoa, ko ngā tika katoa o te Karauna hei mana mō Niu Tireni, me ngā rawa katoa o te Karauna hei mana mō Niu Tireni tae atu ki ngā rawa o te taiao, ngā whenua hoki, ngā kohuke hoki, ngā rawa whaiaro hoki, te pūtea katoa, ka riro ki te Whenua Rangatira ērā rawa katoa me te herenga kore.

(3) I te tīmatanga o tēnei Pouhere, ka riro ngā taumahatanga katoa, ngā herenga katoa hoki o te Karauna hei mana mō Niu Tireni ki te Whenua Rangatira.

(4) He pānga o te rerenga (2) ki ngā whaikaupapa ture whenua mō ngā whai nohonga me ngā pānga mehemea ka riro i te Whenua Rangatira te tūranga o te Karauna hei whakatinana tonu i aua whaikaupapa.

(5) I te tīmatanga o tēnei Pouhere ka whakakorehia ngā mana whakahaere katoa i mahia ai e te hunga Minita i raro i te mana o te Kawa Upoko

(6) This Article is subject to Article 101.

43 Citizenship

(1) Nothing in this Constitution prevents a citizen of the country from also being a citizen of another country.
(2) An Act of Parliament determines the acquisition, loss, and restoration of citizenship.
(3) Nothing in this Constitution prevents citizens of the Cook Islands or Niue or Tokelau from holding Aotearoa New Zealand citizenship.

44 The languages of Aotearoa New Zealand

(1) The official languages of the country are te reo Māori, English, and New Zealand Sign Language.
(2) Provision may be made from time to time by Act of Parliament for the use of any official languages for any one or more official purposes.

Part 5 The Head of State / Kaitiaki of the Nation

45 The Head of State

(1) This Article establishes the office of Head of State of Aotearoa New Zealand.
(2) The Head of State is responsible for protecting this Constitution and is the Guardian or Kaitiaki of the Nation.
(3) The Head of State is appointed to office for a fixed single term of five years by a two-thirds majority of voting members of Parliament on a free vote, that is to say a personal vote on a conscience issue.
(4) The Head of State must—
    (a) be a citizen of Aotearoa New Zealand; and
    (b) reside within Aotearoa New Zealand while holding the office.

Ariki o Ingarangi.
(6) He pānga o tēnei Whiti ki te Whiti 101.

43 Te kirirarautanga

(1) Kāore rawa he mea kei roto i tēnei Pouhere ka ārai i tētahi kirirarau o te whenua kia noho hei kirirarau nō whenua kē atu.
(2) Mā tētahi Ture a te Pāremata e whakatau ai te whiwhinga, te rironga hoki, te whakahokinga hoki o te kirirarautanga.
(3) Kāore rawa he mea kei roto i tēnei Pouhere ka ārai i ngā kirirarau o Rarotonga-Kuki Airani, o Niue rānei, o Tokerau/Tokelau rānei kia pupuri kirirarautanga nō Aotearoa Niu Tireni.

44 Ngā reo o Aotearoa Niu Tireni

(1) Ko te reo Māori, ko te reo Ingarihi hoki, ko te reo Rotarota o Niu Tireni ngā reo whai mana ā-ture o te whenua.
(2) I ētahi wā mā te Ture a te Pāremata e āhei ai te whakamahi i ngā reo whai mana ā-ture i roto i ngā kaupapa ōkawa.

Wāhanga 5 Te Upoko o Te Whenua Rangatira / Te Kaitiaki o te Motu Whānui

45 Te Upoko o Te Whenua Rangatira

(1) Ka whakatū tēnei Whiti i te tūranga o Te Upoko o Te Whenua Rangatira o Aotearoa Niu Tireni.
(2) Ka noho haepapa Te Upoko o Te Whenua Rangatira mō te whakamarumaru i tēnei Pouhere, ā, ko ia hoki te Kaitaki o te Motu Whānui.
(3) Ka kopoua Te Upoko o Te Whenua Rangatira mō tētahi wā pūmau tapatahi e rima tau te roa, mā tētahi pōtitanga herenga kore o ngā mema Pāremata, kia rua hautoru hoki te rahi me pōti mōna, arā, kei tēnā mema, kei tēnā mema tōna mana kia pōti mō tāna e hiahia ai.
(4) Ko tā Te Upoko o Te Whenua Rangatira—
  (a) me noho rawa hei kirirarau nō Aotearoa Niu Tireni ka tika;
  (b) me noho ā-tinana rawa hoki i roto i Aotearoa Niu Tireni i a ia e kawe ana i te tūranga.

46 Death, resignation, or removal of Head of State

(1) Upon the death, resignation, or removal of the Head of State, a new Head of State must be appointed for a five year term.
(2) The Head of State may resign from office, for any reason, by giving notice of resignation to the Prime Minister.
(3) The Head of State may not be removed from office except by a resolution of Parliament, which resolution may be moved only on the grounds of misbehaviour or of incapacity to discharge the functions of office.

47 Functions and arrangements of the Head of State

(1) The Head of State has only the powers, duties, and functions conferred on the office by this Constitution or by Act of Parliament.
(2) The Head of State must—
   (a) subject to Article 49, sign all Bills and subordinate legislation made by Cabinet that are presented for signature:
   (b) on receipt of the report of the Speaker of Parliament, appoint as the Prime Minister the person elected to that office by Parliament:
   (c) accept the resignation of the Prime Minister when tendered by the Prime Minister:
   (d) appoint to, and remove from, the office of Minister the persons whose names are submitted by the Prime Minister:
   (e) on advice of the Prime Minister, issue writs for parliamentary elections:
   (f) on the recommendation of the Prime Minister, confer honours, awards, decorations, and distinctions:
   (g) represent the State at special occasions, celebrations, and commemorations:

46 Te matenga, te rīhainatanga rānei, te tangohanga rānei o Te Upoko o Te Whenua Rangatira

(1) I te matenga, te rīhainatanga rānei, te tangohanga rānei o Te Upoko o Te Whenua Rangatira, me kopou rawa tētahi tangata hou hei Upoko o Te Whenua Rangatira mō tētahi wā e rima tau te roa.

(2) Ka āhei Te Upoko o Te Whenua Rangatira te rīhaina i te tūranga, ahakoa te take, mā te tuku whakamōhiotanga mō te rīhainatanga ki te Pirimia.

(3) Kāore Te Upoko o Te Whenua Rangatira e tangohia i te tūranga, atu mā tētahi whakataunga o te Pāremata, arā, he whakataunga ka mōtinihia i runga i ngā take hīanga, i ngā take āhei kore rānei, i ngā take whakatutuki kore i ngā āheinga o te tūranga.

47 Ngā āheinga me ngā whakaritenga o Te Upoko o Te Whenua Rangatira

(1) Kei Te Upoko o Te Whenua Rangatira ngā mana whakahaere anake, ngā kawenga hoki, ngā āheinga hoki ka tukuna ki te tūranga mā tēnei Pouhere, mā tētahi Ture a te Pāremata rānei.

(2) Ko tā Te Upoko o Te Whenua—
 (a) e ai ki te Whiti 49, me waitohu rawa ngā Pire katoa, ngā waeture katoa ka hangā e Te Rūnanga Kāwanatanga ka tāpaea mai kia waitohua:
 (b) i te whiwhinga o te pūrongo a te Mana Whakawā o te Pāremata, me kopou rawa hei Pirimia te tangata i pōtihia mō taua tūranga e te Pāremata:
 (c) kia whakaae atu ki te rīhainatanga o te Pirimia i te wā ka tukuna mai e te Pirimia:
 (d) me kopou rawa, me tango rawa hoki i te tūranga Minita ngā tāngata nō rātou ngā ingoa ka tukuna e te Pirimia:
 (e) me tuku kārero rawa mō ngā pōtitanga Pāremata, i runga i te whakatakoto whakaaro o te Pirimia:
 (f) me tuku rawa ngā honoretanga, ngā whakawhiwhinga hoki, ngā tohu whakanui hoki, ngā tohu rongonui hoki, i runga i te tūtohunga o te Pirimia:
 (g) me tae atu rawa hei kanohi kitea mō te Whenua Rangatira ki ngā ahurei whakahirahira, ki ngā kaupapa whakanui hoki, ki ngā kaupapa whakamaumahara hoki:

(h) exchange ideas and information with the country's diverse communities and organisations by delivering speeches and communicating with leaders and members of communities and organisations:
(i) after consultation with the Prime Minister, represent the State overseas.

(3) In the period that starts on the day after the first declaration of the official results of a general election of the members of Parliament and ends on the day before the first meeting of Parliament, the Head of State may appoint as the Prime Minister the person whose appointment is, in the opinion of the Head of State, likely to be supported by a majority of the members of Parliament.

(4) A person appointed as Prime Minister under paragraph (3) remains in office until such time as the Head of State receives the report from the Speaker described in Article 47(2)(b).

(5) The Head of State must, in performing the functions of the Head of State, act as a non-partisan symbol of unity.

(6) The Head of State must never be without ministerial advisers and must exercise all functions, powers, and duties other than those conferred by Article 48 or 49, on the advice of those Ministers.

48 Head of State to be kept informed and entitled to advise Ministers

(1) The Prime Minister must keep the Head of State informed on the general conduct of the Government, and must make available to the Head of State information the Head of State may request with respect to any particular matter relating to the Government of the State.

(2) The Head of State may give advice and comment on affairs of State in private to the Prime Minister and to other Ministers.

(h) me whakawhitiwhiti whakaaro rawa, me whakawhitiwhiti pārongo rawa hoki me te kanorau o ngā hapori, o ngā rōpū whakahaere hoki o te whenua, mā te kauhau, mā te whakawhitiwhiti kōrero me ngā kaiārahi me ngā mema o ngā hapori me ngā rōpū whakahaere:
(i) me tae atu rawa ki tāwāhi hei kanohi kitea mō te Whenua Rangatira, whai muri i te whiriwhiri kōrero me te Pirimia.

(3) I roto i te wā ka tīmata i te rā whai i muri mai i te whakapuakitanga tuatahi o ngā putanga ōkawa mō te pōtitanga ā-motu o ngā mema o te Pāremata, ā, ka mutu i te rā i mua i te huinga tuatahi o te Pāremata, ka āhei Te Upoko o Te Whenua Rangatira te kopou i tētahi tangata hei Pirimia, e ai ki ngā whakaaro o Te Upoko o Te Whenua Rangatira, ka tautokona tōna kopoutanga e te nuinga o ngā mema o te Pāremata.

(4) Ka noho tonu tētahi tangata kua kopoua hei Pirimia i raro i te rerenga (3) ki te tūranga, tae noa ki te wā ka whiwhi Te Upoko o Te Whenua Rangatira i tētahi pūrongo nā te Mana Whakawā, ka kōrerohia i roto i te Whiti 47(2)(b).

(5) Me noho here kore rawa hei tohu whakakotahi Te Upoko o Te Whenua Rangatira i roto i āna mahi hei Upoko o Te Whenua Rangatira.

(6) Me kaua rawa Te Upoko o Te Whenua Rangatira e noho wehe i ōna kaitohutohu minitatanga, ā, me mahi rawa e ia ngā āheinga katoa, ngā mana whakahaere katoa, ngā kawenga katoa, atu i ērā ka tukuna e te Whiti 48, 49 rānei, i runga i te whakatakoto whakaaro o aua Minita.

48 Ka whai pārongo Te Upoko o Te Whenua Rangatira, ka āhei te whakatakoto whakaaro ki ngā Minita

(1) Me whakamōhio atu rawa Te Upoko o Te Whenua Rangatira e te Pirimia mō te āhuatanga whānui o te Kāwanatanga, ā, me tuku rawa hoki kia wātea ki Te Upoko o Te Whenua Rangatira ngā pārongo ka tonoa e Te Upoko o Te Whenua Rangatira, mō ngā take katoa e pā ana ki te Kāwanatanga o te Whenua Rangatira.

(2) Ka āhei Te Upoko o Te Whenua Rangatira te whakatakoto whakaaro, te whakapuaki whakaaro hoki tūmataiti nei ki te Pirimia, ki Minita kē atu hoki, mō ngā take e pā ana ki Te Whenua Rangatira.

49 Head of State may refer constitutionality of Bill to Supreme Court

(1) If the Head of State, after consultation with the Prime Minister, is of the view that any Bill passed by Parliament and submitted for the signature of the Head of State may be contrary to this Constitution, the Head of State may refer to the Supreme Court the question whether one or more provisions of the Bill appear to be contrary to this Constitution.

(2) A reference to the Supreme Court under paragraph (1) may not be made later than the tenth working day after the date on which the Bill concerned is presented to the Head of State for signature.

(3) After giving the Head of State, the Government and any other party that the Supreme Court considers should be heard an opportunity to be heard, the Supreme Court must determine the question as soon as practicable and, in any case, not later than the 60th day after the date on which the reference was made.

(4) The Head of State must not sign the Bill concerned if the Supreme Court determines that any provision of the Bill referred to the Court appears to be contrary to the Constitution.

50 Administrator of the Government

In the absence or incapacity of the Head of State or if the office of the Head of State is vacant, the President of the Court of Appeal acts as administrator of the Government, or if that person is unavailable, the next most senior judge of that Court.

Part 6 Parliament

51 Parliament

(1) The institution that, before the commencement of this Constitution, was known as the House of Representatives is, by this Article, established as the Parliament of Aotearoa New Zealand.

(2) Subject to the provisions of this Constitution, Parliament has full power to make laws.

49 Ka āhei Te Upoko o Te Whenua Rangatira te pare atu i te pouheretanga o te Pire ki te Kōti Mana Nui

(1) Mehemea ka whakaaro Te Upoko o Te Whenua Rangatira, whai i muri mai i te whiriwhiri kōrero me te Pirimia, ka takahi pea i tēnei Pouhere tētahi Pire ka whakaturetia e te Pāremata kātahi ka tukuna kia waitohua e Te Upoko o Te Whenua Rangatira, ka āhei Te Upoko o Te Whenua Rangatira te pare atu ki te Kōti Mana Nui te pātai mehemea kotahi āheinga, neke atu rānei, o te Pire kei te takahi pea i tēnei Pouhere.

(2) E kore e taea te tuku parenga ki te Kōti Mana Nui i raro i te rerenga (1) i muri mai i te rā tuangahuru whai i muri mai i te rā i tāpaea ai taua Pire nei ki Te Upoko o Te Whenua Rangatira kia waitohua.

(3) Whai i muri mai i te tuku wāhanga ki Te Upoko o Te Whenua Rangatira, ki te Kāwanatanga rānei, ki a wai ake rānei e whakaaro ana te Kōti Mana Nui me whai wāhi kia rangona, me whakatau rawa e te Kōti Mana Nui te pātai, ki ōna taumata e taea ana te tere, ahakoa te aha hoki, kia kaua e hipa atu i te rā 60 whai i muri mai i te rā i tukuna ai te parenga.

(4) Me kaua rawa e waitohu e Te Upoko o Te Whenua Rangatira te Pire e kōrerotia ana mehemea ka whakatau te Kōti Mana Nui ka takahi pea tētahi āheinga o te Pire ka parea ki te Kōti i te Pouhere.

50 Te kaiwhakahaere o te Kāwanatanga

Mehemea e ngaro ana, e āhei kore ana rānei Te Upoko o Te Whenua Rangatira, e wātea ana rānei te tūranga o Te Upoko o Te Whenua Rangatira, ka noho te Tumu o Te Kōti Pīra hei kaiwhakahaere o te Kāwanatanga, ka noho rānei te kaiwhakawā matua kei raro i a ia i taua Kōti mehemea kāore taua tangata i te wātea.

Wāhanga 6 Te Pāremata

51 Te Pāremata

(1) Ko taua hinonga whakahaere i mōhiotia nei i mua i te tīmatanga o tēnei Pouhere ko te Whare Pāremata tōna ingoa, mā tēnei Whiti e poua ai ko te Pāremata o Aotearoa Niu Tireni.

(2) Mā ngā āheinga o tēnei Pouhere, kei te Pāremata te tino mana whakahaere ki te hanga ture.

52 Meetings of Parliament

(1) Parliament is regarded as always in existence.
(2) Parliament does not require to be summoned and may exercise its legislative power in accordance with this Constitution.
(3) After any general election of the members of Parliament, Parliament must meet no later than 21 days after the first declaration of the official results, on a date to be fixed by the Clerk of Parliament.
(4) Parliament meets regularly in accordance with a published timetable which it has agreed.

53 Members of Parliament

Members of Parliament are elected from time to time in accordance with this Constitution and the provisions of an Act of Parliament governing the conduct of parliamentary elections.

54 Purpose of Parliament

The principal functions of Parliament include the following:
  (a) debating issues of importance:
  (b) scrutinising and passing legislation:
  (c) approving State expenditure, taxation, and loans:
  (d) providing for the redress of grievances:
  (e) electing the Prime Minister:
  (f) holding Ministers to account:
  (g) voting on motions of confidence or no confidence in the Government, or a Minister or the Prime Minister.

55 Election of Speaker

Parliament at its first meeting after any general election of its members, and immediately after any vacancy occurs in the office of Speaker, elects, by secret ballot, a Member of Parliament as Speaker, and every such election is effective on being confirmed by the Head of State.

52 Ngā huinga o te Pāremata

(1) Ko te whakaaro ka toitū tonu te Pāremata.
(2) Ehara i te mea me karanga atu kia huihui te Pāremata, ā, ka āhei te whakamahi i tōna mana whakahaere mō te whakature e ai ki tēnei Pouhere.
(3) Whai i muri mai i ngā pōtitanga ā-motu o ngā mema o te Pāremata, me hui rawa te Pāremata kia kaua e hipa atu i ngā rā 21 whai i muri mai i te whakapuakinga tuatahi o ngā putanga ōkawa, i tētahi rā ka whakaritea e te Karaka o te Pāremata.
(4) Ka auau te huihui a te Pāremata e ai ki tētahi rātaka e whakaaetia ana ka whakaputaina.

53 Ngā mema o te Pāremata

I tēnā wā, i tēnā wā ka pōtihia ngā mema o te Pāremata e ai ki tēnei Pouhere me ngā āheinga o tētahi Ture a te Pāremata e ārahi ana i te whakahaere pōtitanga pāremata.

54 Te aronga o te Pāremata

Ko ngā āheinga matua o te Pāremata tae atu ki ēnei e whai ake nei:
    (a) ko te tautohetohe mō ngā take whakahirahira:
    (b) ko te tātari, ko te whakaturetanga hoki:
    (c) ko te whakaae atu ki tā te Whenua Rangatira whakapau pūtea, mahi tāke hoki, tuku pūtea taurewa hoki:
    (d) ko te tuku whakaoranga mō ngā nawe:
    (e) ko te pōtitanga mō te Pirimia:
    (f) ko te here i ngā Minita kia noho haepapa:
    (g) ko te pōti mō ngā mōtini tuku tautoko, tautoko kore rawa rānei mō te Kāwanatanga, mō tētahi Minita rānei, mō te Pirimia rānei.

55 Te pōtitanga mō te Mana Whakawā o Te Pāremata

I te huinga tuatahi o te Pāremata whai i muri mai i tētahi pōtitanga ā-motu o ōna mema, whai muri tonu mai i tētahi wāteatanga o te tūranga o te Mana Whakawā o te Pāremata, ka pōtihia tētahi Mema o te Pāremata hei Mana Whakawā mā tētahi pōtitanga muna, ā, ka tūturu ia pōtitanga pērā mā te whakatau a Te Upoko o Te Whenua Rangatira.

56 Functions of the Speaker

The Speaker presides impartially over proceedings of Parliament, keeps order, makes rulings, lays claims to the privileges of Parliament, and carries out such other duties prescribed by law or the Standing Orders of Parliament.

57 Speaker to continue in office

A person who is in office as Speaker immediately before Parliament adjourns for a general election of its members continues in office until the next Speaker is elected.

58 Clerk of the Parliament

(1) The Clerk of Parliament advises the Speaker and provides advice to Members of Parliament and Select Committees.

(2) The Clerk of Parliament is appointed by the Parliamentary Services Commission referred to in Article 63.

59 Leader of the Opposition

A Member of Parliament who is the leader of the largest parliamentary party represented in Parliament that is not in Government, nor in coalition with a Government party, nor subject to any agreement for confidence and supply, is recognised by the Speaker as Leader of the Opposition.

60 Parliamentary privilege

(1) Parliament and its members have the rights, powers, privileges and jurisdiction vested in the House of Representatives immediately before the commencement of this Constitution, except so far as they are inconsistent with this Constitution.

(2) Amendments made to parliamentary privilege must be consistent with this Constitution.

61 Parliamentary procedure

Subject to this Constitution and any Act of Parliament, Parliament may regulate its own procedure and for that purpose make and publish Standing Orders.

56 Ngā āheinga o te Mana Whakawā o Te Pāremata

Ka noho matatika te Mana Whakawā i roto i ngā whakahaerenga o te Pāremata, ka tiaki tikanga hoki, ka whakatau tikanga hoki, ka hao hoki i ngā painga o te Pāremata, ka mahi hoki i ngā kawenga pērā ki ērā ka whakatakotoria e te ture, e ngā Whakataunga Tū Roa o te Pāremata.

57 Ka noho tonu te Mana Whakawā o Te Pāremata ki tōna tūranga

Ko te tangata e noho ana ki te tūranga hei Mana Whakawā i mua tonu mai i te whakatārewatanga o te Pāremata mō tētahi pōtitanga ā-motu o ōna mema, ka noho tonu ia ki taua tūranga tae noa ki te pōtitanga o tētahi Mana Whakawā anō.

58 Te Karaka o te Pāremata

(1) Ka whakatakoto whakaaro te Karaka o te Pāremata ki te Mana Whakawā o Te Pāremata, ā, ka whakatakoto whakaaro ki ngā Mema o te Pāremata me ngā Kōmiti Kōwhiri.

(2) Ka kopoua te Karaka o te Pāremata e Te Kōmihana Ratonga Pāremata ka kōrerotia i roto i te Whiti 63.

59 Te kaiārahi o te Āpitihana

Ko tētahi Mema Pāremata e noho ana hei kaiārahi o te rōpū pāremata nui kei roto i te Pāremata engari ehara i te Kāwanatanga, kāore hoki i te noho hei hoa ngātahi me tētahi rōpū Kāwanatanga, kāore hoki i te whai i tētahi whakaaetanga mō te tuku tautoko me te hoatutanga, ka whakaūngia e te Mana Whakawā o te Pāremata ko ia te Kaiārahi o te Āpitihana.

60 Painga ā-Pāremata

(1) Ka riro ki te Pāremata me ōna mema ngā tika, ngā mana whakahaere hoki, ngā painga hoki, te whai mana hoki kei Te Whare Pāremata i mua tonu mai i te tīmatanga o tēnei Pouhere, atu i ērā kāore i te hāngai ki tēnei Pouhere.

(2) Me hāngai rawa ngā whakahoutanga o ngā painga ā-pāremata ki tēnei Pouhere.

61 Te tukanga Pāremata

Mā tēnei Pouhere, mā tētahi Ture a te Pāremata hoki, e whakariterite ai tāna ake tukanga, ā, ka hanga, ka whakaputa hoki i ētahi Whakataunga Tū Roa mō taua aronga nei.

62 Parliamentary Committees

Parliament may establish any committees of its members that it thinks fit.

63 The administration of Parliament

(1) The affairs of Parliament are administered by a Parliamentary Service Commission headed by the Speaker as provided for by Act of Parliament.

(2) The Chief Executive of the Parliamentary Service Commission advises the Speaker and assists Members of Parliament with the discharge of their duties.

Parliamentary elections

64 Parliamentary elections

(1) Elections for membership of Parliament are conducted by equal suffrage and secret ballot under the Mixed Member Proportional system as provided for by Act of Parliament.

(2) An Act of Parliament provides for the electoral system and also for an independent Electoral Commission that includes the following objectives:
    (a) to facilitate participation in parliamentary democracy:
    (b) to administer election broadcasting rules:
    (c) to promote understanding and public awareness of the electoral system and associated matters:
    (d) to provide advice, reports, and public education on electoral matters:
    (e) to maintain confidence in the impartial and professional administration of parliamentary elections.

(3) The Electoral Commission must act independently in performing its statutory functions and duties, and in exercising its statutory powers.

(4) It is the duty of every person who is eligible to vote to—
    (a) register to vote:
    (b) vote at each parliamentary election.

(5) The duty established in paragraph (4) may be regulated by Act of Parliament.

62 Ngā Kōmiti Pāremata

Ka āhei te Pāremata te whakatū kōmiti o ōna mema ki tōna e whakaaro ai.

63 Te whakahaere i te Pāremata

(1) Ka whakahaeretia ngā take Pāremata e tētahi Kōmihana Ratonga Pāremata ka ārahina e te Mana Whakawā o te Pāremata e ai ki tētahi Ture a te Pāremata.

(2) Ka whakatakoto whakaaro te Tumu Whakahaere o te Kōmihana Ratonga Pāremata ki te Mana Whakawā o te Pāremata, ā, ka āwhina i ngā Mema o te Pāremata ki te mahi i ā rātou kawenga.

Ngā pōtitanga Pāremata

64 Ngā pōtitanga Pāremata

(1) Ka whakahaeretia ngā pōtitanga mō ngā mema o te Pāremata i runga i te tika tuku pōti ōrite me te pōti muna i raro i te Tikanga Pōti Whirirua e ai ki te Ture a te Pāremata.

(2) Mā tētahi Ture a te Pāremata e tuku tikanga ai mō tētahi pūnaha pōtitanga, mō tētahi Kōmihana Pōtitanga hoki ka tū motuhake tae atu ki ngā whāinga e whai ake nei:
  (a) kia whakahaere i te whaiuru ki roto i te manapori pāremata:
  (b) kia whakahaere i ngā ritenga mō te whakapāhō i te wā pōtitanga:
  (c) kia toko ake te māramatanga, te mōhiotanga o te iwi mō te pūnaha pōtitanga me ngā take whai pānga:
  (d) kia whakatakoto whakaaro, kia tuku pūrongo hoki, kia tuku mātauranga tūmatanui hoki mō ngā take pōtitanga:
  (e) kia tautoko tonu i te whakahaere matatika, te whakahaere ngaio hoki i ngā pōtitanga pāremata.

(3) Me noho motuhake rawa te Kōmihana Pōtitanga i roto i āna mahi, i āna kawenga hoki, i roto hoki i tāna whakamahi i ōna mana whakahaere ā-ture mā te Pāremata.

(4) Kei ia tangata e whai mana ana ki te pōti te kawenga kia—
  (a) rēhita ki te pōti:
  (b) pōti i ia pōtitanga pāremata.

(5) Ka āhei te whakariterite i te kawenga ka whakatūria i roto i te rerenga (4) mā tētahi Ture a te Pāremata.

65 Timing for general elections

(1) A general election of the members of Parliament must be held in the fourth calendar year following the calendar year in which the last preceding general election was held.
(2) The polling day for a general election of the members of Parliament is the second Saturday in November.
(3) Paragraphs (1) and (2) are subject to Article 66.
(4) Parliament cannot meet in the period commencing on the 25th working day before polling day and ending on the day after the date of the first official declaration of the results of the general election unless an emergency has been declared under Article 113.

66 Early general elections

(1) An early general election may be held only if it is required to take place by this Article.
(2) An early general election is required to take place if Parliament by a majority of 75 percent of all its members passes a motion in the following form: 'That there is to be an early general election.'
(3) An early general election is also required to take place if—
    (a) Parliament passes a motion set out in paragraph (4); and
    (b) the period of 14 days after the day on which the motion is passed ends without Parliament passing a motion set out in paragraph (5).
(4) The form of the motion for the purposes of paragraph (3)(a) is—'That this Parliament has no confidence in the Government.'
(5) The form of the motion for the purposes of paragraph (3)(b) is—'That this Parliament has confidence in the Government.'
(6) When an early general election is required to take place, the Cabinet must as soon as practicable determine and publish the polling day for that election.
(7) In Article 65 and in this Article, 'early general election' means a general election of the members of Parliament that is held earlier than November in the fourth calendar year following the calendar year in which the last preceding general election was held.

65 Te wā o ngā pōtitanga ā-motu

(1) Me tū rawa tētahi pōtitanga ā-motu o ngā mema o te Pāremata ia tau maramataka tuawhā whai i muri mai i te tau maramataka i tū ai tērā o ngā pōtitanga ā-motu.

(2) Ko te Rāhoroi tuarua o te marama o Whiringa ā-rangi te rā pōti o tētahi pōtitanga ā-motu o ngā mema o te Pāremata.

(3) He pānga o ngā rerenga (1), (2) hoki ki te Whiti 66.

(4) Kāore e taea e te Pāremata te hui tahi i te wā ka tīmata mai i te rā mahi 25 i mua i te rā pōti, ā, ka mutu i te rā whai i muri mai i te whakapuakitanga ōkawa mō ngā putanga o te pōtitanga ā-motu, māna ka whakapuakina tētahi take ohotata i raro i te Whiti 113.

66 He pōtitanga ā-motu tōmua

(1) Ka āhei te whakatū pōtitanga ā-motu tōmua mehemea me tū rawa ka tika e ai ki tēnei Whiti.

(2) Me tū rawa tētahi pōtitanga ā-motu tōmua ka tika mehemea ka tautokona tētahi mōtini e te 75 ōrau o ngā mema o te Pāremata i runga i te kōrero e whai ake nei: 'Kia tū tētahi pōtitanga ā-motu tōmua.'

(3) Me tū rawa tētahi pōtitanga ā-motu tōmua ka tika mehemea-
   (a) ka tautoko te Pāremata i tētahi mōtini ka whakatakotoria i roto i te rerenga (4);
   (b) ka mutu hoki te wā 14 rā te roa i muri i te rā ka tautokona te mōtini, me te tautoko kore a te Pāremata i tētahi mōtini ka whakatakotoria i roto i te rerenga (5).

(4) Mō ngā aronga o te rerenga (3)(a) ko te āhua o te mōtini ko te - 'Kāore tēnei Pāremata i te tautoko i te Kāwanatanga.'

(5) Mō ngā aronga o te rerenga (3)(b) ko te āhua o te mōtini ko te - 'Kei te tautoko tēnei Pāremata i te Kāwanatanga.'

(6) I te wā me tū rawa tētahi pōtitanga ā-motu tōmua ka tika, me tere whakatau rawa, me tere whakaputa atu rawa hoki e Te Rūnanga Kāwanatanga ki ōna e taea ana te rā pōtitanga o taua pōtitanga ā-motu.

(7) I roto i te Whiti 65, i roto hoki tēnei Whiti, ko te 'pōtitanga ā-motu tōmua' tētahi pōtitanga ā-motu o ngā mema o te Pāremata ka tū i mua i te marama o Whiringa ā-rangi i roto i te tau maramataka tuawhā whai i muri i te tau maramataka i tū ai tērā o ngā pōtitanga ā-motu.

67 Representation Commission

(1) There continues to be an independent Commission known as the Representation Commission.
(2) The function of the Representation Commission is to provide for the periodical readjustment of the representation of the electoral districts in Parliament.
(3) The Representation Commission must ensure that electoral boundaries are fairly drawn to secure equal representation as far as practicable and to avoid gerrymandering.

Part 7 The Government

Institutions of central government

68 Constitution and powers of Government

(1) The Government consists of the following institutions:
    (a) the Cabinet:
    (b) the Prime Minister:
    (c) the office of each Minister designated by Act of Parliament or by the Prime Minister.
(2) All powers exercised by, or on behalf of, an institution of the Government must be authorised by this Constitution or by or under an Act of Parliament.
(3) A person who is authorised to perform any function, conferred by this Constitution or by or under an Act of Parliament on—
    (a) an institution of the Government; or
    (b) a department of the public service, including any statutory officer located within a department; or
    (c) any other institution of the State that is established, otherwise than as a legal entity, by or under an Act of Parliament to implement legislation or policies.
    (d) may, for the purpose of taking any action that is required for, or that is incidental to, or consequential on the performance of that function, act in the name of the State and exercise the powers that the State has as a legal entity.

67 Te Kōmihana Whakatau Rohe Pōti

(1) Ka tū tonu tētahi Kōmihana motuhake e kīia nei ko Te Kōmihana Whakatau Rohe Pōti.

(2) Ko te āheinga o Te Kōmihana Whakatau Rohe Pōti ko te tuku panoni kauteatea o te āhuatanga o ngā rohe pōti i roto i te Pāremata.

(3) Me whakaū rawa e Te Kōmihana Whakatau Rohe Pōti he tōkeke te tā i ngā rohe kia ōrite ai te rahinga tangata, ki ōna taumata e taea ana, kia kore ai hoki e whai atu i te *gerrymandering*.

Wāhanga 7 Te Kāwanatanga

Ngā hinonga whakahaere o te kāwanatanga ā-motu

68 Te Pouhere me ngā mana whakahaere o te Kāwanatanga

(1) Ko ngā hinonga whakahaere o te Kāwanatanga ko ēnei e whai ake nei:
 (a) ko Te Rūnanga Kāwanatanga:
 (b) ko te Pirimia:
 (c) ko te tari o ia Minita ka tohua e tētahi Ture a te Pāremata, e te Pirimia rānei.

(2) Me whai mana rawa e tēnei Pouhere, i raro rānei i tētahi Ture a te Pāremata, ngā mana whakahaere katoa ka mahia e tētahi hinonga whakahaere o te Kāwanatanga, ka mahia rānei mā tētahi hinonga whakahaere o te Kāwanatanga.

(3) Ko tētahi tangata ka whakamanatia ki te mahi i tētahi āheinga, ka tukuna e tēnei Pouhere, i raro rānei i tētahi Ture a te Pāremata mā—
 (a) tētahi hinonga whakahaere o te Kāwanatanga;
 (b) tētahi tari rānei o te ratonga tūmatanui, tae atu ki ngā āpiha kei roto i tētahi tari;
 (c) tētahi atu hinonga whakahaere rānei o te Whenua Rangatira kua whakatūria, atu i te tū hei hinonga ā-ture, e tētahi Ture a te Pāremata rānei, i raro rānei i tētahi Ture a te Pāremata hei whakatinana ture, hei whakatinana kaupapa here rānei.
 (d) te aronga pea o te whai atu i tētahi mahi e tika ana hei mahi i taua āheinga, e whai take ai rānei, nā konā ka whai hua rānei i te mahi i taua āheinga, ka mahi rānei i roto i te ingoa o te Whenua Rangatira me te mahi i ngā mana whakahaere o te Whenua Rangatira hei hinonga ā-ture.

69 Cabinet

(1) This Article establishes the Cabinet.
(2) The Cabinet consists of the persons who hold current warrants as Ministers, but does not include Ministers designated under paragraph (6) or (7).
(3) The Cabinet—
    (a) determines the general direction of the Government:
    (b) develops and implements government policy:
    (c) co-ordinates and directs, subject to any Act of Parliament, the functions of institutions of the Government, the public service, and other institutions of the State established to implement legislation or policies:
    (d) initiates and develops Government Bills:
    (e) makes subordinate legislation under authority conferred on it by this Constitution or by Act of Parliament.
(4) The Cabinet is collectively responsible to Parliament for the performance by the Government of its responsibilities.
(5) The Cabinet may appoint any committees that it considers necessary or required to assist the Cabinet in the discharge of its responsibilities; the Prime Minister must report the purpose, membership, and terms of reference of the committees to Parliament.
(6) The Prime Minister may designate Ministers as associate Ministers to the principal Minister in a portfolio with responsibilities delegated by the principal Minister.
(7) The Prime Minister may designate Ministers outside Cabinet with responsibilities designated by the Prime Minister.
(8) Ministers referred to in paragraphs (6) and (7) may be appointed to Cabinet committees, but are not thereby members of Cabinet.
(9) The Cabinet must from time to time approve and issue a Cabinet Manual that provides a guide to the processes and procedures of Cabinet.

69 Te Rūnanga Kāwanatanga

(1) Ka whakatū tēnei Whiti i Te Rūnanga Kāwanatanga.

(2) Kei roto i Te Rūnanga Kāwanatanga ngā tāngata e pupuri ana i ngā whakamananga o nāianei hei Minita, engari kāore i reira ngā Minita ka tohua i raro i te rerenga (6), (7) rānei.

(3) Ko tā Te Rūnanga Kāwanatanga ko te—
   (a) whakatakoto huarahi hei ahunga mā te Kāwanatanga:
   (b) hanga kaupapa here kāwanatanga, ko te whakatinana kaupapa here kāwanatanga hoki:
   (c) whakarite, ko te tohutohu hoki, e ai ki ngā Ture a te Pāremata, i ngā āheinga o ngā hinonga whakahaere o te Kāwanatanga, o te ratonga tūmatanui hoki, o hinonga whakahaere kē atu hoki o te Whenua Rangatira ka whakatūria hei whakatinana i ngā ture, i ngā kaupapa here rānei:
   (d) tīmata ki te hanga, ko te whakawhanake hoki i ngā Pire Kāwanatanga:
   (e) hanga waeture i raro i te mana i tukuna e tēnei Pouhere, e tētahi Ture a te Pāremata rānei.

(4) Ka noho haepapa ā-tōpū Te Rūnanga Kāwanatanga ki te Pāremata mō te mahi a te Kāwanatanga mō ōna haepapatanga.

(5) Ka āhei Te Rūnanga Kāwanatanga te kopou i ngā kōmiti e tika ana ki ōna whakaaro, me whakatū rawa rānei ka tika, hei āwhina i Te Rūnanga Kāwanatanga ki te kawe i ōna haepapatanga: me tuku pūrongo rawa e te Pirimia mō te aronga, mō ngā mema hoki, mō ngā paearu hoki o ngā kōmiti, ki te Pāremata.

(6) Ka āhei te Pirimia te tohu Minita hei Minita tuarua ki te Minita matua i roto i tētahi kohinga haepapatanga ka tuaritia e te Minita matua.

(7) Ka āhei te Pirimia te tohu Minita ka noho i waho atu i Te Rūnanga Kāwanatanga kia whai haepapatanga ka tohua e te Pirimia.

(8) Ka kopoua pea ngā Minita ka kōrerotia i roto i ngā rerenga (6), (7) hoki ki ngā kōmiti o Te Rūnanga Kāwanatanga, engari ehara i te mea ka noho hei mema mō Te Rūnanga Kāwanatanga.

(9) I ētahi wā me whakaae rawa, me whakaputa rawa hoki e Te Rūnanga Kāwanatanga tētahi Puka Rūnanga Kāwanatanga hei tuku aratohu mō ngā hātepe me ngā tukanga a Te Rūnanga Kāwanatanga.

70 The Office of Prime Minister

(1) This Article establishes the office of Prime Minister.
(2) The Prime Minister is the Head of the Government.
(3) The Prime Minister is appointed to the office by the Head of State in accordance with Article 47.
(4) Following a general election of the members of Parliament and whenever there is a vacancy in the office of Prime Minister, Parliament may, by a majority of the voting members, elect a member of Parliament as the new Prime Minister.
(5) The Prime Minister ceases to hold office—
    (a) if the Prime Minister ceases to be a member of Parliament; or
    (b) on the receipt by the Head of State of a letter of resignation from the Prime Minister; or
    (c) when a new Prime Minister is appointed by the Head of State under Article 47.

71 Roles, functions, and responsibilities of the Prime Minister

The roles, functions, and responsibilities of the Prime Minister include the following:
    (a) to oversee the execution of the policies of the Government with and through the appropriate Ministers and the public service:
    (b) to act as chair of Cabinet proceedings:
    (c) to make recommendations on Cabinet and other ministerial appointments and determine departmental responsibilities of Ministers:
    (d) to formulate and manage with Ministers the Government's legislative programme in Parliament:
    (e) to be held to account by Parliament for the performance of public duties:
    (f) to be responsible for the standards of ministerial conduct:
    (g) to represent the people and Government of the State of Aotearoa New Zealand overseas:
    (h) to perform any other roles, functions, and duties that may be required.

70 Te Tari o Te Pirimia

(1) Ka whakatū tēnei Whiti i te tari o te Pirimia.
(2) Ko te Pirimia te Upoko o te Kāwanatanga.
(3) Ka kopoua te Pirimia ki te tari e Te Upoko o Te Whenua Rangatira e ai ki te Whiti 47.
(4) Whai i muri i tētahi pōtitanga ā-motu o ngā mema o te Pāremata, ā, i ngā wā ka wātea te tūranga o te Pirimia, ka āhei te Pāremata te pōti i tētahi mema o te Pāremata hei Pirimia hou mā tētahi pōtitanga a te nuinga o ngā mema ka pōti.
(5) Ka mutu te tūranga o te Pirimia—
    (a) mehemea ka mutu te Pirimia i tana mahi hei mema Pāremata;
    (b) ka whiwhi rānei Te Upoko o Te Whenua Rangatira i tētahi reta rīhainatanga nā te Pirimia;
    (c) i te wā rānei ka kopoua tētahi Pirimia hou e Te Upoko o Te Whenua Rangatira i raro i te Whiti 47.

71 Ngā mahi, ngā āheinga hoki, ngā haepapatanga hoki o te Pirimia

Ko ngā mahi, ngā āheinga hoki, ngā haepapatanga hoki o te Pirimia tae atu ki ēnei e whai ake nei:
  (a) kia mātai iho i te whakamahinga o ngā kaupapa here o te Kāwanatanga me ngā Minita tika me te ratonga tūmatanui, mā ngā Minita tika hoki me te ratonga tūmatanui:
  (b) kia noho hei heamana mō ngā whakahaerenga o Te Rūnanga Kāwanatanga:
  (c) kia tuku tūtohunga mō ngā kopoutanga ki Te Rūnanga Kāwanatanga, ki ngā tūranga Minita hoki, kia whakatau hoki i ngā haepapatanga ā-tari o ngā Minita:
  (d) kia whakakaupapa tahi, kia whakahaere tahi hoki me ngā Minita te hōtaka whakature a te Kāwanatanga i roto i te Pāremata:
  (e) kia herea e te Pāremata kia noho haepapa mō te mahinga o ngā kawenga tūmatanui:
  (f) kia noho haepapa mō ngā taumata o ngā whanonga minitatanga:
  (g) kia noho hei kanohi mō te iwi whānui me te Kāwanatanga o te Whenua Rangatira o Aotearoa Niu Tireni ki tāwāhi:
  (h) kia mahi i mahi kē atu, i āheinga kē atu hoki, i kawenga kē atu hoki, e tika ana.

72 Ministers

(1) Ministers are appointed by the Head of State, acting on the advice of the Prime Minister, from among members of Parliament.

(2) The designations of Ministers and their responsibilities are set by the Prime Minister.

(3) A Minister is individually responsible to Parliament for the proper and efficient execution of the Minister's responsibilities.

(4) For the purposes of paragraph (3), a Minister is responsible for any department of the public service or other institution of the State within the Minister's portfolio, but is not responsible for actions that the department or institution is required to take independently.

(5) A Minister ceases to hold office—
   (a) if the Minister ceases, other than in the circumstances described in paragraph (6), to be a member of Parliament for any reason; or
   (b) if removed from office by the Head of State, acting on the advice of the Prime Minister; or
   (c) on the receipt by the Prime Minister of a letter of resignation from the Minister.

(6) Any function, duty, or power exercisable by or conferred on any Minister (by whatever designation that Minister is known) may, unless the context of applicable legislation otherwise requires, be exercised or performed by any other Minister.

(7) Despite paragraph (1)—
   (a) following a general election of the members of Parliament, a person who was a candidate at that election but whose status as a member of Parliament has not yet been determined may be appointed and hold office as a Minister, but if the person is not a member of Parliament by the 40th day after the person's appointment, the person ceases to hold office as Minister at the end of that day:
   (b) a Minister who ceases to be a member of Parliament may continue to hold office as a Minister for 28 days after the day on which the Minister ceased to be a member of Parliament.

72 Ngā Minita

(1) Ka kopoua te Minita e Te Upoko o Te Whenua Rangatira, e whai ana i te whakatakoto whakaaro o te Pirimia, mai i ngā mema o te Pāremata.

(2) Ka tohua e te Pirimia ngā kawenga a ngā Minita me ō rātou haepapatanga.

(3) Ka noho haepapa takitahi ia Minita ki te Pāremata kia tōtika, kia whai hua hoki te whakatutukitanga o ngā haepapatanga Minita.

(4) Mō ngā aronga o rerenga (3), ka noho haepapa tētahi Minita mō tētahi tari o te ratonga tūmatanui, mō tētahi atu hinonga whakahaere rānei o te Whenua Rangatira kei roto i te kōpae a te Minita, engari kāore e noho haepapa mō ngā mahi a te tari, a te hinonga whakahaere rānei e tika ana kia mahia motuhake nei.

(5) Ka mutu te tūranga o tētahi Minita—

    (a) mehemea ka mutu te Minita i tana mahi hei mema Pāremata i runga i ngā āhuatanga o te wā, atu i ngā āhuatanga ka whakamāramatia i roto i te rerenga (6);

    (b) mehemea ka tangohia rānei i te tūranga e Te Upoko o Te Whenua Rangatira e whai ana i te whakatakoto whakaaro o te Pirimia;

    (c) ina ka whiwhi rānei te Pirimia i tētahi reta rīhainatanga nā te Minita.

(6) Ko ngā mahi, ngā kawenga rānei, ngā mana whakahaere rānei ka mahia e tētahi Minita, ka tukuna rānei ki tētahi Minita (mā te kaupapa e mōhiotia ana taua Minita ahakoa he aha) ka āhei e Minita kē atu te whakatutuki, te mahi rānei, māna he rerekē atu te horopaki o ngā ture whai pānga.

(7) Ahakoa te rerenga (1)—

    (a) whai i muri mai i tētahi pōtitanga ā-motu o ngā mema o te Pāremata, ko tētahi tangata i tū ai hei kaitono rohe pōti i taua pōtitanga engari kāore anō kia mārama te āhua o tana tūranga hei mema Pāremata, ka āhei te kopou i a ia ki tētahi tūranga hei Minita, heoi anō, ki te kore ia e eke ki te tūranga hei mema Pāremata i te rā 40 whai i muri mai i te kopoutanga o te tangata, ka mutu te tūranga o te tangata hei Minita i te tōnga o taua rā:

    (b) ka āhei tētahi Minita ka mutu tana mahi hei mema Pāremata kia noho tonu ki te tūranga hei Minita i ngā rā 28 whai i muri mai i te rā i mutu ai tana noho hei mema Pāremata.

The public service

73 Nature and obligations of the public service

(1) The public service is a career-based service driven by a culture of excellence and efficiency, where appointment and promotion is on merit.
(2) The first duty of the public service is to act in accordance with this Constitution and the law.
(3) The public service must act in a spirit of service to the community and with commitment to open democratic government.
(4) The public service is politically neutral and impartial and serves loyally the Government of the day.
(5) The public service must provide Ministers with free and frank advice.
(6) The public service upholds the concept of stewardship, that is active planning and management of medium- and long-term interests, along with associated advice.
(7) The public service and all other institutions of the State must maintain high standards of integrity and conduct.

74 Government Services Commission

(1) This Article establishes a commission to be known as the Government Services Commission.
(2) The Government Services Commission consists of three persons who are each appointed for a single fixed term of five years by the Head of State on the recommendation of the Prime Minister, after consultation with the leaders of the political parties represented in Parliament.
(3) The Government Services Commission—
    (a) is the employer of chief executives of departments of the public service:

Te ratonga tūmatanui

73 Te āhua me ngā herenga o te ratonga tūmatanui

(1) He ratonga rapuara te ratonga tūmatanui ka kōkirihia i runga i tētahi ahurea rapu kounga, i tētahi ahurea pai te karawhiu hoki, e whakanuia ai te tangata ki te kopoutanga, ki te tokonga ake hoki mō tana pukumahi.

(2) Ko te kawenga tuatahi o te ratonga tūmatanui kia mahi e ai ki tēnei Pouhere me te ture.

(3) Me mahi rawa e te ratonga tūmatanui i roto i tētahi wairua whakarato ki te hapori, me te ū tonu kia māhorahora, kia manapori hoki te kāwanatanga.

(4) Ka noho ngākau tapatahi, ka noho matatika hoki te ratonga tūmatanui i ngā āhuatanga tōrangapū, ā, ka noho ngākau pono ki te Kāwanatanga o te wā.

(5) Me tuku rawa e te ratonga tūmatanui te whakatakoto whakaaro utu kore, pono hoki ki ngā Minita.

(6) Ka hāpai ake te ratonga tūmatanui i te tikanga o te kaitiakitanga, arā, ko te kaha whakamahere, ko te whakahaeretanga hoki o ngā whāinga pae waenga, pae tawhiti hoki, me te whakatakoto whakaaro whai pānga.

(7) Me tiaki rawa e te ratonga tūmatanui, e hinonga whakahaere kē atu hoki o te Whenua Rangatira ngā taumata teitei o te ngākau tapatahi me te whanonga.

74 Te Kōmihana Ratonga Kāwanatanga

(1) Ka whakatū tēnei Whiti i tētahi Kōmihana e kīia nei ko Te Kōmihana Ratonga Kāwanatanga.

(2) Tokotoru ngā tāngata ka whai wāhi ki Te Kōmihana Ratonga Kāwanatanga, ka kopoua ia tangata mō tētahi wā pūmau kotahi e rima tau te roa e Te Upoko o Te Whenua Rangatira i runga i te tūtohunga o te Pirimia, whai i muri mai i te whiriwhiri kōrero ki ngā kaiārahi o ngā rōpū tōrangapū kei roto i te Pāremata.

(3) Ko Te Kōmihana Ratonga Kāwanatanga—

    (a) te kaitukumahi o ngā tumu whakarae o ngā tari o te ratonga tūmatanui:

(b) provides leadership to the public service and all other institutions of the State established to implement legislation or policies:
(c) supervises standards of integrity and conduct in the public service and any other institution of the State that it is empowered to supervise by an Act of Parliament.
(4) The Government Services Commission makes decisions independently of Ministers.
(5) An Act of Parliament must provide for the organisation and governance of the Government Services Commission.

Part 8 Local Government

75 Local Government

(1) Aotearoa New Zealand must be divided into defined geographical localities that are governed by local governments under a democratic system of local government based on the following principles:
(a) the principle of subsidiarity, which means that the provision of services and the solution of issues should take place as close to the citizens as is practicable:
(b) the principle of autonomy, which means that Parliament should confer on local governments the power and autonomy to manage a substantial share of public affairs:
(c) the principle of financial sufficiency, which means that the funding of each local government, through financial support, rates, and taxes that it is empowered to raise, should be sufficient for it to function effectively:
(d) the principle of community, which means that each local government should foster a sense of community and provide for the participation of its citizens in decision-making (including through assemblies of citizens, co-governance arrangements, or other participatory means) to ensure that decisions serve the well-being of the community:
(e) the principle of transparency, which means that local governments should govern in an open and transparent manner

(b) ka tuku ārahitanga mō te ratonga tūmatanui me ērā atu hinonga whakahaere katoa hoki o te Whenua Rangatira ka whakatūria hei whakatinana ture, hei whakatinana kaupapa here rānei:
(c) ka whakahaere tikanga i ngā taumata o te ngākau tapatahi, o te whanonga hoki i roto i te ratonga tūmatanui me ērā atu o ngā hinonga whakahaere o te Whenua Rangatira ka whakamanatia e tētahi Ture a te Pāremata ki te whakahaere tikanga.
(4) Ka noho motuhake Te Kōmihana Ratonga Kāwanatanga i ngā Minita ki te whakatau.
(5) Me tuku rawa e tētahi Ture a te Pāremata mō te whakahaere, mō te mana ārahi hoki o Te Kōmihana Ratonga Kāwanatanga.

Wāhanga 8 Kāwanatanga ā-Rohe

75 Kāwanatanga ā-Rohe

(1) Me whakawehe rawa a Aotearoa Niu Tireni hei wāhi matawhenua ka mahi kāwana ngā kāwanatanga ā-rohe i raro i tētahi pūnaha manapori kāwanatanga ā-rohe ka takea mai i ngā mātāpono e whai ake nei:
(a) ko te mātāpono o te turuki, arā, ka noho tata te tuku ratonga me te tuku rongoā mō ngā take ki ngā kirirarau ki ōna taumata e taea ana:
(b) ko te mātāpono o te motuhaketanga, arā, me tuku e te Pāremata te mana whakahaere me te motuhaketanga ki runga i ngā kāwanatanga ā-rohe hei whakahaere i tētahi rahinga o ngā take tūmatanui:
(c) ko te mātāpono o te rawaka ā-pūtea, arā, me rawaka pai te pūtea ki ia kāwanatanga ā-rohe mā te tautoko ā-pūtea, mā ngā reiti hoki, mā ngā tāke hoki, e whakamanatia ai kia kohikohi kia tōtika ai tana mahi:
(d) ko te mātāpono o te hapori, arā, me poipoi e ia kāwanatanga ā-rohe tētahi wairua hāpai hapori, me tuku hoki kia whaiuru ai ōna kirirarau i roto i ngā whakatau (tae atu mā ngā huinga kirirarau, mā ngā whakaritenga mana ārahi tōpū rānei, mā huarahi whakauru kē atu rānei) kia whakaū ai ka whai oranga te hapori i ngā whakatau:
(e) ko te mātāpono o te taiahoaho, arā, me ārahi ā-kāwana e ngā kāwanatanga ā-rohe mā roto i tētahi āhuatanga māhorahora, i tētahi āhuatanga taiahoaho hoki, kia noho haepapa hoki ki ō

and be accountable to their electors.
(2) This Constitution recognises the importance of a sound relationship between the Government and local governments and to that end—
   (a) before any new responsibility is placed on local governments by an Act of Parliament or a decision of Ministers, the Government must adequately consult representatives of local governments about the proposed responsibility and provide estimates of the financial and administrative costs of the proposed responsibility:
   (b) before introducing to Parliament a Government Bill or a Member's Bill that would change legislation relating to local government legislation or otherwise significantly affect local governments, the Government or the Member of Parliament promoting the Bill must adequately consult representatives of local governments about the contents of the proposed Bill.

Part 9 *The Judiciary*

76 Judicial authority

(1) The judicial authority of the State is vested in the courts.
(2) Acts of Parliament may provide for tribunals to exercise the judicial authority of the State.
(3) Acts of Parliament may provide for a Judge to be appointed as a member of a tribunal.
(4) The courts and the tribunals are independent and subject only to the Constitution and the law, which they must apply independently, impartially and without fear, favour or prejudice.
(5) The procedures and jurisdiction of all courts and tribunals function under the authority of Acts of Parliament.
(6) The Chief Justice of the State is the head of the judiciary. The Chief Justice is a member of, and presides over, the Supreme Court.
(7) Acts of Parliament may confer investigatory and decision-making functions of a non-judicial nature upon a court or tribunal.

rātou kaipōti.

(2) Ka whakaū tēnei Pouhere i te whakahirahira o tētahi hononga pāmārō kei te Kāwanatanga me ngā kāwanatanga ā-rohe, ā, nā whai anō—

  (a) i mua i te taunga o ētahi haepapatanga hou ki runga i ngā kāwanatanga ā-rohe mā tētahi Ture a te Pāremata, mā tētahi whakatau rānei a ngā Minita, me whiriwhiri kōrero rawa e te Kāwanatanga ki ngā kanohi o ngā kāwanatanga ā-rohe mō te haepapatanga kei te whakaarotia, me te tuku nama mō te nui pea o te pūtea me ngā whakapaunga utu mō te whakahaere i te haepapa kei te whakaarotia:

  (b) i mua i te whakauru i tētahi Pire Kāwanatanga, i tētahi Pire nā tētahi mema o te Pāremata rānei ki te Pāremata, me kī, he Pire e panoni ai i tētahi Ture e pā ana ki te kāwanatanga ā-rohe, ka kaha rānei te pānga ki ngā kāwanatanga ā-rohe, me whiriwhiri kōrero rawa e te Kāwanatanga, e te Mema o te Pāremata rānei e toko ake ana i te Pire, ki ngā kanohi o ngā kāwanatanga ā-rohe mō te kiko o te Pire kei te whakaarotia.

Wāhanga 9 Te Hunga Whakawā ā-Ture

76 Te mana whakatau

(1) Ka riro ki ngā kōti te mana whakawā ā-ture o te Whenua Rangatira.

(2) Mā ngā Ture a te Pāremata e tuku ai pea ki ngā taraipiunara te āhei kia whakatinana i te mana whakatau o te Whenua Rangatira.

(3) Mā ngā Ture a te Pāremata e tuku ai pea kia kopoua tētahi Kaiwhakawā hei mema mō tētahi taraipiunara.

(4) Ka noho motuhake ngā kōti me ngā taraipiunara i runga i te here ki te Pouhere me te ture anake, me motuhake rawa, me matatika rawa hoki, me mataku kore rawa hoki, me mariu kore rawa hoki, me whakatakē kore rawa hoki tā rātou whakatinana i ērā.

(5) Ka mahia ngā tukanga me ngā mana whakatau o ngā kōti katoa, o ngā taraipiunara katoa hoki i te mana o ngā Ture a te Pāremata.

(6) Ko te Tumu Whakawā o te Whenua Rangatira te upoko o te hunga whakawā ā-ture. He mema te Tumu Whakawā o te Kōti Mana Nui, ā, kei a ia te mana whakahaere.

(7) Mā ngā Ture a te Pāremata e āhei ai te tuku i ngā āheinga hōpara, i ngā āheinga whakatau o tētahi āhuatanga whakawā kore ki tētahi kōti, ki tētahi taraipiunara rānei.

(8) Acts of Parliament must limit the number of Judges in each court and tribunal. Changes to those numbers may only be made by Act of Parliament.

77 Courts of general jurisdiction

(1) There continue to be the following courts of general jurisdiction which exercise the judicial authority of the State within the jurisdiction conferred upon them by this Constitution and by Acts of Parliament:
  (a) the District Court:
  (b) the High Court:
  (c) the Court of Appeal:
  (d) the Supreme Court.
(2) The Supreme Court is the court of final appeal. Any decision of the Supreme Court is final and binding on all other courts.
(3) The Supreme Court is not bound by its previous decisions.
(4) Courts of general jurisdiction have the power to develop the common law in a manner that is compatible with the Constitution.
(5) Parliament has the power to alter the common law.

78 Other courts and tribunals

(1) Those courts and tribunals in existence at the commencement of this Constitution continue in existence with the powers, privileges, and jurisdiction conferred upon them until such time as they are reorganised by Acts of Parliament.
(2) Subject to this Constitution, Acts of Parliament may establish any other courts (other than courts of general jurisdiction) and tribunals as are considered appropriate for the administration of justice within the country and make provisions for matters related to their administration and jurisdiction.
(3) No tribunal, other than a military tribunal, may determine a criminal charge. A military tribunal may only determine a criminal charge against military law.

(8) Me whakawhāiti rawa e ngā Ture a te Pāremata te tokomaha o ngā Kaiwhakawā kei roto i ia kōti, i ia taraipiunara hoki. Mā ngā Ture a te Pāremata anake e panoni ai taua tokomaha.

77 Ngā kōti whakawā whānui

(1) Ka tū tonu ngā kōti whakawā whānui e whai ake nei, ka whakatinana i te mana whakatau o te Whenua Rangatira i roto i te whai mana ka tukuna ki aua kōti e tēnei Pouhere me ngā Ture a te Pāremata:
 (a) ko te Kōti ā-Rohe:
 (b) ko te Kōti Teitei:
 (c) ko te Kōti Pīra:
 (d) ko te Kōti Mana Nui.

(2) Ko te Kōti Mana Nui te kōti pīra whakamutunga. He mea mutu rawa atu, he mea mau tonu ngā whakatau a te Kōti Mana Nui ki ngā kōti katoa.

(3) Kāore te Kōti Mana Nui i te herea e ōna whakatau o mua.

(4) Kei ngā kōti whakawā whānui te mana whakahaere ki te waihanga ture noa i runga i tētahi āhuatanga e hāngai ana ki te Pouhere.

(5) Kei te Pāremata te mana whakahaere ki te panoni i te ture noa.

78 Ko kōti kē atu, ko taraipiunara kē atu hoki

(1) Ko aua kōti, ko aua taraipiunara hoki e tū ana i te tīmatanga o tēnei Pouhere ka tū tonu me ngā mana whakahaere, ngā painga hoki, te whai mana hoki ka tukuna ki ērā tae atu ki te wā ka whakahaeretia anōtia e ngā Ture a te Pāremata.

(2) Ka āhei te Pāremata i runga i tēnei Pouhere, i ngā Ture a te Pāremata hoki, te whakatū i kōti kē atu (atu i ngā kōti whakawā whānui) me ngā taraipiunara e tika ana hei whakahaere i te mana ture i roto i te whenua, kia waihanga āheinga hoki mō ngā take e pā ana ki te whakahaere, ki te whai mana hoki o ērā.

(3) Atu i tētahi taraipiunara ngārahu, kāore rawa tētahi taraipiunara e whakatau i tētahi whakawhiunga taihara. Ka āhei tētahi taraipiunara ngārahu te whakatau i tētahi whakawhiunga taihara e ai ki te ture ngārahu anake.

79 Judicial Appointments Commission and judicial appointments

(1) An Act of Parliament must establish, and provide for, a Judicial Appointments Commission.

(2) The Act of Parliament must—
  (a) provide that members of the Commission consist of persons who are members of the judiciary, the legal profession, Parliament and the general public:
  (b) set out procedures for the Commission to identify candidates for judicial office to be selected on merit, having regard to the candidate's personal qualities, legal ability, and experience, and the desirability that the judiciary reflect gender, cultural, and ethnic diversity:
  (c) require the Commission to produce a short list of candidates whom it considers suitable for appointment to a judicial vacancy.

(3) No person may be appointed as a Judge of any court unless that person's name appears upon the short list for that vacancy produced by the Commission.

(4) Judges are appointed to office by the Head of State, upon recommendation by the Attorney-General.

80 Protection of Judges against removal from office

(1) No Judge may be removed from office except by the Head of State acting upon a resolution of Parliament, which resolution may be moved only on the grounds of that Judge's misbehaviour or of that Judge's incapacity to discharge the functions of office.

(2) An Act of Parliament must establish an independent panel to inquire into and report upon the conduct or capacity of Judges.

79 Te Kōmihana Kopoutanga Whakawā ā-Ture me ngā kopoutanga whakawā ā-ture

(1) Me whakatū rawa e tētahi Ture a te Pāremata, me tuku rawa hoki tētahi Kōmihana Kopoutanga Whakawā ā-Ture.
(2) Me tuku rawa e te Ture a te Pāremata kia—
    (a) tuku he mema nō te hunga whakawā ā-ture, nō te ngaiotanga ā-ture hoki, nō te Pāremata hoki, nō te iwi whānui hoki ngā mema o te Kōmihana:
    (b) whakatakoto tukanga mā te Kōmihana hei tautohu i ngā kaitono mō te tūranga whakawā ā-ture kia kōwhiria mō te angitū, me te aro atu ki ngā kounga whaiaro o te kaitono, tana āhei ā-ture hoki, tana wheako hoki, me te hiahia kia whai kanorau ā-ira – tāne mai, wahine mai, aha mai hoki ā-ahurea hoki, ā-mātāwaka hoki:
    (c) herea te Kōmihana ki te waihanga i tētahi rārangi poto o ngā kaitono ki ōna whakaaro e pai ana kia kopoua ki tētahi wāteatanga whakawā ā-ture.
(3) Kāore tētahi tangata e kopoua hei Kaiwhakawā mō tētahi kōti māna kei runga tana ingoa i tētahi rārangi poto mō taua wāteatanga, ka whakaputaina e te Kōmihana.
(4) Ka kopoua ngā Kaiwhakawā ki taua tūranga e Te Upoko o Te Whenua Rangatira, i runga i te tūtohunga o te Rōia Matua.

80 Te whakamarumaru i ngā Kaiwhakawā kia kore ai e tangohia i te tūranga

(1) Kāore tētahi Kaiwhakawā e tangohia i te tūranga māna ka tangohia e Te Upoko o Te Whenua Rangatira e mahi ana i runga i tētahi whakatau a te Pāremata, ka mōtinihia mō te whanonga kino o taua Kaiwhakawā te take, i runga rānei i te āhei kore o taua Kaiwhakawā te mahi i ngā āheinga o te tūranga.
(2) Me whakatū rawa e tētahi Ture a te Pāremata tētahi kāhui motuhake hei uiui, hei tuku pūrongo hoki mō te whanonga, mō te āheitanga hoki o ngā Kaiwhakawā.

(3) A resolution under paragraph (1) may not be moved unless—
   (a) it is moved by the Attorney-General; and
   (b) the independent panel established under paragraph (2) has stated in a report submitted to the Attorney-General that the panel is of the opinion that consideration of the removal of the Judge is justified.
(4) An Act of Parliament must provide for a judicial retirement age of 72.
(5) The independence of tribunals must be secured by Act of Parliament, but members of tribunals, including Judges, may be appointed for limited terms.

81 Salaries of Judges not to be reduced

The salary of a Judge must not be reduced, and no other adverse changes made in other conditions of service, during the Judge's tenure of office.

82 Government's duty to protect the courts and tribunals

(1) The Government is under a duty to protect the courts and tribunals to ensure their independence, impartiality, dignity, accessibility, and effectiveness.
(2) The Attorney-General has a particular responsibility to ensure that this duty is discharged.

Part 10 Integrity and Transparency

Law Officers

83 Attorney-General and Solicitor-General

(1) The law officers of the State are the Attorney-General and Solicitor-General.
(2) The law officers are responsible for—
   (a) ensuring the integrity of the legal system:
   (b) protecting the rule of law:
   (c) safeguarding the independence of the judiciary.

(3) Kāore e mōtinihia tētahi whakataunga ā-takitini i raro i te rerenga (1) māna—
   (a) ka mōtinihia e te Rōia Matua;
   (b) ka whakapuakina hoki e te kāhui motuhake ka whakatūria i raro i te rerenga (2), i roto i tētahi pūrongo ka tukuna atu ki te Rōia Matua, ki ngā whakaaro o te kāhui he tika kia tangohia te Kaiwhakawā.
(4) Me tuku rawa e tētahi Ture a te Pāremata tētahi rītaiatanga whakawā ā-ture i te tau 72 tau te pakeke.
(5) Me whakamarumaru rawa te motuhake o ngā taraipiunara e tētahi Ture a te Pāremata, engari ka āhei te kopou i ngā mema o ngā taraipiunara, tae atu ki ngā Kaiwhakawā, mō ētahi wā pūmau.

81 Ka kore e whakahekea te utu mā ngā Kaiwhakawā

Me kaua rawa e whakahekea te utu o tētahi Kaiwhakawā, e panonihia kinotia rānei āhuatanga kē atu o te mahi, i te roanga o te noho a te Kaiwhakawā ki te tūranga.

82 Te kawenga o te Kāwanatanga ki te whakamarumaru i ngā kōti me ngā taraipiunara

(1) Ka noho kawenga te Kāwanatanga ki te whakamarumaru i ngā kōti me ngā taraipiunara kia whakaū ai i te motuhake, i te matatika hoki, i te tū rangatira hoki, i te āheitanga hoki, i te tōtika hoki o ērā.
(2) Ka noho haepapa rawa te Rōia Matua ki te whakaū ka mahia tēnei kawenga.

Wāhanga 10 Te Ngākau Tapatahi me te Taiahoaho

Ngā Āpiha Ture

83 Te Rōia Matua me Te Rōia Tianara

(1) Ko te Rōia Matua me te Rōia Tianara ngā āpiha ture o te Whenua Rangatira.
(2) Ka noho haepapa ngā āpiha ture kia—
   (a) whakaū i te ngākau tapatahi o te pūnaha ture:
   (b) whakamarumaru i te ritenga o te ture:
   (c) tiaki i te motuhake o te hunga whakawā ā-ture.

(3) The Solicitor-General alone is responsible for supervision and oversight of the machinery for criminal prosecutions.

Officers of Parliament

84 Officers of Parliament

(1) Officers of Parliament are appointed by the Head of State on the recommendation of Parliament and are responsible to Parliament.

(2) An officer of Parliament may report the officer's findings and recommendations to Parliament.

(3) The following officers continued or established by this Constitution are officers of Parliament:

    (a) the Controller and Auditor-General, provided for in Article 85:

    (b) the Ombudsmen, provided for in Article 86:

    (c) the Commissioner for the Environment, provided for in Article 87:

    (d) the Commissioners for Human Rights, who are each members of the Commission provided for in Article 88.

(4) An Act of Parliament may establish further officers of Parliament.

85 The Controller and Auditor-General

(1) An officer, who may be known as the Controller and Auditor-General, must audit the public accounts of the State and of local governments and report to Parliament to ensure that—

    (a) public monies are properly spent and accounted for:

    (b) taxpayers receive value for money:

    (c) public money is lawfully expended.

(2) An Act of Parliament must provide for the office in accordance with these principles.

86 The Ombudsmen

(1) In order to protect the public from unfair decisions and enhance the quality of administrative decision-making, an Act of Parliament must continue to empower Ombudsmen to investigate administrative actions

(3) Ka noho haepapa te Rōia Tianara anake mō te whakahaere tikanga, mō te tirotiro tikanga hoki o te whakahaerenga o ngā whakawhiunga taihara.

Ngā Āpiha o te Pāremata

84 Ngā Āpiha o te Pāremata

(1) Ka kopoua ngā āpiha o te Pāremata e Te Upoko o Te Whenua Rangatira i runga i te tūtohunga o te Pāremata, ā, ka noho haepapa ki te Pāremata.

(2) Ka āhei tētahi āpiha o te Pāremata te tuku pūrongo mō ngā kitenga, mō ngā tūtohunga hoki o te āpiha ki te Pāremata.

(3) Ka noho tonu ngā āpiha e whai ake nei, ka whakatūria rānei e tēnei Pouhere hei āpiha Pāremata:

    (a) ko te Tumuaki o te Mana Arotake, ka tukuna i roto i te Whiti 85:

    (b) ko ngā Kaitiaki Mana Tangata, ka tukuna i roto i te Whiti 86:

    (c) ko te Kaikōmihana mō te Taiao, ka tukuna i roto i te Whiti 87:

    (d) ko ngā Kaikōmihana mō ngā Tika Tangata, ka noho hoki ko tēnā, ko tēnā hei mema mō te Kāhui ka tukuna i roto i te Whiti 88.

(4) Ma tētahi Ture a te Pāremata e whakatū ai ētahi āpiha anō o te Pāremata.

85 Te Tumuaki o te Mana Arotake

(1) Me āta tirotiro rawa e tētahi āpiha, e kīia nei ko ia te Tumuaki o te Mana Arotake, ngā puka kaute tūmatanui o te Whenua Rangatira, o ngā kāwanatanga ā-rohe hoki, ā, ka tuku pūrongo ki te Pāremata kia whakaū ai—

    (a) he tika te whakapau pūtea, he tika hoki te kaute pūtea mō ngā moni tūmatanui:

    (b) ka whiwhi hua ngā kaiutu tāke i taua moni:

    (c) ka whāia te ture i te whakapau moni tūmatanui.

(2) Me tuku rawa e tētahi Ture a te Pāremata ki te tūranga e ai ki ēnei mātāpono.

86 Ngā Kaitiaki Mana Tangata

(1) Me tū tonu rawa tētahi Ture a te Pāremata ki te whakakaha i ngā Kaitiaki Mana Tangata ki te whakatewhatewha i ngā mahi whakahaere ka pā kaha ki te tangata me tōna whaiarotanga, ka mahia rānei e ngā tari o te

that affect persons in their personal capacity and are taken by departments of the public service, local governments, and other organisations named by or under the Act.

(2) Parliament must appoint a Chief Ombudsman.

87 The Commissioner for the Environment

In order to enhance the protection of the environment, an Act of Parliament must continue to empower the Commissioner for the Environment to monitor—
- (a) the adequacy of the systems established by the Government for managing the environment:
- (b) the performance of public authorities in maintaining and promoting the quality of the environment.

88 Commission for Human Rights

(1) In order to enhance the protection of human rights, an Act of Parliament must provide for a Commission for Human Rights to monitor and report on human rights issues and interact with the Government and Parliament. The Act of Parliament may confer other functions and powers on the Commission.

(2) Parliament must appoint a Chief Commissioner for Human Rights. The Chief Commissioner for Human Rights chairs the Commission for Human Rights.

(3) In order to assist the Government and Parliament bring about the rights set out in Article 29, the Commission for Human Rights may assess—
- (a) the social, economic, and health of sections of society and consider whether policy responses are required to progress the realisation of those rights:
- (b) whether proposed policies or Bills are likely to contribute towards, or detract from, realising those rights:
- (c) the impact of existing policies or legislation on the realisation of those rights.

ratonga tūmatanui, o ngā kāwanatanga ā-rohe hoki, o rōpū whakahaere kē atu rānei ka whakaingoatia, i raro rānei i te Ture, hei whakamarumaru i te iwi whānui i ngā whakatau makihuhunu, hei whakarākei hoki i te kounga o te whakatau whakahaere.

(2) Me kopou rawa e te Pāremata tētahi Kaitiaki Matua mō te Mana Tangata.

87 Te Kaikōmihana mō te Taiao

Me mana tonu rawa tētahi Ture a te Pāremata hei whakamarumaru ake i te taiao, hei whakakaha ake hoki i te Kaikōmihana mō te Taiao ki te aroturuki i—
- (a) te pai o ngā pūnaha ka whakatūria e te Kāwanatanga hei whakahaere i te taiao:
- (b) te mahi a ngā mana tūmatanui ki te tiaki, ki te toko ake hoki i te kounga o te taiao.

88 Kāhui Tika Tangata

(1) Me tuku rawa e tētahi Ture a te Pāremata mō tētahi Kāhui Tika Tangata hei aroturuki, hei tuku pūrongo hoki mō ngā take tika tangata, kia pāhekoheko ki te Kāwanatanga me te Pāremata, hei whakakaha ake i te whakamarumaru i ngā tika tangata. Mā tētahi Ture a te Pāremata e tuku ai ētahi atu āheinga, ētahi atu mana whakahaere hoki ki te Kāhui.

(2) Me kopou rawa e te Pāremata tētahi Kaikōmihana Matua mō ngā Tika Tangata. Ka noho te Kaikōmihana Matua mō ngā Tika Tangata hei kaihautū mō te Kāhui Tika Tangata.

(3) Hei āwhina i te Kāwanatanga me te Pāremata ki te whakatinana i ngā tika ka whakatakotoria i roto i te Whiti 29, ka āhei te Kāhui Tika Tangata te whakamātau—
- (a) i ngā wāhanga pāpori, ōhanga hoki, hauora hoki o te porihanga, ā, ka whakaaro mehemea e tika ana kia rapu urupare ā-kaupapa here hei kōkiri ake i te whakatinanatanga o aua tika:
- (b) mehemea mā aua kaupapa here, Pire rānei ka whakaarotia e whai hua ai, e raru ai rānei te whakatinanatanga o aua tika:
- (c) i te kaha o te pānga o ngā kaupapa here e tū kē ana, o ngā ture e tū kē ana rānei, ki te whakatinanatanga o aua tika.

Availability of information concerning the Government, local governments, and other organisations

89 Official information

(1) An Act of Parliament must give the public as much access as practicable to information held by the Government, public service, institutions of the State, local governments, and by any other institutions and organisations that are accountable to Parliament, the Government, or to a local government, in order to—
   (a) enable members of the public to participate more effectively in the making and administration of laws and policies:
   (b) promote the responsibility and accountability of Ministers and elected and unelected officials:
   (c) enhance respect for the law and to promote good governance.

(2) In accordance with these principles, the Act must—
   (a) provide for the availability of official information and enable individuals and bodies corporate to access information concerning themselves:
   (b) provide for the establishment of an independent Information Authority:
   (c) empower the Information Authority to review decisions to deny information and to release information if it considers that to be the right course of action under the Act, with Ministers having no power of veto:
   (d) require the Authority to provide appropriate education, guidance and advice to agencies and the public on the application of the Act.

(3) The Act must also provide for access to information concerning Parliament, including the office of the Speaker, the office of the Clerk, Parliamentary Services, the Parliamentary Counsel Office, and all officers of Parliament.

Te wāteatanga o ngā pārongo e pā ana ki te Kāwanatanga, ki ngā kāwanatanga ā-rohe hoki, ki rōpū whakahaere kē atu hoki

89 Pārongo Ōkawa

(1) Me tuku rawa e tētahi Ture a te Pāremata, ki ōna taumata e taea ana, te āhei kia whai pārongo ka puritia e te Kāwanatanga, e te ratonga tūmatanui hoki, e ngā hinonga whakahaere hoki o te Whenua Rangatira, e ngā kāwanatanga ā-rohe hoki, e hinonga whakahaere kē atu hoki me ngā rōpū whakahaere hoki ka noho haepapa ki te Pāremata, ki te Kāwanatanga rānei, ki tētahi kāwanatanga ā-rohe rānei, kia—

    (a) āhei ngā mema o te iwi whānui kia kaha ake te whaiuru ki roto i te waihanga, i te whakahaere hoki, i ngā ture me ngā kaupapa here:

    (b) toko ake i te haepapatanga me te noho haepapa o ngā Minita me ngā āpiha ka pōtihia, kāore e pōtihia rānei:

    (c) whakakaha ake i te whakaute i te ture me te toko ake i te mana ārahi kia pai.

(2) I runga i ēnei mātāpono, ko tā te Ture me—

    (a) tuku rawa kia wātea te pārongo ōkawa, kia āhei hoki te tangata takitahi, ngā rangatōpū hoki te whiwhi pārongo mō rātou anō:

    (b) tuku rawa kia whakatūria tētahi Mana Pārongo motuhake:

    (c) whakamana rawa te Mana Pārongo ki te arotake i ngā whakatau kia whakatoitoi pārongo, kia tuku hoki te pārongo kia rere mehemea ki ōna whakaaro koirā te huarahi tika kia whāia i raro i te Ture, me te kore āhei o ngā Minita te whakahē:

    (d) herea rawa te Mana Pārongo ki te tuku mātauranga, ki te tuku tohutohu hoki, ki te tuku whakaaro hoki e tika ana ki ngā pokapū, ki te iwi whānui hoki mō te whakatinanatanga o te Ture.

(3) Me tuku rawa e te Ture kia āhei te whiwhi pārongo e pā ana ki te Pāremata, tae atu ki te tūranga o te Mana Whakawā o Te Pāremata, ki te tūranga o te Karaka hoki, ki Ngā Ratonga Pāremata hoki, ki te Tari Tohutohu Pāremata hoki, ki ngā āpiha katoa hoki o te Pāremata.

Intelligence and security

90 Oversight over intelligence and security agencies

(1) Any intelligence and security agency of the Government must be established by Act of Parliament.
(2) In order to protect the liberty of the people, an Act of Parliament establishing a security and intelligence agency must—
  (a) limit the functions and powers of the agency within reasonable bounds:
  (b) subject the agency to effective oversight mechanisms:
  (c) provide for regular reviews of the agency's functions and powers.

Part 11 Fundamental functions of the State

Law-making

91 Legislative procedures

(1) Subject to this Constitution, a Bill becomes law when it is passed by an affirmative vote of a voting majority of members of Parliament and is signed by the Head of State.
(2) Subject to this Constitution and any Act of Parliament, any subordinate legislation made by Cabinet becomes law when it is signed by the Head of State.

92 Information concerning Government legislation

At least five working days before introducing to Parliament a Bill that contains a new legislative scheme or a Bill that contains significant or extensive amendments to an existing Act, the Government must make publicly available information concerning the proposed legislation, including but not limited to—
  (a) the detailed nature of the proposals:
  (b) the policy papers relating to the changes:
  (c) the administrative arrangements proposed:
  (d) the fiscal costs of the new measures:
  (e) an analysis whether the proposals comply with this Constitution.

Te matataua me te whakamarumaru

90 Te tirotiro i ngā pokapū matataua me ngā pokapū whakamarumaru

(1) Me whakatū rawa e tētahi Ture a te Pāremata ngā pokapū matataua, ngā pokapū whakamarumaru hoki.

(2) Hei whakamarumaru i te noho here kore o te iwi whānui, mā tētahi Ture a te Pāremata ka whakatū i tētahi pokapū whakamarumaru, i tētahi pokapū matataua hoki me—
- (a) whakawhāiti rawa i ngā āheinga me ngā mana whakahaere o te pokapū ki ōna taupā e taea ana:
- (b) tuku rawa te pokapū ki ngā huarahi tōtika hei tirotiro:
- (c) tuku rawa kia auau te arotakenga o ngā āheinga me ngā mana whakahaere o te pokapū.

Wāhanga 11 Ngā tino āheinga o te Whenua Rangatira

Te hanga ture

91 Ngā tukanga whakature

(1) E ai ki tēnei Pouhere, ka whakaturetia tētahi Pire i te wā ka tautokona e tētahi pōtitanga o te nuinga o ngā mema o te Pāremata ka pōti, ā, ka waitohua e Te Upoko o Te Whenua Rangatira.

(2) E ai ki tēnei Pouhere me ngā Ture a te Pāremata, ka whakaturetia tētahi waeture e Te Rūnanga Kāwanatanga i te wā ka waitohua e Te Upoko o Te Whenua Rangatira.

92 Ngā pārongo e pā ana ki ngā ture Kāwanatanga

E rima rā neke atu rānei i mua i te whakauru i tētahi Pire ki te Pāremata, me kī, he Pire kei roto rā tētahi hōtaka ture hou, ko ētahi whakahoutanga nui, ko ētahi whakahoutanga tino kaha rānei ki tētahi Ture e tū ana kē, me whakawātea rawa e te Kāwanatanga ngā pārongo ki te iwi whānui mō te ture kei te whakaarotia, tae atu ki ēnei engari kāore e whakawhāitihia ki—
- (a) te āhuatanga āmiki o ngā whakatakotoranga whakaaro:
- (b) ngā pepa kaupapa here e pā ana ki ngā panoni:
- (c) ngā whakaritenga whakahaere kei te whakaarotia:
- (d) te utu ā-pūtea o ngā whakahoutanga:
- (e) tētahi tātaritanga mehemea ka hāngai ngā whakatakotoranga whakaaro ki tēnei Pouhere.

93 Attorney-General to report to Parliament where Bill appears to be inconsistent with Bill of Rights or te Tiriti o Waitangi/the Treaty of Waitangi

(1) Where any Bill is introduced into Parliament, the Attorney-General must bring to the attention of Parliament any provision in the Bill that appears—
   (a) to subject any of the rights and freedoms contained in Part 2 of this Constitution to a limit that cannot be demonstrably justified in a free and democratic society; or
   (b) to be inconsistent with any rights arising from te Tiriti o Waitangi/the Treaty of Waitangi.
(2) The Attorney-General must comply with paragraph (1)—
   (a) in the case of a Government Bill, on the introduction of that Bill:
   (b) in any other case, as soon as practicable after the introduction of the Bill.
(3) The Standing Orders of Parliament must provide procedures to bring to the attention of Parliament the provisions of an amendment to a Bill that would appear to have the effects set out in paragraphs (1)(a) or (1)(b).

94 Legislative programme

For each calendar year, the Government must publish its proposed legislative programme.

95 Urgency

(1) When a motion for urgency to expedite the consideration of legislation is moved, the Speaker must rule whether it is in the public interest to set aside the ordinary processes of Parliament, including Article 92, because of the particular circumstances stated or referred to in the motion.
(2) The Speaker must give reasons for the ruling.

96 Legislation to be accessible and comprehensible

(1) All legislation must be drafted in clear and understandable language.
(2) Systems must be in place that allow the people to have ready access to the text of all legislation.
(3) Paragraph (2) also applies to subordinate legislation.

93 Ka tuku pūrongo te Rōia Matua ki te Pāremata i ngā wā kāore pea te Pire i te tino hāngai ki Te Pire Tika Tangata, ki Te Tiriti o Waitangi/The Treaty of Waitangi rānei

(1) I ngā wā ka horahia tētahi Pire ki te Pāremata, me whakamōhio rawa e te Rōia Matua ki te Pāremata ngā āheinga kei roto i te Pire ko te āhua nei—
   (a) ka tuku kia herea tētahi tika, tētahi māhorahora rānei kei roto i te Wāhanga 2 o tēnei Pouhere, ā, kāore rawa e tino whakaaturia he tika kia pērā i roto i tētahi porihanga māhorahora, i tētahi porihanga manapori hoki;
   (b) kāore i te hāngai rānei ki ngā tika ka ahu mai i Te Tiriti o Waitangi/The Treaty of Waitangi.
(2) Me whai rawa e te Rōia Matua te rerenga (1)—
   (a) mō tētahi Pire Kāwanatanga, i te horanga o taua Pire:
   (b) mō take kē atu, ki ōna taumata e taea ana i muri i te whakaurunga o te Pire.
(3) Me tuku rawa e ngā Whakataunga Tū Roa o te Pāremata ngā tukanga hei whakamōhio atu ki te Pāremata ngā āheinga o tētahi whakahoutanga o tētahi Pire ko te āhua nei he pānga ōna ka whakatakotoria i roto i ngā rerenga (1)(a), (1)(b) rānei.

94 Te hōtaka whakature

Mō ia tau maramataka, me whakaputa rawa e te Kāwanatanga tana hōtaka o ngā whakaturetanga kei te whakaarotia.

95 Te whāwhaitanga

(1) I te wā ka mōtinihia kia whāwhai te kōkiri i te whakaaro mō tētahi ture, me whakatau rawa e te Mana Whakawā o Te Pāremata mehemea he aronga tūmatanui kia whakatahangia te hātepe māori o te Pāremata, tae atu ki te Whiti 92, nā ngā āhuatanga i kīia, i kōrerotia rānei i roto i te mōtini kia pērā ai.
(2) Me whakatakoto rawa e te Mana Whakawā o Te Pāremata ngā take mō te whakataunga.

96 Ka āhei te whiwhi, ka mārama hoki ngā ture

(1) Me mahea rawa, me mārama hoki te reo ā-tuhi o ngā ture katoa.
(2) Me whakarite rawa ngā pūnaha kia āhei ai te tangata te whiwhi i ngā tuhinga o ngā ture katoa.
(3) Ka hāngai hoki te rerenga (2) ki ngā waeture.

97 Subordinate legislation

(1) Acts of Parliament may authorise the Cabinet, a Minister, or other person or body to regulate specified matters by subordinate legislation.
(2) Parliament may disallow or amend any subordinate legislation authorised or purporting to be authorised by an Act of Parliament. The manner in which Parliament exercises these powers may be provided for by Act of Parliament or Standing Orders.
(3) Paragraph (2) does not apply to resolutions passed by Parliament or to by-laws made by a local government.

Public finance and taxation

98 Parliamentary control of public finance

It is not lawful for the Government, except by or under an Act of Parliament,—
   (a) to levy a tax; or
   (b) to raise a loan or to receive any money as a loan from any person; or
   (c) to spend any public money.

99 Public finance controls

An Act of Parliament determines the detailed control of public finance which—
   (a) provides a framework for Parliamentary scrutiny of—
      (i) the Government's expenditure proposals:
      (ii) the Government's management of its assets and liabilities:
   (b) establishes lines of responsibility for effective and efficient management of public financial resources:
   (c) specifies the principles for responsible fiscal management in the conduct of fiscal policy and requires regular reporting on the extent to which the Government's fiscal policy is consistent with those principles.

97 Ngā waeture

(1) Mā tētahi Ture a te Pāremata e whakamana Te Rūnanga Kāwanatanga, ko tētahi Minita rānei, ko tētahi atu tangata, ko tētahi atu rangatōpū rānei ki te whakariterite take i āta tohua mā te waeture.

(2) Mā te Pāremata e whakakāhore, e whakahou rānei tētahi waeture ka whakamanatia, ko te āhua nei ka whakamanatia rānei e tētahi Ture a te Pāremata. Mā tētahi Ture a te Pāremata, mā ngā Whakataunga Tū Roa rānei e tuku te āhuatanga o tā te Pāremata whakamahi i ēnei mana whakahaere.

(3) Kāore te rerenga (2) i te hāngai ki ngā whakatau ka tautokona e te Pāremata, ki ngā ture ā-rohe rānei ka waihangatia e tētahi kāwanatanga ā-rohe.

Te pūtea tūmatanui me te tāke

98 Te mana whakahaere o te Pāremata i te pūtea tūmatanui

Atu nā tētahi Ture a te Pāremata, i raro rānei i tētahi Ture a te Pāremata, ka kore whai te Kāwanatanga i te ture,—

(a) ki te hanga i tētahi tāke hou;
(b) ki te tono moni pūtea taurewa rānei, ki te whiwhi moni rānei hei pūtea taurewa i tētahi tangata;
(c) ki te whakapau moni tūmatanui rānei.

99 Ngā whakahaerenga mō te pūtea tūmatanui

Mā tētahi Ture a te Pāremata e whakatau te whakahaere āmiki i te pūtea tūmatanui e—

(a) whakatakoto ai tētahi anga hei tirotiro mā te Pāremata mō—
 (i) ngā whakaaro o te Kāwanatanga hei whakapau pūtea:
 (ii) tā te Kāwanatanga whakahaerenga o ōna rawa, o ōna taumahatanga hoki:
(b) whakatū ai ngā kāwai noho haepapa kia tōtika ai, kia pai ai hoki te whakahaere i ngā rawa pūtea tūmatanui:
(c) āta tohu ai i ngā mātāpono mō te whakahaere pūtea me te noho haepapa i roto i te āhua o te kaupapa here mō te pūtea, e herea ana hoki kia auau te tuku pūrongo mō te kaha o tā te Kāwanatanga kaupapa here mō te pūtea ki te hāngai tonu ki aua mātāpono.

100 Taxation and the budget

(1) For each financial year, the Minister of Finance must prepare a budget that includes proposals with respect to the raising of revenue and government expenditure for that financial year.

(b) The Minister of Finance must present the budget, when approved by Cabinet, to Parliament.

International Relations

101 Aotearoa New Zealand's international position not affected by Constitution

Nothing in this Constitution affects Aotearoa New Zealand's—
   (a) status at international law:
   (b) rights and obligations at international law:
   (c) membership of international organisations.

102 Conduct of international relations

(1) The Government has responsibility for the conduct of the international relations of the State and for the conduct of all forms of diplomacy.

(2) The State accepts the generally recognised principles of international law as its rule of conduct in its relations with other States.

(3) The Head of State, acting on the advice of the Prime Minister or the Minister of Foreign Affairs, has responsibility for—
   (a) appointing Ambassadors and other Heads of Mission and Post to represent the State overseas:
   (b) receiving duly accredited representatives from other states, territories, and international organisations.

103 Treaties

(1) The State must not ratify or otherwise consent to be legally bound by a treaty unless the treaty has first been approved by a resolution of Parliament.

100 Te tāke me te tahua pūtea

(1) Mō ia tau pūtea, me whakarite rawa e te Minita Tahua Pūtea tētahi tahua, tae atu ki ngā tono, me te whakaaro anō hoki ki te mahi kohikohi moni, ko tā te kāwanatanga whakapau moni hoki mō taua tau pūtea.

(2) Me tāpae atu e te Minita Tahua Pūtea te tahua ki te Pāremata i te wā ka whakaaetia e Te Rūnanga Kāwanatanga.

Ngā Hononga ki te Ao

101 Kāore te tūranga o Aotearoa Niu Tireni i roto i te Ao e panonihia e te Pouhere

Kāore kau tēnei Pouhere e panoni ai i ō Aotearoa Niu Tireni—
(a) tūranga ki te ture ā-Ao:
(b) tika, herenga hoki ki te ture ā-Ao:
(c) noho hei mema ki ngā rōpū whakahaere ā-Ao.

102 Te āhua o te whakahaere i ngā hononga ki te Ao

(1) Ka noho haepapa te Kāwanatanga mō te āhua o te whakahaere i ngā hononga o te Whenua Rangatira ki te Ao, mō te āhua hoki o ngā momo whakahangahanga katoa.

(2) Ka whakaae te Whenua Rangatira ki ngā mātāpono ture o te Ao kua whakaūngia noatia hei ritenga mō te whakahaere i ōna hononga ki Whenua kē atu.

(3) I runga i te whai i te whakatakoto whakaaro o te Pirimia, o te Minita mō Ngā Take Tāwāhi, ka noho haepapa Te Upoko o Te Whenua Rangatira mō—

    (a) te kopou Māngai Kāwanatanga, te kopou Upoko Kaupapa kē atu, Upoko Aka Aorere hoki hei māngai mā te Whenua Rangatira ki tāwāhi:

    (b) te whakamanuhiri i ngā māngai whai mana nō whenua kē, nō rohe nui kē hoki, nō rōpū whakahaere ā-ao kē hoki.

103 Ngā Tiriti

(1) Me kaua rawa te Whenua Rangatira e whakapūmau, e whakaae rānei kia herea e tētahi tiriti māna kua whakaaetia kētia e tētahi whakatau a te Pāremata.

(2) An obligation created by a treaty is binding in domestic law only if it is incorporated by legislation.

(3) For the purposes of this Constitution, the term 'treaty' means any document of whatever name that creates binding legal obligations for the State under international law when entered into, whether by ratification or by any other procedure signifying consent to be bound.

Policing

104 Police

(1) An Act of Parliament must provide for the organisation and governance of the Police based on the following principles:
  (a) principled, effective, and efficient policing services are a cornerstone of a free and democratic society under the rule of law:
  (b) effective policing relies on a wide measure of public support and confidence:
  (c) policing services are provided under a national framework but also have a local community focus:
  (d) policing services are provided in a manner that respects human rights:
  (e) policing services are provided independently and impartially:
  (f) in providing policing services every Police employee is required to act professionally, ethically, and with integrity:
  (g) constables in carrying out their duties and exercising their discretion act under the principle of constabulary independence.

(2) The Police are held to account among other ways by an independent authority established and provided for by an Act of Parliament.

(2) Ka waihangatia tētahi kawenga mā tētahi tiriti, he herenga ōna i roto i te ture taiwhenua mehemea ka whakaurua ki roto i tētahi ture.

(3) Mō ngā aronga o tēnei Pouhere, ko te tikanga o te kupu "tiriti" ko tētahi puka, ahakoa te ingoa, ka waihangatia ngā kawenga ā-ture mō te Whenua Rangatira i raro i te ture ā-Ao i te wā ka whāia rawatia, ahakoa nā te whakapūmau, nā tētahi atu tukanga rānei e tohu mai ana i te whakaaetanga kia herea.

Mahi Pirihimana

104 Pirihimana

(1) Me tuku rawa e tētahi Ture a te Pāremata mō te whakahaere, mō te mana ārahi hoki i ngā Pirihimana takea mai ai i ngā mātāpono e whai ake nei:
- (a) he whai mātāpono, he tōtika hoki, he pai hoki ngā ratonga pirihimana, koinei te pūtake o tētahi porihanga māhorahora, o tētahi porihanga manapori rānei i raro i te ritenga o te ture:
- (b) he pai te mahi pirihimana ka āwhinatia mā te taunaki, mā te tautoko hoki o te iwi whānui:
- (c) ka tukuna ngā ratonga pirihimana i raro i tētahi anga ā-motu engari ka aro ki te hapori:
- (d) ka tukuna ngā ratonga pirihimana i runga i tētahi āhuatanga ka whakautehia ngā tika tangata:
- (e) ka tukuna ngā ratonga pirihimana kia motuhake, kia matatika hoki:
- (f) mā te tuku i ngā ratonga pirihimana ka herea ia kaimahi Pirihimana kia ngaio te mahi, kia whai tikanga hoki, kia ngākau tapatahi hoki:
- (g) ka mahi ngā kātipa i ā rātou kawenga, ka mahi i runga hoki i tāna e pai ai, i raro i te mātāpono o te motuhake o te kaupapa kātipa.

(2) Ka herea ngā Pirihimana mō te noho haepapa ki tētahi mana whakahaere motuhake, atu i ētahi atu tikanga, ka whakatūria, ka tukuna hoki e tētahi Ture a te Pāremata.

Defence

105 The Armed Forces

(1) Subject to this Constitution and Acts of Parliament, the State may continue to raise, maintain, and use Armed Forces.
(2) The Head of State is the titular head of the Armed Forces.
(3) The Head of State appoints, in accordance with an Act of Parliament, an officer of the Armed Forces as the Chief of Defence Force
(4) An Act of Parliament may require the appointment of other officers to be made by the Head of State.
(5) The Armed Forces are under the control of the Government, acting through the Prime Minister and the Minister of Defence, who exercise their control through the Chief of Defence Force in accordance with an Act of Parliament.
(6) The Armed Forces must be politically neutral and impartial and must serve loyally the Government of the day.

106 Use of the Armed Forces

(1) The purposes of the Armed Forces are—
    (a) to defend Aotearoa New Zealand:
    (b) to defend ships or aircraft of Aotearoa New Zealand or people in or from Aotearoa New Zealand, wherever that may be required:
    (c) to defend another state, at the request of that state, if—
        (i) the State of Aotearoa New Zealand is, by legislation, responsible for the defence of that state or territory; or
        (ii) the State of Aotearoa New Zealand is, under a treaty, obliged to assist that state; or
        (iii) the Government determines that it is in the interests of Aotearoa New Zealand to accede to the request:
    (d) to contribute to any action involving the defence of another state or the maintenance of international peace and security if—
        (i) the action is in accordance with the purposes and principles of the United Nations; and

Te whakamarumaru

105 Te Ope Kātua

(1) E ai ki tēnei Pouhere me ngā Ture a te Pāremata, ka āhei te Whenua Rangatira te kohikohi, te tiaki hoki, te whakamahi hoki i Te Ope Kātua.

(2) Kei Te Upoko o Te Whenua Rangatira te taitara hei upoko mō Te Ope Kātua.

(3) Ka kopoua e Te Upoko o Te Whenua Rangatira, e ai ki tētahi Ture a te Pāremata, tētahi āpiha o Te Ope Kātua hei Tumu mō Te Ope Kātua.

(4) Mā tētahi Ture a te Pāremata e tuku ai kia kopoua e Te Upoko o Te Whenua Rangatira ētahi atu āpiha.

(5) Ka noho Te Ope Kātua i raro i te mana whakahaere o te Kāwanatanga, mā te Pirimia me te Minita mō te Kaupapa Waonga e mahi ai i tō rāua mana whakahaere mā te Tumu o Te Ope Kātua e ai ki tētahi Ture a te Pāremata.

(6) Me noho motuhake rawa, me noho matatika rawa hoki Te Ope Kātua i ngā āhuatanga tōrangapū, ā, me tōmau rawa te whakaapi.

106 Te whakamahi i Te Ope Kātua

(1) Ko ngā aronga o Te Ope Kātua kia—
  (a) papare i Aotearoa Niu Tireni:
  (b) papare i ngā kaipuke, i ngā waka rererangi rānei o Aotearoa Niu Tireni, i ngā tāngata rānei kei roto, nō Aotearoa Niu Tireni rānei, ahakoa kei hea:
  (c) papare i whenua kē atu, mehemea ka tonoa e taua whenua, mehemea—
    (i) ka noho haepapa ā-ture te Whenua Rangatira o Aotearoa Niu Tireni mō te papare i taua whenua, i taua rohe nui rānei;
    (ii) ka herea rānei Te Whenua Rangatira o Aotearoa Niu Tireni i raro i tētahi tiriti ki te āwhina i taua whenua:
    (iii) ka whakatau rānei te Kāwanatanga ka whai painga a Aotearoa Niu Tireni i te whakaae atu ki te tono:
  (d) tuku āwhina mō tētahi mahi hei papare i whenua kē atu, hei tiaki rānei i te rongomau, i te whakamarumaru rānei ki tāwāhi mehemea—
    (i) ka hāngai te mahi ki ngā aronga me ngā mātāpono o Te Rūnanga Whakakotahi i ngā Iwi o te Ao;

(ii) the Government determines that it is in the interests of Aotearoa New Zealand to contribute to that action:
(e) to participate in, or provide assistance to, a peace operation if the Government determines that it is in the interests of Aotearoa New Zealand to do so, and the peace operation is approved by—
(i) the United Nations Security Council; or
(ii) a regional organisation; or
(iii) a group of states.
(2) Where the deployment of the Armed Forces outside Aotearoa New Zealand for any of the purposes set out in paragraph (1)(c) to (e) is likely to involve the use of lethal force or coercion, Parliament must first, by resolution, authorise the deployment.
(3) When Parliament considers a draft resolution under paragraph (2), the Attorney-General must table in Parliament the Attorney-General's opinion as to whether the proposed deployment of the Armed Forces complies with this Constitution and with international law.

107 Use of Armed Forces in support of the civil power

(1) The Armed Forces may be used to provide public services within the country or overseas, including, but not limited to, search and rescue, disaster relief, humanitarian assistance, and development assistance.
(2) The Armed Forces may also be used, subject to procedures and limitations set out in legislation, to provide—
(a) assistance to agencies of the State in enforcing the law of Aotearoa New Zealand applicable in the territorial Sea, the contiguous zone, the exclusive economic zone, and the continental shelf:
(b) assistance to the civil authorities within the country in times of emergency.
(3) Where the Armed Forces are exercising powers under paragraph (2), the Armed Forces must not take any action involving the use of lethal force or coercion unless that action is taken under an Act of Parliament on behalf of another office holder of the State who is lawfully authorised to take that action.

(ii) ka whakatau hoki te Kāwanatanga ka whai painga a Aotearoa Niu Tireni i te āwhina atu ki taua mahi:
(e) whaiuru ki roto, ka tuku āwhina atu rānei, i tētahi kauhanga rongomau ka whakatau te Kāwanatanga ka whai painga a Aotearoa Niu Tireni i te mahi pērā, ā, ka whakaaetia te kauhanga rongomau e—
(i) te Kaunihera Whakamarumaru o Te Rūnanga Whakakotahi i ngā Iwi o te Ao;
(ii) tētahi rōpū whakahaere ā-rohe rānei;
(iii) tētahi huinga whenua rānei.

(2) Tuatahi, me whakamana rawa e te Pāremata mā tētahi whakataunga kia tukuna Te Ope Kātua kia haere ki waho atu i Aotearoa Niu Tireni mō ngā take ka whakatakotoria i roto i te rerenga (1)(c) e whawhai ai pea, e kūmea ai pea kia whawhai.

(3) I ngā wā ka whakaaro te Pāremata i tētahi whakataunga hukihuki i raro i te rerenga (2), me whakatakoto rawa e te Rōia Matua ki te Pāremata ko tō te Rōia Matua whakaaro mehemea e hāngai ana te tukunga o Te Ope Kātua ki tēnei Pouhere, ki te ture ā-Ao hoki.

107 Te whakamahi i Te Ope Kātua hei tautoko i te mana hiwhiri

(1) Ka āhei te whakamahi i Te Ope Kātua hei tuku ratonga tūmatanui i roto i tēnei whenua, ki tāwāhi rānei, tae atu rā, engari kāore i te whakawhāitihia rawatia ki te rapu me te whakaora, te tuku āwhina hoki i ngā wā o te parekura, te āwhina tangata hoki, te tuku āwhina whakawhanake hoki.

(2) Ka āhei hoki te whakamahi i Te Ope Kātua, e ai ki ngā tukanga me ngā whāititanga ka whakatakotoria i roto i ngā ture, ki te tuku—
(a) āwhina ki ngā pokapū o te Whenua Rangatira ki te uruhi i te ture o Aotearoa Niu Tireni e hāngai ana ki te rohenga Moana, ki te rohe tūtata hoki, ki te rohe ōhanga motuhake hoki, ki te paenga paparahi hoki:
(b) āwhina ki ngā mana hiwhiri i roto i tēnei whenua i ngā wā ohotata.

(3) I ngā wā ka mahia e Te Ope Kātua ngā mana whakahaere i raro i te rerenga (2), me kaua rawa Te Ope Kātua e whawhai, e kūmea rānei kia whawhai māna ka mahia taua mahi i raro i tētahi Ture a te Pāremata hei tautoko i tētahi atu tangata whai tūranga o te Whenua Rangatira kua whai mana ā-ture ki te mahi pērā.

Part 12 Status and revision of Constitution

108 Constitution is supreme

Where there is an inconsistency between any law and any provision of this Constitution, the provision of this Constitution prevails unless a declaration under Article 111 is for the time being in force.

109 Courts determine consistency of laws and conduct with Constitution

(1) The High Court has original jurisdiction to determine the question whether any law or conduct is inconsistent with this Constitution.

(2) All courts have jurisdiction to determine the question whether any law or conduct is inconsistent with this Constitution if it arises in the course of proceedings that otherwise fall within their jurisdiction. An Act of Parliament may confer similar jurisdiction upon a tribunal.

(3) When deciding a constitutional matter within its jurisdiction, a court or tribunal—

  (a) if satisfied that any law or conduct is inconsistent with the Constitution, must declare the law or conduct invalid to the extent of its inconsistency:

  (b) may make any order that is just and equitable in order to remedy the consequences or effects of that inconsistency:

  (c) may make any order that is just and equitable to limit the effects of a declaration of invalidity or of a remedial order including—

    (i) an order prospectively limiting the retrospective effect of the declaration of invalidity or of the remedial order:

    (ii) an order suspending the declaration of invalidity or of the remedial order for any period and on any conditions, to allow the competent authority to correct the inconsistency.

(4) Despite anything in this Article, if, in accordance with a declaration under Article 111, a provision in an Act of Parliament prevails for the

Wāhanga 12 Te tūnga me te whakahoutanga o te pouhere

108 He mana nūnui rawa atu tō te Pouhere

I ngā wā he hāngai kore nō tētahi ture ki ngā āheinga o tēnei Pouhere, kei runga ake te mana o te āheinga o tēnei Pouhere māna ka whakamahia tētahi whakapuakitanga mō tētahi wā i raro i te Whiti 111.

109 Ka whakatau ngā kōti i te hāngai tonu o ngā ture me ngā whanonga ki te Pouhere

(1) He whai mana taketake te Kōti Teitei hei whakatau i te pātai mehemea kāore i te hāngai tētahi ture, tētahi whanonga rānei ki tēnei Pouhere.

(2) He whai mana ngā kōti katoa hei whakatau i te pātai mehemea kāore i te hāngai tētahi ture, tētahi whanonga rānei ki tēnei Pouhere mehemea ka ahu mai tētahi take i roto i te whai i ngā whakahaerenga ka noho noa i raro i tō rātou e whai mana ai. Mā tētahi Ture a te Pāremata e tuku ai ka whai mana pērā tētahi taraipiunara.

(3) I ngā wā e whakatauria ana tētahi take pouhere i roto i tōna e whai mana ai, ko tā te kōti, ko tā te taraipiunara rānei—

   (a) mehemea ka kite atu he hāngai kore tētahi ture, tētahi whanonga rānei ki te Pouhere, me whakapuaki rawa he mana kore te ture, te whanonga rānei i runga i te āhua o tōna hāngai kore:

   (b) ka āhei te tuku i tētahi whakahau e pono ana, e matatika ana hoki hei whakatika ake i ngā putanga, i ngā pānga rānei o taua hāngai kore:

   (c) ka āhei te tuku i tētahi whakahau e pono ana, e matatika ana hoki hei whakawhāiti i ngā pānga o tētahi whakapuakitanga whakanoa, mō tētahi whakahau tikanga whakaora rānei tae atu ki—

      (i) tētahi whakahau hei whakawhāiti pea i te pānga o mua o te whakapuakitanga whakanoa, o tētahi whakahau tikanga whakaora rānei:

      (ii) tētahi whakahau e whakatārewa ana i te whakapuakitanga whakanoa, mō tētahi whakahau tikanga whakaora rānei mō tētahi wā ahakoa te roa, ahakoa he aha rānei, hei tuku i te mana whai matatau ki te whakatika i te hāngai kore.

(4) Ahakoa ngā mea katoa kei roto i tēnei Whiti, mehemea e ai ki tētahi whakapuakitanga i raro i te Whiti 111, kei runga ake te mana o tētahi

time being over any Article or paragraph of this Constitution, no court may do anything that would be inconsistent with the declaration under Article 111.

(5) If a declaration or order described in paragraph (3) concerns the consistency of an Act of Parliament with this Constitution and is made by a tribunal or by a court other than the Supreme Court, the declaration or order does not take effect unless it is confirmed by the Supreme Court.

(6) The Supreme Court has power to confirm, vary, modify, or set aside any declaration or order that it is asked to confirm.

(7) The procedure for confirmation by the Supreme Court may be regulated by Act of Parliament.

110 Entrenchment and Amendment

No Article or part of this Constitution may be repealed or amended unless the Bill for the repeal or amendment—
- (a) was published at least 90 days before being voted on in Parliament and is then passed by a majority of 75 percent of all the members of Parliament; or
- (b) has been carried by a majority of the valid votes cast at a poll of electors eligible to vote.

111 Act may prevail over Constitution for limited period

(1) Parliament may, following a determination under Article 109 that an Act of Parliament, in whole or in part, is inconsistent with this Constitution or a determination under Article 49(3) following a referral of a Bill by the Head of State that a Bill, in whole or in part, appears to be contrary to this Constitution, in an Act that is passed by a majority of 75 per cent of all Members of Parliament, expressly declare that one or more specified provisions which were the subject of the Supreme Court's determination prevail over one or more provisions of this Constitution.

(2) The power conferred on Parliament may be exercised on one or more occasions in respect of the same provisions.

āheinga i roto i tētahi Ture a te Pāremata mō tētahi wā i ngā Whiti, i ngā rerenga rānei o tēnei Pouhere, kāore e āhei tētahi kōti te mahi i tētahi mahi hāngai kore ki te whakapuakitanga i raro i te Whiti 111.

(5) Mehemea ka mahia e tētahi taraipiunara, e tētahi kōti rānei atu i te Kōti Mana Nui, tētahi whakapuakitanga, tētahi whakahau rānei ka kōrerotia i roto i te rerenga (3), he pānga o tērā ki te hāngai o tētahi Ture a te Pāremata ki tēnei Pouhere, kāore e whai mana te whakapuakitanga, te whakahau rānei māna ka whakaūngia e te Kōti Mana Nui.

(6) Kei te Kōti Mana Nui te mana whakahaere ki te whakaū, ki te panoni rānei, ki te whakahou ake rānei, ki te whakataha rānei i tētahi whakapuakitanga, i tētahi whakahau rānei, e tonoa ai te kōti kia whakaū.

(7) Ka whakariteritea e tētahi Ture a te Pāremata te tukanga ka whakaūngia e te Kōti Mana Nui.

110 Te whakamau me te Whakahou

Kāore e āhei te whakakore, te whakahou rānei i ngā Whiti, i ngā wāhanga rānei o tēnei Pouhere māna ko taua Pire nei ka whakakorengia, ka whakahoungia rānei—

(a) i whakaputaina e 90 rā neke atu i mua i te pōtitanga i roto i te Pāremata, kātahi ka tautokona e te nuinga o te 75 ōrau o ngā mema katoa o te Pāremata;

(b) kua whakamanatia rānei e te nuinga o ngā pōti whai mana i te wā o tētahi pōtitanga o ngā kaipōti e whai mana ana ki te pōti.

111 Kei runga ake te mana o tētahi Ture i te Pouhere mō tētahi wā poto

(1) Ka āhei te Pāremata te āta whakapuaki kei runga ake te mana o tētahi āheinga neke atu rānei ka āta tohua, i noho ai hei mea whakatau e te Kōti Mana Nui, i tētahi atu āheinga neke atu rānei i āta tohua ai o tēnei Pouhere, whai i muri i te whakataunga i raro i te Whiti 109 i ngā wā he hāngai kore tētahi Ture a te Pāremata, katoa mai, wāhanga mai rānei, ki te Pouhere, ki tētahi whakataunga i raro i te Whiti 49(3) whai i muri i tētahi tukunga o tētahi Pire nā Te Upoko o Te Whenua Rangatira ko tētahi Pire, katoa mai, wāhanga mai rānei, ko te āhua nei kāore i te hāngai ki tēnei Pouhere, i roto i tētahi Ture ka tautokona e te nuinga o te 75 ōrau o ngā Mema katoa o te Pāremata.

(2) Ka āhei te whakamahi i te mana whakahaere ka tukuna ki te Pāremata i tētahi wā neke atu rānei i runga i te āhua o aua āheinga.

(3) Every declaration, enacted in accordance with paragraph (1), has effect for a period that ends on the day that is five years after the declaration comes into force or such earlier date provided for in the declaration.

(4) No provision of an Act or declaration within an Act of Parliament may prevail over Articles 109 or 110 or this Article.

(5) A Bill that contains a declaration described in paragraph (1) may be referred to the Supreme Court by the Head of State under Article 49.

112 Periodic revisions of Constitution

(1) The Constitution must be reconsidered every ten years, although changes may be made at other times.

(2) An Act of Parliament must establish a commission to consider amendments to this Constitution ('the Consitutional Commission').

(3) Particular consideration must be given to the question of the appropriate position of social and economic rights in this Constitution, and whether the list of grounds of discrimination prohibited under Article 16(1) is adequate.

(4) Every ten years, following the year in which this Constitution comes into force, Parliament must appoint representatives of the political parties represented in the Parliament to be members of the Constitutional Commission.

(5) The number of representatives of each political party serving as members of the Constitutional Commission must be proportionate to the political party's strength in the Parliament.

(6) The other members of the Constitutional Commission are the Head of State, the Speaker, the Chief Justice, the Chairperson of the Waitangi Tribunal, the Chief Ombudsman, the Controller and Auditor-General, the Solicitor-General, the Chair of the Government Services Commission, the Commissioner for the Environment and the Chief Commissioner for Human Rights.

(7) After the representatives of the political parties are appointed to the Constitutional Commission, an Assembly must be convened of 100 citizens randomly selected from the electoral roll from each region in approximately the same proportion as the proportion of the population of that region bears to the total population of Aotearoa New Zealand.

(3) Ka whai mana ia whakapuakitanga, ka whakamanatia e ai ki te rerenga (1), mō tētahi wā ka mutu i te rā e rima tau whai i muri i te whakatinanatanga o te whakapuakitanga, i tētahi rā i whakaritea i mua mai rānei i roto i te whakapuakitanga.

(4) Kāore tētahi Ture, tētahi whakapuakitanga rānei i roto i tētahi Ture a te Pāremata e noho mana ake i runga ake i ngā Whiti 109, 110 rānei, o tēnei Whiti rānei.

(5) Ka āhei Te Upoko o Te Whenua Rangatira te tuku atu i tētahi whakapuakitanga ka kōrerotia i roto i te rerenga (1) ki te Kōti Mana Nui i raro i te Whiti 49.

112 Ngā whakahoutanga kauteatea o te Pouhere

(1) Me whakaaroaro rawa anō mō te Pouhere ia tekau tau, otirā i ētahi atu wā ka āhei te panoni.

(2) Me whakatū rawa e tētahi Ture a te Pāremata tētahi Kōmihana hei whakaaro i ngā whakahoutanga ki tēnei Pouhere (arā, ko "te Kōmihana Pouhere").

(3) Me āta whakaaro rawa mō te pātai e pā ana ki te wāhi tika o ngā tika pāpori, o ngā tika ōhanga hoki i roto i tēnei Pouhere, ā, mehemea e pai ana te rārangi o ngā take toihara kua āraitia i raro i te Whiti 16(1).

(4) Ia tekau tau, whai i muri mai i te tau ka whakamanatia tēnei Pouhere, me kopou rawa e te Pāremata ētahi māngai nō ngā rōpū tōrangapū kei roto i te Pāremata hei mema mō te Kōmihana Pouhere.

(5) Me rite rawa te rahi o ngā māngai o ia rōpū tōrangapū e noho ana hei mema mō te Kōmihana Pouhere, ki te rahi o te rōpū tōrangapū i roto i te Pāremata.

(6) Ko Te Upoko o Te Whenua Rangatira rātou ko te Mana Whakawā o Te Pāremata, ko te Tumu Whakawā, ko te Kaihautū o Te Rōpū Whakamana i te Tiriti o Waitangi, ko te Kaitiaki Matua mō te Mana Tangata, ko te Tumuaki o te Mana Arotake, ko te Rōia Matua, ko te Kaihautū o te Kōmihana Ratonga Kāwanatanga, ko te Kaikōmihana mō te Taiao, ko te Kaikōmihana Matua mō ngā Tika Tangata hoki ērā atu mema o te Kōmihana Pouhere.

(7) Whai i muri i te kopoutanga o ngā māngai nō ngā rōpū tōrangapū ki te Kōmihana Pouhere, ka karangatia tētahi Huinga 100 ngā kirirarau ka kōwhiria noatia i te rārangi pōti o ia rohe i runga i te rite o te rahi me te rahi o te taupori o ngā tāngata o taua rohe me te rahi o te taupori katoa o Aotearoa Niu Tireni.

(8) The Assembly must be adequately supported by the Government and must consider and report on how the Constitution is working and what improvements could be made.
(9) Within six months after being convened, the Assembly must report to the Constitutional Commission on the Assembly's findings.
(10) In considering any recommendations for constitutional amendments, the Commission must take into account the report of the Assembly, but is not restricted to the matters raised in that report.
(11) No later than one year after the appointment of representatives of political parties, the Constitutional Commission must report its finding and recommendations to Parliament.

Part 13 Emergencies

113 Emergencies and suspension of parts of the Constitution

(1) This paragraph applies if, in the opinion of the Prime Minister, there is within Aotearoa New Zealand or any part of it—
   (a) an actual, or imminent, grave threat to national security or public order; or
   (b) an actual, or imminent, grave civil emergency.
(2) If paragraph (1) applies, the Cabinet may make an order wholly or partly suspending any of the provisions of this Constitution set out in paragraph (10), but only to the extent strictly required by the exigencies of the situation and reasonably justified in a democratic society.
(3) The order may be subject to conditions.
(4) If it is practicable to refer a draft of a proposed order to Parliament, the order must not be made unless it has been approved in draft form by a majority of 75 percent of all the members of Parliament.
(5) An order that is made without approval under paragraph (4) ceases to have effect on the 14th day after the day on which it comes into force unless it is confirmed before that day by Parliament by a majority of 75 percent of all its members.

(8) Me tautoko rawa e te Kāwanatanga te Huinga, ā, me whakaaro rawa, me tuku pūrongo rawa hoki mō te āhuatanga pai o te Pouhere me ngā wāhanga kia whakapaingia ake.

(9) Me tuku pūrongo rawa e te Huinga ki te Kōmihana Pouhere mō ngā kitenga o te Huinga, i roto i te ono marama whai i muri mai i te wā ka karangatia.

(10) Me whai whakaaro rawa e te Kōmihana te pūrongo a te Huinga mō ō rātou whakaaro i ngā tūtohunga mō ngā whakahoutanga pouhere, engari kāore e ārikarika te kōrero ki ngā take ka ahu mai i taua pūrongo.

(11) Me kaua rawa e roa ake i te kotahi tau whai i muri i te kopoutanga o ngā māngai nō ngā rōpū tōrangapū me tuku pūrongo e te Kōmihana Pouhere mō ōna kitenga, mō ōna tūtohunga hoki, ki te Pāremata.

Wāhanga 13 Ngā Ohotata

113 Ngā ohotata me te tārewa i ētahi wāhanga o te Pouhere

(1) Ka hāngai tēnei rerenga mehemea e ai ki ngā whakaaro o te Pirimia, i roto i Aotearoa Niu Tireni, i roto rānei i tētahi wāhanga, arā—
  (a) tētahi āhuatanga mōrearea tūturu, ka puta mai pea rānei, ka pā kino ki te whakamarumaru ā-motu, ki te tikanga tūmatanui rānei;
  (b) tētahi ohotata hiwhiri rānei ka pā kino, he ohotata tūturu, ka puta mai pea rānei.

(2) Mehemea ka hāngai te rerenga (1), ka āhei Te Rūnanga Kāwanatanga te mahi i tētahi whakahau e whakatārewa ana, katoa mai, wāhanga mai rānei, i ngā āheinga o tēnei Pouhere ka whakatakotoria i roto i te rerenga (10), engari tae atu ki ngā āhuatanga e tika ana i runga i ngā āhuatanga o te wā, e tika ana hoki i roto i tētahi porihanga manapori.

(3) Ka whai pānga pea tēnei whakahau ki ētahi āhuatanga.

(4) Mehemea ki ōna taumata e taea ana ka tukuna tētahi mea hukihuki o tētahi whakahau kei te whakaarotia ki te Pāremata, me kaua rawa e mahia te whakahau māna kua whakaaetia hei mea hukihuki e te nuinga o te 75 ōrau o ngā mema katoa o te Pāremata.

(5) Ko tētahi whakahau ka mahia me te kore whakaae i raro i te rerenga (4) ka mutu tērā i te rā 14 whai i muri i te rā i whakamanatia ai māna ka whakaūngia i mua i taua rā e te Pāremata mā te nuinga o te 75 ōrau o ōna mema katoa.

(6) Every order must specify a date on which it expires, which must be no later than 30 days after the order comes into force.

(7) Before the order expires, the Cabinet may, by written notice and only once, extend the expiry date of the order by not more than 30 days if advised by the Prime Minister that paragraph (1) continues to apply.

(8) For the purposes of any proceeding in Parliament under paragraph (4) or (5), a member of Parliament may be present by any method of communication that allows the member to participate effectively during the whole of the proceeding.

(9) The validity of an order made under this Article may be challenged in proceedings for judicial review.

(10) Subject to paragraph (11), only the following provisions may be suspended under this Article—

    (a) Part 2, Articles 2 to 36 concerning the Bill of Rights:

    (b) Article 49 concerning the referral power of the Head of State:

    (c) Articles 64 to 66 concerning elections of members of Parliament:

    (d) Article 75 concerning local government:

    (e) Article 92 concerning the availability of legislative information:

    (f) Article 95 concerning urgency.

(11) The following provisions of the Bill of Rights must not be suspended under this Article—

    (a) Article 2 Right not to be deprived of life:

    (b) Article 3 Right not to be subjected to torture or cruel treatment:

    (c) Article 4 Right not to be subjected to medical or scientific experimentation:

    (d) Article 6 Right not to be held in slavery:

    (e) Article 8 Freedom of thought, conscience and religion:

    (f) Article 15 Equality before the law:

    (g) Article 16 Freedom from discrimination:

    (h) Article 19 Liberty of the person:

    (i) Article 21 Rights of persons charged:

    (j) Article 22 Minimum standards of criminal procedure:

    (k) Article 23 Retroactive penalties and double jeopardy.

(6) Me āta tohu rawa ia whakahau te rā ka pau tōna mana, me kaua rawa e hipa atu i te 30 rā whai i muri mai i te wā ka mana te whakahau.
(7) I mua i te paunga o te whakahau, ka āhei Te Rūnanga Kāwanatanga, mā tētahi pānui ā-tuhi kotahi anake, te whakaroa ake i te wā mutunga o te whakahau kia kaua e roa ake i te 30 rā mehemea ka whakatakoto whakaaro te Pirimia ka hāngai tonu te rerenga (1).
(8) Mō ngā aronga o ngā tukanga i roto i te Pāremata i raro i te rerenga (4), (5) rānei, ka āhei tētahi mema o te Pāremata te whakawhitiwhiti kōrero ahakoa mā te aha, e taea ai e te mema te kaha whaiuru ki roto i te tukanga katoa.
(9) Ka āhei te whakapātaritari i te mana o tētahi whakahau ka mahia i raro i tēnei Whiti i roto i ngā whakahaerenga arotake whakawā ā-ture.
(10) I runga i te rerenga (11), ka āhei te whakatārewa i ngā āheinga e whai ake nei anake i raro i tēnei Whiti—
    (a) Wāhanga 2, ngā Whiti 2 ki te 36 e pā ana ki te Pire Tika Tangata:
    (b) Whiti 49 e pā ana ki te tuku i te mana whakahaere ki Te Upoko o Te Whenua Rangatira:
    (c) Ngā Whiti 64 ki te 66 e pā ana ki ngā pōtitanga o ngā mema o te Pāremata:
    (d) Whiti 75 e pā ana ki te kāwanatanga ā-rohe:
    (e) Whiti 92 e pā ana ki te wāteatanga o ngā pārongo whakature:
    (f) Whiti 95 e pā ana ki te whāwhaitanga.
(11) Me kaua rawa e whakatārewa ngā āheinga o te Pire Tika Tangata e whai ake nei i raro i tēnei Whiti—
    (a) Whiti 2 Te tika kia kaua e whakamatea:
    (b) Whiti 3 Te tika kia kaua e whakamamaetia, tūkinotia rānei:
    (c) Whiti 4 Te tika kia kaua e whakamātauria mahi rata nei, pūtaiao nei hoki:
    (d) Whiti 6 Te tika kia kaua e mauheretia kia noho hei taurekareka:
    (e) Whiti 8 Te māhorahora o te whakaaro, o te ngākau manako hoki, o te wairuatanga hoki:
    (f) Whiti 15 Te noho ōrite i raro i te ture:
    (g) Whiti 16 Te noho māhorahora i te toihara:
    (h) Whiti 19 Te noho here kore o te tangata:
    (i) Whiti 21 Ngā tika o te tangata ka whiua ki te ture:
    (j) Whiti 22 Ngā paerewa mōkito o te tukanga taihara:
    (k) Whiti 23 Ngā hāmenetanga o mua me te tukurua.

Part 14 Miscellaneous Provisions

Remuneration of office holders

114 Independent determination of salaries and expenses

The remuneration and expenses of the Head of State, the Prime Minister, the Speaker, Ministers, Members of Parliament, the Judges, and all public officers established under this Constitution must be set by an independent authority established by Act of Parliament.

Commencement

115 Commencement

If the proposal to approve this Constitution is carried by a majority of the valid votes cast by electors eligible to vote at the poll conducted under the Act of Parliament enacted for that purpose, this Constitution comes into force on the date specified in that Act for the commencement of this Constitution.

Transitional provisions

[The necessary transitional provisions and consequential amendments have not been drafted at this stage. There will be extensive changes to New Zealand statute law.]

Wāhanga 14 He Āheinga Anō

Te utu i ngā kainoho tūranga

114 Te whakatau motuhake i ngā utu ā-tau me ngā whakapaunga

Me whakatū rawa e tētahi mana ka noho motuhake ka whakatūria e tētahi Ture a te Pāremata te utu me ngā whakapaunga o Te Upoko o Te Whenua Rangatira, te Pirimia hoki, te Mana Whakawā o Te Pāremata hoki, ngā Minita hoki, ngā Mema o te Pāremata hoki, ngā Kaiwhakawā hoki, me ngā āpiha tūmatanui katoa ka whakatūria i raro i tēnei Pouhere.

Te Tīmatanga

115 Te Tīmatanga

Mehemea ka tautokona te whakaaro kia whakaaetia tēnei Pouhere e te nuinga o ngā pōti ka tukuna e ngā kaipōti whai mana ki te pōti ki te pōtitanga ka whakahaeretia i raro i tētahi Ture a te Pāremata i whakaturetia mō taua aronga, ka whai mana tēnei Pouhere i te rā ka āta tohua i roto i taua Ture a te Pāremata mō te tīmatanga o tēnei Pouhere.

Ngā Āheinga Whakawhiti

[I tēnei wā kāore anō kia tuhia ngā āheinga whakawhiti me ngā whakahoutanga whai haere e tika ana. Ko te tikanga he maha ngā panoni ki ngā ture o Niu Tireni.]

A note on the translation

The translation of this proposed draft Constitution for Aotearoa New Zealand is based on terminology sourced from a variety of relevant resources including Te Ture mō Te Reo Māori: Māori Language Act 2016 (the first piece of legislation to be fully translated into Māori), Te Pokapū Reo Ture: A Dictionary of Māori Legal Terms, and other Māori language dictionaries and resources. This was also conducted in consultation with the writers of this book (for clarification of specific legal terms and legislative language), Māori legal academics, and other Māori language specialists where necessary and appropriate.

This translation should be considered by the reader as an example of what a Māori language version of a Constitution may look like, and it is open to adaptation according to one's preferences regarding grammar, terminology and phrases. In saying this, it is important to remind the reader that the genre of Māori legal language continues to evolve as it is increasingly applied to legislation, policy, legal contracts and of course constitutional documents.

In this instance attempts have been made to ensure the Māori language used in this proposed Constitution not only meets the language requirements of a modern constitutional document but that it is as natural as possible in its delivery within the context of the purpose of the proposed Constitution. An example of this is the use of 'hoki' (for '. . . ; and') and 'rānei' (for '. . . ; or'). Ordinarily, in English-language-based legislation, such terms would appear at the end of a series of text as a lead-in to a related idea or concept. This type of structure and format, however, is unnatural in te reo Māori in both verbal and written forms. Instead, words such as 'hoki' and 'rānei' have been incorporated as best as possible into the structure of applicable sentences. This practice, which is consistent with Te Ture mō Te Reo Māori: Māori Language Act 2016, is encouraged of any translators who endeavour to translate future legislative, policy, legal and constitutional documents.

Afterword

Democracy is based on the theory that the governed consent to being governed. So, people have a say in how the framework for making decisions by the State should be organised.

New Zealand has never yet had a deep national conversation about its constitutional arrangements. This book is based on the view that we should have that conversation, before emergencies or troubles arise that challenge our values and way of life. It will take effort and commitment to see such a process through.

Obviously New Zealand can continue with its existing arrangements. The existing arrangements will endure with minor adjustments over time, unless a deliberate and carefully planned process is undertaken to revise them.

The country is relatively well governed, a condition that makes it harder to persuade people that change is needed. We are convinced New Zealand would be better governed if the ship of state had clearer navigation lights to guide it, with increased constitutional protections.

Nevertheless, the preservation of flexibility in line with our traditions in an important value. That is why we have put a lot of emphasis on getting the constitutional amendment and revision process right.

We hope people will ask for change. We have made our case and what happens next rests with the people.

Meetings around New Zealand

19 May 2016—Constitutional Symposium, Faculty of Law, Victoria University of Wellington

22 August 2016—Open Source/Open Society Conference, Michael Fowler Centre, Wellington

7 September 2016—Briefing Environmental NGOs at headquarters of the Royal Forest and Bird Protection Society

21 September 2016—Secondary school children from Wellington area at Victoria University of Wellington

21 September 2016—Launch of Constitution Aotearoa, Grand Hall at Parliament

30 September 2016—University of the Third Age, Takaka

30 September 2016—Nelson launch of Constitution Aotearoa, Nelson Marlborough Institute of Technology

5 October 2016—Unity Books, Wellington

5 October 2016—Auckland Launch of Constitution Aotearoa, The New Zealand Initiative, hosted at Russell McVeagh, Auckland

11 October 2016—Australasian Study of Parliament Group, Parliament

14 October 2016—Professor Janet McLean's Advanced Public Law class at the University of Auckland

22 November 2016—Scorpio Books, Christchurch

22 November 2016—Canterbury Westland branch of New Zealand Law Society, Christchurch

28 November 2016—Public Service Association, Wellington

30 November 2016—Meeting with law students and Faculty, University of Otago

30 November 2016—public meeting, Otago Public Museum

9 December 2016—public meeting, Civic Chambers, Palmerston North

9 February 2017—public meeting, Queenstown Events Centre

29 February 2017—Continuing Education, Hamilton

13 March 2017—Political Science students studying New Zealand government at Victoria University

15 March 2017—Friends of Hastings Libraries, Hastings War Memorial Library

20 March 2017—Students at the University of Waikato

23 March 2017—Conference on improving intergenerational governance, Parliament

26 March 2017—Public Law students, Victoria University of Wellington

29 March 2017—public meeting for students, University of Auckland

31 March 2017—Annual Conference of Judges' Clerks, Supreme Court, Wellington

4 May 2017—Local Government New Zealand Forum, Wellington

17 May 2017—McGuinness Foundation meeting on civics, Wellington

22 May 2017—Transparency International, Wellington

29 June 2017—University of the Third Age, Christchurch

29 June 2017—Network Waitangi, Otautahi, Christchurch

30 June 2017—Chapman Tripp, lawyers and staff, Wellington.

3 July 2017—Shaping Aotearoa katakana, Youth meeting, Porirua

1 August 2017—Democracy Week Panel, Victoria University, 'Constitutional Blueprints'

5 August 2017—UN Youth High Schools Politics event, University of Auckland

8 August 2017—Annual Meeting, Environmental Defence Society, Auckland

16 August 2017—Wise Response Meeting at Parliament

26 August 2017—Annual Meeting of ECO, Nelson

30 August 2017—Meeting arranged by Westpac New Zealand, Auckland

6 September 2017—Centre for Public Law, Victoria University, Constitutional Roundtable

13 September 2017—talk to students at South Wellington Intermediate School

8 September 2017—Te Papa launch of 'The Ninth Floor.'

29 September 2017—Māori Women's Welfare League, Hui a Tau, New Plymouth

9 October 2017—TEDxVUW talk, Wellington

12 October 2017—Pacific Women's Watch with University of Auckland Public Policy Institute, Auckland

26 October 2017—Law Society Panel on public sector governance, Wellington

Acknowledgements

This list acknowledges people and groups who have made valuable input into this project. We are very grateful for their comments and advice. The fact that a name is on the list is not to be taken as an indication of acceptance of what we have advanced.

Several people have provided help and advice that has been invaluable on this project but wish to remain unacknowledged. We thank them for their assistance.

Public Law Scholars Roundtable at Victoria University of Wellington

- Professor Gordon Anderson
- Dr Joel Colón-Ríos
- Dr Dean Knight
- Dr Elizabeth McLeay
- Professor Geoff McLay
- Dr Grant Morris
- Dr Leonid Sirota
- Professor Tony Smith
- Dr Edward Willis
- Professor Margaret Wilson
- Jannik Zerbst

Contributions from others

- Professor Tony Angelo
- Professor Robert Blackburn QC
- Professor Jonathan Boston
- Professor Richard Boast QC
- Professor Andrew Geddis
- Elana Geddis
- Professor Mark Hickford
- Hugo Hoffman
- Emeritus Professor Peter Hogg QC
- Dr Carwyn Jones
- Professor Philip Joseph
- Colin Keating

Acknowledgements

- Rt Hon Sir Kenneth Keith QC
- Lina Kim
- Bill Mansfield
- Professor Janet McLean
- Rebecca McMenamin
- Rebekah Palmer
- Dame Alison Quentin-Baxter
- Bernard Steeds
- Māmari Stephens
- Brigadier Kevin Riordan
- Sir Anand Satyanand
- Amnesty International New Zealand
- Members of the 2017 LAWS320: Advanced Public Law class at Victoria University of Wellington
- Local Government New Zealand
- Māori Women's Welfare League
- Transparency International New Zealand

Translation

- Kiwa Hammond

Others

- The New Zealand Law Foundation, Executive Director: Lynda Hagen
- Victoria University Press, Fergus Barrowman, Kirsten McDougall and Holly Hunter
- New Zealand Centre for Public Law
- Victoria University of Wellington Faculty of Law
- Harbour Chambers
- Russell McVeagh
- West Egg Ltd
- Margaret Palmer

Public Engagement

- Australasian Study of Parliament Group
- Bound Books & Records, Queenstown
- Canterbury/Westland Branch of the New Zealand Law Society
- Catalyst Trust, Queenstown

- Chapman Tripp, Wellington
- Continuing Education, Hamilton
- Environment and Conservation Organisation of Aotearoa New Zealand
- Environmental Defence Society
- Friends of Hastings Public Library
- Māori Women's Welfare League
- Nelson Marlborough Institute of Technology
- New Zealand Forest and Bird Society, Inc
- New Zealand Fish and Game Council
- The New Zealand Initiative
- Pacific Women's Watch
- Page & Blackmore Booksellers, Nelson
- Palmerston North City Council
- Poppies Book Store, Hamilton
- Public Service Association
- Scorpio Books, Christchurch
- TEDxVUW
- University of Auckland
- University of Otago
- UN Youth New Zealand
- Unity Books, Wellington and Auckland
- University Book Store, Dunedin
- University of Otago Faculty of Law
- University of the Third Age, Takaka
- Volume Booksellers, Nelson
- Waikato University
- Westpac New Zealand

Index

abuse of public power *see* integrity and transparency; public power
accident compensation scheme, 263
  deficiency of legislation, 102
Adoption Act 1955, 131
Afghanistan, 243
Against Elections (Van Reybrouck), 242–44, 273n21
Aikman, Dr Colin, 212
alternative facts, 9
amendment of constitution
  adoption of written, codifed constitution *see* constitutional change process
  Bill of Rights context, 155–56
  entrenchment, 17–18, 34–36
  periodic review, 22, 270–72
Ardern, Jacinda, 15
Argentina, 228
armed forces, overseas deployment, 21, 93–94
'Ask Away', 279
Atkinson case (family carer policy and law), 154, 172–73, 213
Attorney-General
  Bill vetting function, 101, 171
    socio-economic rights, 162, 163
  function and duties, 21, 140–41
  Head of State referrals of Bill to Supreme Court, 135
  non-lawyer as, 71
  proposed overseas deployment of armed forces, 94
Auditor-General, 21, 151–52
Austin, Jack, 29
Australia
  bicameral Parliament, 107, 108
  Commonwealth Parliament's Main Committee, 119
  compulsory voting, 228
  constitutional amendment, 18
  election of Speaker of House of Representatives, 96
  judicial strike-down power, 127, 155
Austria, 227
authoritarianism, 8, 122, 247

Bagehot, Walter, 73
Baird, Natalie, 30
Baron, Dominic Paul, 30
Baron, Steve, 30
Barton, Andrew, 44
Beer, Andrew, 31–32
Belgium, 228
Belich, James, 111
Bell, Sir Francis Dillon, 111, 122
Bennett, Paula, 14
'big data' use in political campaigns, 252–53
Bill of Rights
  1963 proposal for, 113
  as check on Cabinet power, 71
  Constitution Aotearoa, drafting issue, 171–72
  corporations and human rights, 170–71
  inconsistent Bills
    Attorney-General's vetting function, 101, 162, 163, 171
    passage, 104, 154
  inconsistent legislation
    'declarations of inconsistency', 131–32
    limits to judicial strike-down power, 154–56
  need for strengthened protection for rights, 153–56
  diversity of society and, 206
  observance, 51
  revised proposals, summary, 18
  scope of protected rights, 157–70
    children's rights, 169–70
    environmental rights, 163–66
    gender identity and expression, 158
    need for expansion, 157–58
    privacy rights, 167–68
    property rights, 166–67
    socio-economic rights, 151, 159–63
biodiversity, 164
Blackburn, Professor Robert, 266n14
Bolger, Jim, 56n2
Bolivia, 16n11
Bolton, Matthew, 215n11, 282
Booth, James, 30, 43
Boshier, Judge Peter, 149
Bosselmann, Professor Klaus, 28–29

Brandeis, Louis, 145
Brazil, 228
Brexit, 9, 34–35, 132, 225, 231, 238, 246, 252-253, 276
Brown, David, 40
Browning, Claire, 164, 165
Brownlie, Professor Ian, 176
Burke, Edmund, 238–39, 247n1
Burrows, John, 262
Business New Zealand, 209
Butler, Dr Andrew, 26

Cabinet *see* Government
Cambridge Analytica, 253
Canada
  bicameral Parliament, 107, 108
  citizen engagement in constitutional change, 273
  election of Speaker of House of Commons, 96
  judicial strike-down power, 127, 128–29, 135
  'notwithstanding mechanism', 137
Canadian Charter of Rights and Freedoms (1982), 35–36
  protection of Treaty and aboriginal rights, 189, 191, 192, 203
Canterbury earthquakes, 9–10, 167
Carribean Commonwealth, 127
Catt, Helena, 227
Caygill, David, 114n29
Chen, Mai, 58n7, 59
children's rights, 169–70
Chile, 228, 269
Chilwell, Justice, 179
citizen juries or assemblies, 22, 239–40, 264
  overseas models, 272–79
'civic culture', 64
civic literacy and engagement, 209–16
  community activism, 215
  democracy and *see* democratic renewal
  demographic categories, 209–10
  elements to be taught, 213–15
  government review recommendations, 210–11
  public misunderstandings about existing systems of government, 28, 213
  role of written codified constitution and, 50, 215–16

student knowledge and achievement, 211–12
Clark, Helen, 56n2
climate change, 8, 14–15, 157, 163
  deficiency of legislation, 103–4
Cody, John, 46–47
Cole, Cimino, 36
Collins, Justice, 148–49
Commonwealth countries, 60
compulsory voting, 227–30
conservation, 164
  Treaty references in legislation, 179
Conservative Party campaign, 233
constitution
  current unwritten constitution *see* New Zealand constitution
  definition, 7
  revised draft written constitution *see* Constitution Aotearoa
Constitutional Advisory Panel (2013), 12, 27, 87, 153n2, 155, 158, 211, 256, 262, 281
Constitutional Arrangements Committee (2005), 210–11, 256, 262
constitutional change process
  citizen juries or assemblies, 22, 264
  clean slate approach, 261–62
  Commission of Inquiry model, 262–64
  Constitutional Commission, 22, 162–63, 271–72
  Constitutional Committee, 266–67
  Constitutional Engagement Group, 264, 267
  democratic renewal and, 256–57
  disagreement: 'incompletely theorised agreements', 280–82
  drafting of Bill and select committee scrutiny, 268
  future revisions, 270–72
  generally, 22–23
  Government-led inquiries, 256
  interference by political elites, 268–69
  issues to be addressed and whether incremental change appropriate, 259–62
  need for deep public engagement, 256
  New Zealand initiatives for citizen engagement, 279
  overseas models for citizen engagement, 272–79

Index

phases, 265–70
popularisation difficulty, 32–33
public appetite for change, 256
public inclusivity and degree of involvement of political elites, 257–59
public referenda, 268–70
technical legal issues, 261
Treaty issues, 264–66
constitutional conventions
  Cabinet, 72
  generally, 72
  ministerial responsibility, 78
Constitution Aotearoa
  accessibility and certainty, 50
  aims, 12, 24, 25–26, 50–52
  as a constitution belonging to the people, 51–52
  Bill of Rights *see* Bill of Rights
  consultation process/publicity for, 12, 13, 27
  emergency suspension, 22
  entrenched law, 17–18, 34–36
  Government *see* Government
  Head of State *see* State
  integrity and transparency *see* integrity and transparency
  Judiciary *see* Judiciary
  local government *see* local government
  Parliament *see* Parliament
  periodic review provision, 22
  Preamble, 16, 53–54
  public submissions on proposals, 12–13, 27–49
    other non-constitutional policy matters, 47–48
  revised proposals, summary, 15–23
    key changes from original draft, 16–17
    simplification and reordering of draft, 15–16
    unchanged issues, 17
  State *see* State
  statement of core values and principles, 52–54
  superior law constitution, 17, 33–34
    Bill of Rights as check on Cabinet power, 71
  Treaty of Waitangi *see* Tiriti o Waitangi/Treaty of Waitangi
  website for, 12
  written codified constitution, 28–33
Cook Islands, 59
corporations
  human rights, 170–71
  influence of multi-nationals on domestic policy, 9
  protection against activities of, 157
  vested interests, 246
corruption
  open government as safeguard against, 10, 145, 247
  political parties, 233–34
Cotter, Catherine, 38
Craig, Colin, 233
customary title, 181–82

Danks Committee (1980), 145–46
Dawes, Gregory, 34, 38
democracy
  accountability of public decision-makers, 51
  approaches, 236
  deepening citizen engagement *see* democratic renewal
  local government and *see* local government
  privacy and, 168
democratic renewal
  challenges facing New Zealand and other western democracies, 8–9, 246–48
  civic literacy and engagement, 25, 214, 215–16
    measurement issue, 237
  constitutional change as contributor, 256–57
  definition and purpose, 237–38
  deliberative democracy, 24, 238–48
    citizen juries or assemblies, 239–40, 264
    definition and origins, 244
    features, 239–40
    Icelandic experience, 276–79
    Irish experience, 275–76
    listening, 241
    Māori legal traditions, 195, 241–42
    purpose, 239, 241–42
    traditional view of representative government, 238–39
  'Democratic Fatigue Syndrome', 242–43
  elections
    'electoral fundamentalism', 243

importance, 24, 236
  sufficiency of, 24, 217, 235, 237
  legitimacy of decision-making, 244–45, 256–57
  media, information and communication, 246, 249–55
  need for, generally, 9–10, 24
  open government, 247–48
  overseas models for citizen engagement, 272–79
  participation, 241, 245–46
  role of written codified constitution in, 24
  spirit of democracy, 23
  trust in institutions, 24, 25, 237, 244–45
Design+Democracy's 'On the Fence' app, 265n13, 279
de Smith, Professor Stanley, 60
diversity of society, 58–59, 204–6
  ethnic population projections, 205
  human rights protection, 206
  local government and, 84–85
Drage, Dr Jean, 85
Dunne, Peter, 56

Eady, Paul, 28
ECO, 164
'econocracy', 246–47
economic nationalism, 9
Ecuador, 16n11
Edgeler, Graeme, 95–96
education, right to, 159, 169
Edwards, John, 168
Edwards, Maakere, 11
elections *see also* MMP electoral system
  2017 election
    alternative facts, 9
    MMP and, 217–24
  broadcasting facilities, 232
  compulsory voting, 227–30
  corruption, avoidance of, 233–34
  'electoral fundamentalism', 243
  lowering the voting age, 226–27
  party lists and candidate selection, 234
  political party funding, 230–33
  sufficiency, in a democracy *see* democratic renewal
  voter turnout, 224–26, 229–30, 246
electoral law, entrenched provisions, 18n12, 113, 127

Elizabeth II, Queen, 38, 55 *see also* State
Ellis, Dr Gavin, 254
emergencies
  suspension of constitution, 22
  use of urgency, 37, 94
Emissions Trading Scheme (ETS), 104
English, Bill, 14
entrenchment of constitution, 17–18, 34–36
Environmental Defence Society (EDS), 164–65
environmental rights, 163–66
Executive Council, 20, 63

Facebook, 250, 251, 253
family carer policy and law (*Atkinson* case), 154, 172–73, 213
Farquhar, Neville, 30, 39
fascism, 238
Federated Farmers, 209
Finlayson, Hon Chris, 31, 207
'foreshore and seabed' case and legislation, 181–82, 183
Franklin, Benjamin, 77
free trade agreement ISDS clauses, 128

Geddis, Professor Andrew, 173, 232–33
gender identity and expression, 158
genetically modified organisms, 263
Germany, 127, 135
Ghahraman, Golriz, 269
Google, 250, 251
Government
  acting in own political interest/domination of House of Representatives, 93
  authoritarianism, 8, 122, 247
  Cabinet, 72–74
    as constitutional convention, 72
    collective decision-making, 76
    committees, 79
    flexibility, 72
    functions, 72–74
    fusion of executive and legislative powers, 73–74
    membership, 71
    MMP, effects of, 73–74, 78–79, 220–21
    Prime Minister's role, 75
    vesting of executive authority in, 20, 63, 73
  challenges facing, 8–10

Index

confidence of the House of Representatives, 75, 94
Crown Entities and other organisations, 81
Department of Prime Minister and Cabinet, 75
Executive Council, 20, 63, 71
   functions and powers, 63, 69–70
   ministers, 63, 77–79
      appointment, 75, 77, 79
      collective responsibility, 77–79
      designation, 79
      functions, 77
      individual responsibility, 78, 79
   Prime Minister, 20, 75–77
      appointment, 75, 76
      as Finance Minister, 71
      confidence of House of Representatives, 75
      management of multi-party Governments, 75
      power to dissolve Parliament, 71
      roles, functions and responsibilities, 71, 75–77
   public service, 20, 79–81
      communications specialists and consultants, 254
      functions, 79
      Government Services Commission, proposal for, 21–22, 71, 80–81
      independence, 80
      provision of free and frank advice to ministers, 22, 71, 79–80
   revised proposals, summary, 20, 70–71
   te ao Māori and, 195–96
   Treaty considerations in decision-making, 182–84
Government Communications Security Bureau (GCSB), 22, 142–45
Governor-General
   appointment of Prime Minister, 75
   refusal of Royal Assent to legislation, 59, 213
Graham, Sir Douglas, 113–14
Grayling, Professor AC, 225–26, 231
Green Party, 14–15, 78, 217, 224

Hailsham, Lord, 222
Hai Xin Huang, 226
Hall, David, 36
Hammond, Kiwa, 11
Harris, Max, 25, 237
Hayward, Associate Professor Bronwyn, 213–14, 248
Head of State *see* State
Hicks, Wally, 45–46
Hobson, Captain, 175, 181n26, 190
Hogg, Emeritus Professor Peter, 35–36, 212
Holden, Lewis, 39, 66
housing affordability, 10
human rights, 15
   ability to restrain abuses of executive power, 104
   Bill of Rights *see* Bill of Rights
   erosion, by government, 8
   gang crackdown policy, 14
   judicial strike-down power *see* Judiciary
   misunderstanding of Queen's power in relation to legislation breaching rights, 59, 213
Human Rights Commission, 22, 151, 152, 156–57
   socio-economic rights, role in respect of, 161, 162, 163
   Staying in the red zones report, 167
Human Rights Foundation, 161

Iceland, citizen engagement in constitutional change, 273, 276–79
India, 16n11, 127, 160, 189
indigenous peoples
   customary title, 181–82
   protection of rights, 190–92
integrity and transparency
   2016 proposals, summary, 139–40
   generally, 51, 139
   intelligence agencies, 22, 142–45
   law officers, 21, 140–41
   open government and information
      as safeguard against corruption, 10, 145, 247
      Information Authority, proposal for, 140, 149–50
      Local Government Official Information and Meetings Act, 147
      Official Information Act, 22, 145–50
      Ombudsmen's function, 149, 150
   Police, 22, 141–42
   revised proposals, summary, 21–22

International Covenant on Civil and Political Rights (1966), 153
International Covenant on Economic, Social and Cultural Rights (1966), 153, 159
international treaties, approval by Parliament, 21, 93
Iraq, 243
Ireland
　amendment of constitution, 155–56
　as Republic, 59–60
　citizen engagement in constitutional change, 260, 268, 273–76
　judicial strike-down power, 127
　referral of Bills by President, for constitutionality determination, 66, 68, 135
　socio-economic rights, 160
Israel, 7
Italy, 127

Jackson, Moana, 197
James, David, 45
Jarden, Fiona, 30
Jennings, Sir Ivor, 212
Jones, Dr Carwyn, 194–95, 204
Jordan, Miraz, 39, 44
Joseph, Professor Philip, 116, 120
Judiciary
　2016 proposals and feedback received, 125–26
　compulsory retirement age of judges, 125
　courts and tribunals, 124
　Head of State referral of Bill to Supreme Court, 62, 66–68, 135–36
　independence, 125
　Judicial Appointments Commission, proposal for, 21, 63, 125–26, 129
　power to strike down legislation, 33–34, 63–64, 126–38, 154–56
　　confirmatory role of Supreme Court, 134
　　discriminatory legislation and limits to 'declarations of inconsistency', 131–32
　　need for judicial oversight, 130–32
　　parliamentary override: 'notwithstanding mechanism', 136–38, 155
　　process, 132–35
　role, 63–64, 124–25
　senior courts, 125

Waitangi Tribunal, 126
jury duty, 244

Kaikoura earthquake, 9–10
Kelsey, Professor Jane, 147–48
Kerkin, Sarah, 245
Key, Sir John, 56n2
Kitteridge, Rebecca, 144
Knight, Dr Dean, 31

Labour Party, 9, 15, 217, 219, 222–23, 224
Laffoy, Justice Mary, 275
Lang, Katy, 211
Lange, David, 56n2
Langman, Ian, 45
Larsen, Andrew, 38
Law Commission
　adoption of a Main Committee recommendation, 120
　interactive submissions process, 265n13
　Official Information Act review, 147
law-making
　accessibility and comprehensibility of laws, 101
　advance information about Government legislation, 20, 100
　Attorney-General's Bill vetting function, 101, 171
　　socio-economic rights, 162, 163
　legislative procedures, 100
　'manner and form' restrictions, 92–93, 128
　parliamentary term and, 100
　policy failures and sub-optimal legislation
　　accident compensation, 102
　　climate change, 103–4
　　human rights, 104
　　Pike River mine, 104–6
　　Resource Management Act, 103
　publication of Government's legislative programme, 20, 97–98, 101
　public submissions on proposals, 96–97
　quality and nature of laws, 10
　　accountability for, 97–100
　　evaluation, 98–99
　quantity of law, 99
　speed, generally, 20, 97, 98
　subordinate legislation, 102
　supplementary order papers, 100, 118
　technical scrutiny, 100

Index

changes to Standing Orders, 120–21
Committee of the Whole, 118–19, 120
Law Society's suggested improvements, 117–20
Main Committee, proposal for, 100, 119, 120
select committee system, 116, 117
upper house scrutiny, proposal for, 114, 115
use of urgency, 36–38, 94–95, 97, 101
Lawrence, Hugo, 33
Levy, Ron, 239n9
Lincoln, Abraham, 52
Lipson, Leslie, 112
lobby groups, 209–10
local government
  co-governance arrangements, 89
  constitutional protection, 20, 64, 85, 86–89
  democratic role, 84
  functions and powers, 21, 83–84
  importance to communities, 83
  LGNZ submission, 84, 87–88
  public participation in, 85–86
  purpose, 83
  regional council responsibilities, 83, 84
  relationship with central government, 85, 86, 87–88, 89–90
  revenue-raising, 89
  revised proposals, summary, 20–21
  subsidiarity and autonomy, 88–89
  territorial council responsibilities, 84
  Treaty references in legislation, 178
Local Government New Zealand (LGNZ), 84, 87–88
Local Government Official Information and Meetings Act 1987, 147
Locke, Keith, 33
Lusby, Stanley Richard, 40

Macauley, Lord, 249
McCully, Murray, 114n29
McGonigal, Racheal, 43
McGuinness Institute, 211–12
McKenzie, Peter, 214–15
McLean, Professor Janet, 57–58
McLeay, Professor Elizabeth, 121–22
McMenamin, Rebecca, 38, 44, 257–58, 268–69

Macpherson, Elizabeth, 30
Mansfield, Bill, 47
Manufacturing New Zealand, 209
Māori and whakapapa, 189–90
Māori constitutional culture, 196
Māori customary rights, 181–82
Māori deliberative forms of decision-making, 195, 241–42
Māori Party, 218, 262
Māori representation
  Māori electorate seats, 14, 115
  Treaty and, 189
  upper house and, 114, 115
Māori Television, 250
Māori values in environmental protection, 164, 165–66
Marine and Coastal Area (Takutai Moana) Act 2011, 182n30
Mark, Emeritus Professor Alan, 45
Massey University, Election Survey, 13–14
Mataparae, Sir Jerry, 56n2
Matike Mai Aotearoa, 196–200, 262, 265
Mattys, Karl, 43
Maynard, Ken, 41
media, information and communication, 246, 249–55
MediaWorks, 250
Mercer, Neil, 42
Merkel, Chancellor Angela, 218n2
Michels, Robert, 222
Midson, Brenda, 219
Miller, Professor Raymond, 222
ministers *see* Government
Mitchell, Mark, 232
MMP electoral system
  2017 election, 217–24
    Cabinet government and, 73–74, 220–21
    collective responsibility and 'agree to disagree' agreements, 78–79
  effects, generally, 122–23
  management of multi-party Governments, 75
  Parliament and, 221–22
  party discipline, 221–22
  policy mandates and, 222–24
  political party membership, 222
monarchy *see* State
Morgan, Dr Gareth, 14, 114–15, 233
Mourant, David Herbert, 37, 39, 41

Muir, Jane, 40
multiculturalism *see* diversity of society
multi-national corporations *see* corporations
Mutu, Margaret, 197

National Council of Women of New Zealand, 34, 156
national identity, 51, 59, 64–65
National Party, 9, 14, 112, 113, 217–18, 219, 222–23
national symbols, 64–65
Newcomb, Bob, 33–34
Newsroom, 251
New Zealand Association of Psychotherapists, Te Tiriti Bi-cultural Committee, 199
New Zealand Bill of Rights Act 1990 *see* Bill of Rights
New Zealand constitution
   adoption of written, codifed constitution *see* constitutional change process
   inherent dangers of, and need for change, 7–10
   nature of, 7
   necessary contents, 10–11
   political party policies calling for written constitution, 14–15
   revised draft written constitution *see* Constitution Aotearoa
New Zealand First, 78, 217, 224
New Zealand Fish and Game Council, 164
New Zealand Law Society, 117–20
New Zealand Press Association, 250
The New Zealand Project (Harris), 25, 237
New Zealand Republic, 66
New Zealand Security Intelligence Service (NZSIS), 22, 142–45
Nicholls, Todd, 39
Niue, 59

Obama, Barack, 215, 248, 252
Officers of Parliament, 22, 151–52
official information *see* integrity and transparency
Ombudsmen, 22, 152
   creation of office, 113
   official information function, 149, 150
Opie, Josh, 161
Opportunities Party (TOP), 14, 114–15, 233
O'Regan, Sir Tipene, 262

Orr, Graeme, 239n9
Otago Daily Times, 250

Pacific Island countries, judicial strike-down power, 127, 128
Page, Professor Alan, 129
paid parental leave entitlements, and use of veto power, 95
Palmer, Sir Geoffrey, 26, 120, 212
Palmer, Dr Matthew, 247
Parihaka, 206–7
Parliament
   2016 proposals, summary, 91–92
   confidence in the Government, 75, 94
   definition, 94
   financial veto power, 95
   functions and powers, 62–63
   Government domination of House of Representatives, 93
   international relations and defence, 21, 93–94
   key functions, 91
   law-making *see* law-making
   legal existence, 94
   legitimacy of powers, 91, 92–93
   membership, 94
   MMP, effects of, 221–22
   parliamentary sovereignty, 92–93
   power to override judicial strike-down power, 136–38, 155
   Press Gallery, 254
   Prime Minister's power to dissolve, 71
   purpose, 94
   revised proposals, summary, 20, 94–96
   size, 116–17
   Speaker
      election, 20, 95–96
      role, 20
      ruling on use of urgency, 95
   term, 20, 36–38, 71, 94, 100
   upper house, arguments for and against *see* upper house
Parliamentary Commissioner for the Environment, 22, 103, 152, 157, 165
Pike River mine disaster, 10, 104–6, 263
   Royal Commission report, 105–6
pluralism *see* diversity of society
Police, 22, 141–42
political parties

Index

'big data' use in campaigns, 252–53
corruption, 233–34
decline in membership, 222
funding, 230–33
party discipline, 221–22
party lists and candidate selection, 234
parties calling for written constitution, 14–15
populism, 132, 238
'post-truth' politics, 9
Prebble, Dr Mark, 147
pressure groups, 209–10
Prime Minister *see* Government
privacy rights, 167–68
Proceedings of the Civics and Media Project (McGuinness Institute), 211–12
property rights, 166–67
Pryor, Dr Judith, 207–8
public broadcasting, 250
public finance and expenditure, 20, 21, 62, 63
public misunderstandings about existing systems of government, 28, 213
public opinion, manipulation of, 9
public power *see also* integrity and transparency
 democratic legitimacy in exercise of, 91
 objectives of, and limits on, 52–54
 parliamentary sovereignty, 93–94
 potential for abuse, 8
 protections against abuse, 51
public service *see* Government

Quentin-Baxter, Dame Alison, 57–58
Quentin-Baxter, Professor RQ, 244
Quinn, Keith, 29

Radio New Zealand (RNZ), 250
Reddy, Dame Patsy, 183–84
referenda
 adoption of constitution, 268–70
 Bill of Rights context, amendment of constitution, 155–56
 direct voter referenda, 35
regional councils *see* local government
regulations
 challenges to validity, 67–68, 102
 signing by Head of State, 67–68
republicanism *see* State
Republican Party (US), 225

Resource Management Act 1991, 103
 Treaty references in, 178
rights and freedoms *see* Bill of Rights; human rights
Roberts (Jr), Hon John G, 129–30
Romanos, Joseph, 58–59
Rosieur, Harvey, 41
Ross Dependency, 59
Royal Commission on the Electoral System (1986), 203–4, 234, 258
 as model for future constitutional change, 262–64
 referenda use recommendation, 270
 report, 219
 Treaty issues and Māori rights recommendation, 203–4, 263–64
Royal Commission on the Pike River Coal Mine Tragedy (2012), 105–6
royal powers *see* State
rule of law, 21, 25, 51–52, 93, 98, 141, 206, 215

safeguards *see* integrity and transparency
Salmond, Dame Anne, 173
Scotland
 judicial strike-down power, 127, 129
 political interests of young people, 227
Scott, David, 28
Scott, Professor KJ, 112, 223
Seddon, Richard, 110
Shaw, James, 14–15
Singapore, compulsory voting, 227–28
Sissons, Jeff, 161
Smith, Dr Nicholas, 193
Smuts-Kennedy, Chris, 29
social media, political use of, 253
socio-economic rights, 151, 159–63
Solicitor-General, 21, 140–41
South Africa, 127, 134, 135
South America, 16n11, 127, 281
Spain, 127, 160
The Spinoff, 251
Spoonley, Professor Paul, 205
State
 constitutional monarchy and concept of 'the Crown', 55
 core institutions, overview, 61–64
 Government *see* Government
 Head of State: 'Guardian' or 'Kaitiaki' of

the nation
functions and powers, 58, 62, 64–68
New Zealander as, 51, 55, 65
public submissions on proposals, 39–40
'referral' power for Bills of doubtful constitutionality, 62, 66–68, 135–36
regulations, signing of, 67–68, 71
revised proposals, summary, 19
selection process, 65–66
symbolism, 64–65
term of office, 65
Judiciary *see* Judiciary
local government *see* local government
move to a Republic
abolition of Realm of New Zealand, 19, 59
effecting, 59–60, 261
effects, 55, 57–58
inevitability, 55–56
Jacinda Ardern on idea, 15
possible process for, 57
public submissions on proposals, 38–40, 56
re-distribution of Crown's powers, 57, 58
Parliament *see* Parliament
revised proposals, summary, 19, 61–64
royal prerogative/powers, 19, 31, 40, 55, 57, 71, 259, 261
source of power, 61
State Services Commission, 21
Stephens, Māmari, 11, 196
subordinate legislation, 102 *see also* regulations
superior law constitution, 17, 33–34
Bill of Rights as check on Cabinet power, 71
Swinburn, Jolyon, 164
Swiss Constitution, amendment of, 35
symbols, 64–65

taxation, 20, 62, 63
territorial authorities *see* local government
This Realm of New Zealand (Quentin-Baxter and McLean), 57–58
Tikanga Pākehā Anglican Diocese of Auckland, Social Justice Working Group, 44
Tiriti o Waitangi/Treaty of Waitangi
consideration in Government decision-making, 182–84
current legal status
international law, 175–76
statute law, 176–79, 182
Treaty settlement legislation, 180
inconsistent Bills, vetting function, 101
Matike Mai Aotearoa work, 196–200
misunderstandings/misinformation about, 28, 190
observance, 51
principles, 177–78, 190
process for clarification of constitutional position, 19, 175, 201–4, 264–66
proposed inclusion in Constitution Aotearoa, 175–76, 184–86
modified proposal, 200–204
public submissions on proposed inclusion, 40–47, 174, 186–96
explicit recognition for tino rangatiratanga, 194–96
opposition to Treaty altogether and response to such views, 186–92
uncertainty issue, 192–94
relevance of history in shaping the future, 206–8
Tokelau, 59
Trans-Pacific Partnership Agreement (TPPA), 128, 147–48
Transparency International, 149, 233
Trump, Donald, 9, 132, 238, 246, 252–253
Twitter, 251, 252, 253

United Future, 218
United Kingdom *see also* Brexit
bicameral Parliament, 106, 107
election of Speaker of House of Commons, 96
fixed parliamentary term, 94
Human Rights Act 1998, 60
transparency in election campaigning, 231
unwritten constitution, 7
United Nations Convention on the Rights of the Child (1989), 169, 170
United Nations Declaration on the Rights of Indigenous Peoples (2007), 190–91
United Nations Human Rights Committee, criticism of New Zealand's lack of judicial strike-down power, 130
United States

constitutional amendment, 18
judicial strike-down power, 127, 155
moderating effect of constitution, 9
political party funding, 230–31
politicisation of judicial appointments, 129
Universal Declaration on Human Rights (1948), 160–61
University of Canterbury Law School, 30, 161
upper house
  arguments for and against, 107–8
  failure of Legislative Council and attempts at revival, 107, 112–15, 121–23
  history of the Legislative Council, 108–12
  improving scrutiny of legislation without need for, 116–21
  Opportunities Party policy, 14, 114–15
  representation of Māori interests, 114, 115, 116
  scrutiny of lower house legislation, 114, 115
urgency, use of *see* law-making

Van Reybrouck, David, 242–44, 273n21
voting *see* elections
Vowles, Professor Jack, 225
Waitangi Tribunal, 126, 177, 180, 184, 188, 190, 203
Wakem, Dame Beverley, 146n6
water quality, 10, 163
Wedderspoon, Wayne, 30
Whanganui River, 164, 180, 186
William and Kate (Duke and Duchess of Cambridge), 56
Willis, Dr Edward, 32, 193–94
Willoughby, Alan, 31, 41–42
Wilson, Professor Margaret, 104
Winiata, Professor Whata, 115
Wood-Bodley, Frankie, 158n8
Woodhouse, Sir Owen, 102
workers' rights, 159–60, 161–62
Wright, David, 39
written codified constitution, public submissions on proposal, 28–33